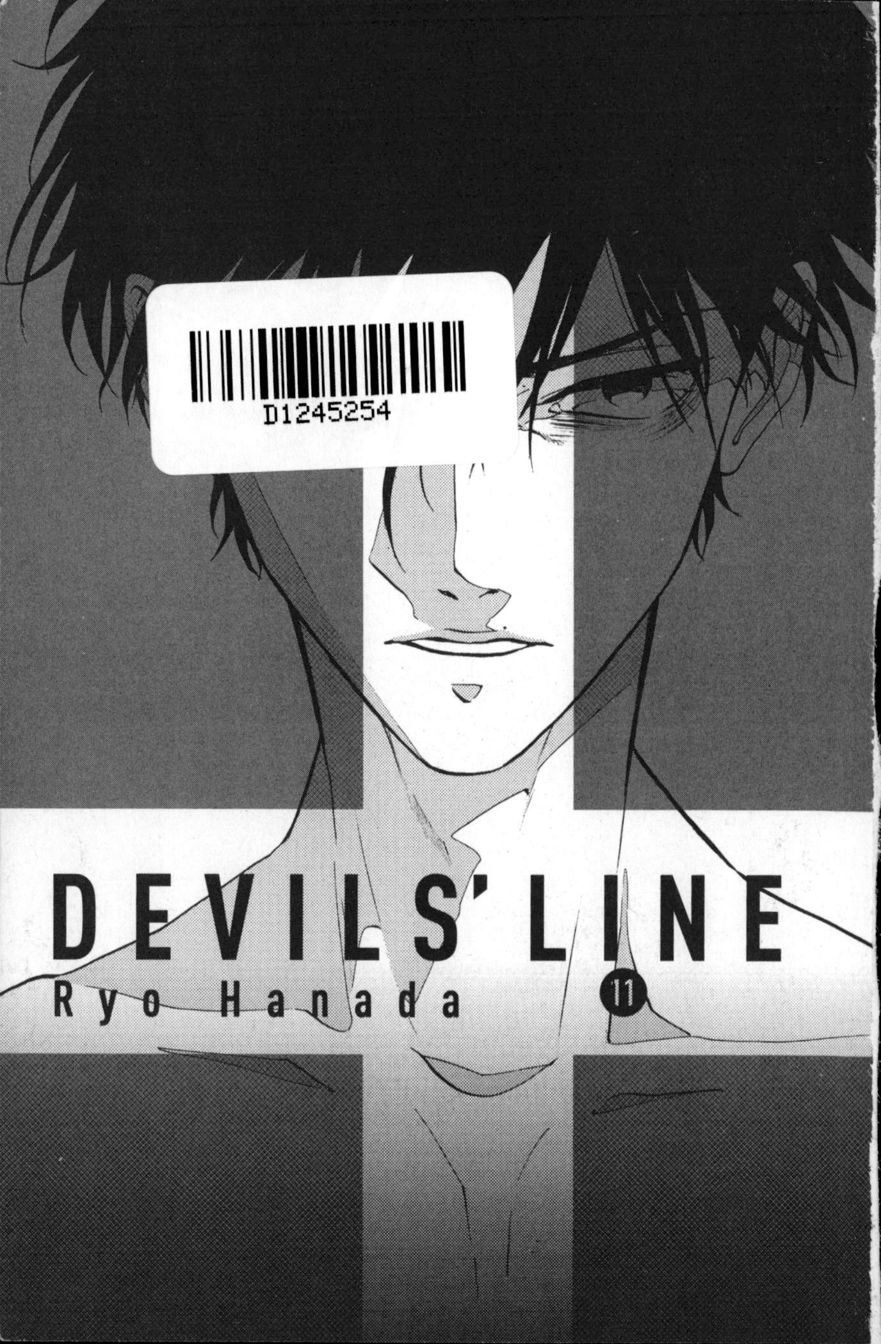
DEVILS' LINE
Ryo Hanada
11

Character and Relationship Diagram

(based on relationships up to the last volume)

TAKESHI MAKIMURA
(Zero Six)

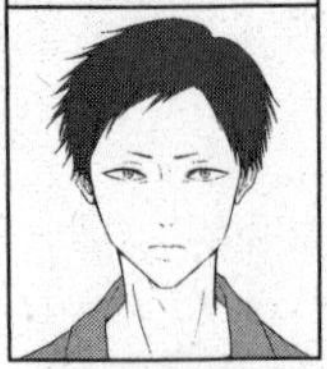

Came into contact with the CCC for an undercover investigation. He is currently in hiding somewhere in Tokyo with Mayu Sumimori.

NAOYA USHIO
(Zero Five)

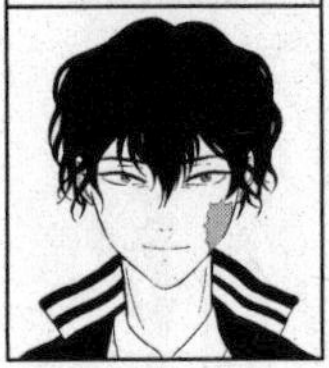

Former CCC member. He is currently under protection and surveillance by the police.

KIRIO KIKUHARA
(Zero Two)

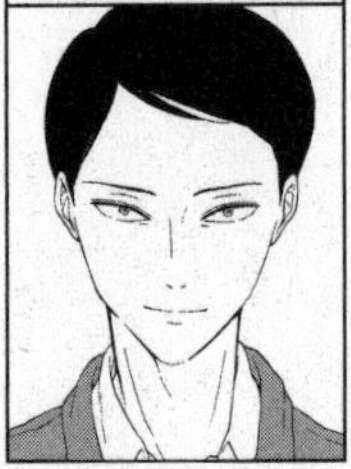

He was the leader of Public Safety Division 5's A Squad, but he was also secretly the commander of the CCC. Someone put a bomb in his car.

YUUKI ANZAI

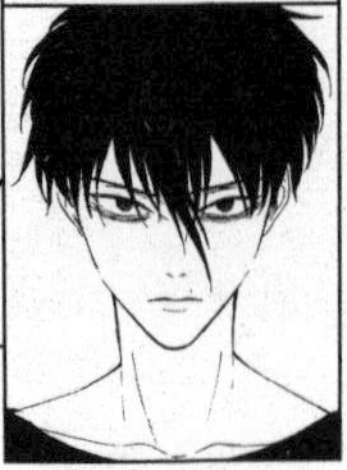

He was with the police's Public Safety Division 5, but since resigned. Half-devil, half-human. He was dating Tsukasa, but they're on a break.

MEGUMI ISHIMARU

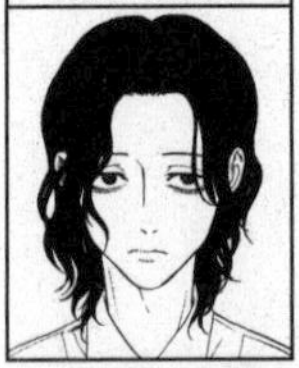

Came into contact with the CCC while working with Division 5 for an undercover investigation. Transferred back to Public Safety General Affairs.

TAKASHI SAWAZAKI

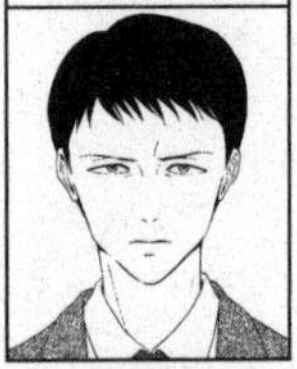

Senior police officer with Public Safety Division 5. Transferred to the General Admin department.

YOUSUKE ASAMI

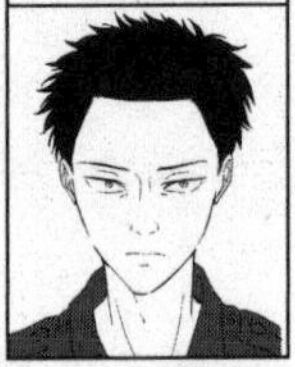

A member of Investigation Division 1, he was assigned to Public Safety Division 5 temporarily.

TOMOAKI OGATA

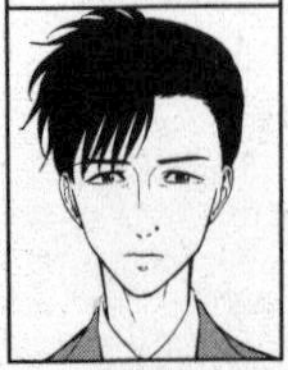

Sergeant with Riot Squad No. 9. Currently assigned to Division 5 as a bodyguard for Anzai.

JULIANA LLOYD

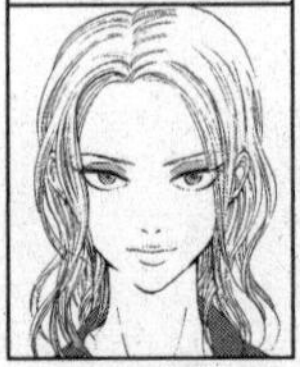

Devil police officer. Born and raised in Japan. She skillfully uses make-up to hide the bags under her eyes.

MIDORI ANZAI

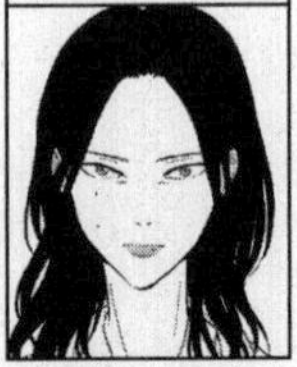

Yuuki Anzai's mother. Researcher at the Obihiro National Laboratory (ONL).

TAMAKI ANZAI

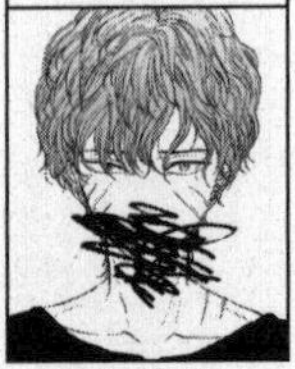

Yuuki Anzai's father. A devil who committed mass murder due to certain circumstances.

KEN'ICHI YOSHII
(Zero Nine)

He fled the CCC with Zero Seven, but is currently under protection and surveillance by the police.

NANAKO TENJO
(Zero Seven)

She was a CCC sniper, but has deserted the group. Currently on the run alone.

MAYU SUMIMORI
(Eleven)

She was responsible for accounting and intel gathering. Makimura's quick thinking saved her life.

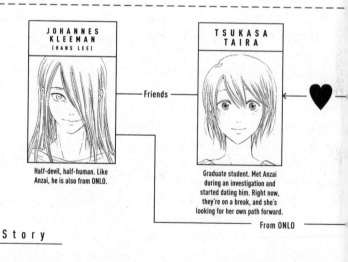

JOHANNES KLEEMAN
(HANS LEE)

Half-devil, half-human. Like Anzai, he is also from ONLO.

— Friends —

TSUKASA TAIRA

Graduate student. Met Anzai during an investigation and started dating him. Right now, they're on a break, and she's looking for her own path forward.

From ONLO

DEVILS'LINE

Story

The existence of devils becomes known to the world at large, dramatically changing society. In the midst of this upheaval, Anzai was fatally wounded in a fierce battle with the CCC, and Tsukasa's blood saved his life. The weight of his actions heavy on his mind, Anzai decides to take leave of the police force as well as break up with Tsukasa for the time being, in order to confront his own devil self. Tsukasa accepts his decision and resolves to also move forward. Both with their own objectives, Tsukasa and Anzai head separately to Obihiro. But they are finally reunited, thanks to guidance from Anzai's mother, Midori. Then, to know each other more deeply, they open the door to a new test.

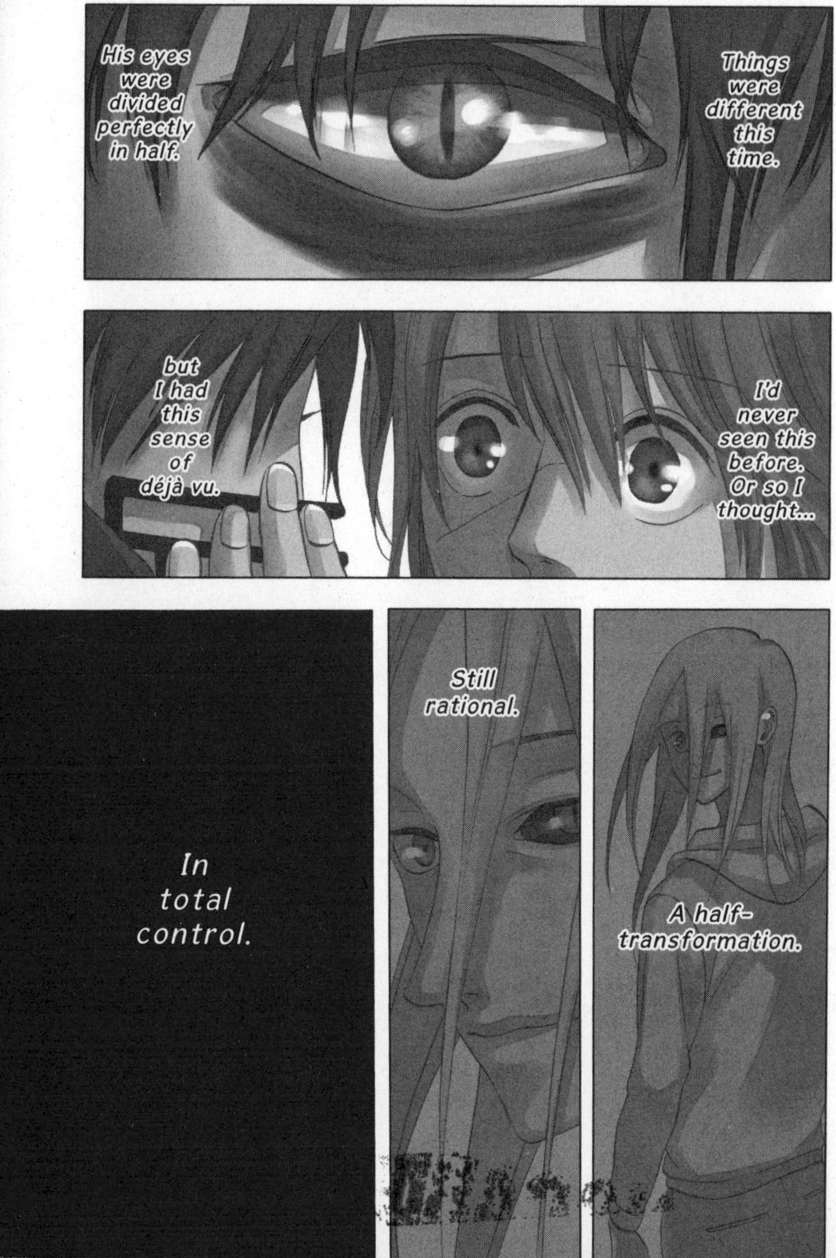
Things were different this time.
His eyes were divided perfectly in half.
I'd never seen this before. Or so I thought...
but I had this sense of déjà vu.
A half-transformation.
Still rational.
In total control.

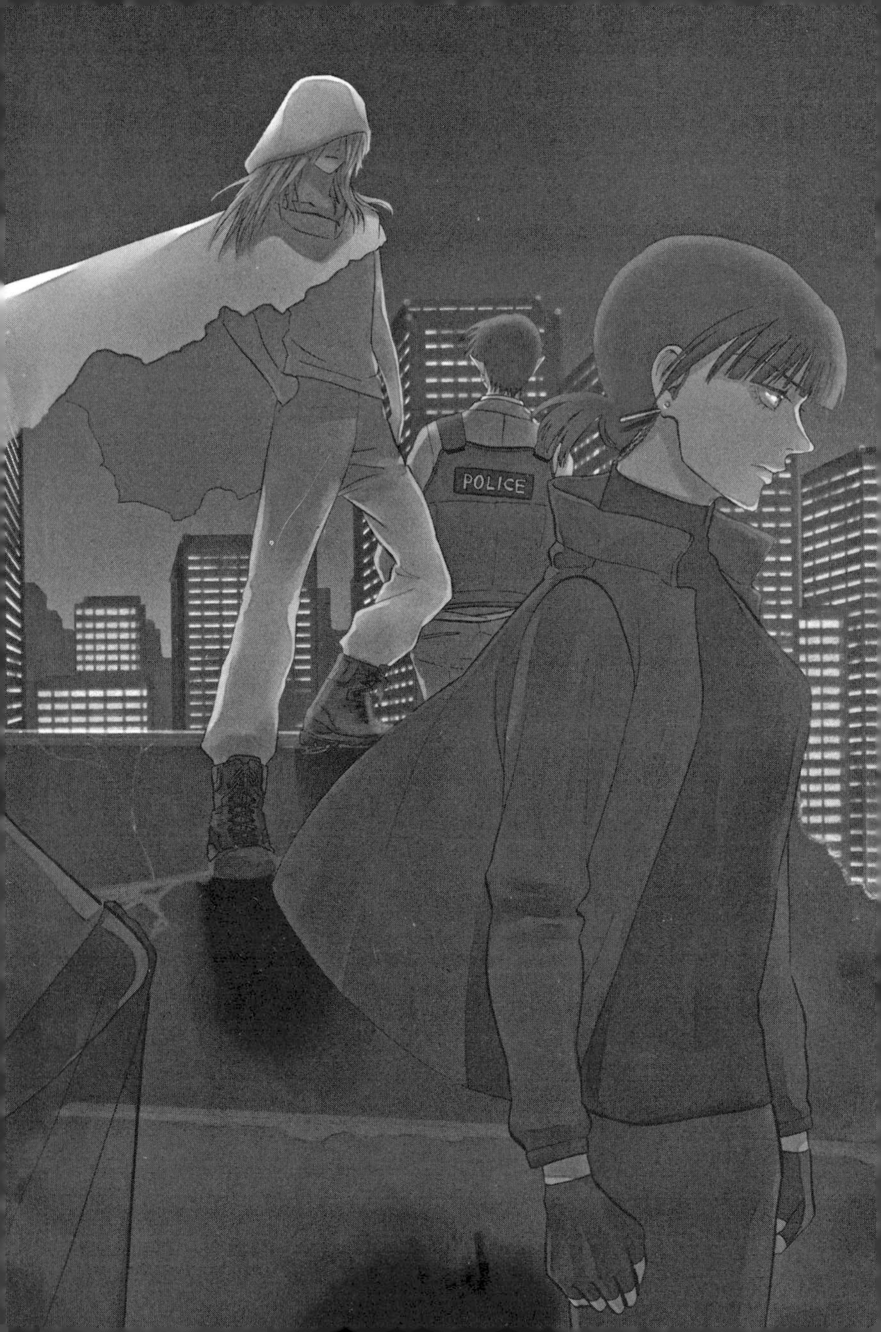
POLICE

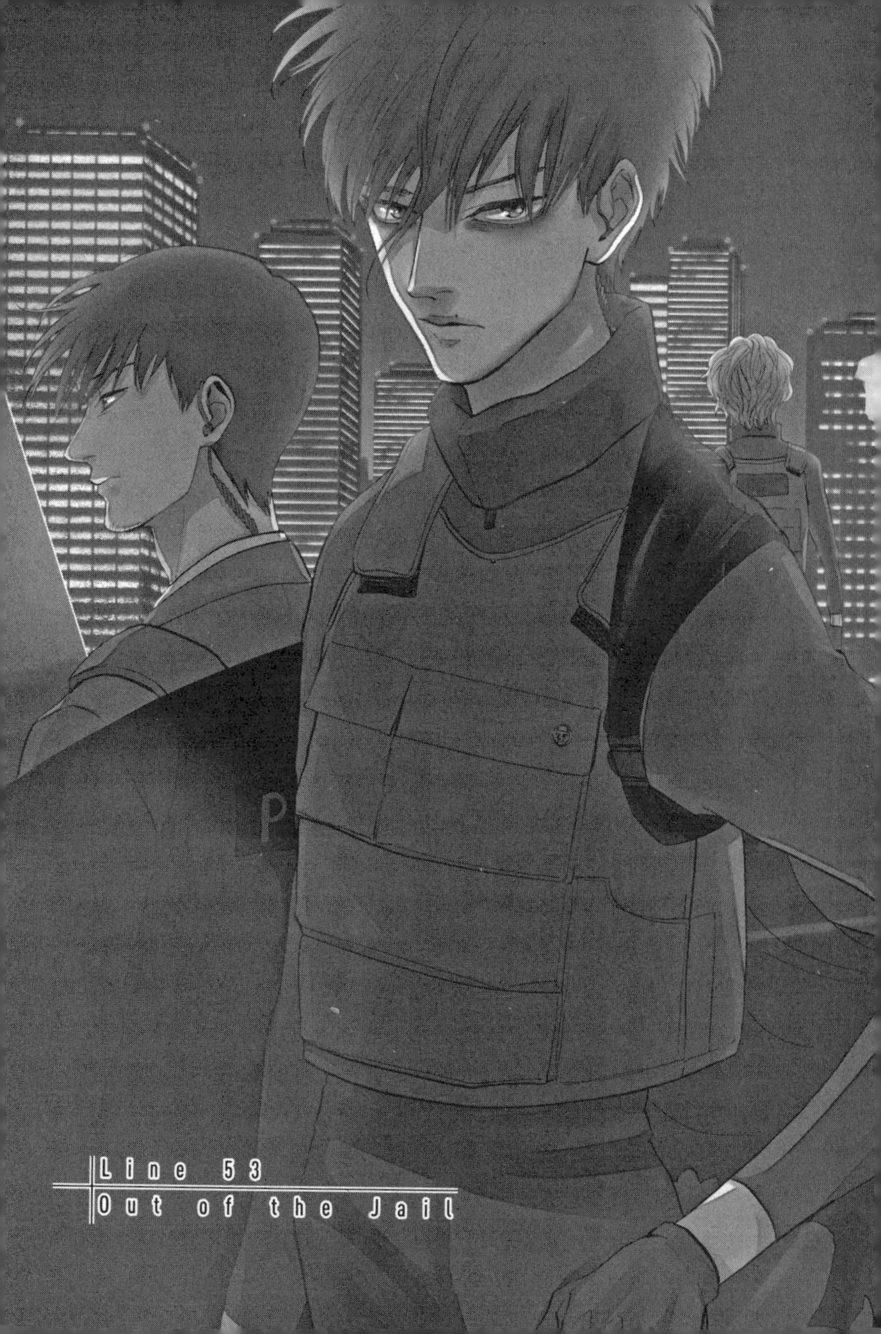
Line 53
Out of the Jail

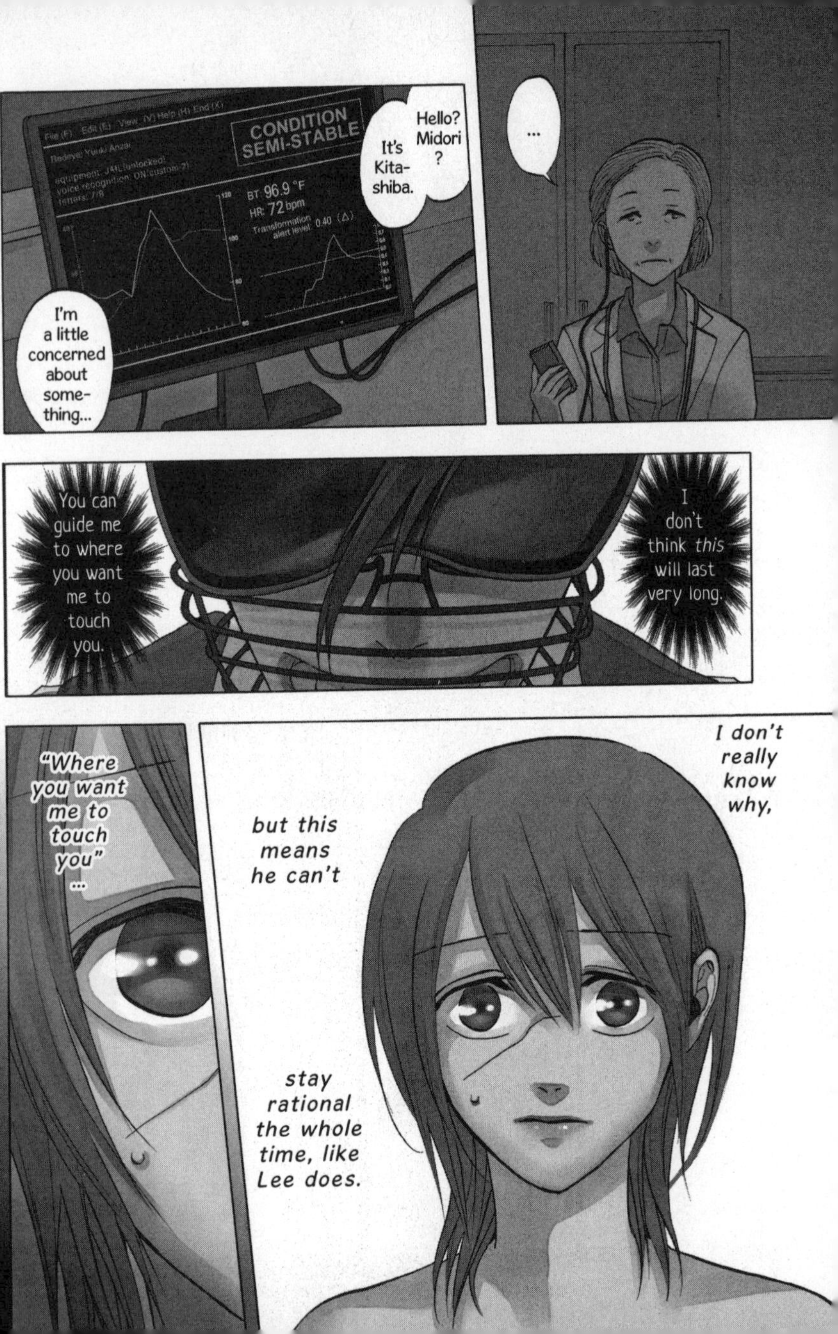
...
CONDITION SEMI-STABLE
BT 96.9 °F
HR: 72 bpm
Transformation alert level: 0.40 (△)
Hello? Midori?
It's Kita-shiba.
I'm a little concerned about something...
I don't think *this* will last very long.
You can guide me to where you want me to touch you.
I don't really know why,
but this means he can't
stay rational the whole time, like Lee does.
"Where you want me to touch you"...

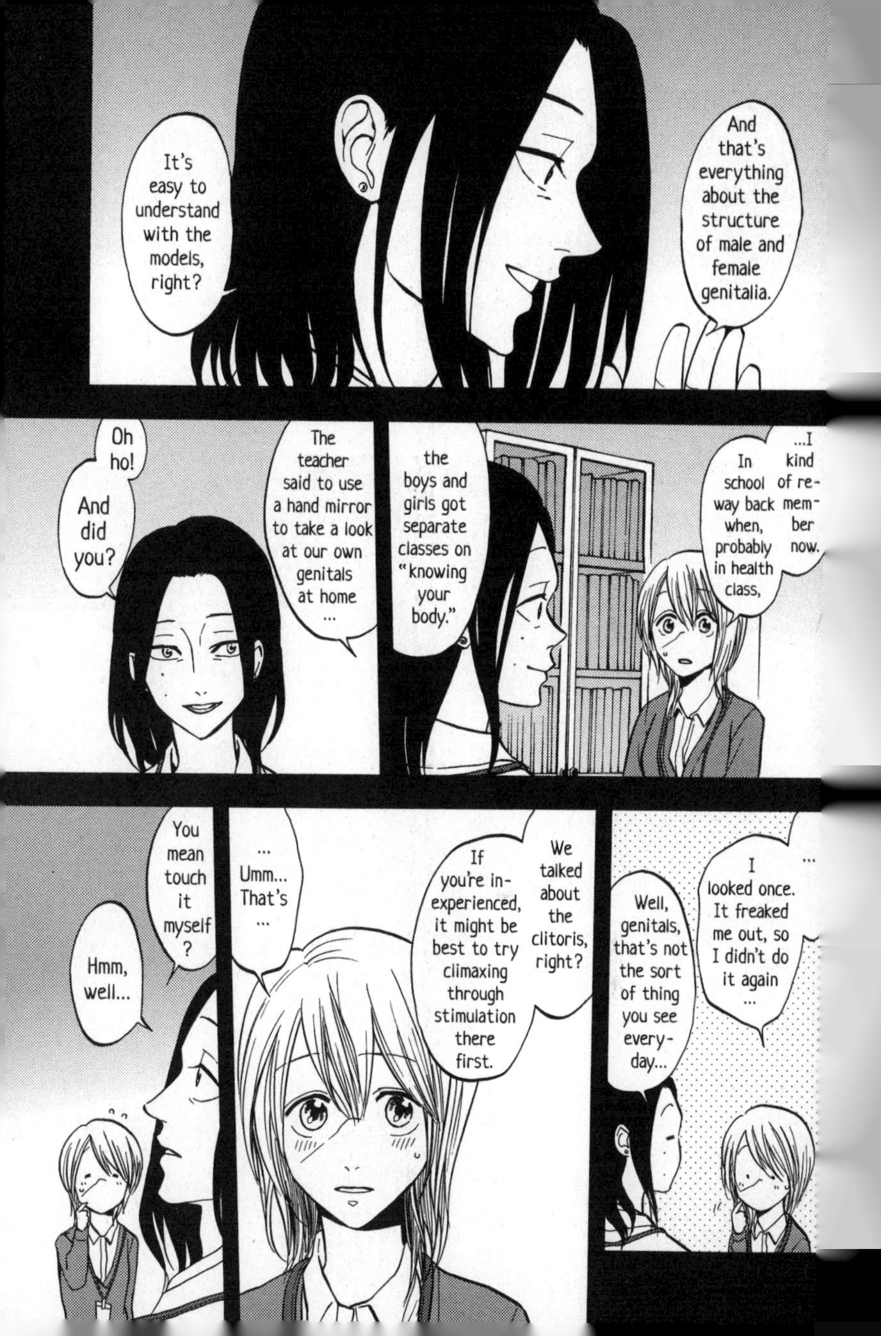

And that's everything about the structure of male and female genitalia.
It's easy to understand with the models, right?
...I kind of remember now.
In school way back when, probably in health class,
the boys and girls got separate classes on "knowing your body."
The teacher said to use a hand mirror to take a look at our own genitals at home ...
Oh ho! And did you?
...
I looked once. It freaked me out, so I didn't do it again ...
Well, genitals, that's not the sort of thing you see everyday...
We talked about the clitoris, right?
If you're inexperienced, it might be best to try climaxing through stimulation there first.
... Umm... That's ...
You mean touch it myself?
Hmm, well...

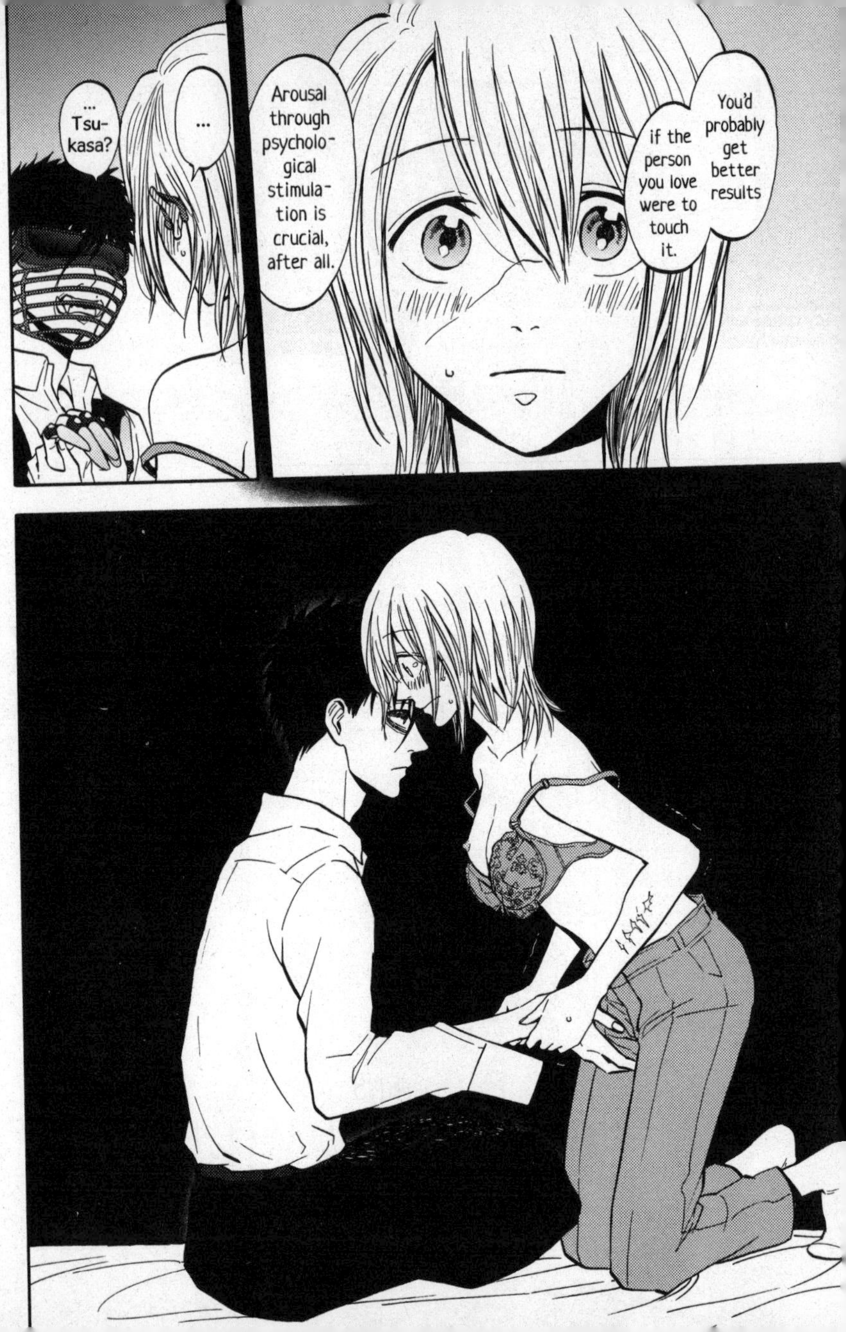
You'd probably get better results
if the person you love were to touch it.
Arousal through psycholo-gical stimula-tion is crucial, after all.
...
... Tsu-kasa?

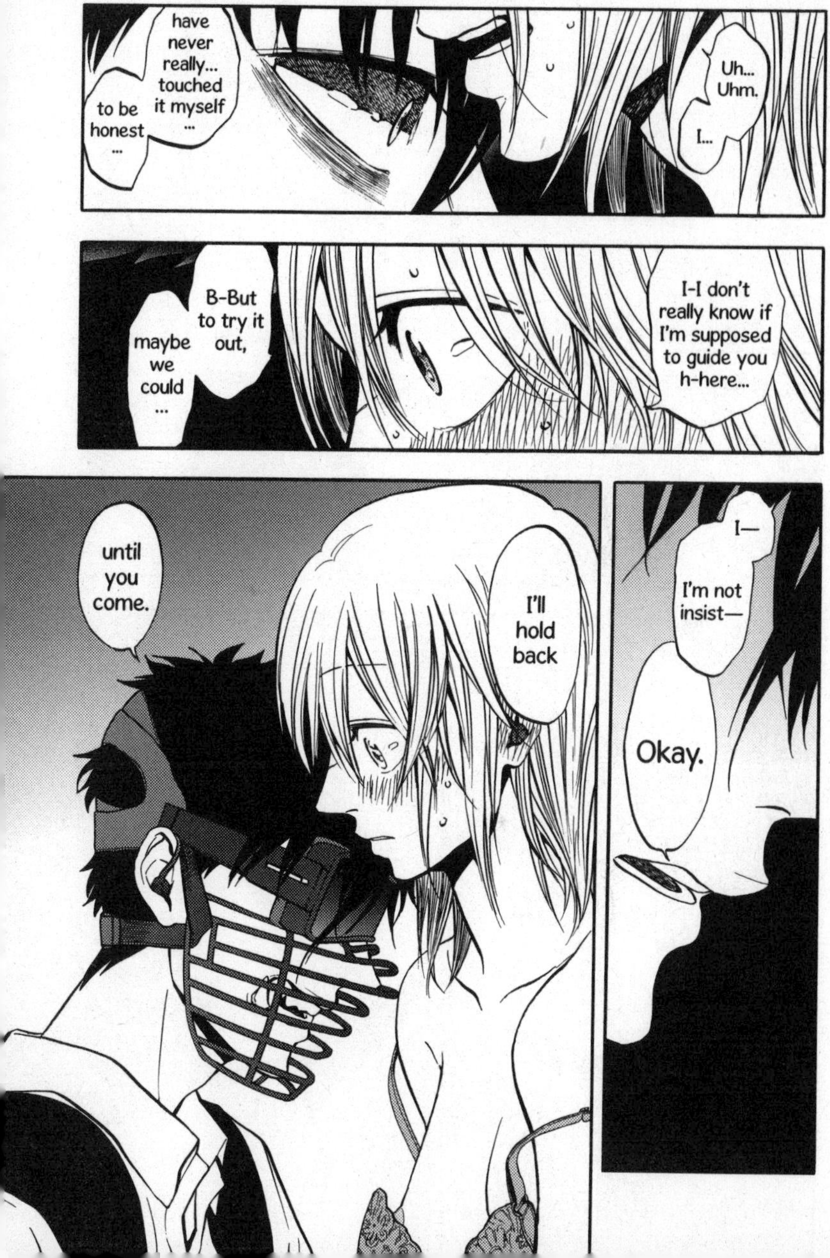
Uh... Uhm.
I...
have never really... touched it myself ...
to be honest ...
I-I don't really know if I'm supposed to guide you h-here...
B-But to try it out,
maybe we could ...
I—
I'm not insist—
Okay.
I'll hold back
until you come.

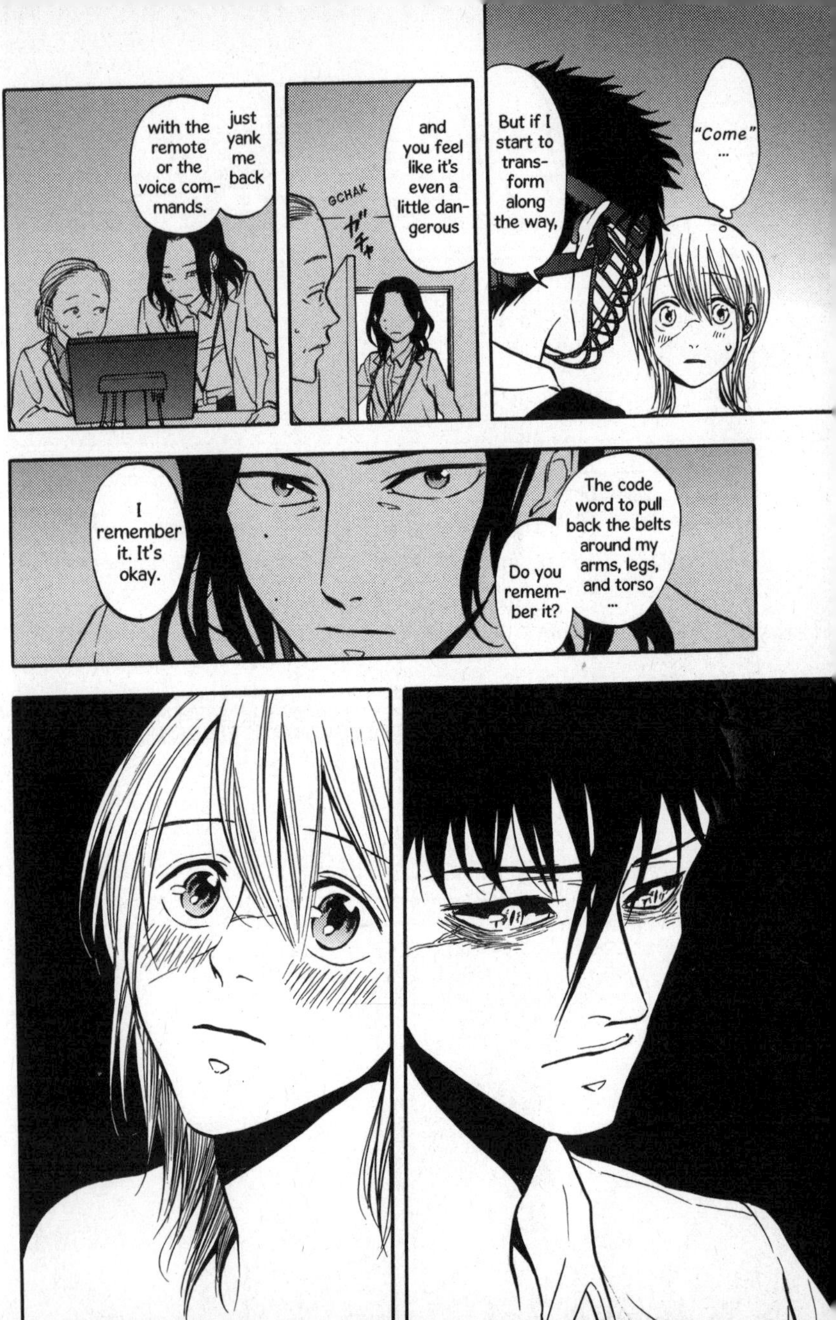
"Come" ...
But if I start to transform along the way,
and you feel like it's even a little dangerous
GCHAK
ガチャ
just yank me back
with the remote or the voice commands.
The code word to pull back the belts around my arms, legs, and torso ...
Do you remember it?
I remember it. It's okay.

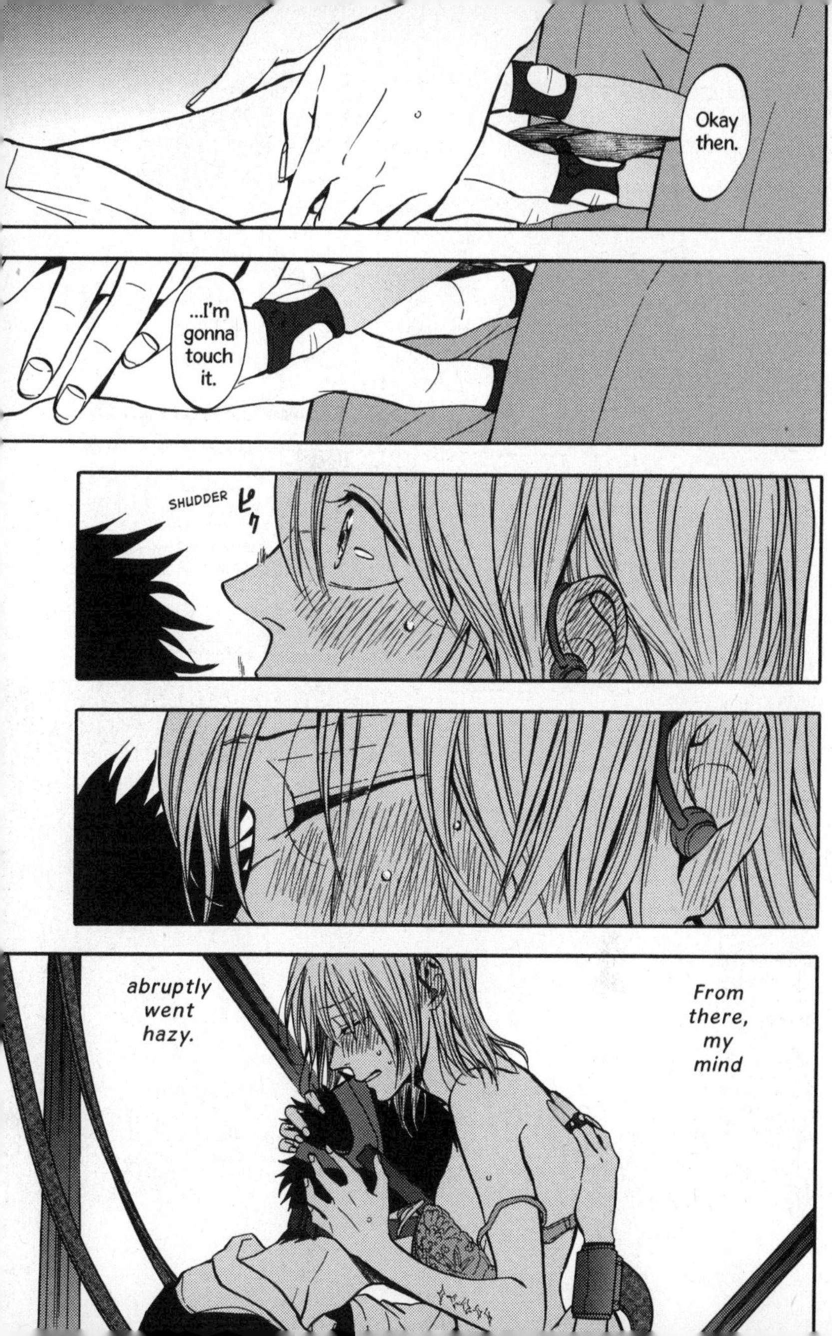
Okay then.
...I'm gonna touch it.
SHUDDER ピク
From there, my mind
abruptly went hazy.

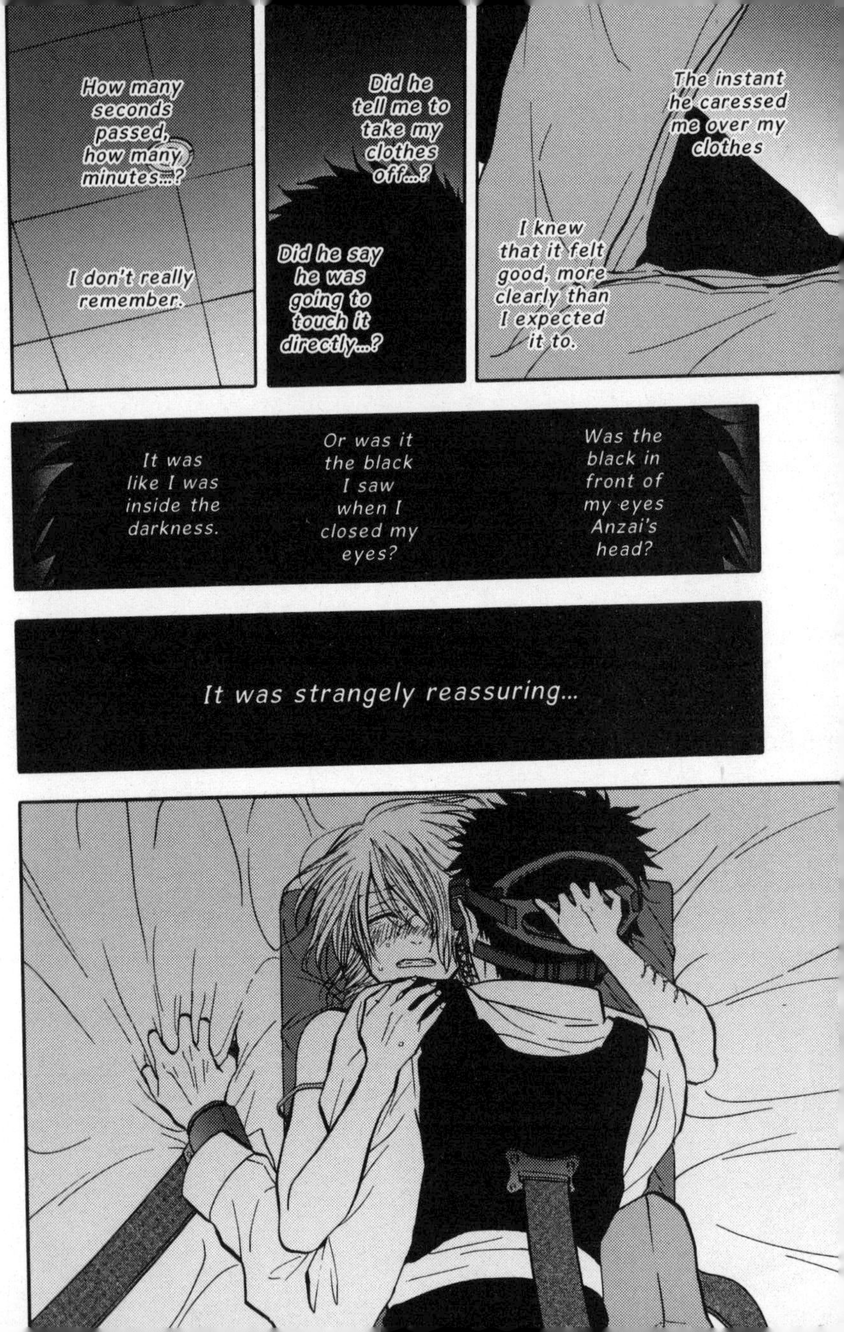
The instant he caressed me over my clothes
I knew that it felt good, more clearly than I expected it to.
Did he tell me to take my clothes off...?
Did he say he was going to touch it directly...?
How many seconds passed, how many minutes...?
I don't really remember.
Was the black in front of my eyes Anzai's head?
Or was it the black I saw when I closed my eyes?
It was like I was inside the darkness.
It was strangely reassuring...

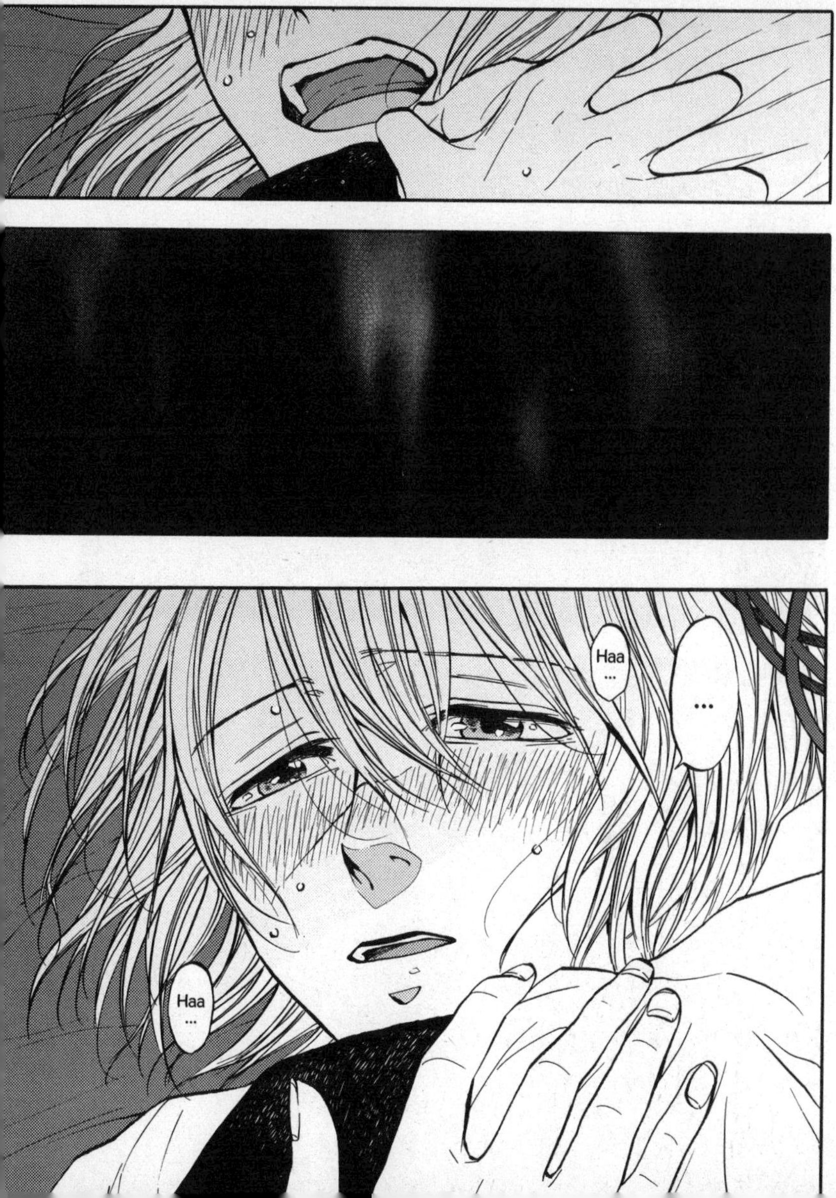
...
Haa...
Haa...

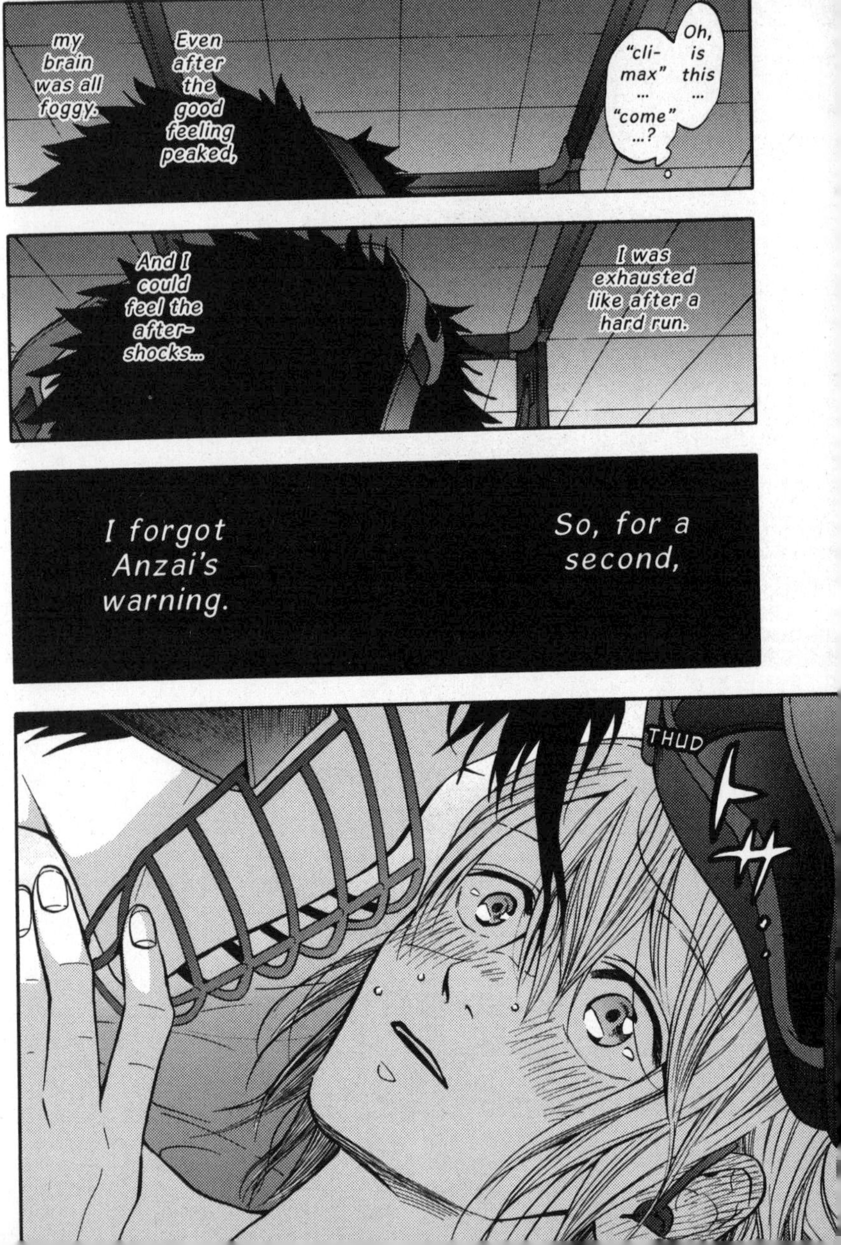
Oh, is this ... "cli-max" ... "come" ...?
Even after the good feeling peaked,
my brain was all foggy.
I was exhausted like after a hard run.
And I could feel the after-shocks...
So, for a second,
I forgot Anzai's warning.
THUD

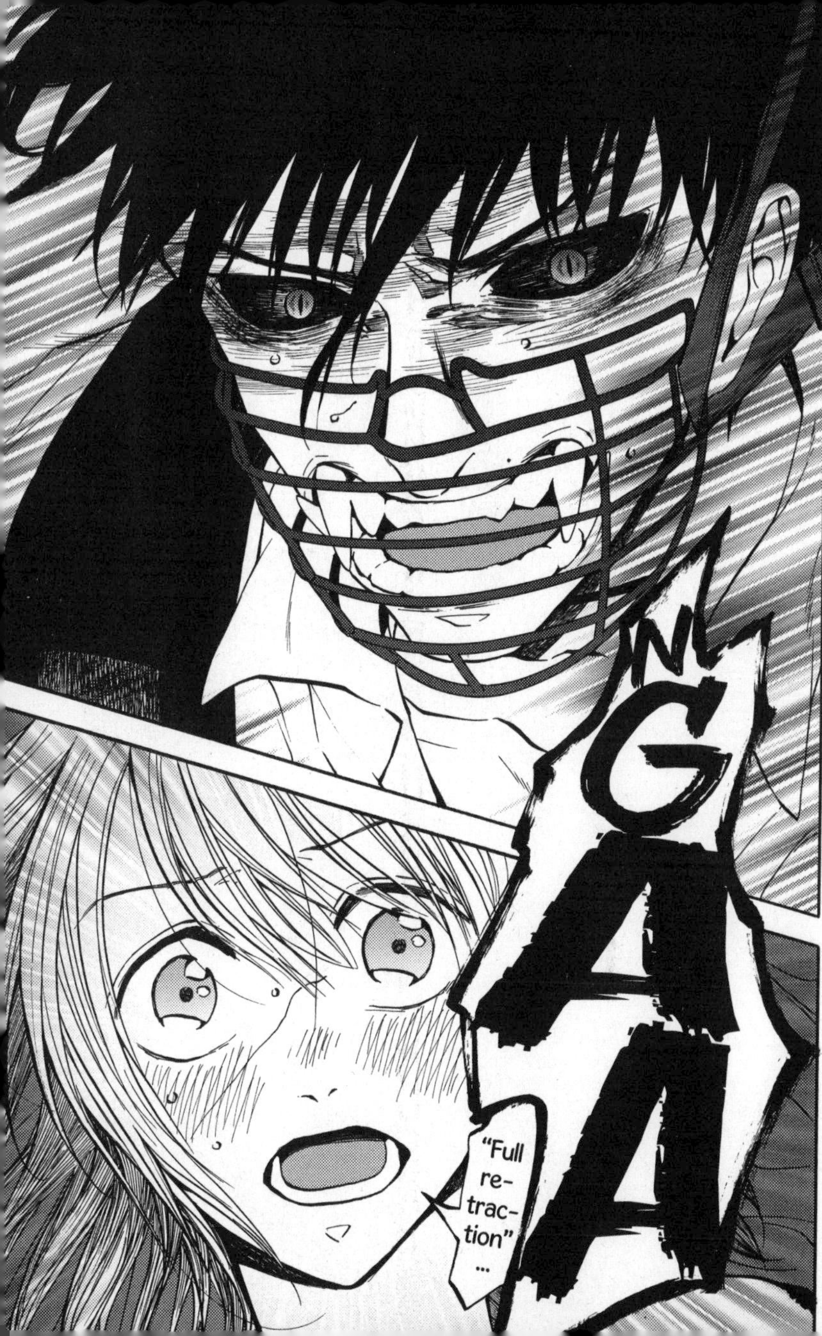
“Full re- trac- tion” ...

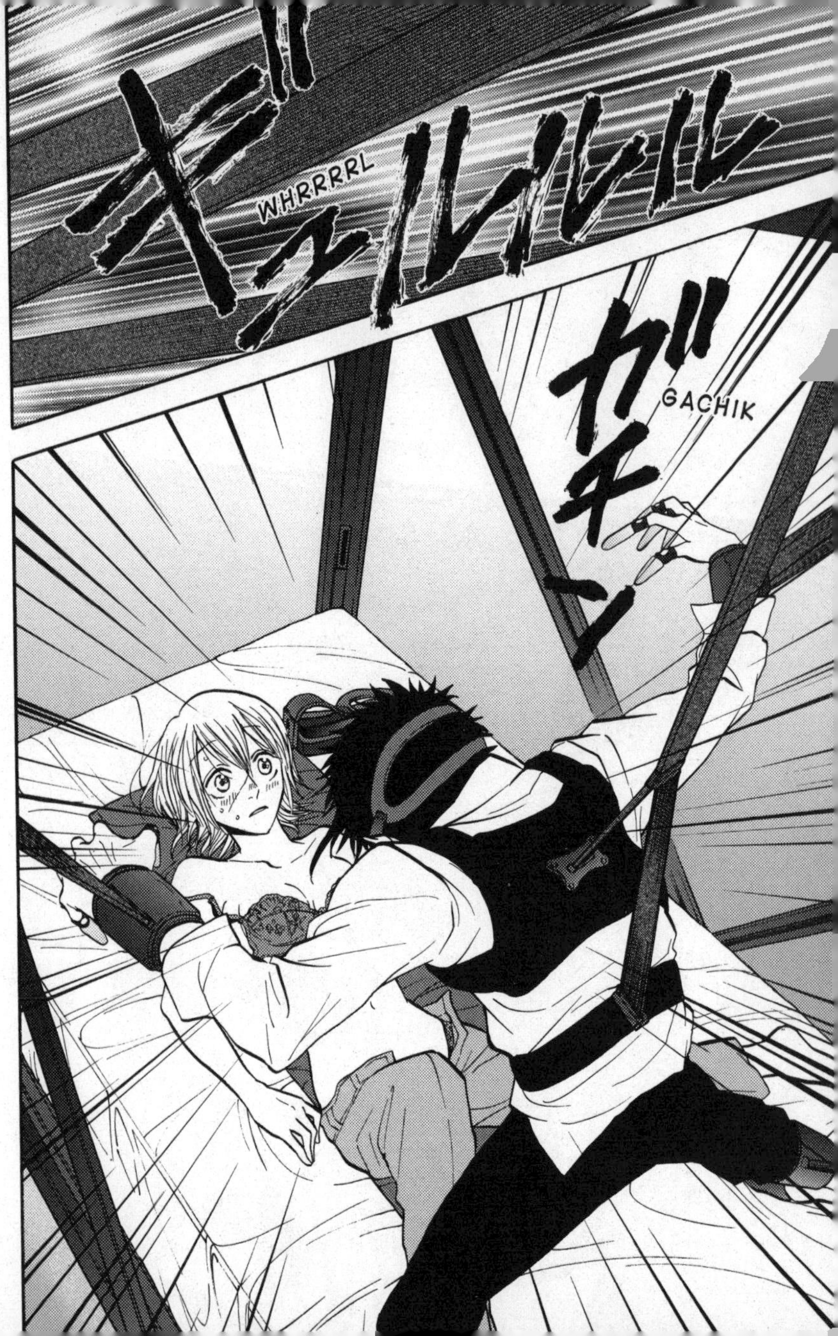
ギュルルルル
WHRRRRL
ガチーン
GACHIK

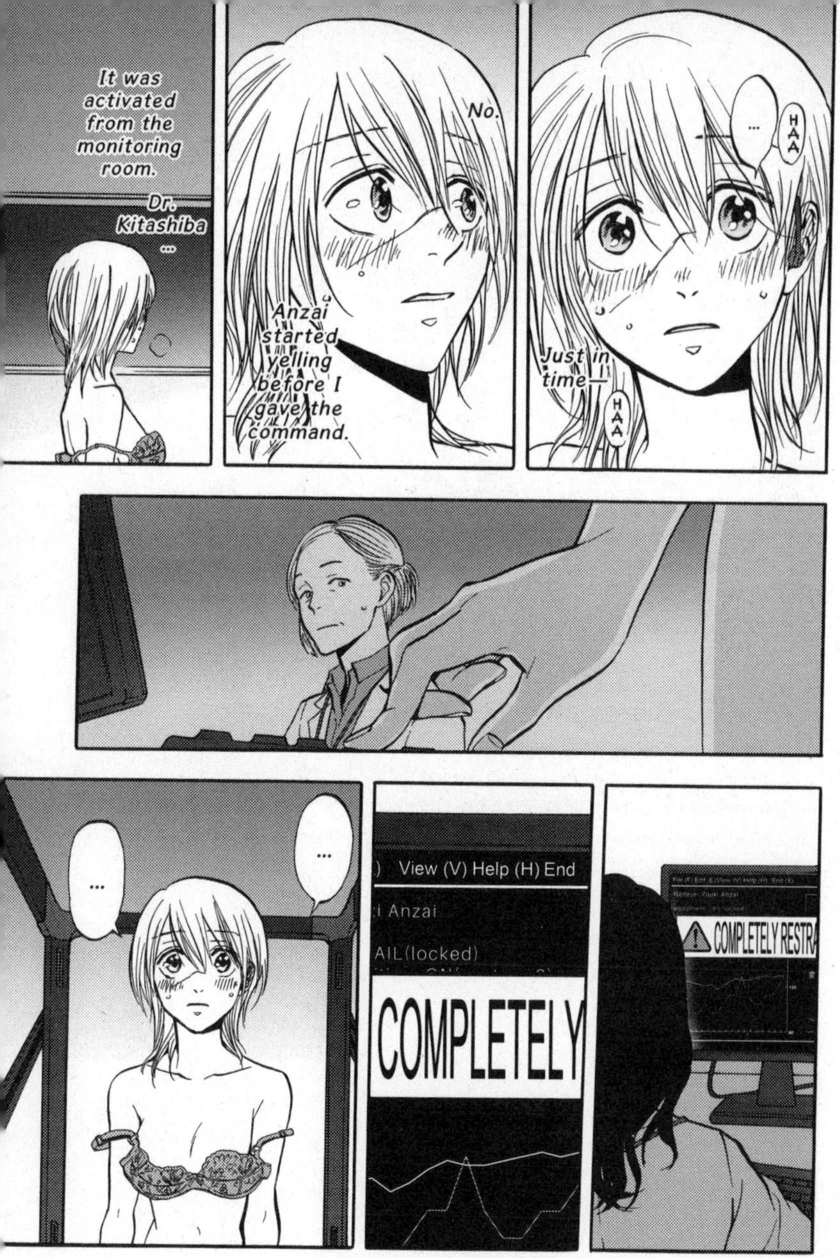
HAA
...
Just in time—
HAA
No.
Anzai started yelling before I gave the command.
It was activated from the monitoring room.
Dr. Kitashiba ...
COMPLETELY RESTRA
) View (V) Help (H) End
i Anzai
AIL(locked)
COMPLETELY
...
...

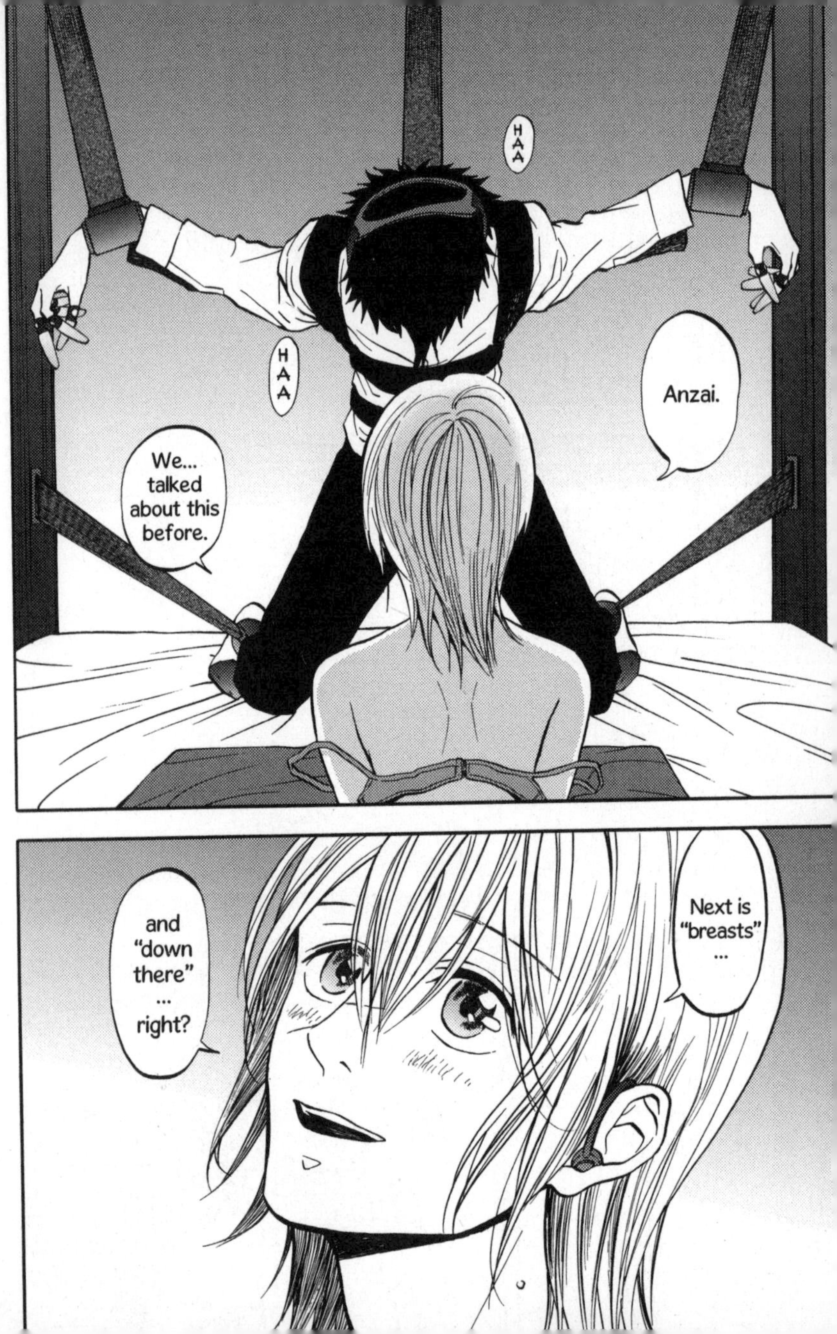
HAA
Anzai.
HAA
We... talked about this before.
Next is "breasts" ...
and "down there" ... right?

TWITCH
ピク...

HAAAA

HAAAA

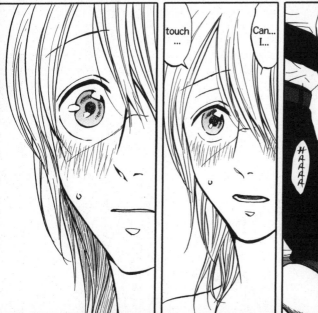

touch
...

Can...
I...

HAAAA

HAAAA

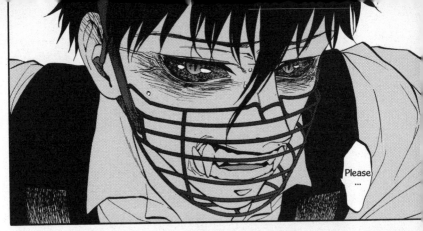

Please ...
ドク…ン
BADUM
And that's everything about how to touch a penis.
That said, it's probably going to be fairly difficult at first.
What's important is com-munication with your partner.
Does it feel good for him? Does it hurt?
When you get aroused yourself, your judgement becomes clouded as well.
You have to watch your partner carefully.
If your partner is in a state where he's able to talk,
you can simply ask.
And you can get clues from what felt good when it was done to you...

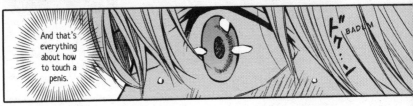

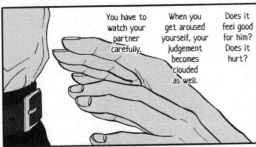

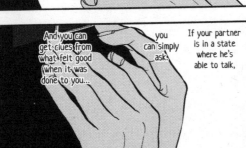

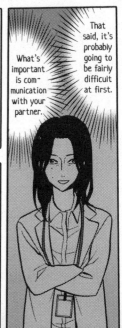

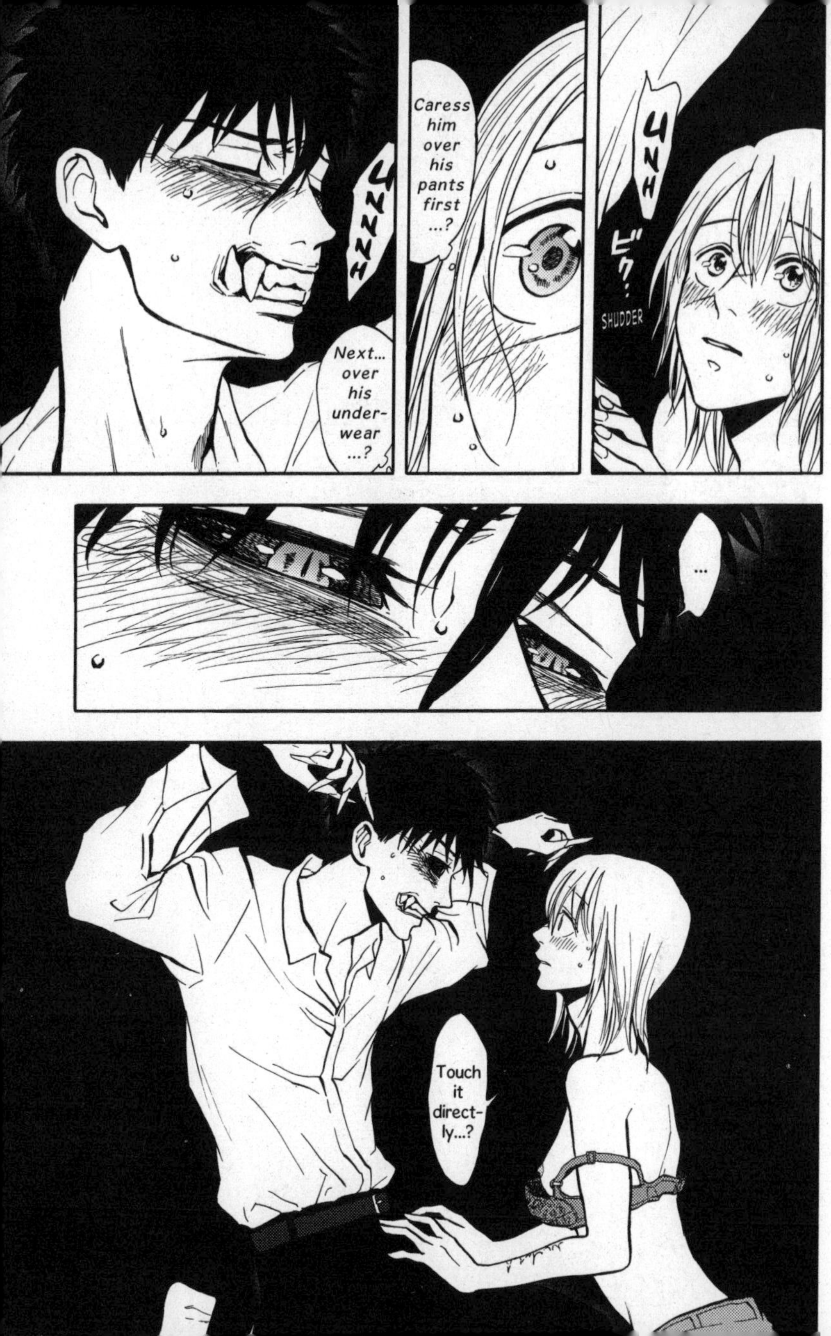
UNH
ビク
SHUDDER
Caress him over his pants first ...?
UNNNH
Next... over his under-wear ...?
...
Touch it direct-ly...?

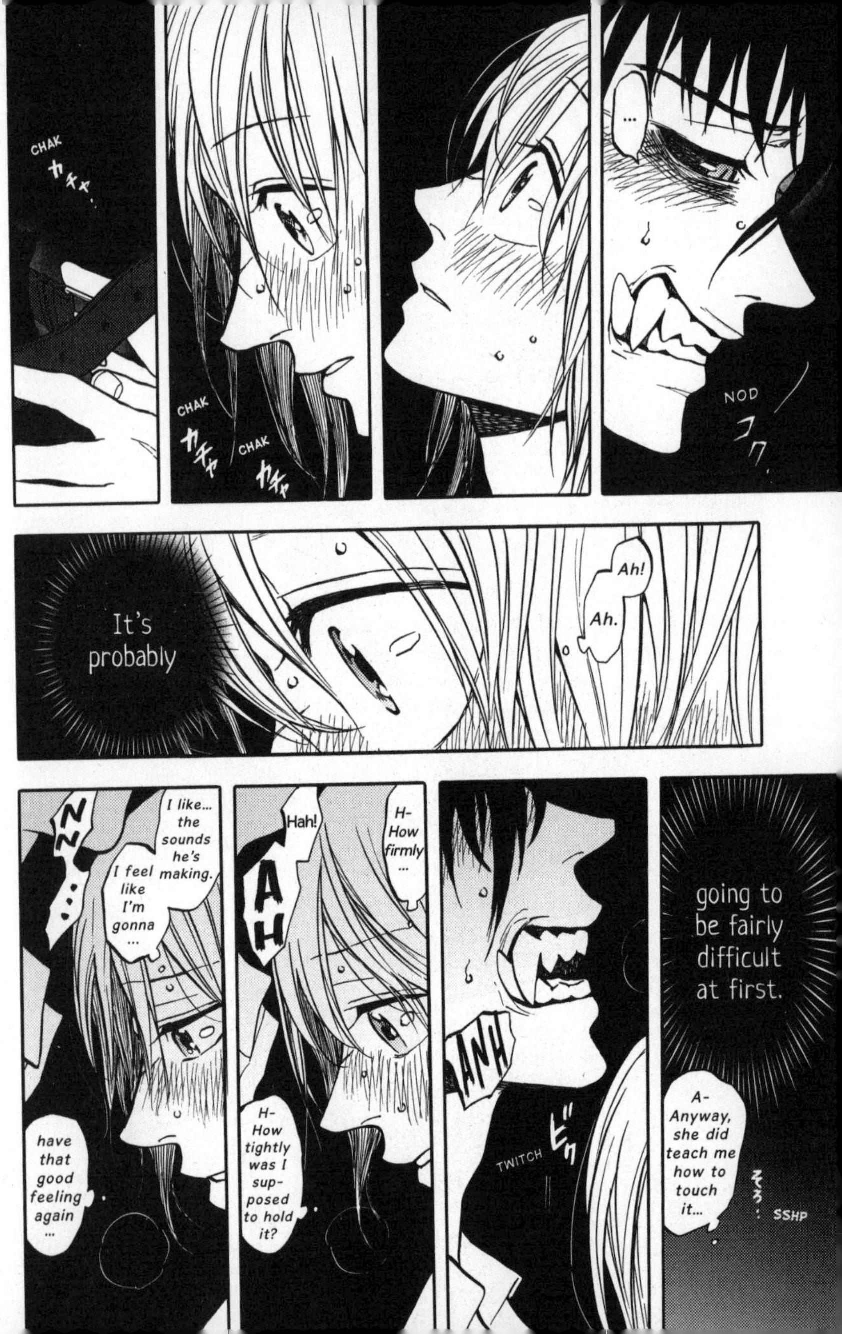
...
NOD
コク
CHAK
カチャ
CHAK
カチャ
CHAK
カチャ...
Ah!
Ah.
It's probably
going to be fairly difficult at first.
A- Anyway, she did teach me how to touch it...
そろ...
SSHP
ANH
TWITCH
ビク
H- How firmly ...
Hah!
AH
H- How tightly was I sup- posed to hold it?
I like... the sounds he's making.
I feel like I'm gonna ...
NN...
have that good feeling again ...

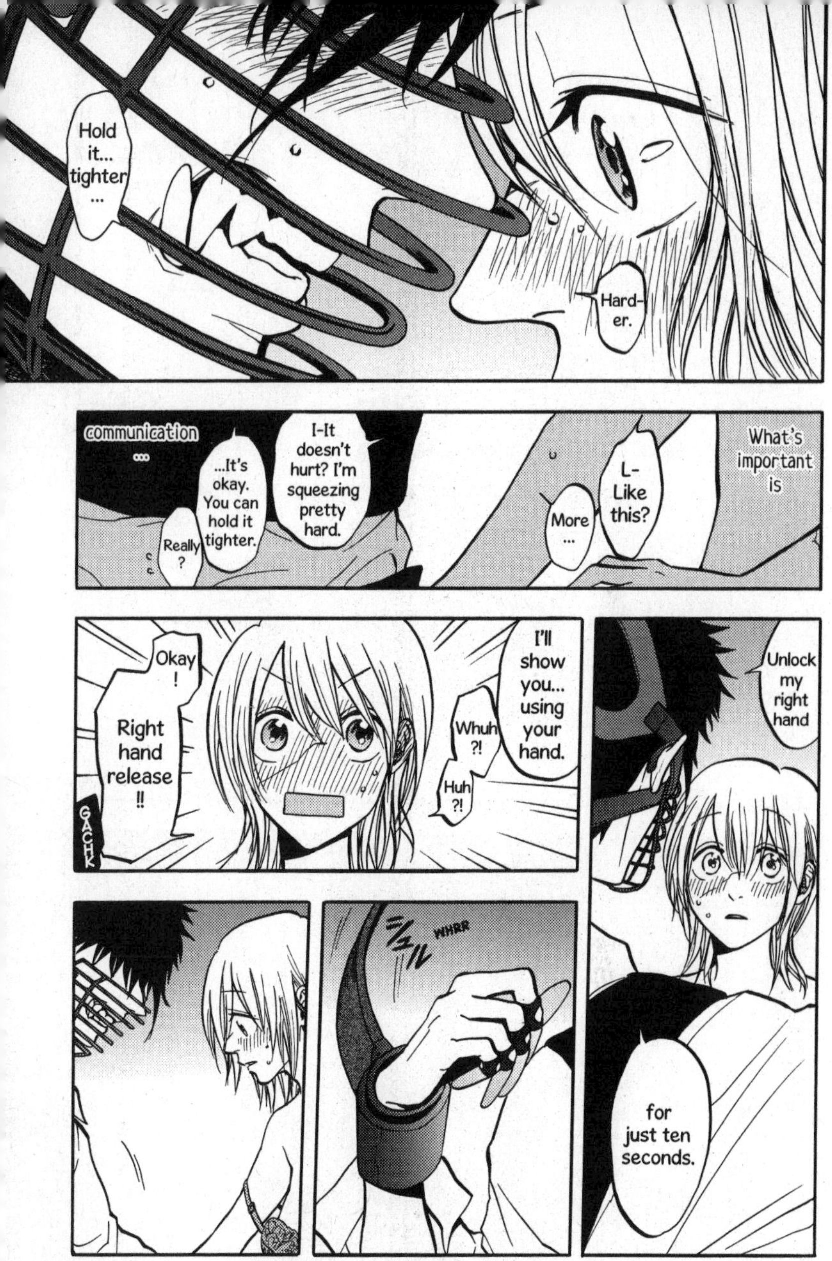
Hold it... tighter...
Harder.
What's important is
L-Like this?
More...
I-It doesn't hurt? I'm squeezing pretty hard.
...It's okay. You can hold it tighter.
Really?
communication...
Unlock my right hand
for just ten seconds.
I'll show you... using your hand.
Whuh?!
Huh?!
Okay!
Right hand release!!
GACHK
WHRR

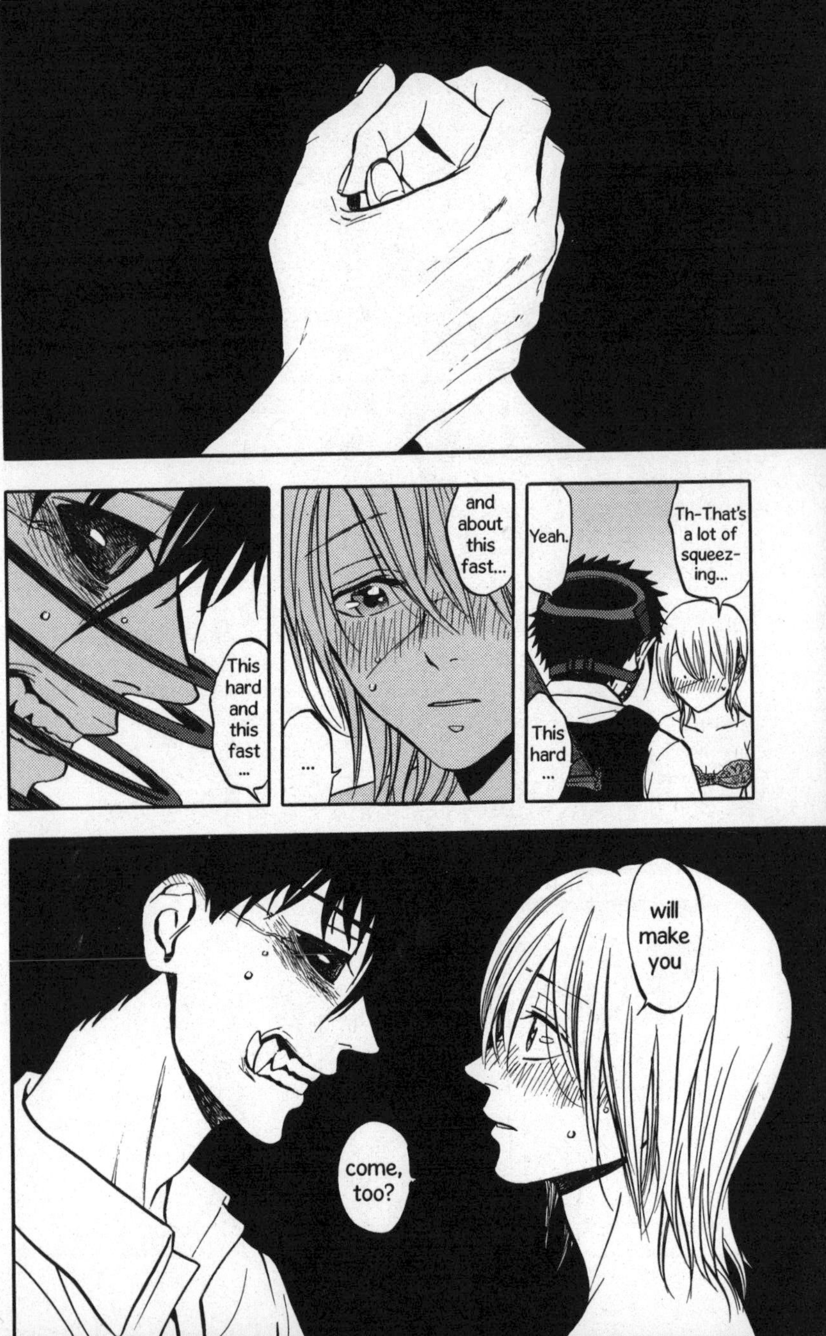
Th-That's a lot of squeez-ing...
Yeah.
This hard ...
and about this fast...
...
This hard and this fast ...
will make you
come, too?

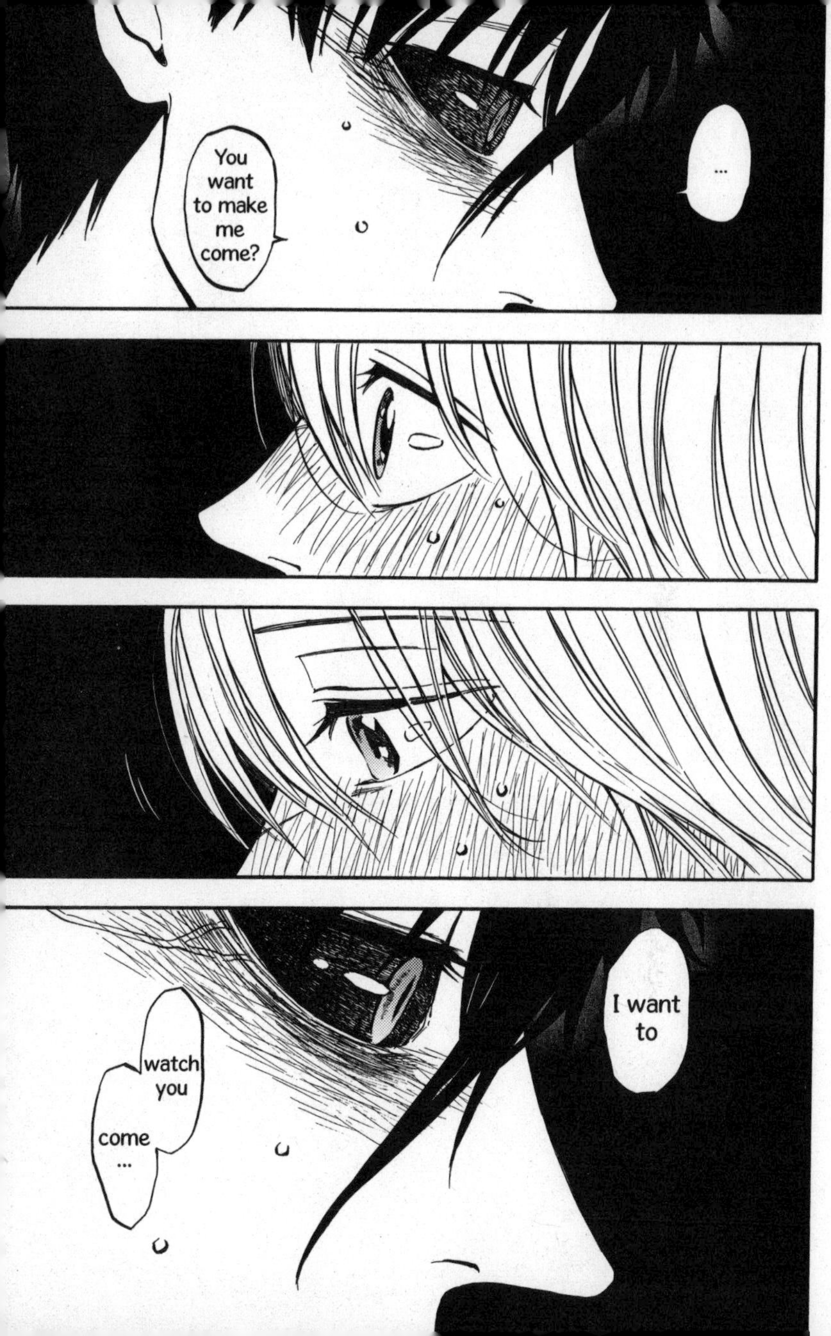
...
You want to make me come?
I want to
watch you come ...

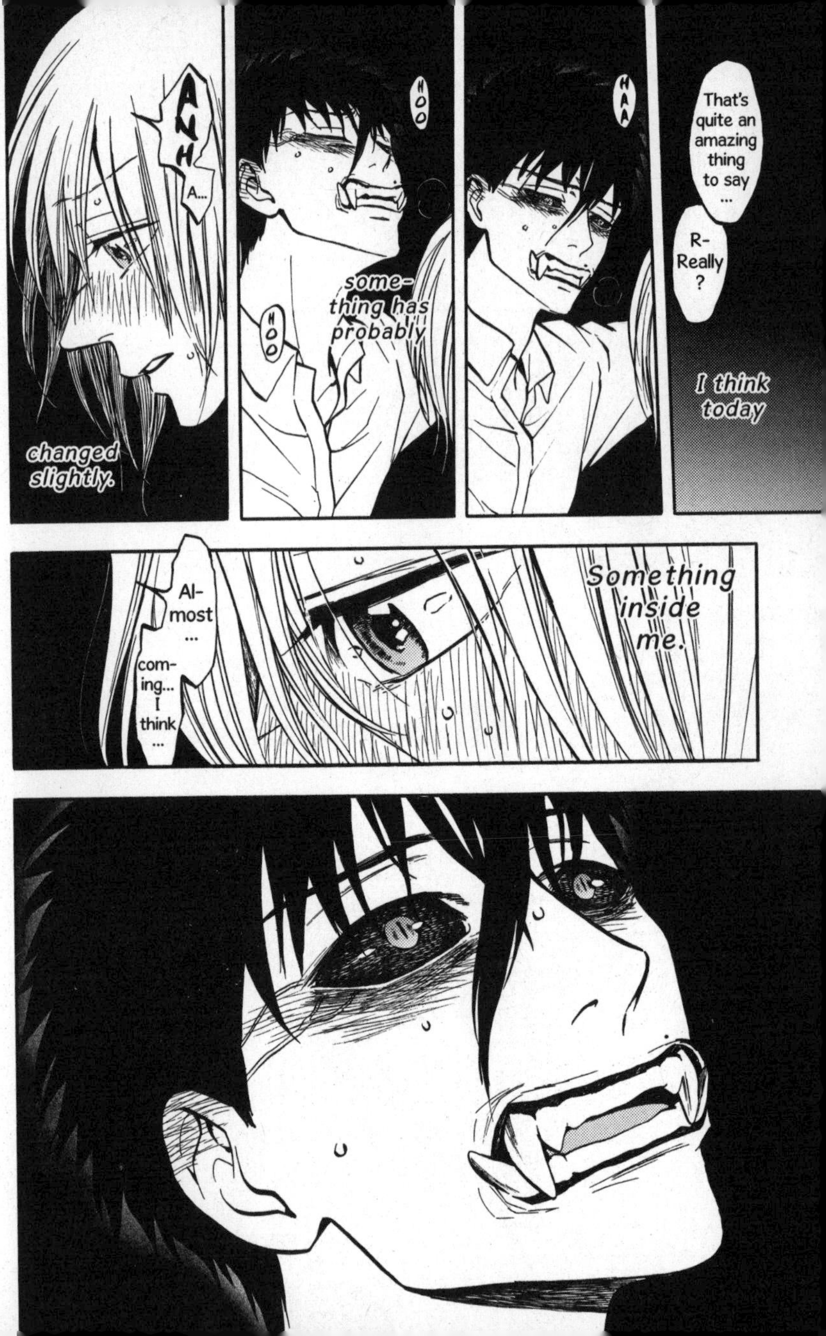
That's quite an amazing thing to say ...
R-Really?
I think today
HAAA
HOO
something has probably
HOO
ANHA
A...
changed slightly.
Something inside me.
Almost ...
coming... I think ...

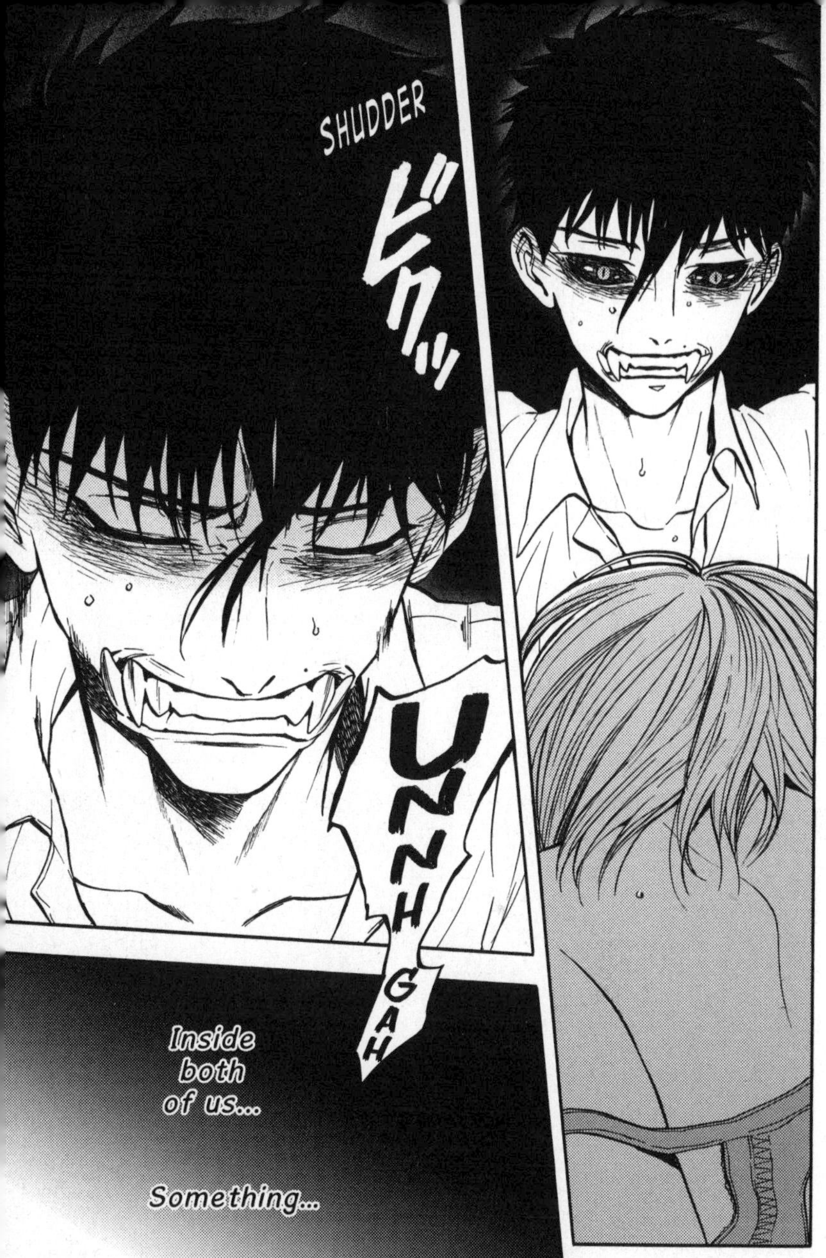
SHUDDER
ビクッ
UNNH GAH
Inside both of us...
Something...

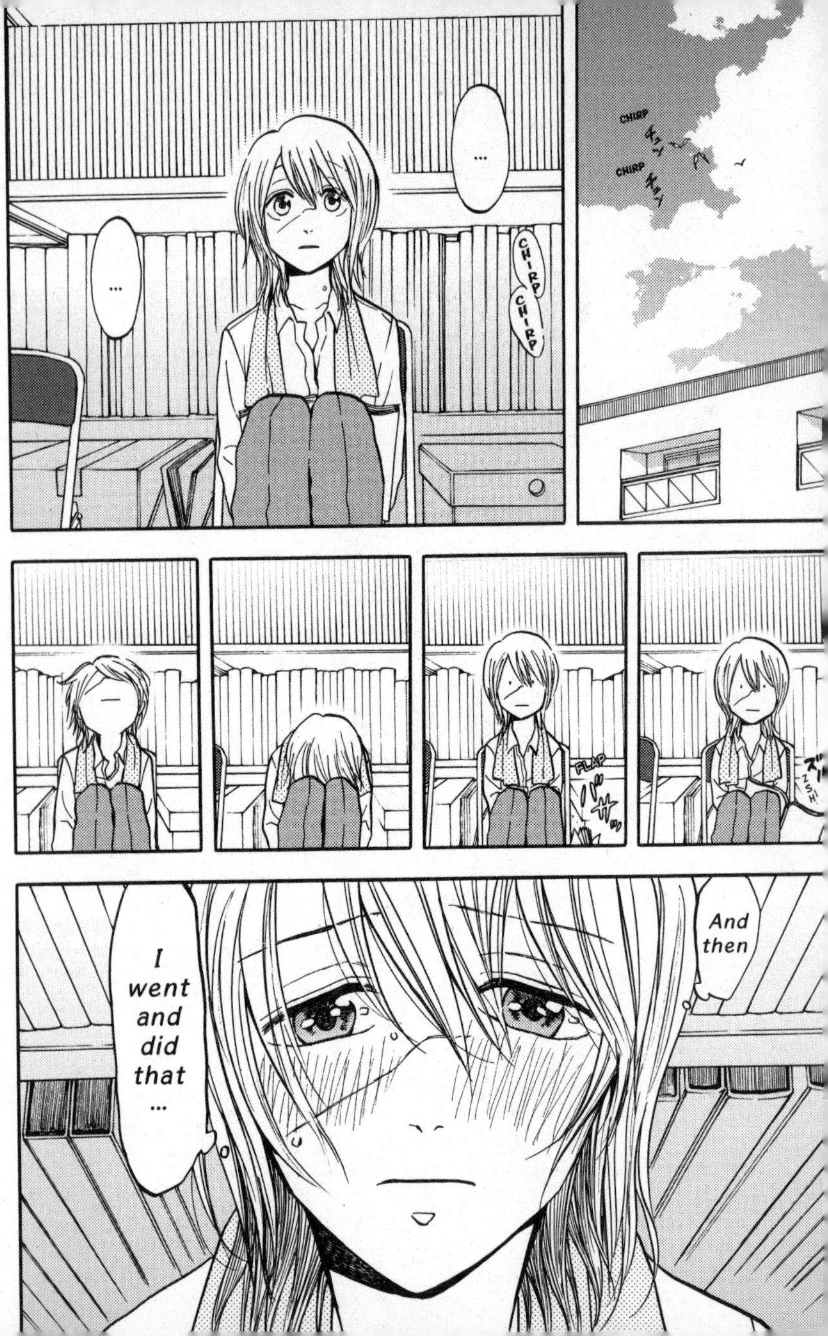
CHIRP
CHIRP
...
CHIRP
CHIRP
...
ZSH!
FLAP
And then
I went and did that ...

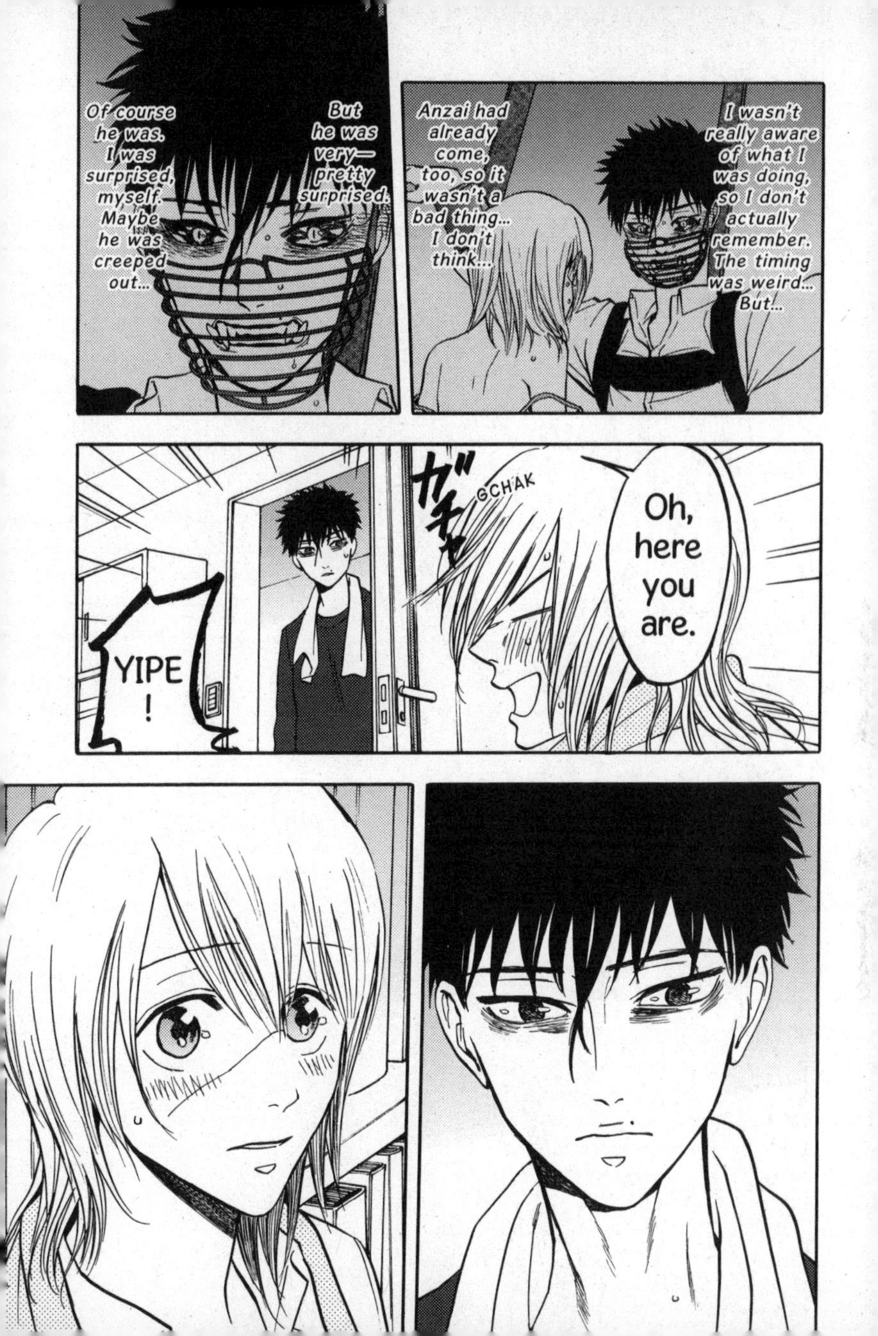
I wasn't really aware of what I was doing, so I don't actually remember. The timing was weird... But...
Anzai had already come, too, so it wasn't a bad thing... I don't think...
But he was very— pretty surprised.
Of course he was. I was surprised, myself. Maybe he was creeped out...
GCHAK
Oh, here you are.
YIPE !

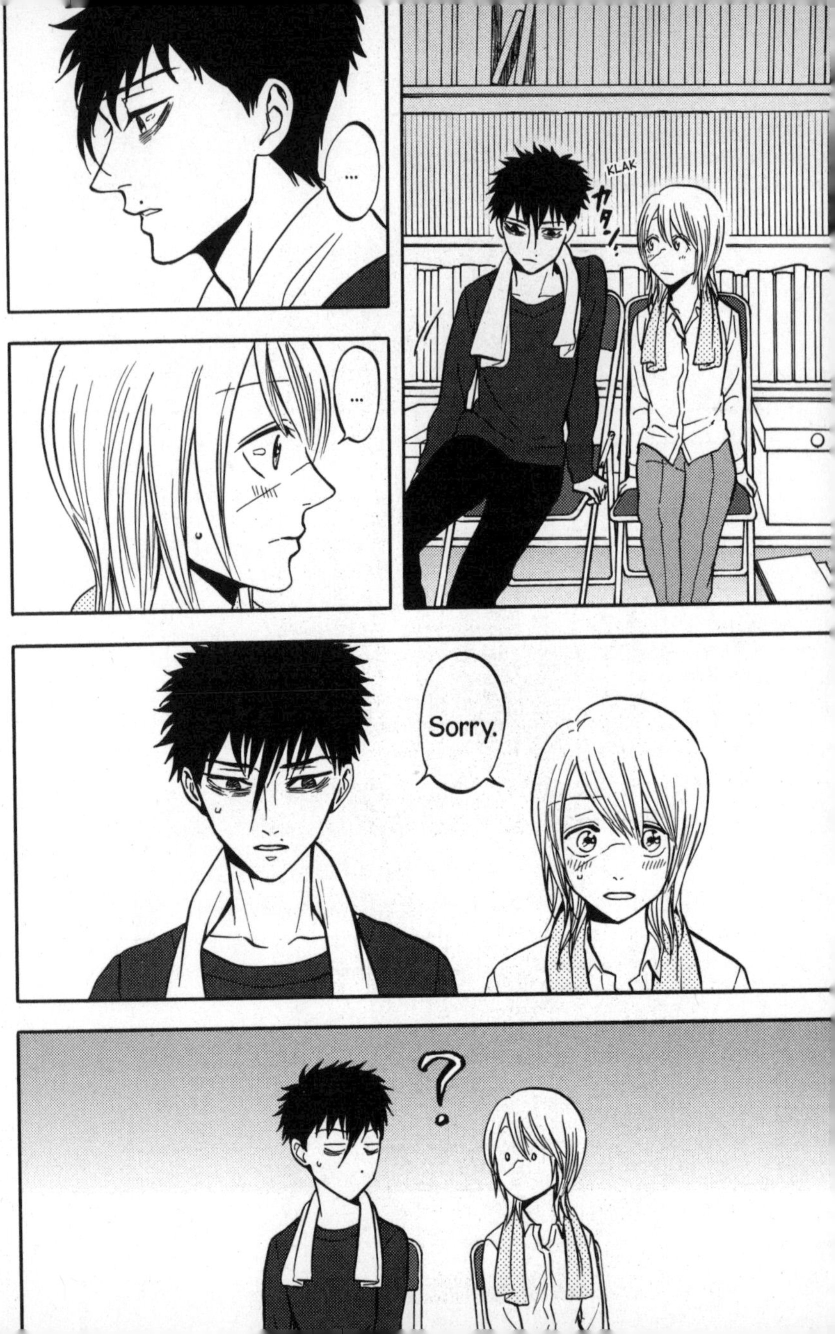
KLAK
ガタ!
...
...
Sorry.
?

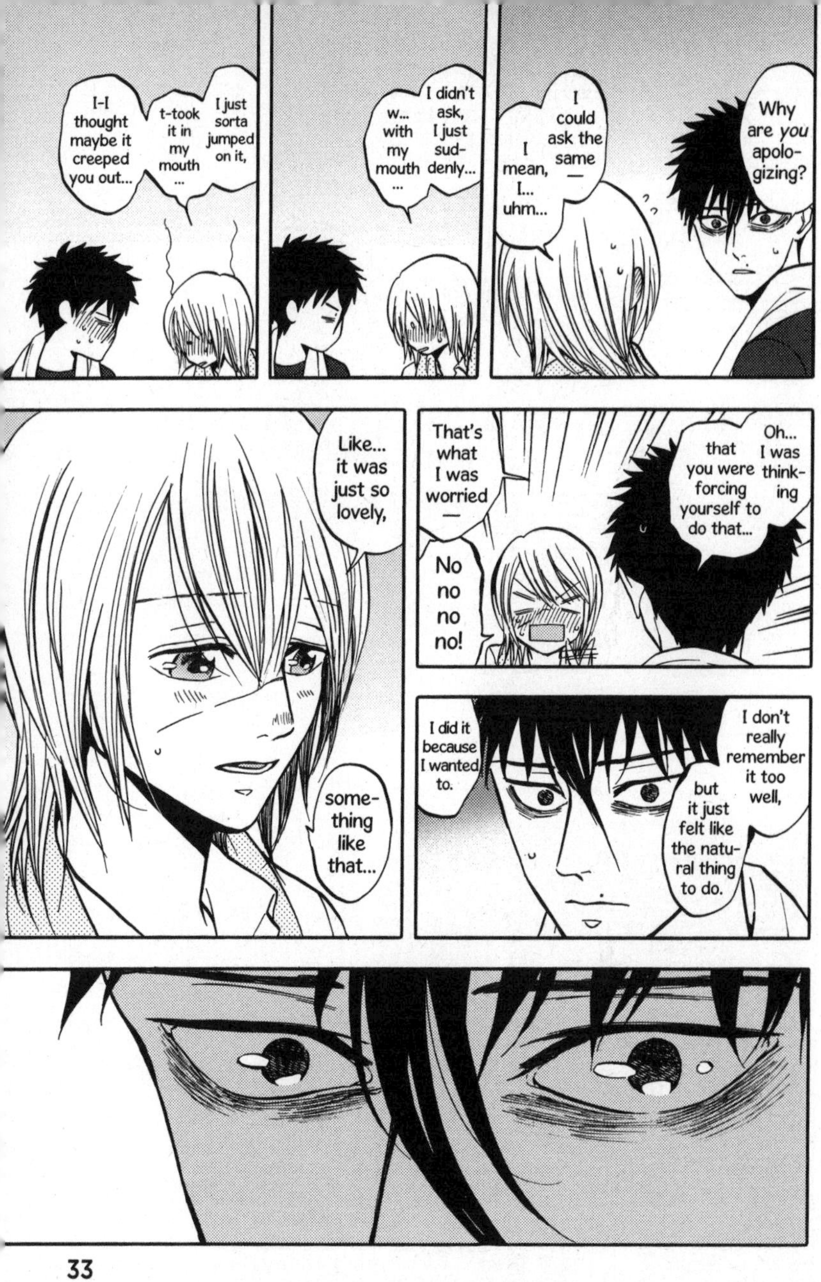
Why are *you* apologizing?
I could ask the same —
I mean, I... uhm...
I didn't ask, I just suddenly...
w... with my mouth ...
I just sorta jumped on it,
t-took it in my mouth ...
I-I thought maybe it creeped you out...
Oh... I was thinking
that you were forcing yourself to do that...
That's what I was worried —
No no no no!
I don't really remember it too well,
but it just felt like the natural thing to do.
I did it because I wanted to.
Like... it was just so lovely,
something like that...

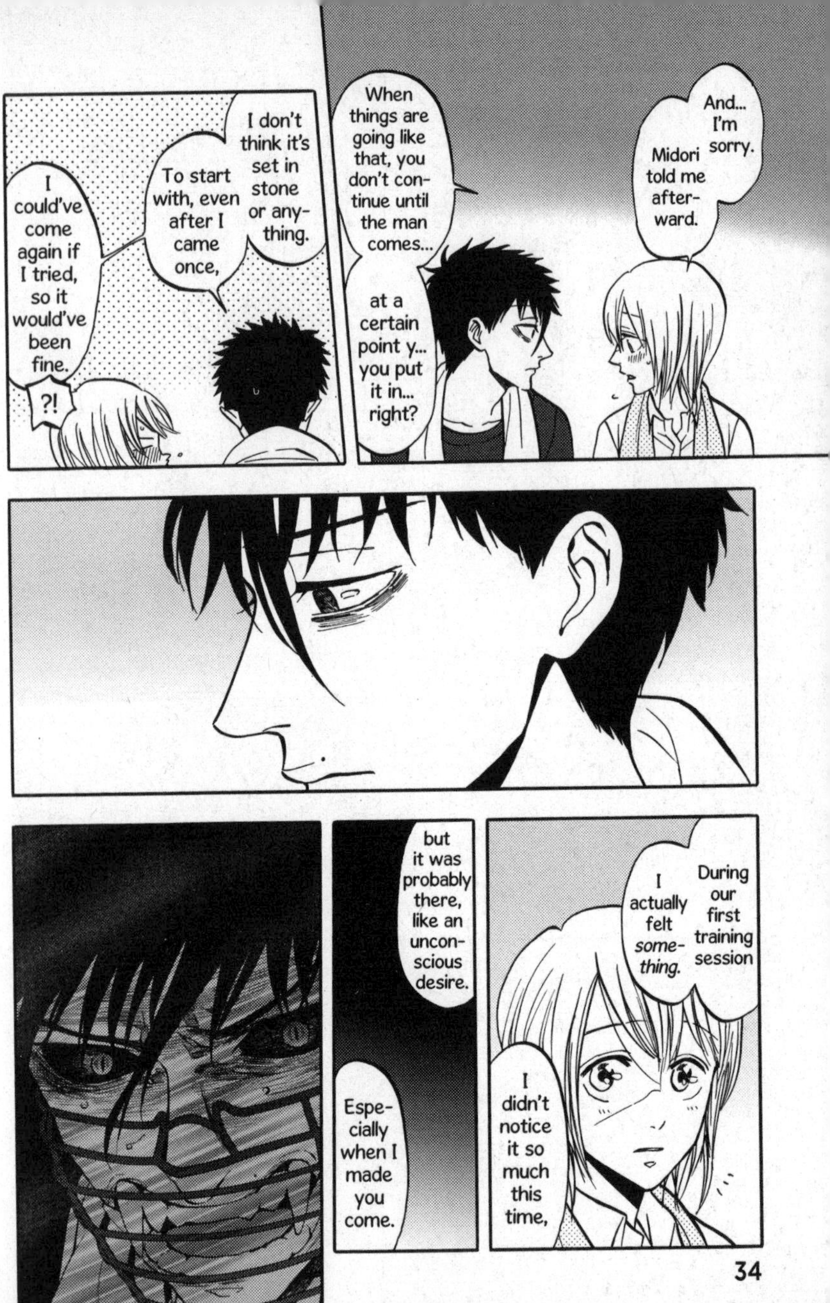
And... I'm sorry.
Midori told me afterward.
When things are going like that, you don't continue until the man comes...
at a certain point y... you put it in... right?
I don't think it's set in stone or anything.
To start with, even after I came once,
I could've come again if I tried, so it would've been fine.
?!
During our first training session
I actually felt *something.*
I didn't notice it so much this time,
but it was probably there, like an unconscious desire.
Especially when I made you come.

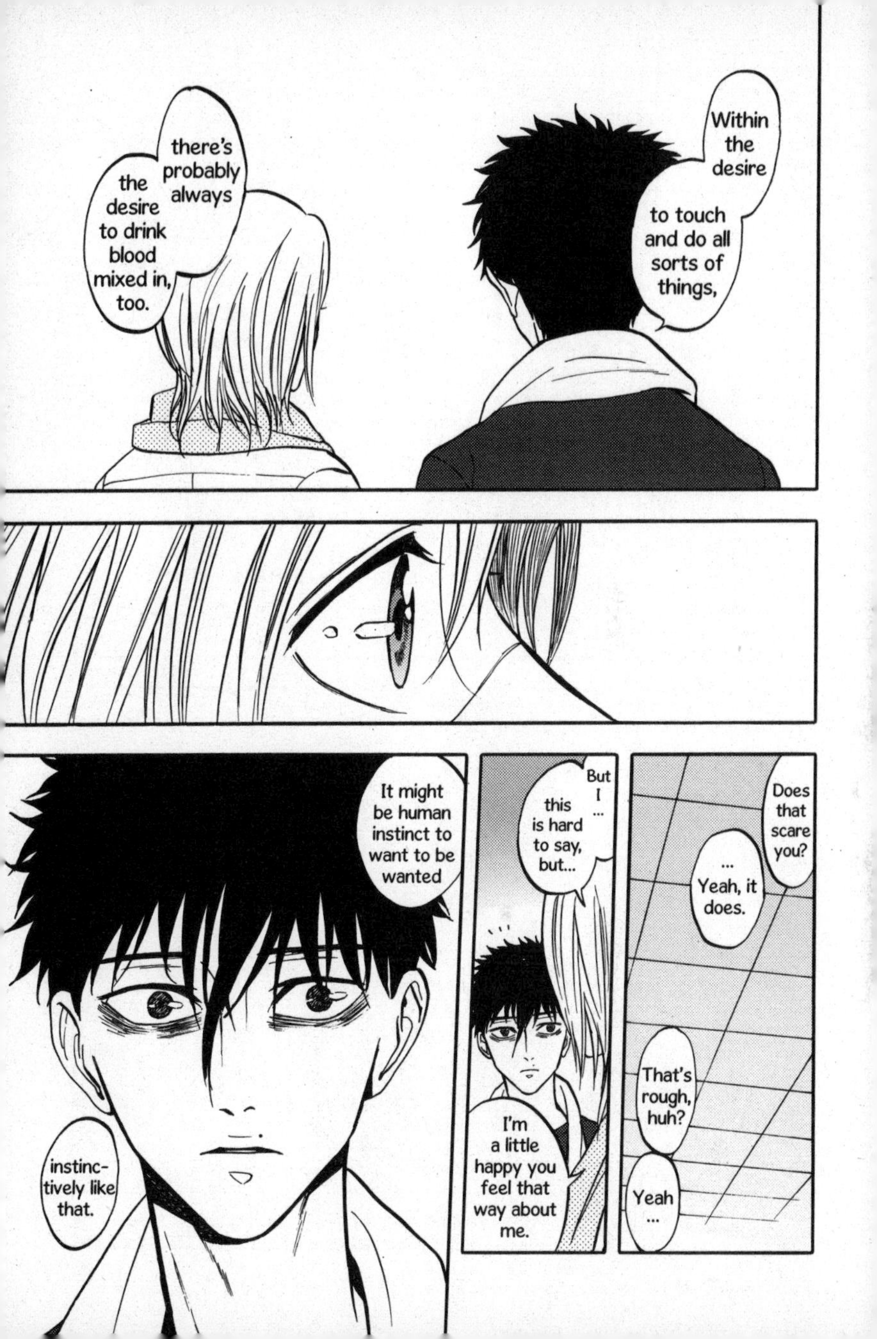
Within the desire
to touch and do all sorts of things,
there's probably always
the desire to drink blood mixed in, too.
Does that scare you?
... Yeah, it does.
That's rough, huh?
Yeah ...
But I ...
this is hard to say, but...
I'm a little happy you feel that way about me.
It might be human instinct to want to be wanted
instinc-tively like that.

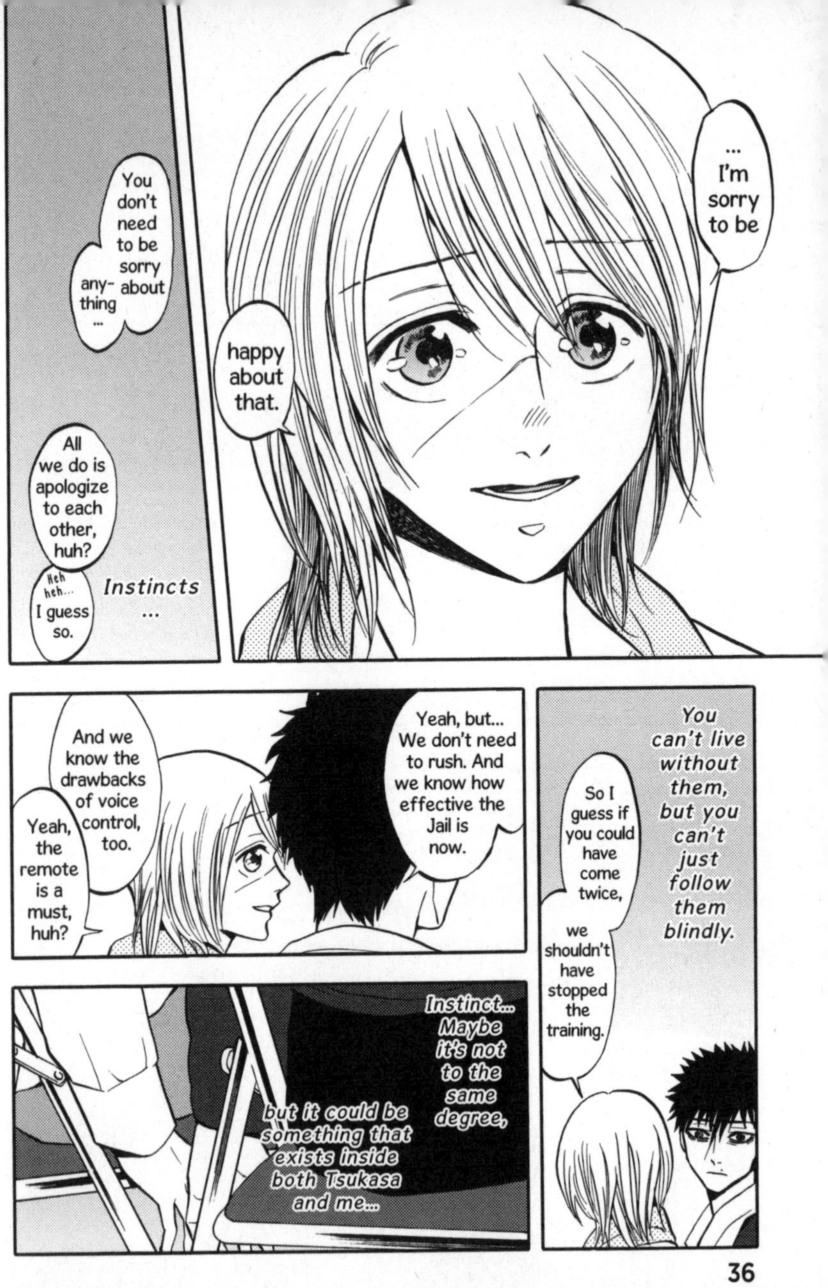
... I'm sorry to be
happy about that.
You don't need to be sorry about anything...
All we do is apologize to each other, huh?
Instincts...
Heh heh... I guess so.
You can't live without them, but you can't just follow them blindly.
So I guess if you could have come twice,
we shouldn't have stopped the training.
Yeah, but... We don't need to rush. And we know how effective the Jail is now.
And we know the drawbacks of voice control, too.
Yeah, the remote is a must, huh?
Instinct... Maybe it's not to the same degree,
but it could be something that exists inside both Tsukasa and me...

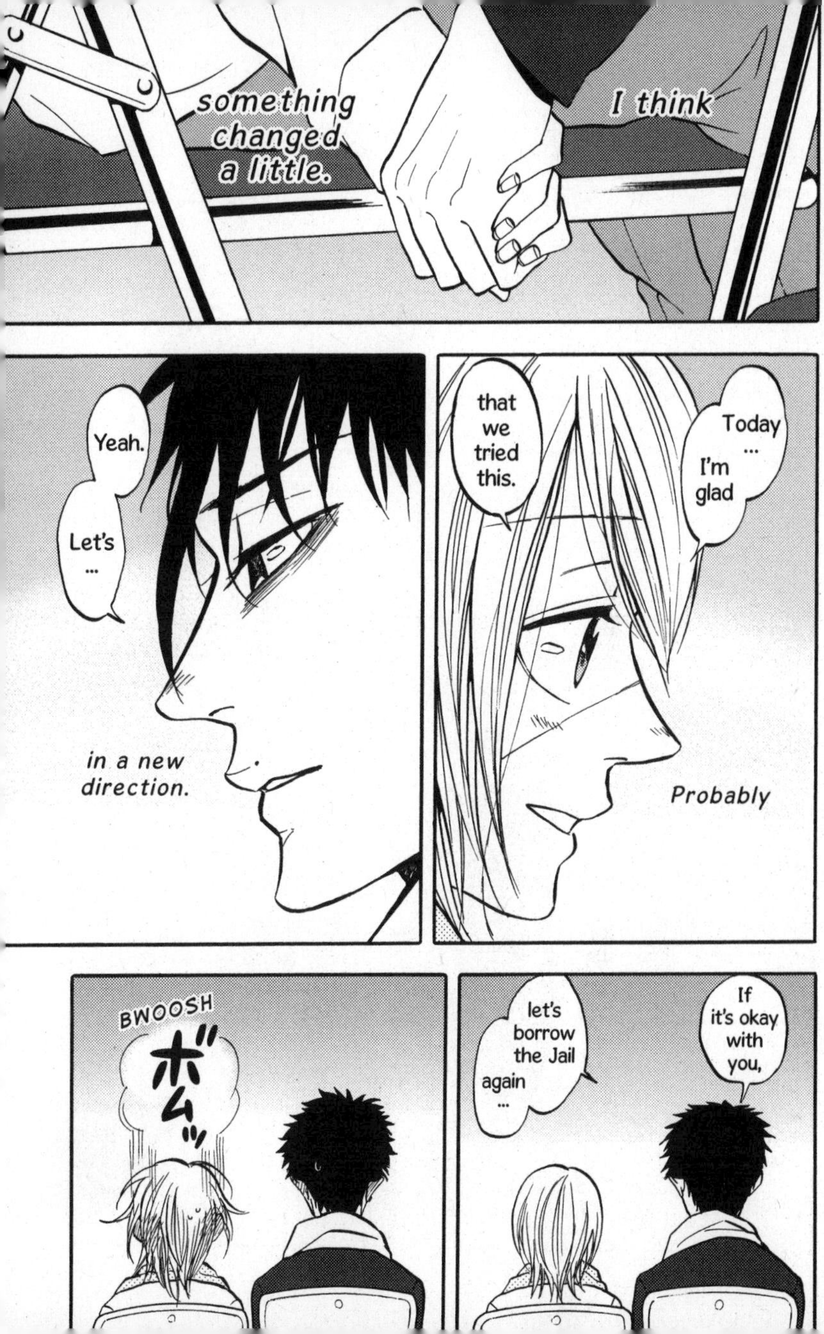

I think
something changed a little.
Today ... I'm glad
that we tried this.
Probably
Yeah.
Let's ...
in a new direction.
If it's okay with you,
let's borrow the Jail again ...
BWOOSH
ボムッ

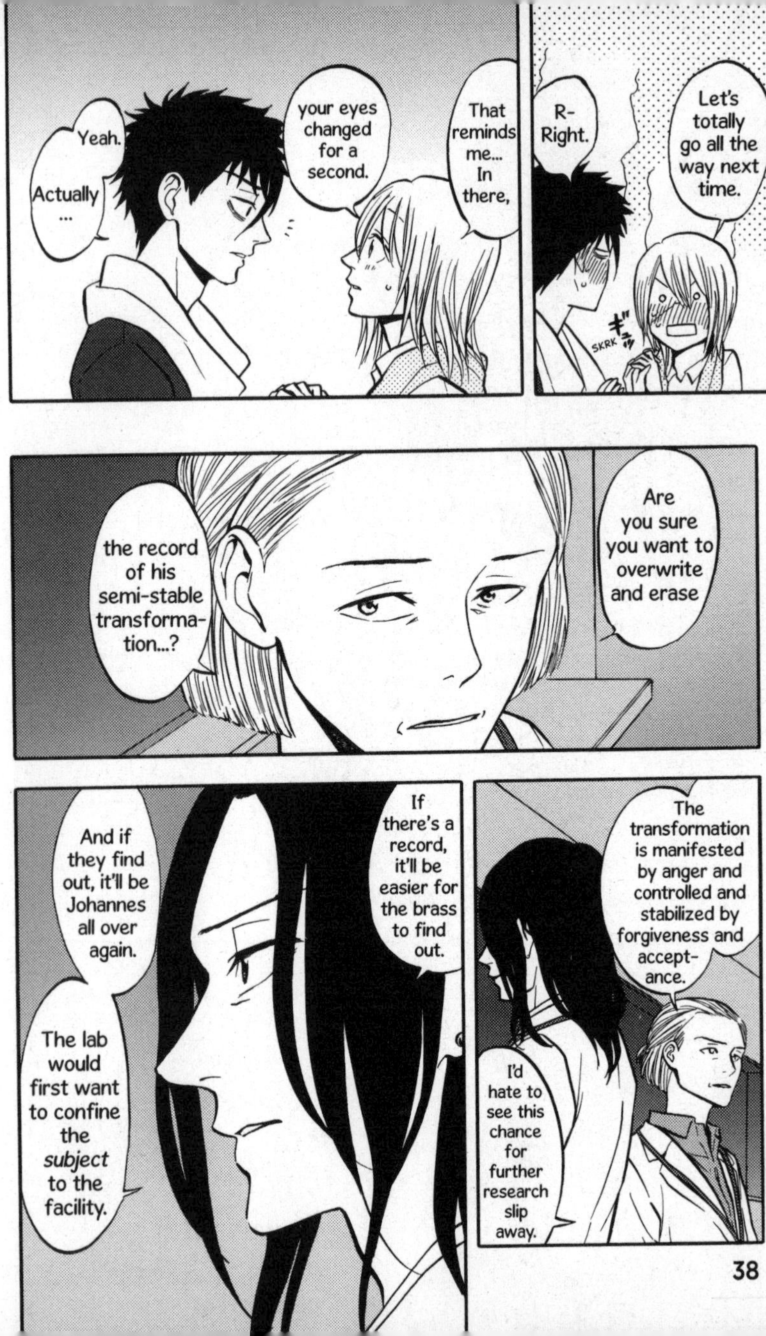
Let's totally go all the way next time.
R- Right.
SKRK
ギュッ
That reminds me... In there,
your eyes changed for a second.
Yeah.
Actually ...
Are you sure you want to overwrite and erase
the record of his semi-stable transformation...?
The transformation is manifested by anger and controlled and stabilized by forgiveness and acceptance.
I'd hate to see this chance for further research slip away.
If there's a record, it'll be easier for the brass to find out.
And if they find out, it'll be Johannes all over again.
The lab would first want to confine the *subject* to the facility.

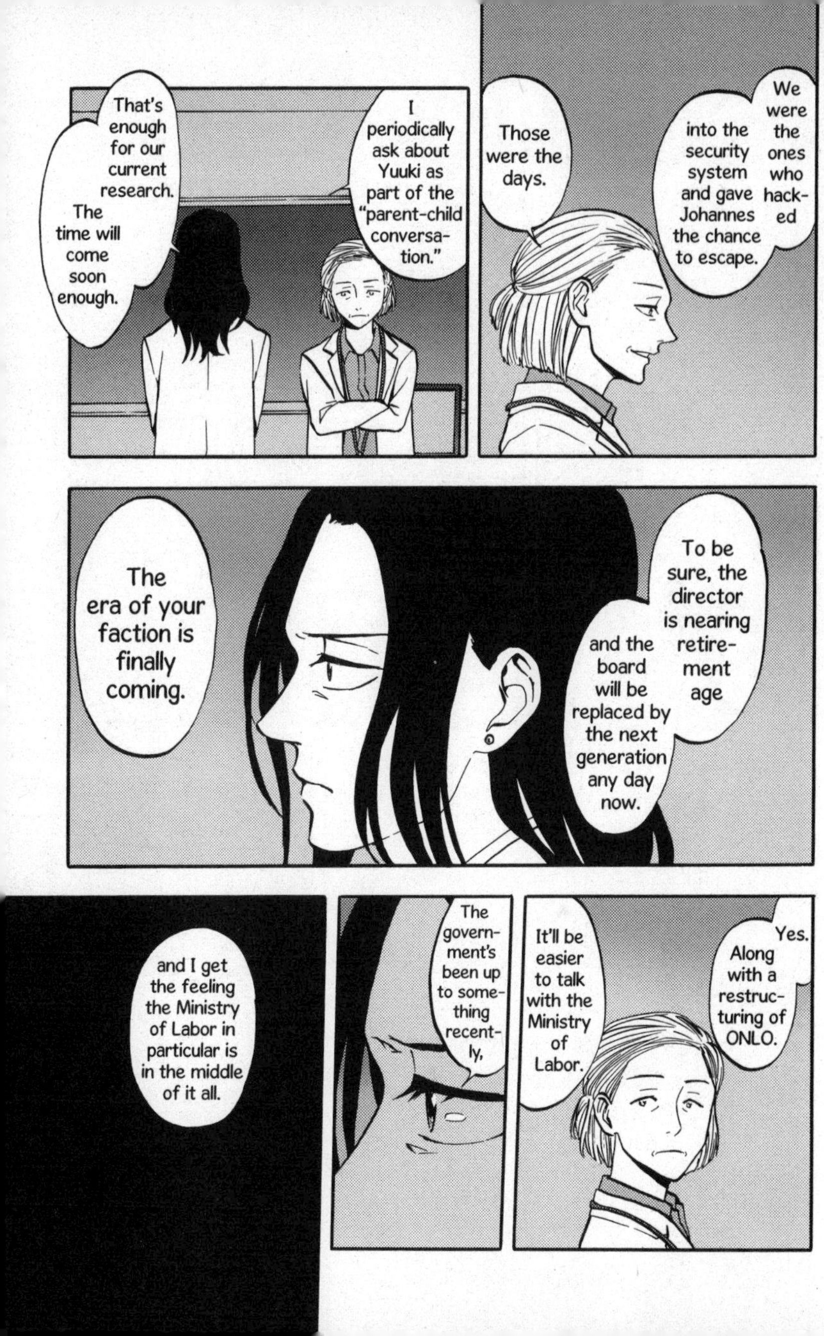
We were the ones who hack-ed into the security system and gave Johannes the chance to escape.
Those were the days.
I periodically ask about Yuuki as part of the "parent-child conversa-tion."
That's enough for our current research. The time will come soon enough.
To be sure, the director is nearing retire-ment age and the board will be replaced by the next generation any day now.
The era of your faction is finally coming.
Yes. Along with a restruc-turing of ONLO.
It'll be easier to talk with the Ministry of Labor.
The govern-ment's been up to some-thing recent-ly,
and I get the feeling the Ministry of Labor in particular is in the middle of it all.

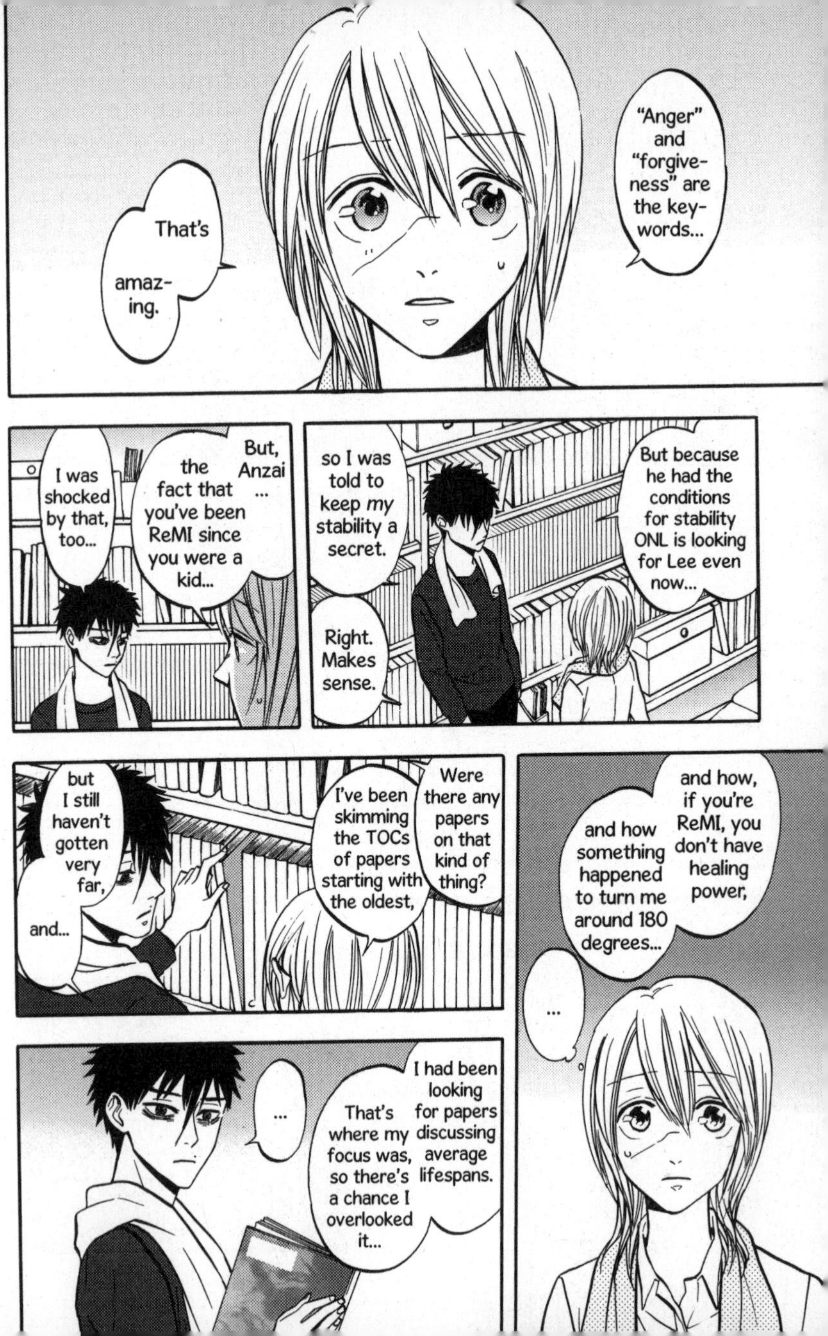
"Anger" and "forgive-ness" are the key-words...
That's amaz-ing.
But because he had the conditions for stability ONL is looking for Lee even now...
so I was told to keep *my* stability a secret.
Right. Makes sense.
But, Anzai ...
the fact that you've been ReMI since you were a kid...
I was shocked by that, too...
and how, if you're ReMI, you don't have healing power,
and how something happened to turn me around 180 degrees...
...
Were there any papers on that kind of thing?
I've been skimming the TOCs of papers starting with the oldest,
but I still haven't gotten very far,
and...
I had been looking for papers discussing average lifespans.
That's where my focus was, so there's a chance I overlooked it...
...

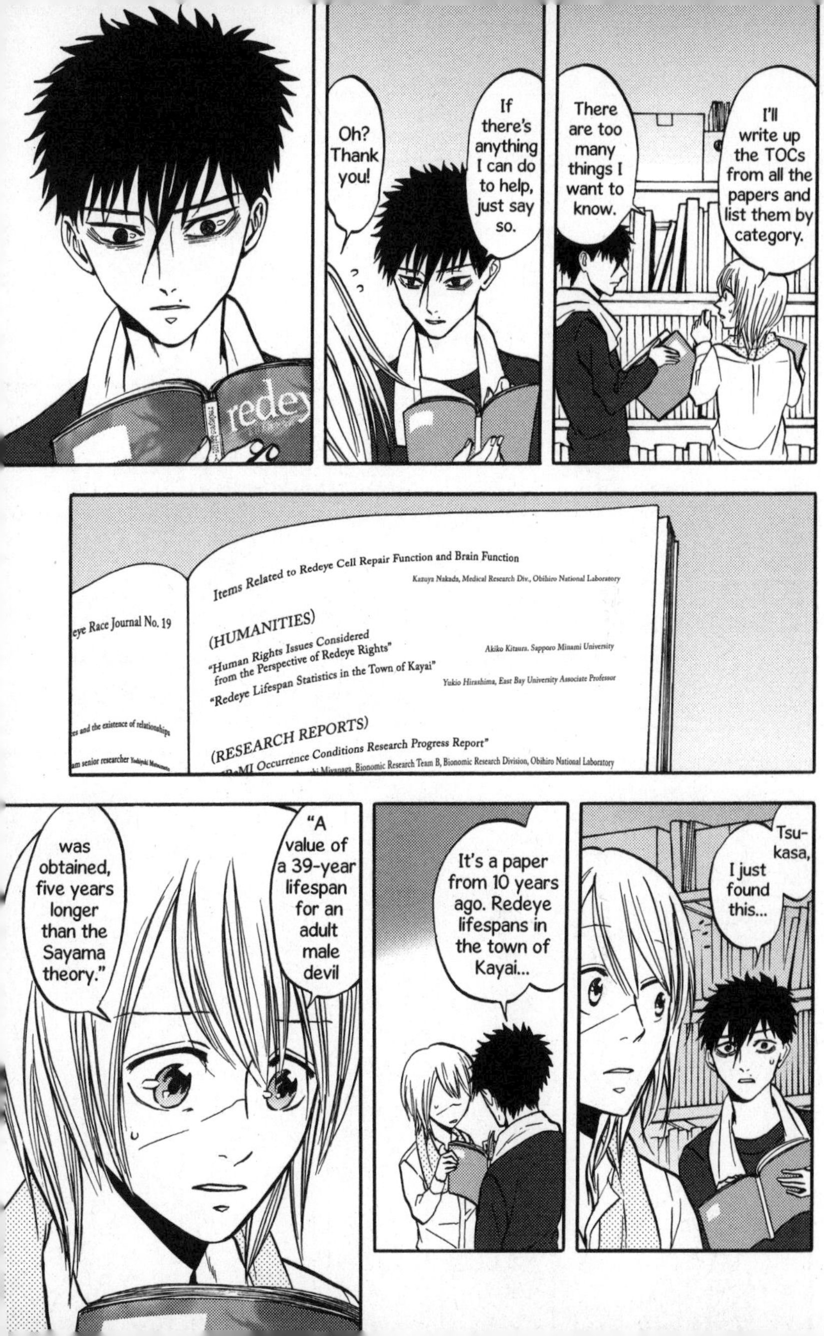
I'll write up the TOCs from all the papers and list them by category.
There are too many things I want to know.
If there's anything I can do to help, just say so.
Oh? Thank you!
eye Race Journal No. 19
Items Related to Redeye Cell Repair Function and Brain Function
Kazuya Nakada, Medical Research Div., Obihiro National Laboratory
(HUMANITIES)
"Human Rights Issues Considered from the Perspective of Redeye Rights"
Akiko Kitaura, Sapporo Minami University
"Redeye Lifespan Statistics in the Town of Kayai"
Yukio Hirashima, East Bay University Associate Professor
(RESEARCH REPORTS)
Occurrence Conditions Research Progress Report"
Bionomic Research Team B, Bionomic Research Division, Obihiro National Laboratory
Tsu-kasa, I just found this...
It's a paper from 10 years ago. Redeye lifespans in the town of Kayai...
"A value of a 39-year lifespan for an adult male devil
was obtained, five years longer than the Sayama theory."

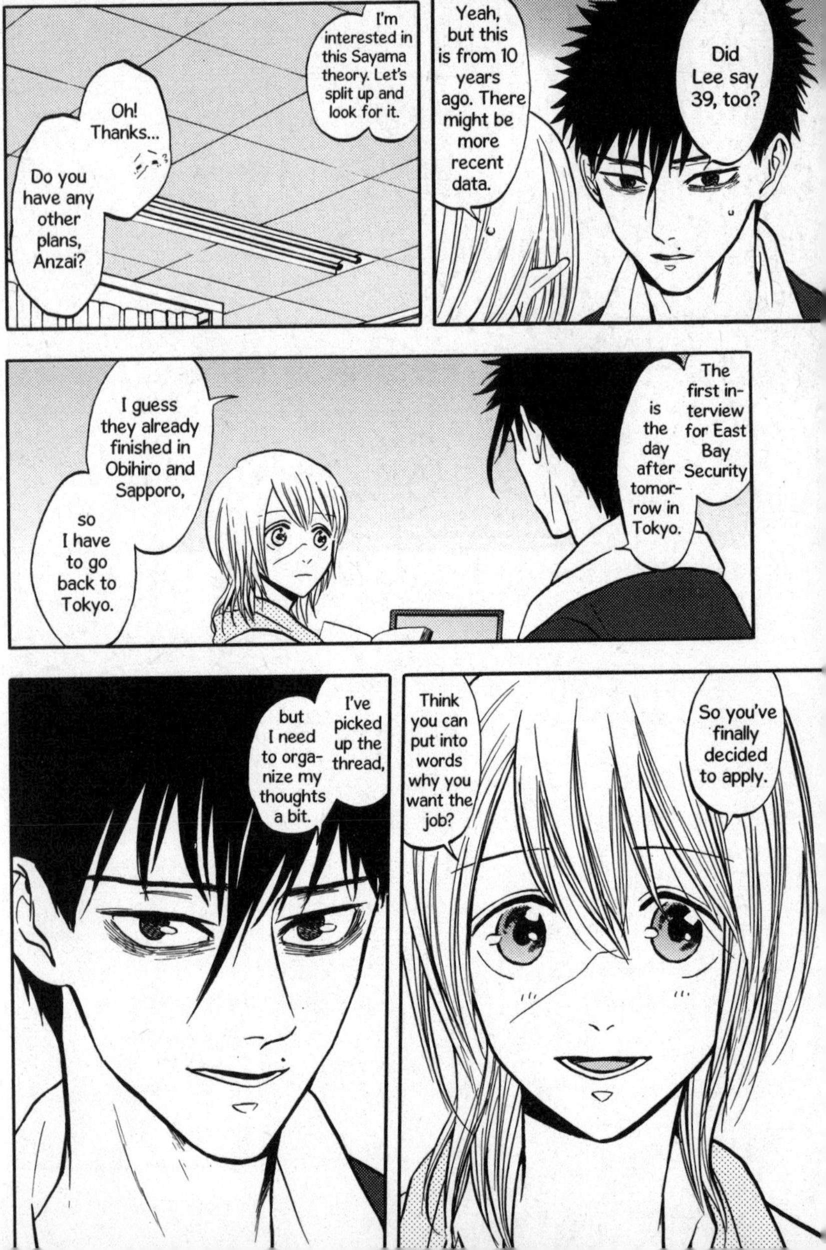
Did Lee say 39, too?
Yeah, but this is from 10 years ago. There might be more recent data.
I'm interested in this Sayama theory. Let's split up and look for it.
Oh! Thanks...
Do you have any other plans, Anzai?
The first interview for East Bay Security
is the day after tomorrow in Tokyo.
I guess they already finished in Obihiro and Sapporo,
so I have to go back to Tokyo.
So you've finally decided to apply.
Think you can put into words why you want the job?
I've picked up the thread,
but I need to organize my thoughts a bit.

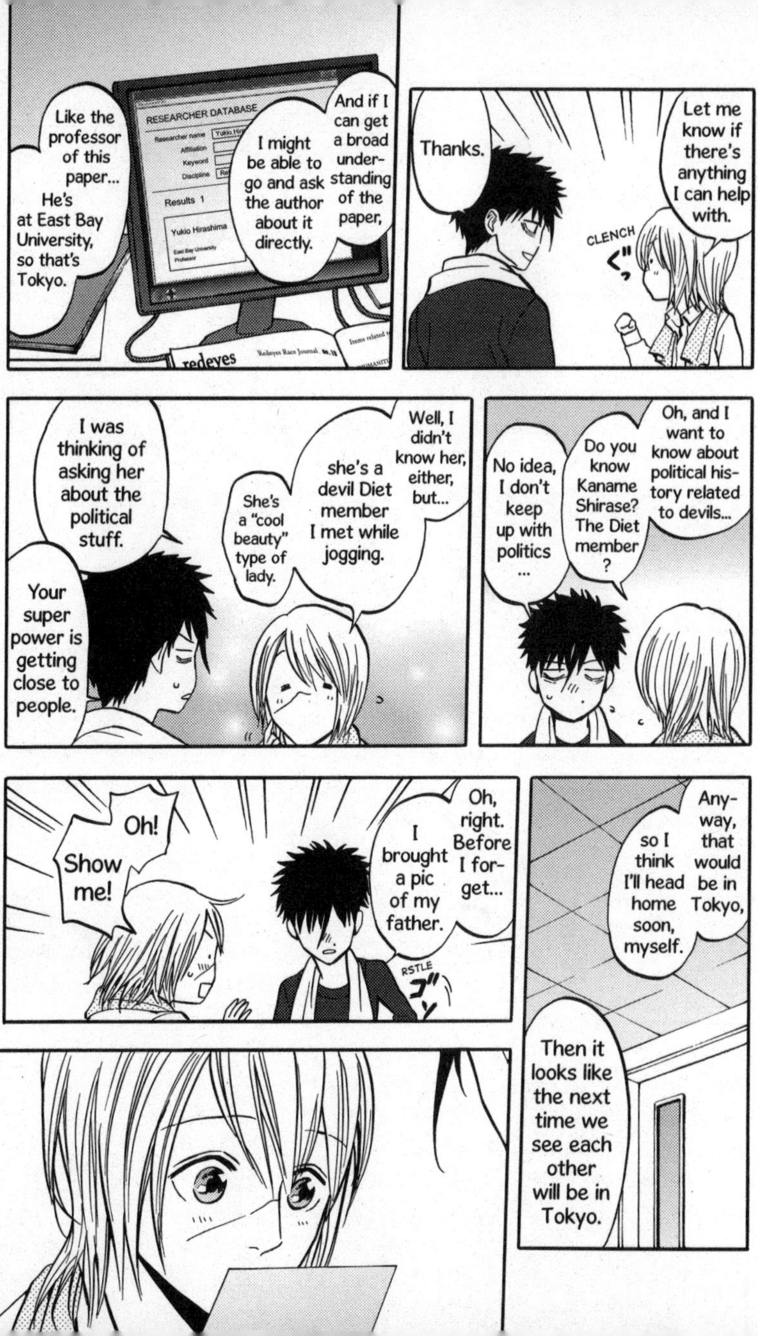

Let me know if there's anything I can help with.
CLENCH
Thanks.
And if I can get a broad understanding of the paper,
I might be able to go and ask the author about it directly.
Like the professor of this paper... He's at East Bay University, so that's Tokyo.
RESEARCHER DATABASE
Researcher name
Affiliation
Keyword
Discipline
Results 1
Yukio Hirashima
East Bay University
Professor
redeyes
Redeyes Race Journal
Items related t
Oh, and I want to know about political history related to devils...
Do you know Kaname Shirase? The Diet member?
No idea, I don't keep up with politics...
Well, I didn't know her, either, but...
she's a devil Diet member I met while jogging.
She's a "cool beauty" type of lady.
I was thinking of asking her about the political stuff.
Your super power is getting close to people.
Anyway, that would be in Tokyo,
so I think I'll head home soon, myself.
Then it looks like the next time we see each other will be in Tokyo.
Oh, right. Before I forget...
I brought a pic of my father.
RSTLE
Oh!
Show me!

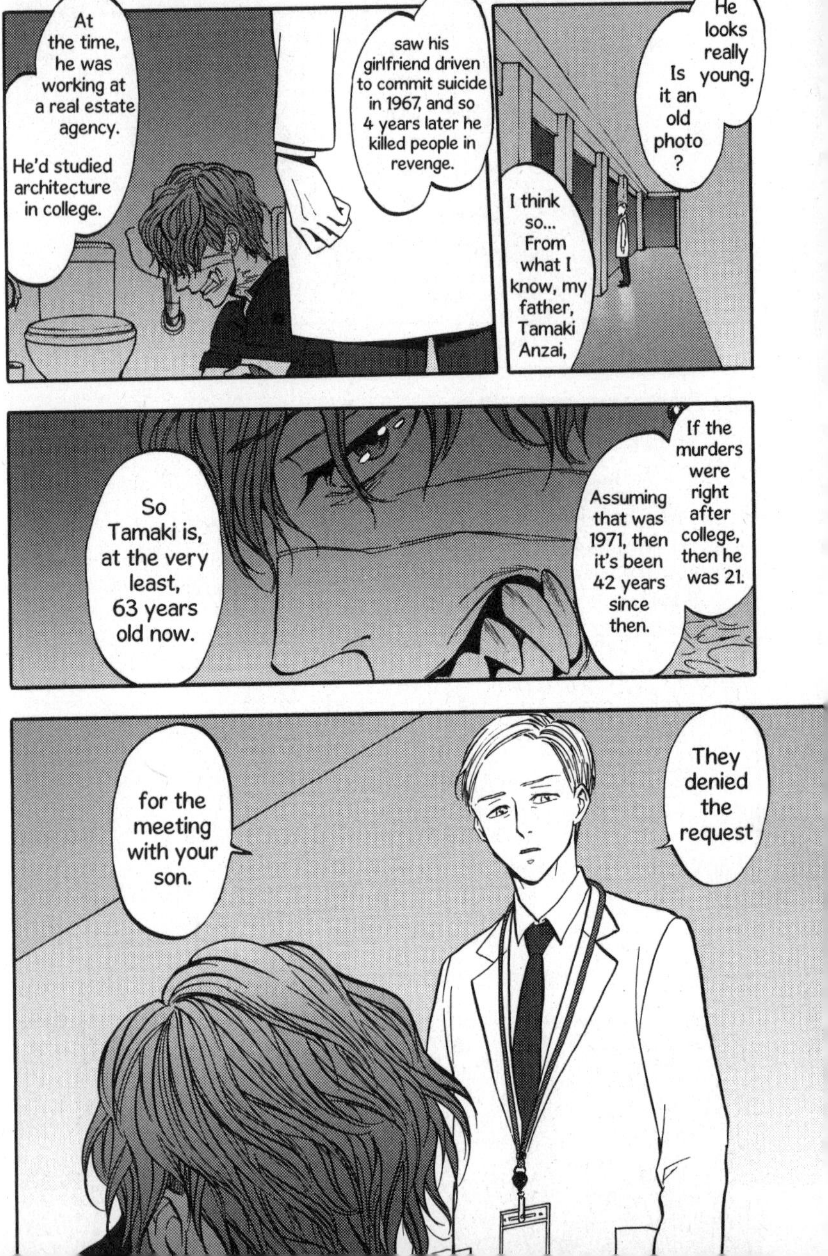
He looks really young. Is it an old photo?
I think so... From what I know, my father, Tamaki Anzai,
saw his girlfriend driven to commit suicide in 1967, and so 4 years later he killed people in revenge.
At the time, he was working at a real estate agency.
He'd studied architecture in college.
If the murders were right after college, then he was 21.
Assuming that was 1971, then it's been 42 years since then.
So Tamaki is, at the very least, 63 years old now.
They denied the request
for the meeting with your son.

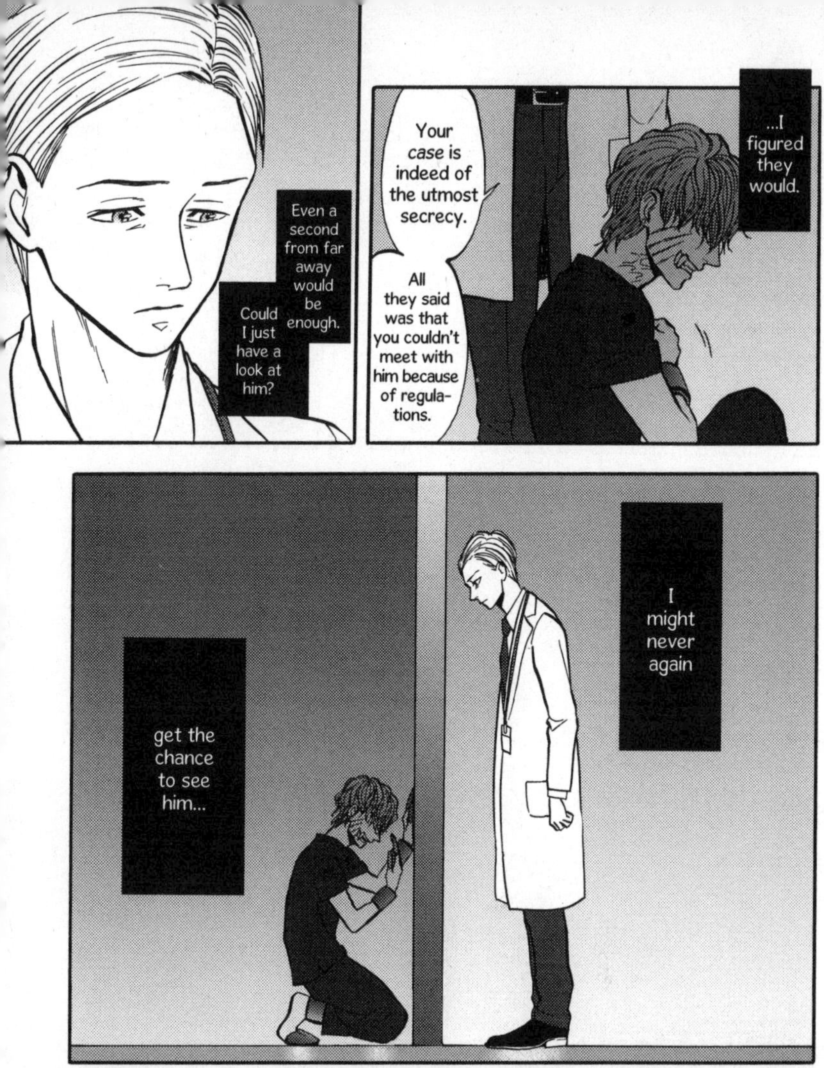
...I figured they would.
Your case is indeed of the utmost secrecy.
All they said was that you couldn't meet with him because of regulations.
Even a second from far away would be enough.
Could I just have a look at him?
I might never again
get the chance to see him...

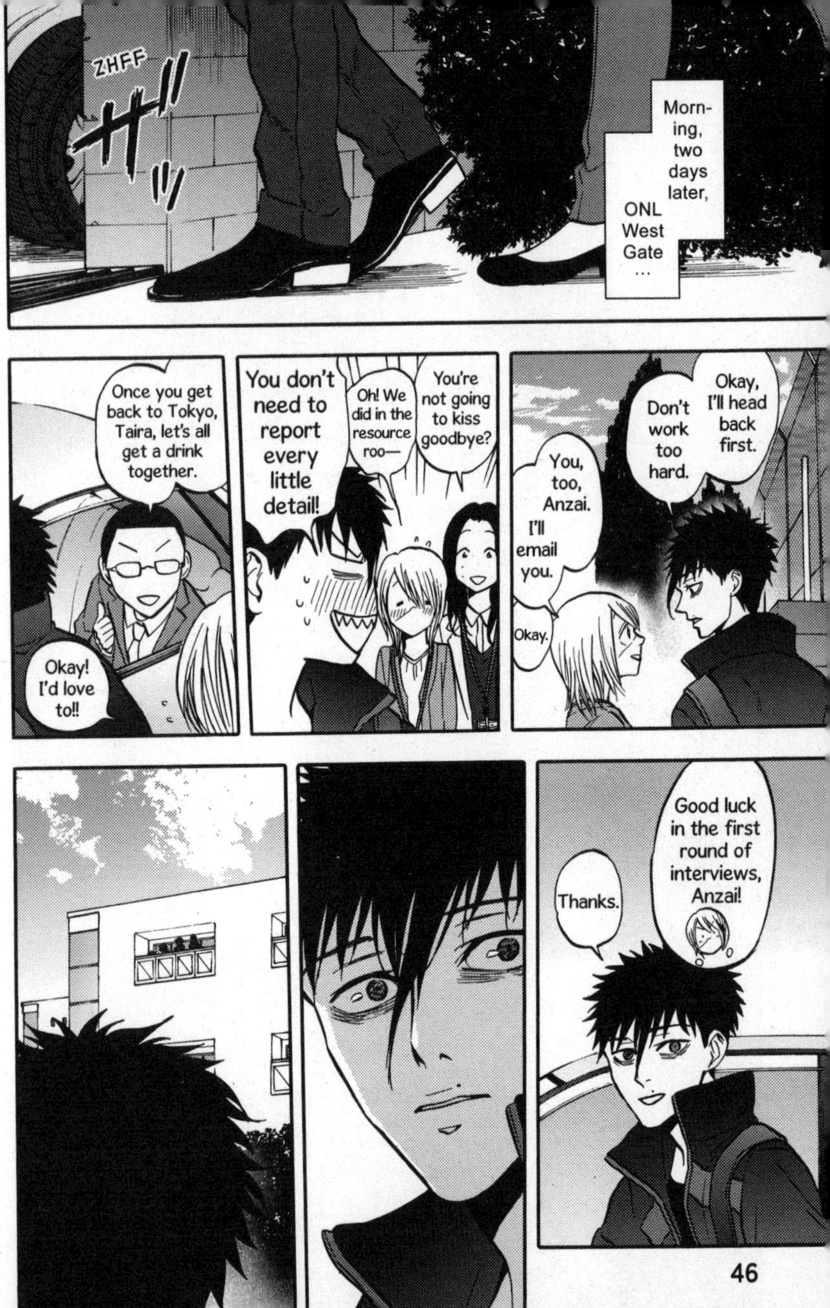
ZHFF
Morning, two days later, ONL West Gate …
Okay, I'll head back first.
Don't work too hard.
You, too, Anzai. I'll email you.
Okay.
You're not going to kiss goodbye?
Oh! We did in the resource roo—
You don't need to report every little detail!
Once you get back to Tokyo, Taira, let's all get a drink together.
Okay! I'd love to!!
Good luck in the first round of interviews, Anzai!
Thanks.

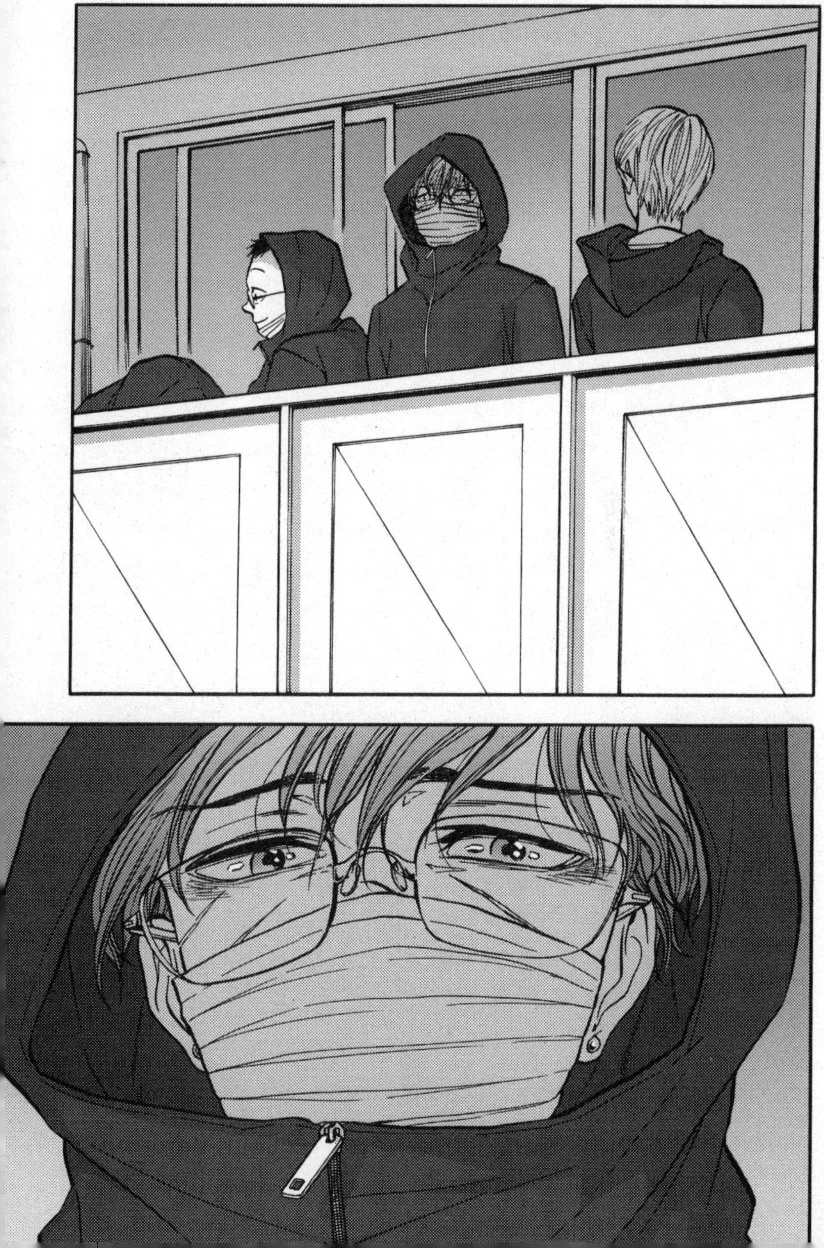

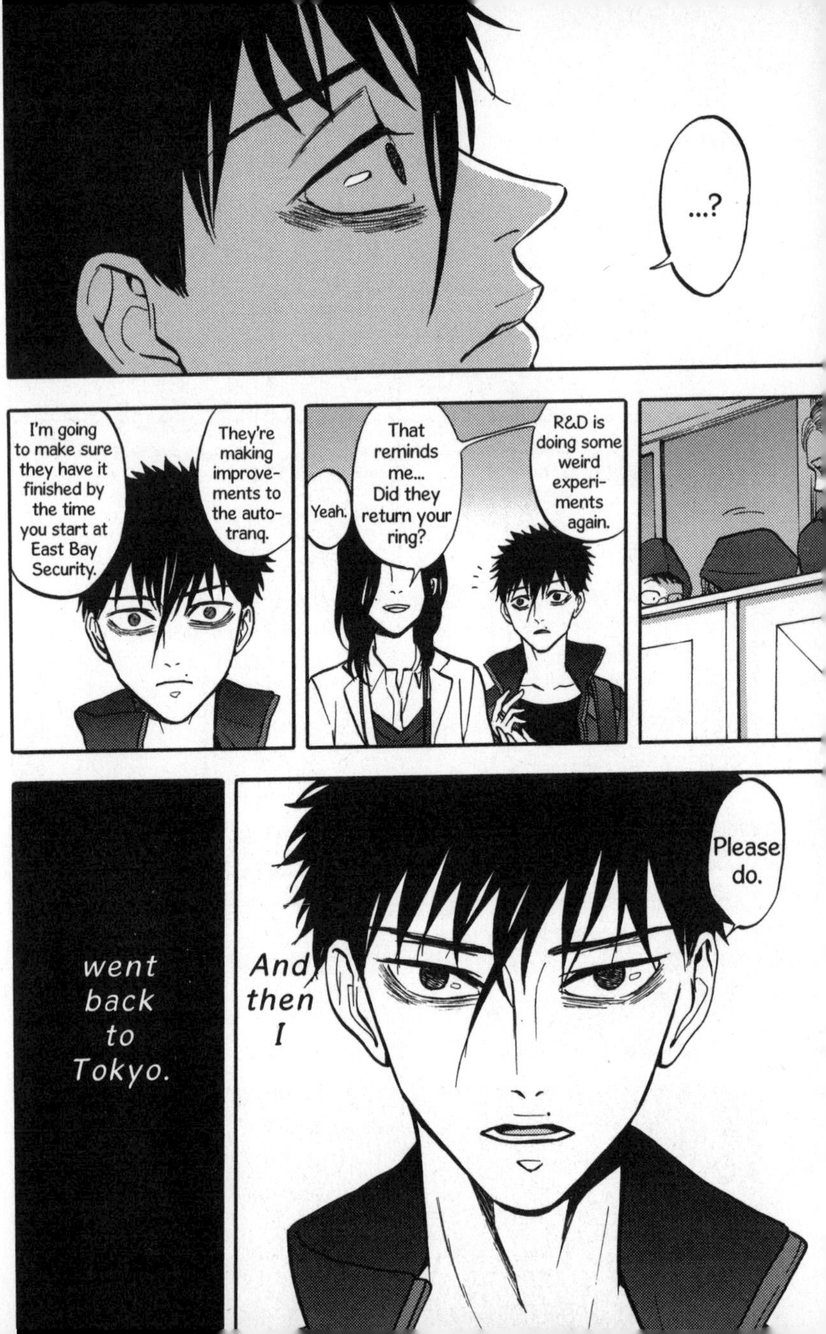
...?
R&D is doing some weird experiments again.
That reminds me... Did they return your ring?
Yeah.
They're making improvements to the auto-tranq.
I'm going to make sure they have it finished by the time you start at East Bay Security.
Please do.
And then I
went back to Tokyo.

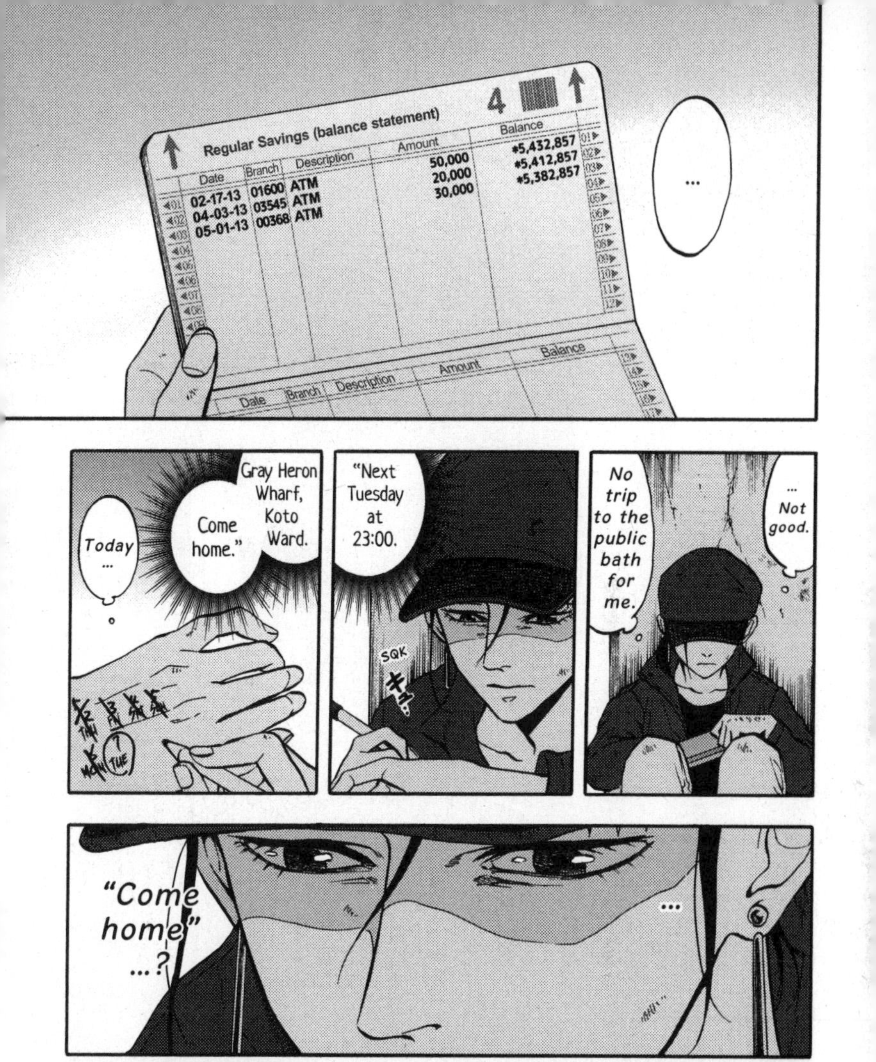
4
Regular Savings (balance statement)
Date Branch Description Amount Balance
02-17-13 01600 ATM 50,000 ¥5,432,857
04-03-13 03545 ATM 20,000 ¥5,412,857
05-01-13 00368 ATM 30,000 ¥5,382,857
Date Branch Description Amount Balance
...
... Not good.
No trip to the public bath for me.
"Next Tuesday at 23:00.
SQK
Gray Heron Wharf, Koto Ward.
Come home."
Today ...
...
"Come home" ...?

Line 54
Ken'ichi

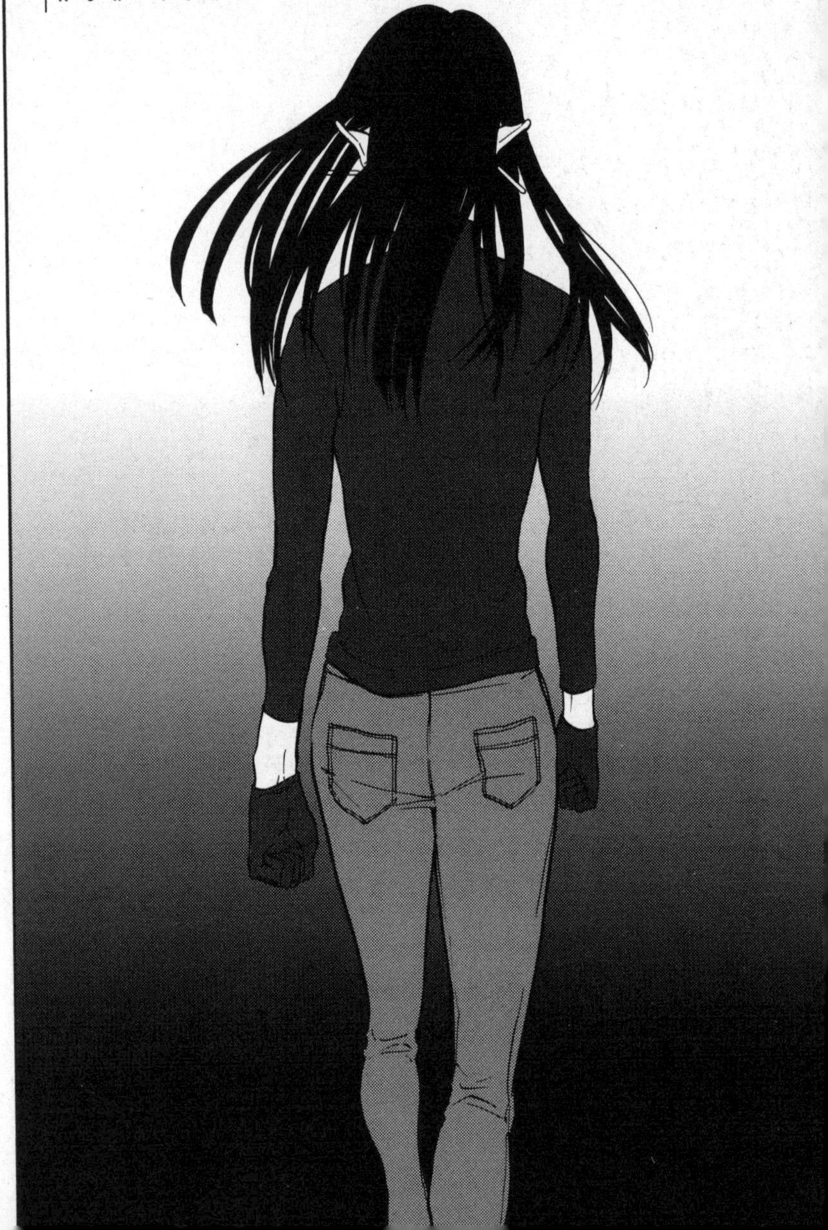

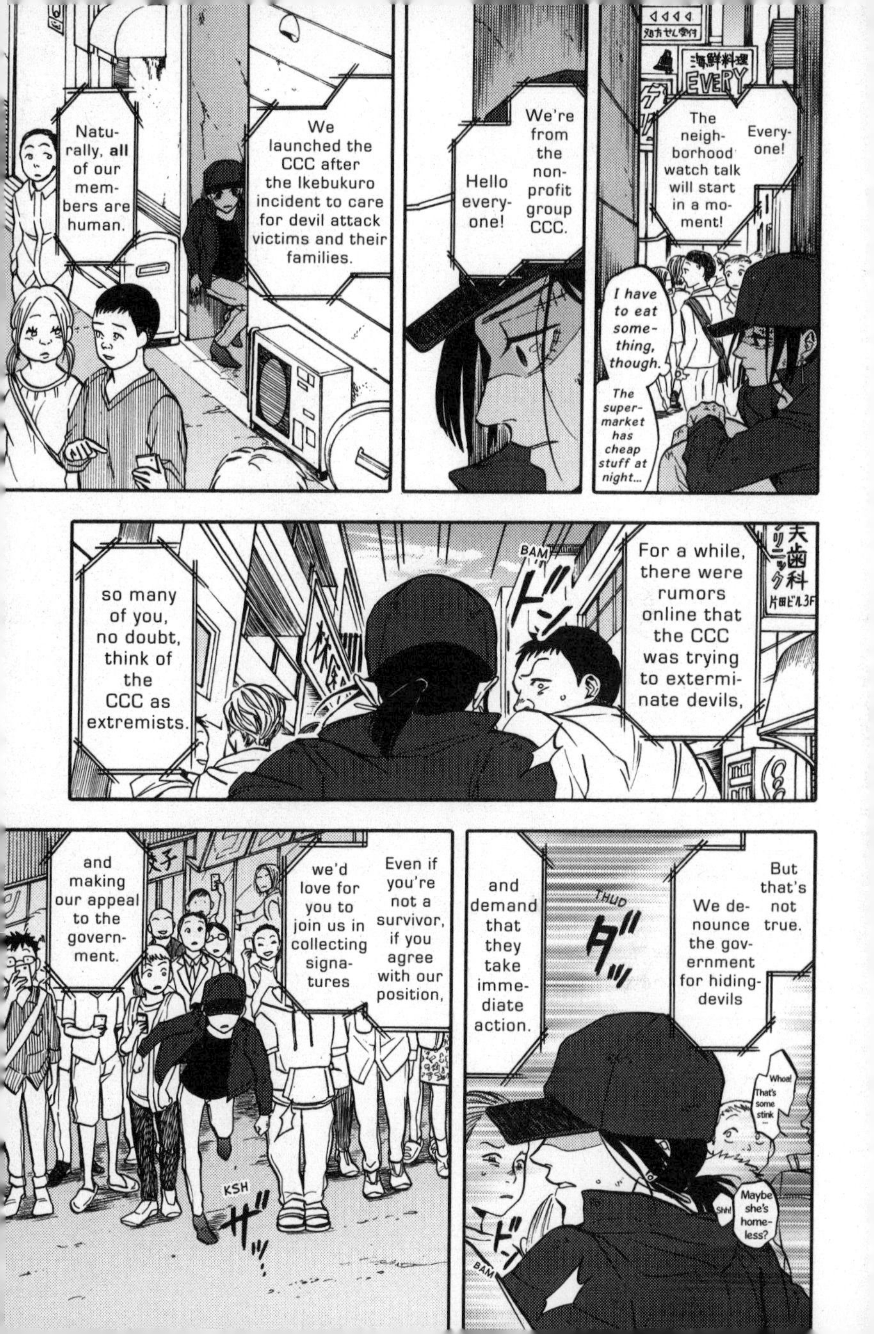

海鮮料理 EVERY
Every-one!
The neighborhood watch talk will start in a moment!
I have to eat something, though.
The supermarket has cheap stuff at night...
We're from the non-profit group CCC.
Hello everyone!
We launched the CCC after the Ikebukuro incident to care for devil attack victims and their families.
Naturally, **all** of our members are human.
For a while, there were rumors online that the CCC was trying to exterminate devils,
BAM
so many of you, no doubt, think of the CCC as extremists.
But that's not true.
We denounce the government for hiding devils
and demand that they take immediate action.
THUD
Whoa! That's some stink...
Shh!
Maybe she's homeless?
BAM
Even if you're not a survivor, if you agree with our position,
we'd love for you to join us in collecting signatures
and making our appeal to the government.
KSH

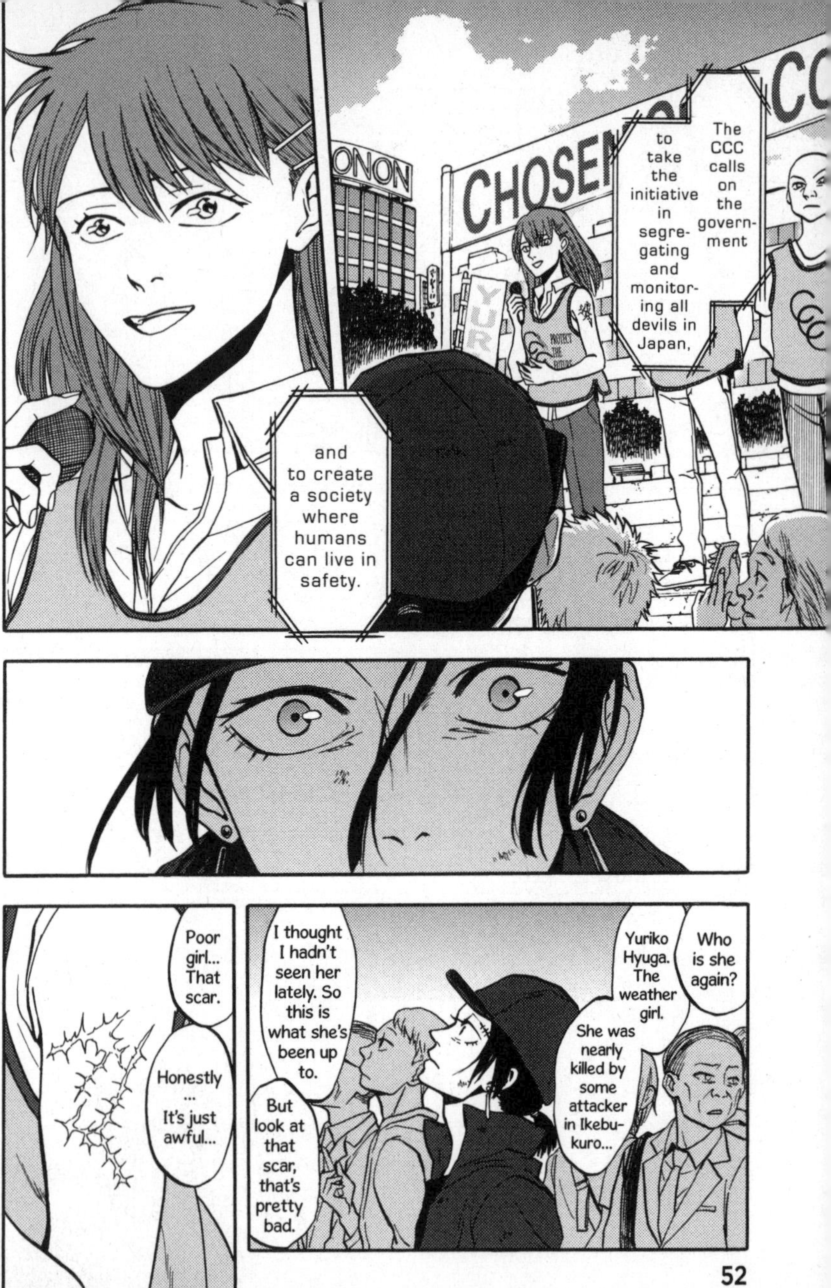
The CCC calls on the government
to take the initiative in segregating and monitoring all devils in Japan,
and to create a society where humans can live in safety.
Who is she again?
Yuriko Hyuga. The weather girl.
She was nearly killed by some attacker in Ikebukuro...
I thought I hadn't seen her lately. So this is what she's been up to.
But look at that scar, that's pretty bad.
Poor girl... That scar.
Honestly... It's just awful...

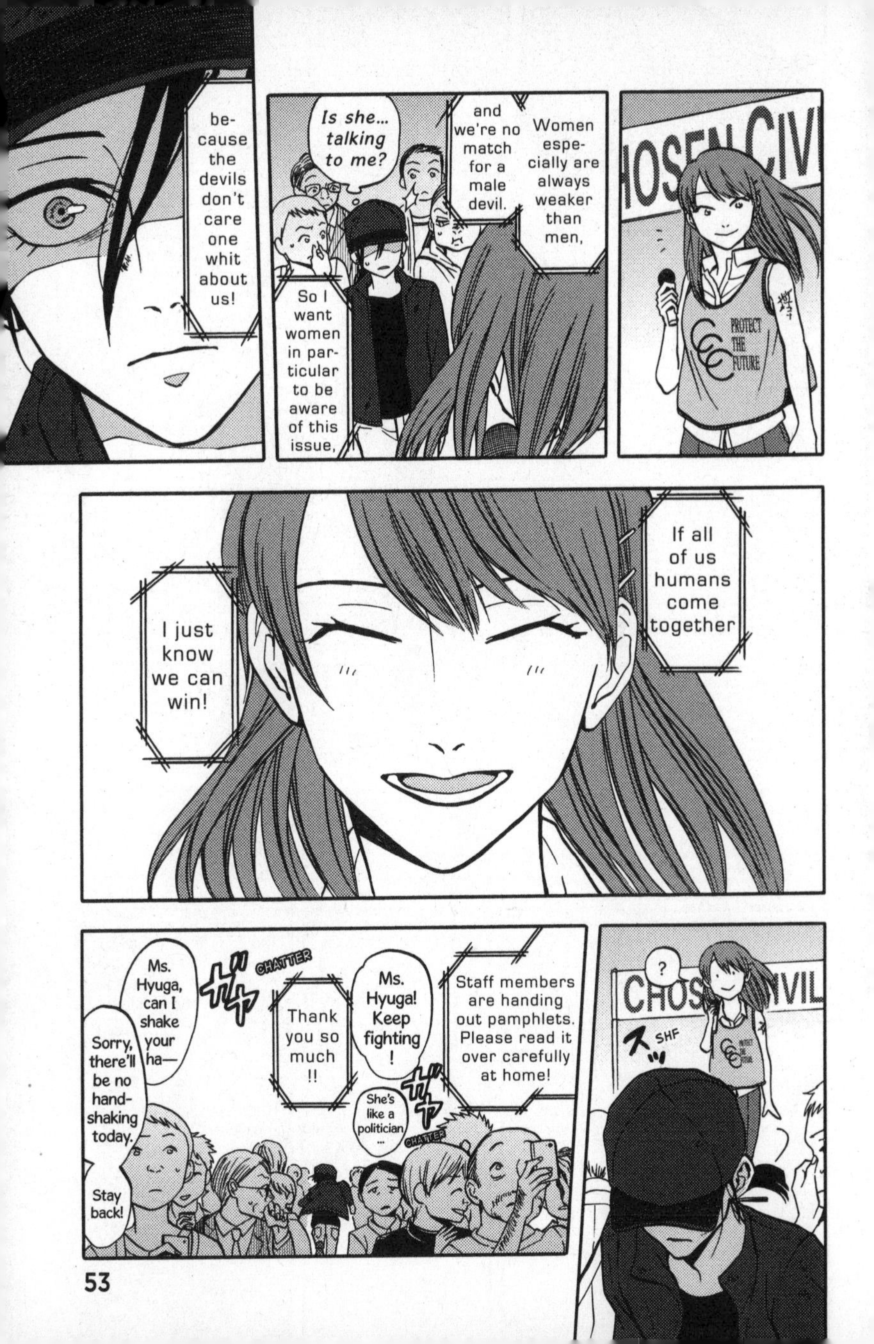

PROTECT THE FUTURE
Women especially are always weaker than men,
and we're no match for a male devil.
Is she... talking to me?
So I want women in particular to be aware of this issue,
be-cause the devils don't care one whit about us!
If all of us humans come together
I just know we can win!
?
SHF
Staff members are handing out pamphlets. Please read it over carefully at home!
Ms. Hyuga! Keep fighting!
She's like a politician...
CHATTER
Thank you so much!!
CHATTER
Ms. Hyuga, can I shake your ha—
Sorry, there'll be no hand-shaking today.
Stay back!

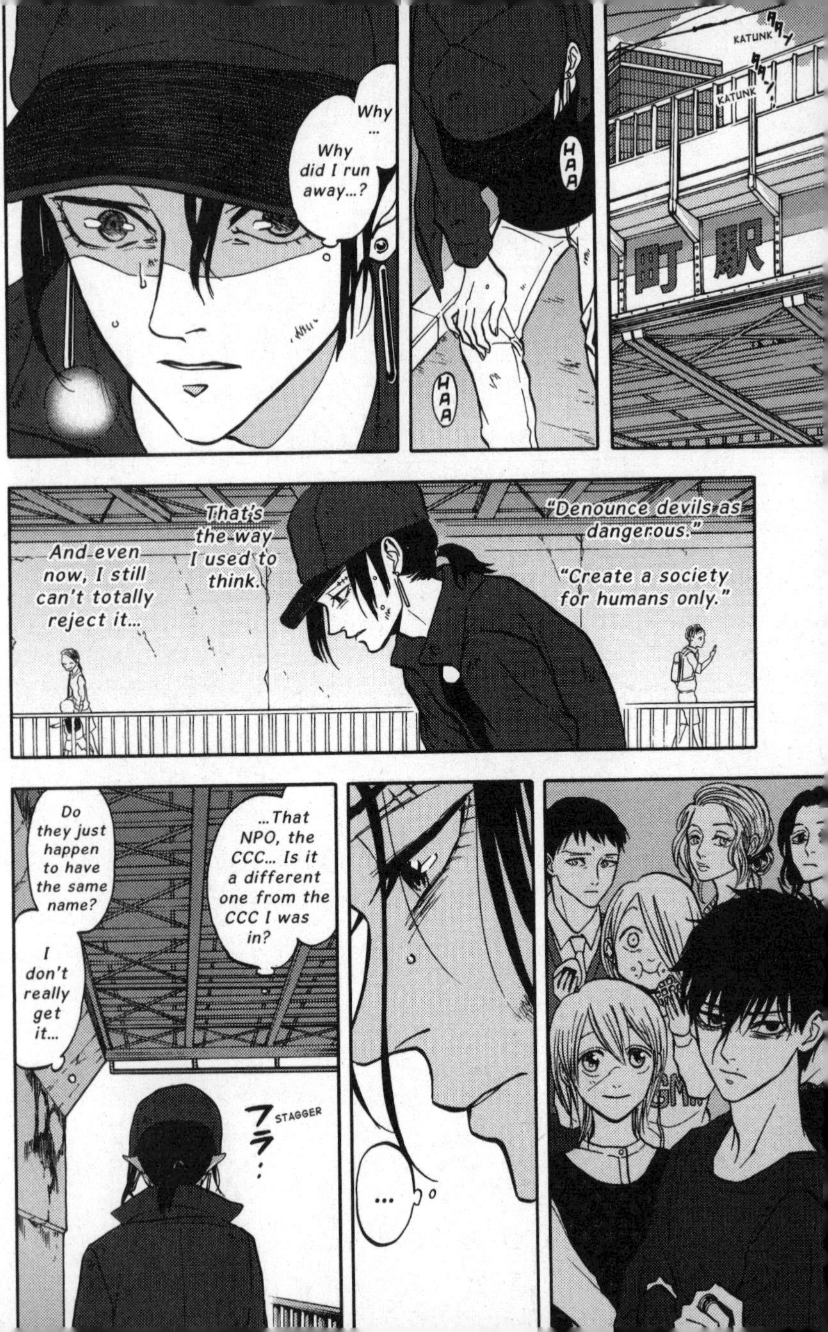
KATUNK
KATUNK
町 駅
HAA
HAA
Why... Why did I run away...?
"Denounce devils as dangerous."
"Create a society for humans only."
That's the way I used to think.
And even now, I still can't totally reject it...
...
...That NPO, the CCC... Is it a different one from the CCC I was in?
Do they just happen to have the same name?
I don't really get it...
STAGGER

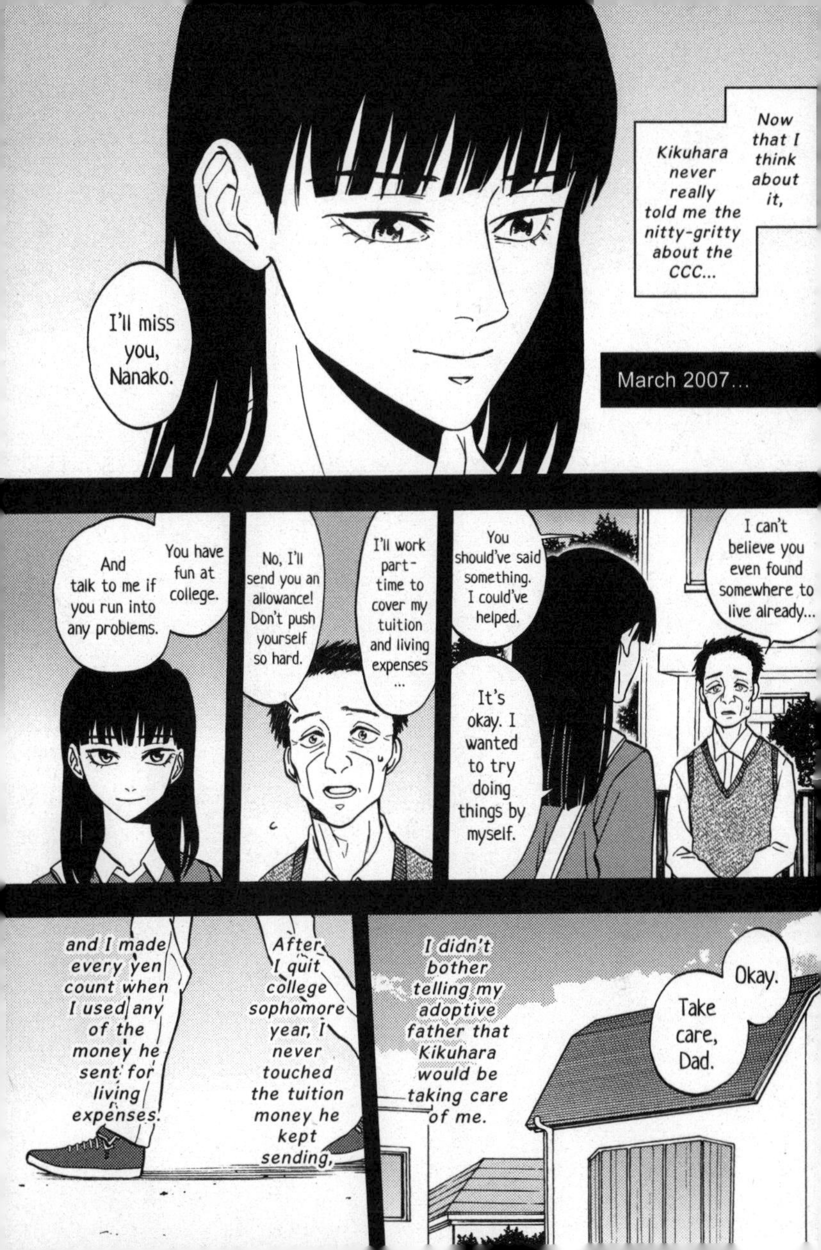
Now that I think about it,
Kikuhara never really told me the nitty-gritty about the CCC...
March 2007...
I'll miss you, Nanako.
I can't believe you even found somewhere to live already...
You should've said something. I could've helped.
It's okay. I wanted to try doing things by myself.
I'll work part-time to cover my tuition and living expenses...
No, I'll send you an allowance! Don't push yourself so hard.
You have fun at college.
And talk to me if you run into any problems.
Okay.
Take care, Dad.
I didn't bother telling my adoptive father that Kikuhara would be taking care of me.
After I quit college sophomore year, I never touched the tuition money he kept sending,
and I made every yen count when I used any of the money he sent for living expenses.

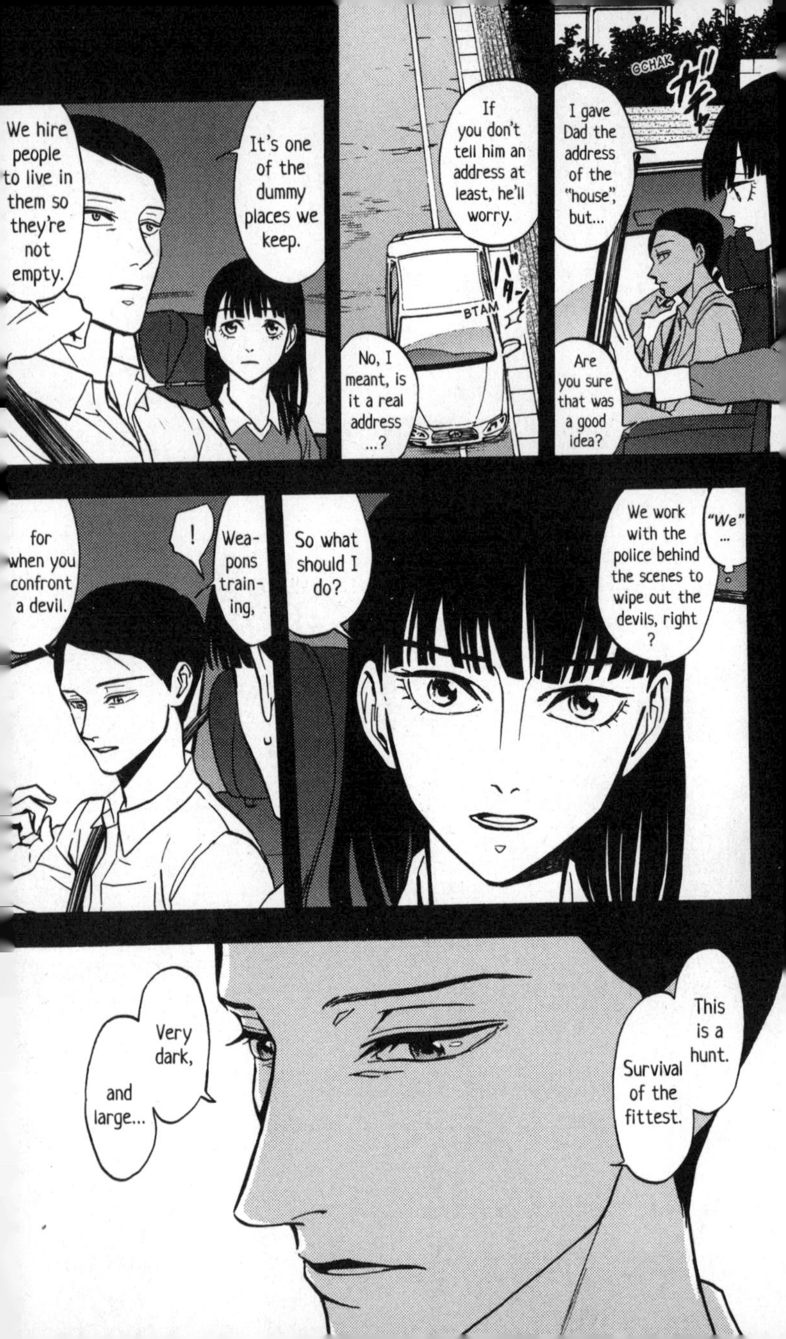
GCHAK
I gave Dad the address of the "house", but...
Are you sure that was a good idea?
If you don't tell him an address at least, he'll worry.
BTAM
No, I meant, is it a real address ...?
It's one of the dummy places we keep.
We hire people to live in them so they're not empty.
We work with the police behind the scenes to wipe out the devils, right?
"We" ...
So what should I do?
Weapons training,
!
for when you confront a devil.
This is a hunt.
Survival of the fittest.
Very dark,
and large...

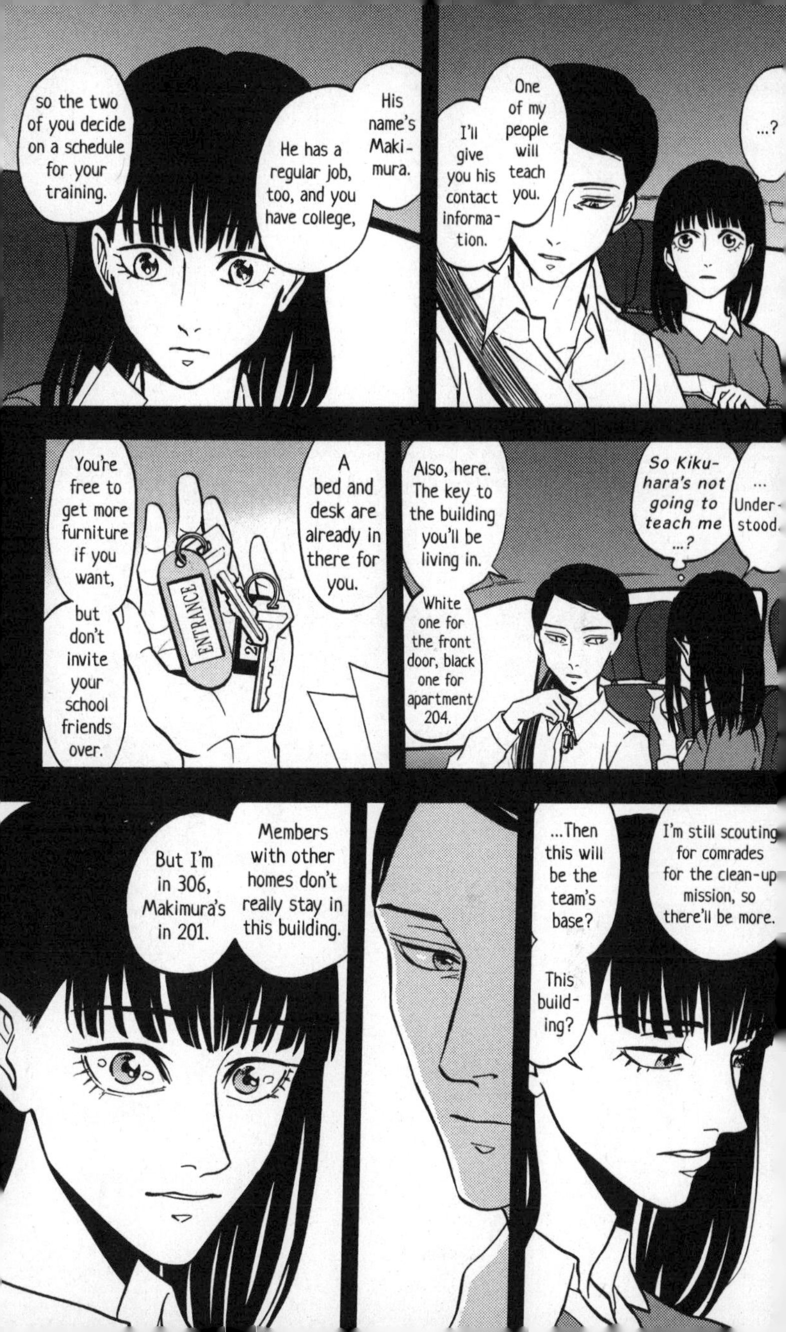
...?
One of my people will teach you.
I'll give you his contact information.
His name's Makimura.
He has a regular job, too, and you have college,
so the two of you decide on a schedule for your training.
... Understood.
So Kikuhara's not going to teach me ...?
Also, here. The key to the building you'll be living in.
White one for the front door, black one for apartment 204.
A bed and desk are already in there for you.
You're free to get more furniture if you want,
ENTRANCE
but don't invite your school friends over.
I'm still scouting for comrades for the clean-up mission, so there'll be more.
...Then this will be the team's base?
This building?
Members with other homes don't really stay in this building.
But I'm in 306, Makimura's in 201.

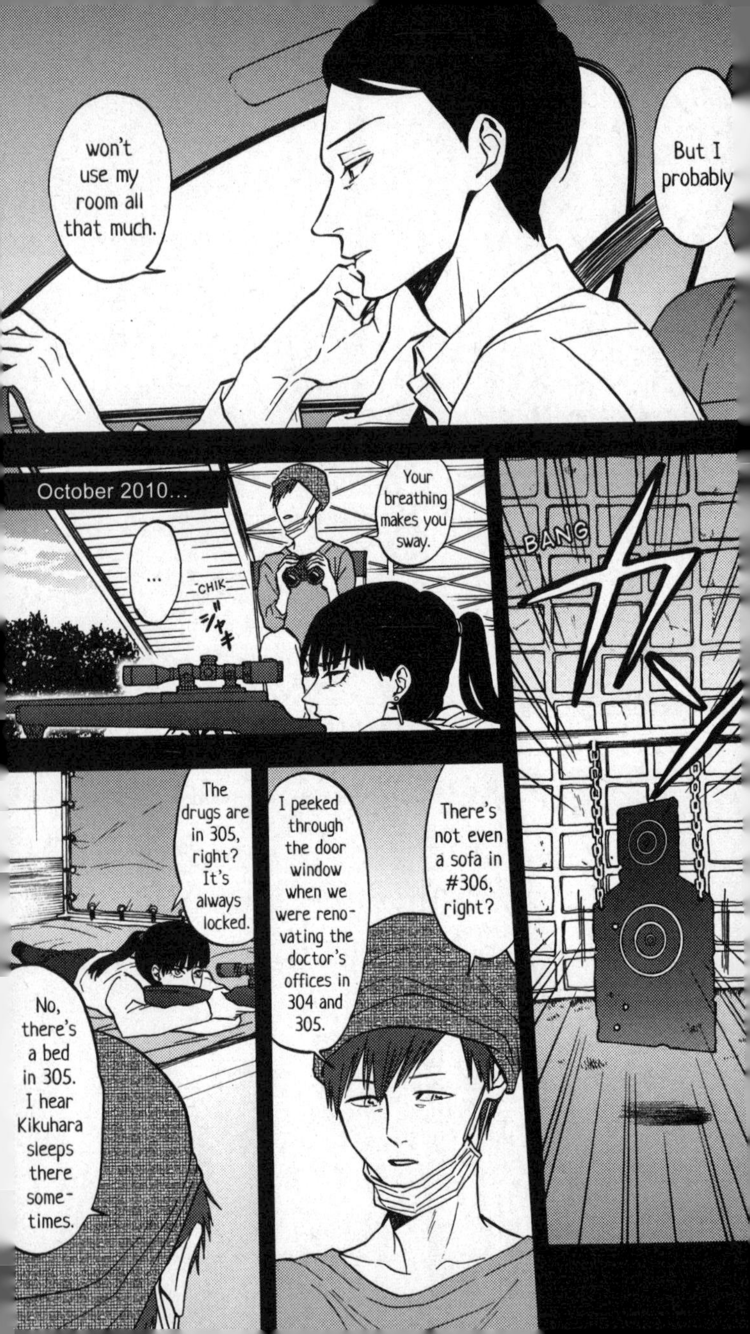
But I probably
won't use my room all that much.
BANG
Your breathing makes you sway.
October 2010…
...
CHIK
ジャキ
There's not even a sofa in #306, right?
I peeked through the door window when we were renovating the doctor's offices in 304 and 305.
The drugs are in 305, right? It's always locked.
No, there's a bed in 305. I hear Kikuhara sleeps there sometimes.

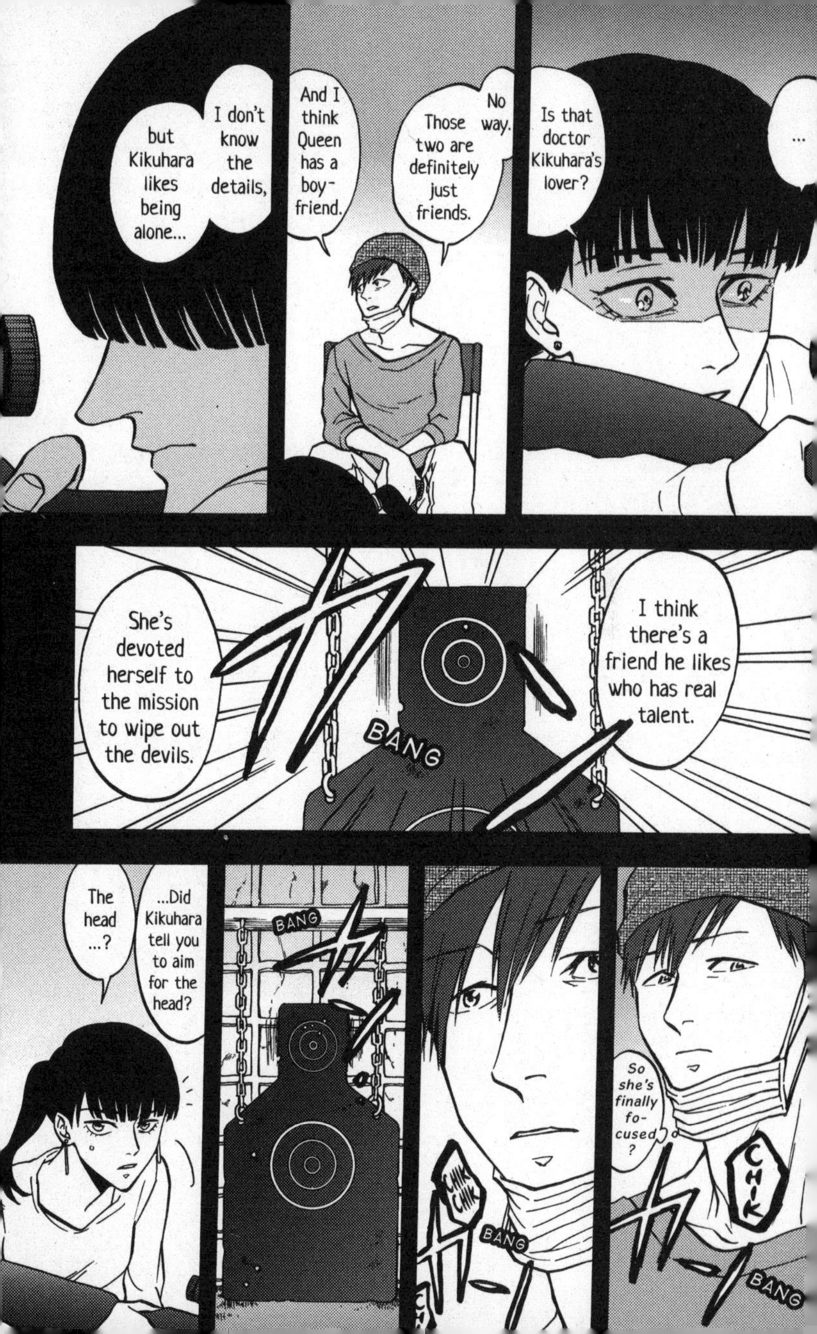
...
Is that doctor Kikuhara's lover?
No way.
Those two are definitely just friends.
And I think Queen has a boy-friend.
I don't know the details,
but Kikuhara likes being alone...
I think there's a friend he likes who has real talent.
She's devoted herself to the mission to wipe out the devils.
BANG
CHIK
So she's finally fo-cused?
BANG
CHIK CHIK
BANG
BANG
...Did Kikuhara tell you to aim for the head?
The head ...?

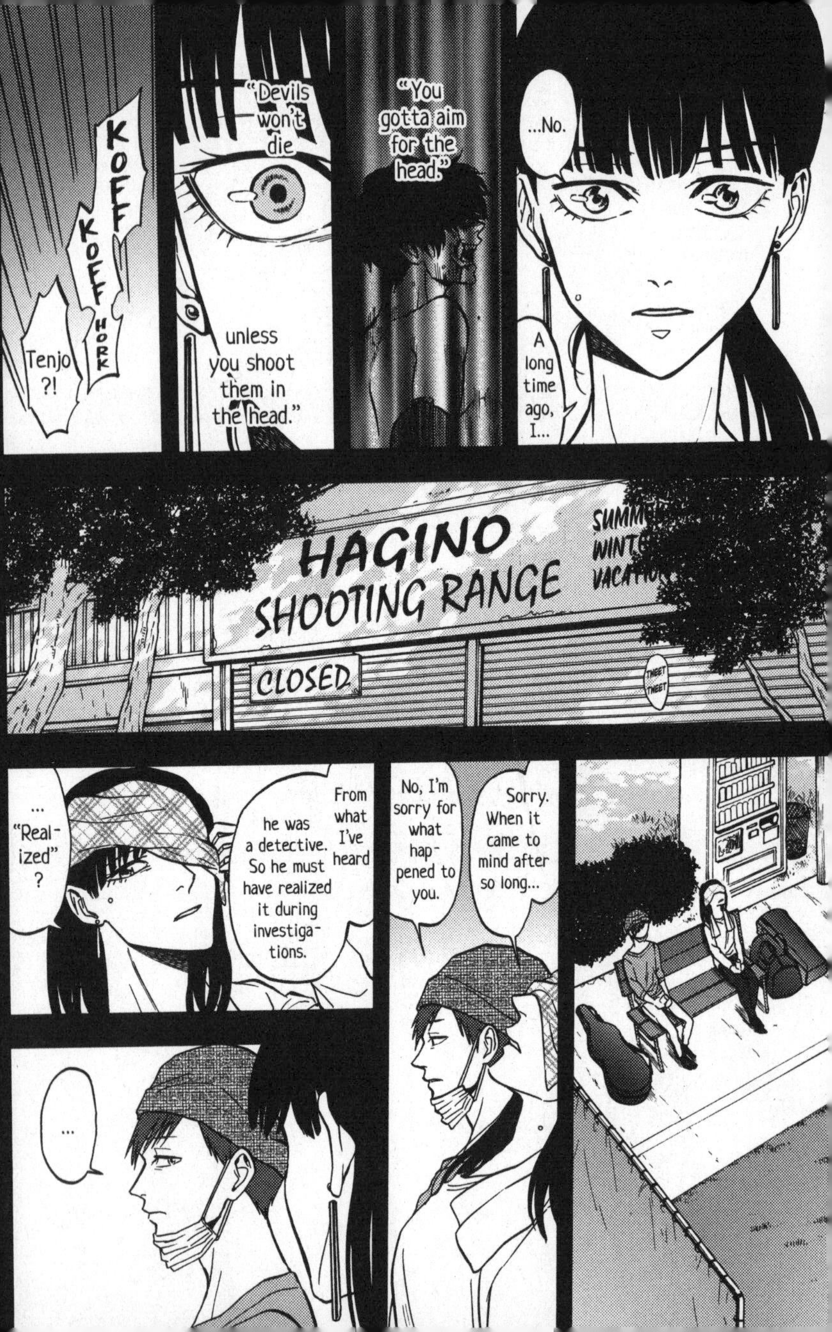
...No.
A long time ago, I...
"You gotta aim for the head."
"Devils won't die
unless you shoot them in the head."
KOFF
KOFF
HORK
Tenjo?!
HAGINO SHOOTING RANGE
CLOSED
TWEET TWEET
Sorry. When it came to mind after so long...
No, I'm sorry for what hap-pened to you.
From what I've heard
he was a detective. So he must have realized it during investiga-tions.
..."Real-ized"?
...

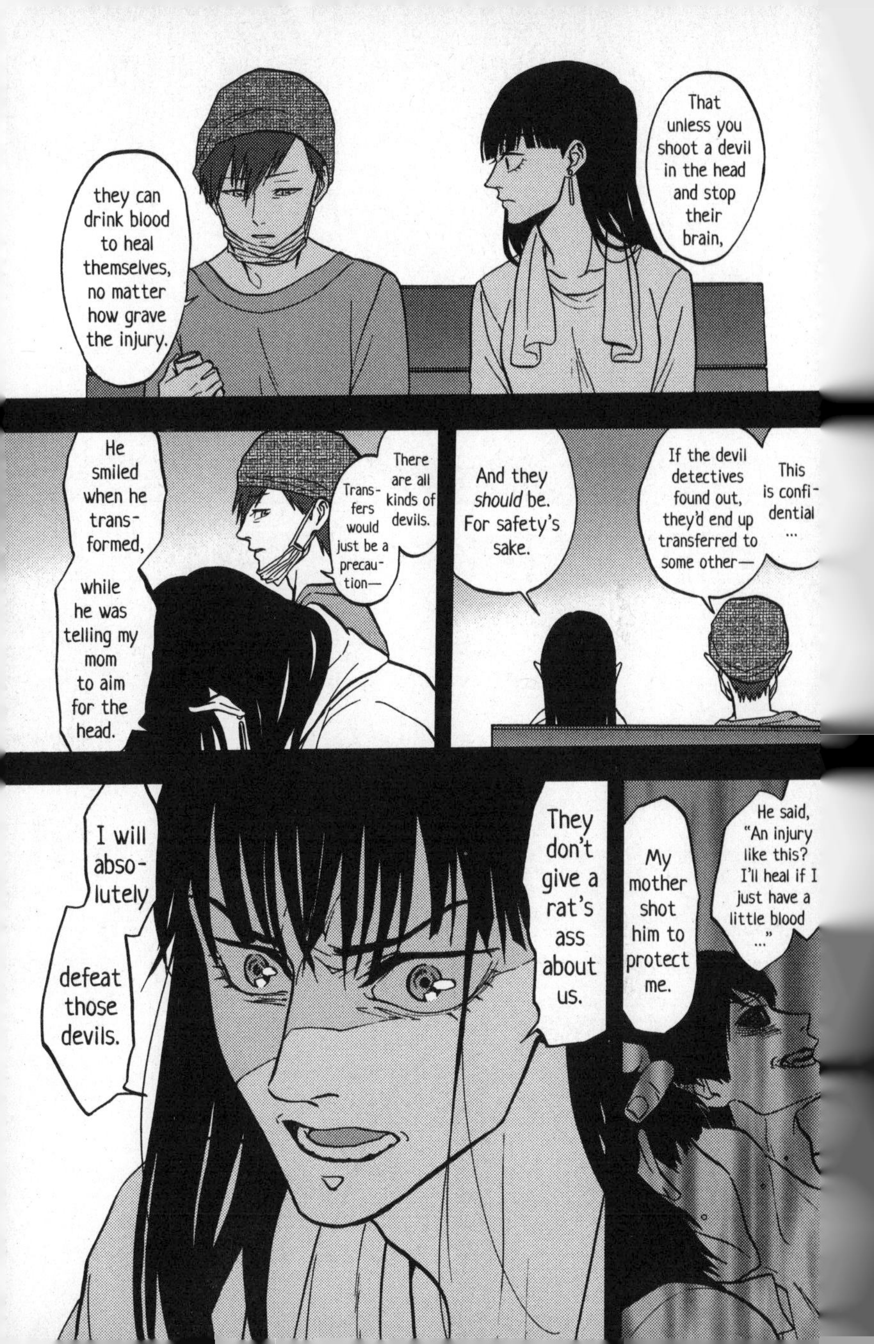
That unless you shoot a devil in the head and stop their brain,
they can drink blood to heal themselves, no matter how grave the injury.
This is confi-dential ...
If the devil detectives found out, they'd end up transferred to some other—
And they *should* be. For safety's sake.
There are all kinds of devils.
Trans-fers would just be a precau-tion—
He smiled when he trans-formed,
while he was telling my mom to aim for the head.
He said, "An injury like this? I'll heal if I just have a little blood ..."
My mother shot him to protect me.
They don't give a rat's ass about us.
I will abso-lutely
defeat those devils.

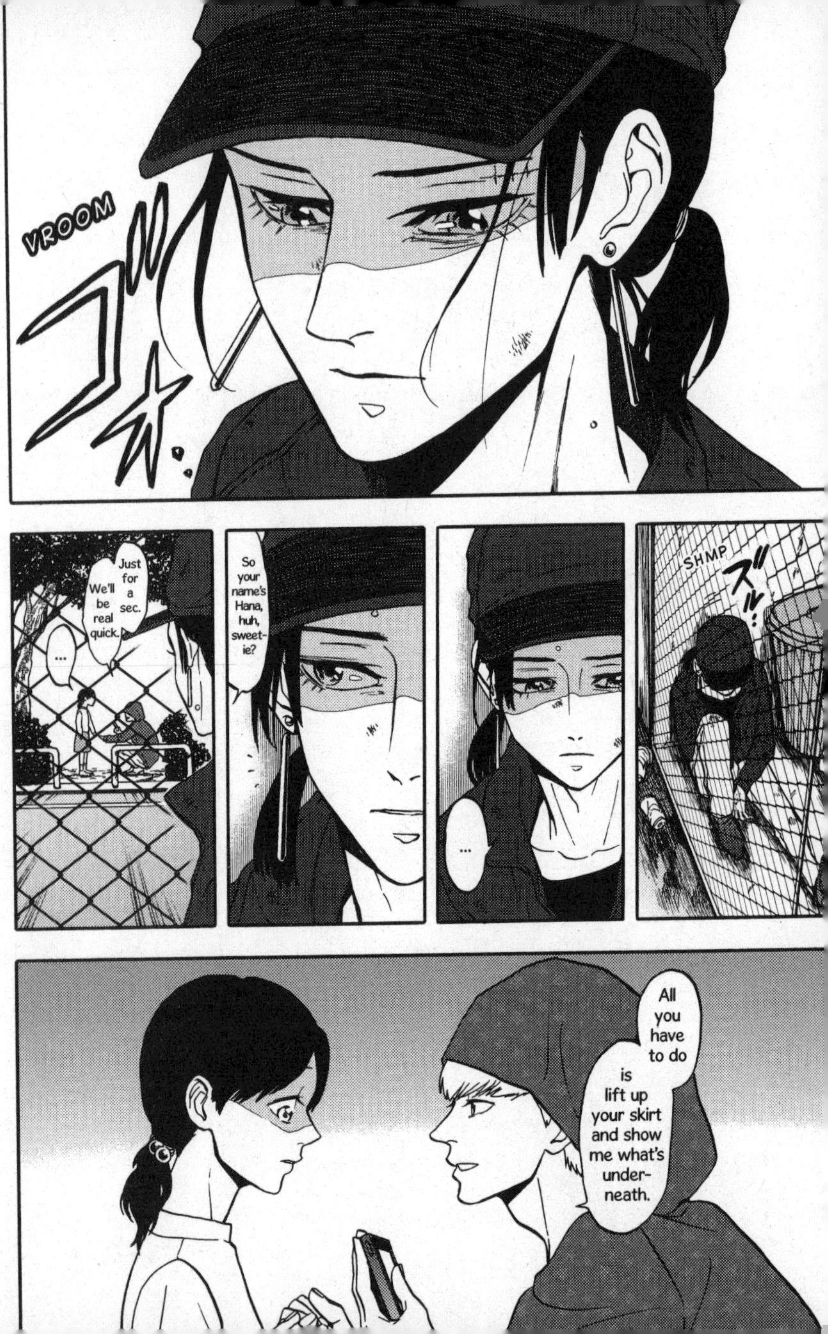
VROOM
SHMP
...
So your name's Hana, huh, sweetie?
Just for a sec.
We'll be real quick.
...
All you have to do is lift up your skirt and show me what's underneath.

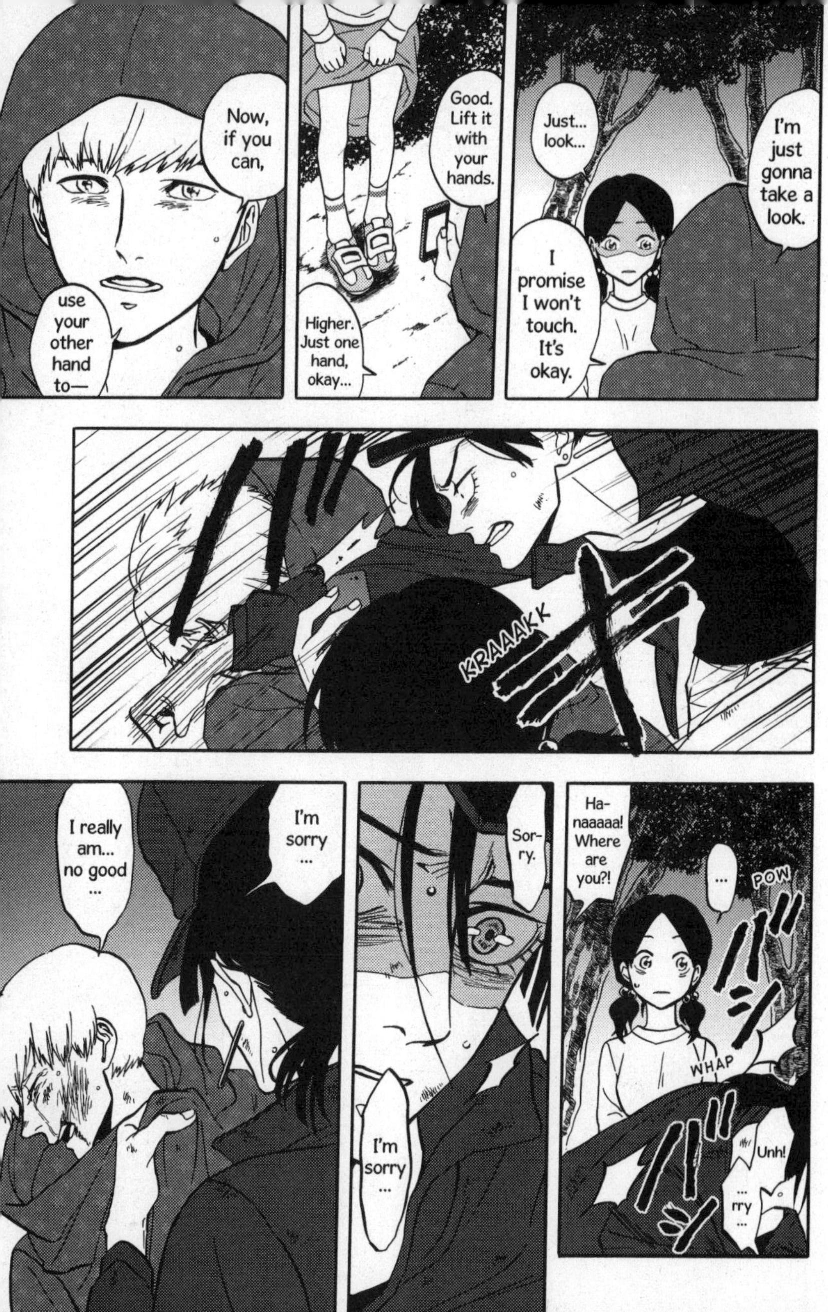
I'm just gonna take a look.
Just... look...
I promise I won't touch. It's okay.
Good. Lift it with your hands.
Higher. Just one hand, okay...
Now, if you can,
use your other hand to—
KRAAAKK
Ha-naaaaa! Where are you?!
...
POW
WHAP
Unh!
...rry...
Sor-ry.
I'm sorry...
I'm sorry...
I really am... no good...

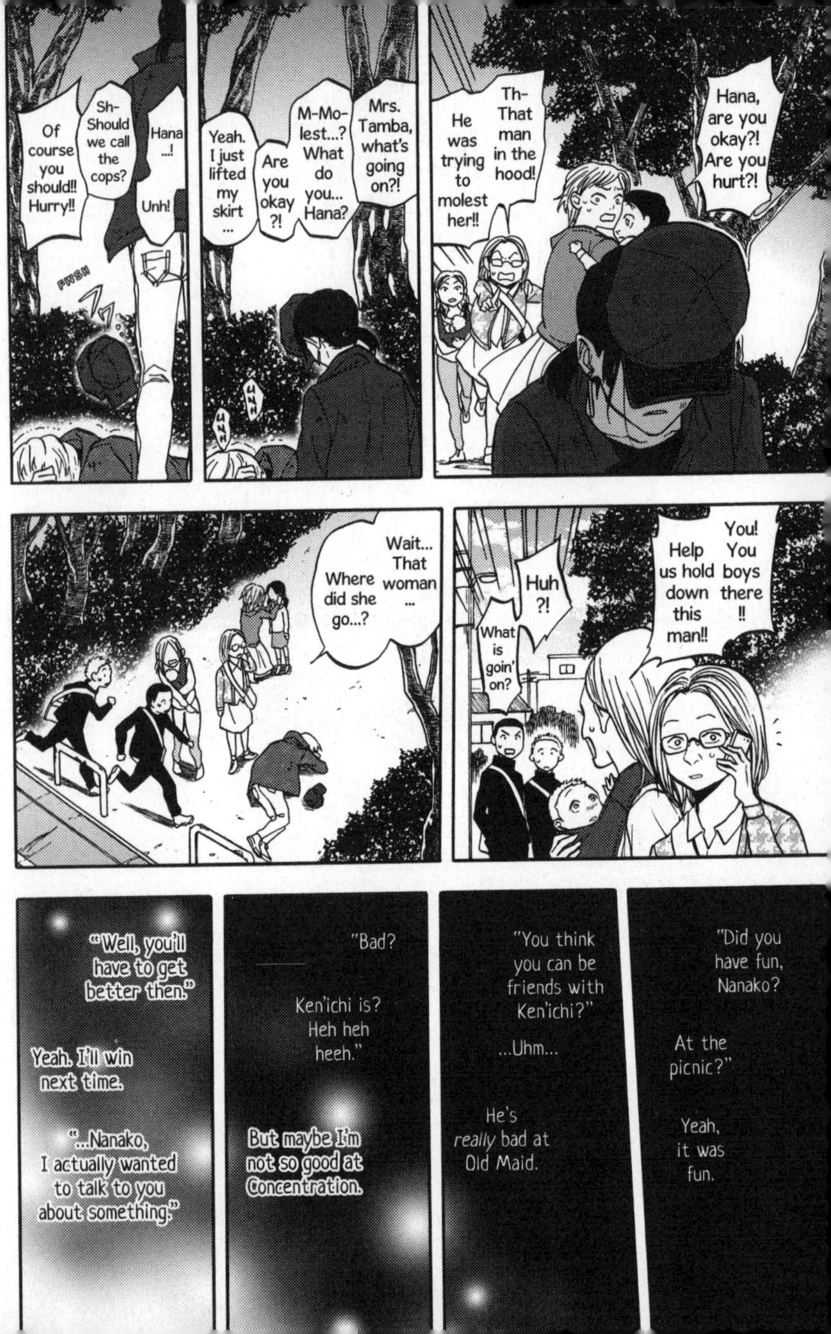
Hana, are you okay?! Are you hurt?!
Th- That man in the hood!
He was trying to molest her!!
Mrs. Tamba, what's going on?!
M-Mo- lest...? What do you... Hana?
Are you okay ?!
Yeah. I just lifted my skirt ...
Hana ...!
Unh!
Sh- Should we call the cops?
Of course you should!! Hurry!!
FWSH
You! You boys there !!
Help us hold down this man!!
Huh ?!
What is goin' on?
Wait... That woman ...
Where did she go...?
"Did you have fun, Nanako?
At the picnic?"
Yeah, it was fun.
"You think you can be friends with Ken'ichi?"
...Uhm...
He's *really* bad at Old Maid.
"Bad?
Ken'ichi is? Heh heh heeh."
But maybe I'm not so good at Concentration.
"Well, you'll have to get better then."
Yeah. I'll win next time.
"...Nanako, I actually wanted to talk to you about something."

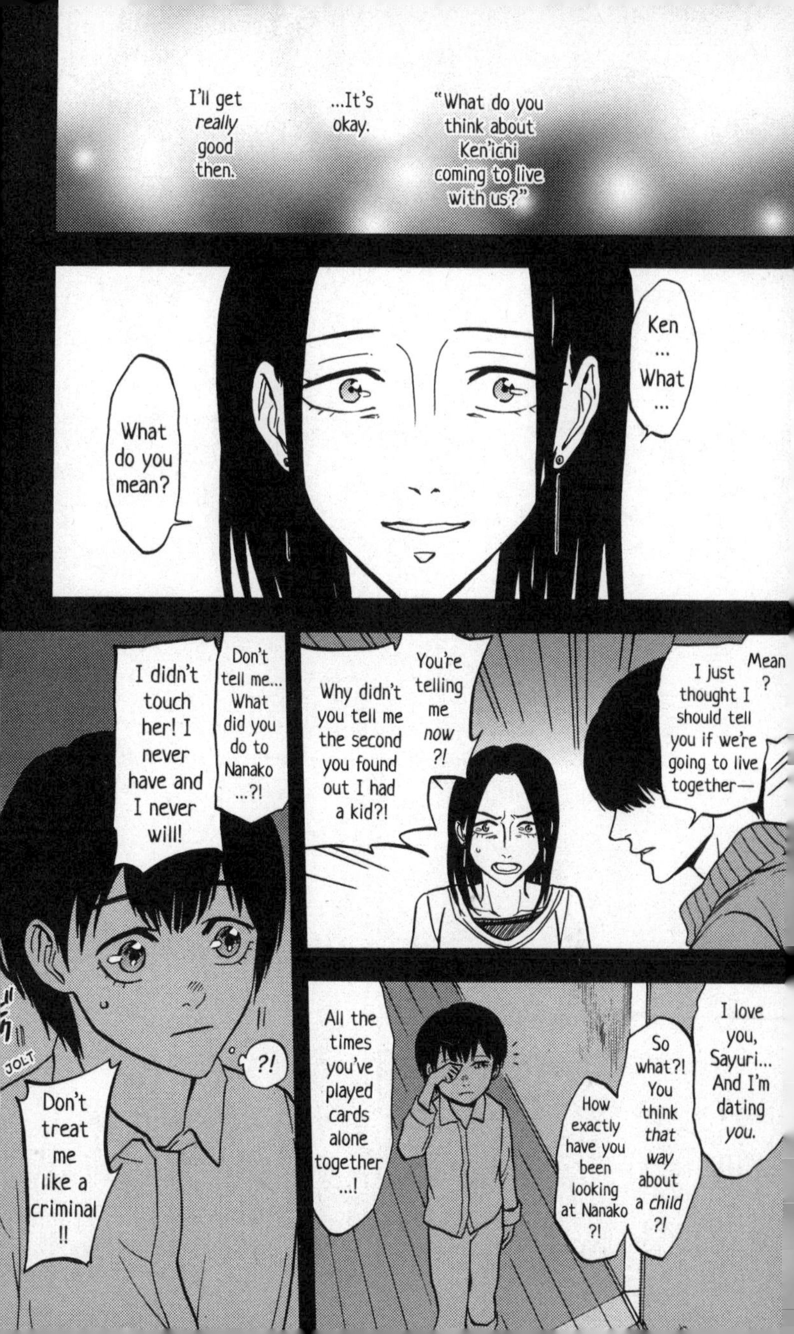
"What do you think about Ken'ichi coming to live with us?"
...It's okay.
I'll get *really* good then.
Ken... What...
What do you mean?
Mean?
I just thought I should tell you if we're going to live together—
You're telling me *now*?!
Why didn't you tell me the second you found out I had a kid?!
I love you, Sayuri... And I'm dating *you*.
So what?! You think *that* way about a *child*?!
How exactly have you been looking at Nanako?!
All the times you've played cards alone together...!
Don't tell me... What did you do to Nanako...?!
I didn't touch her! I never have and I never will!
?!
JOLT
Don't treat me like a criminal!!

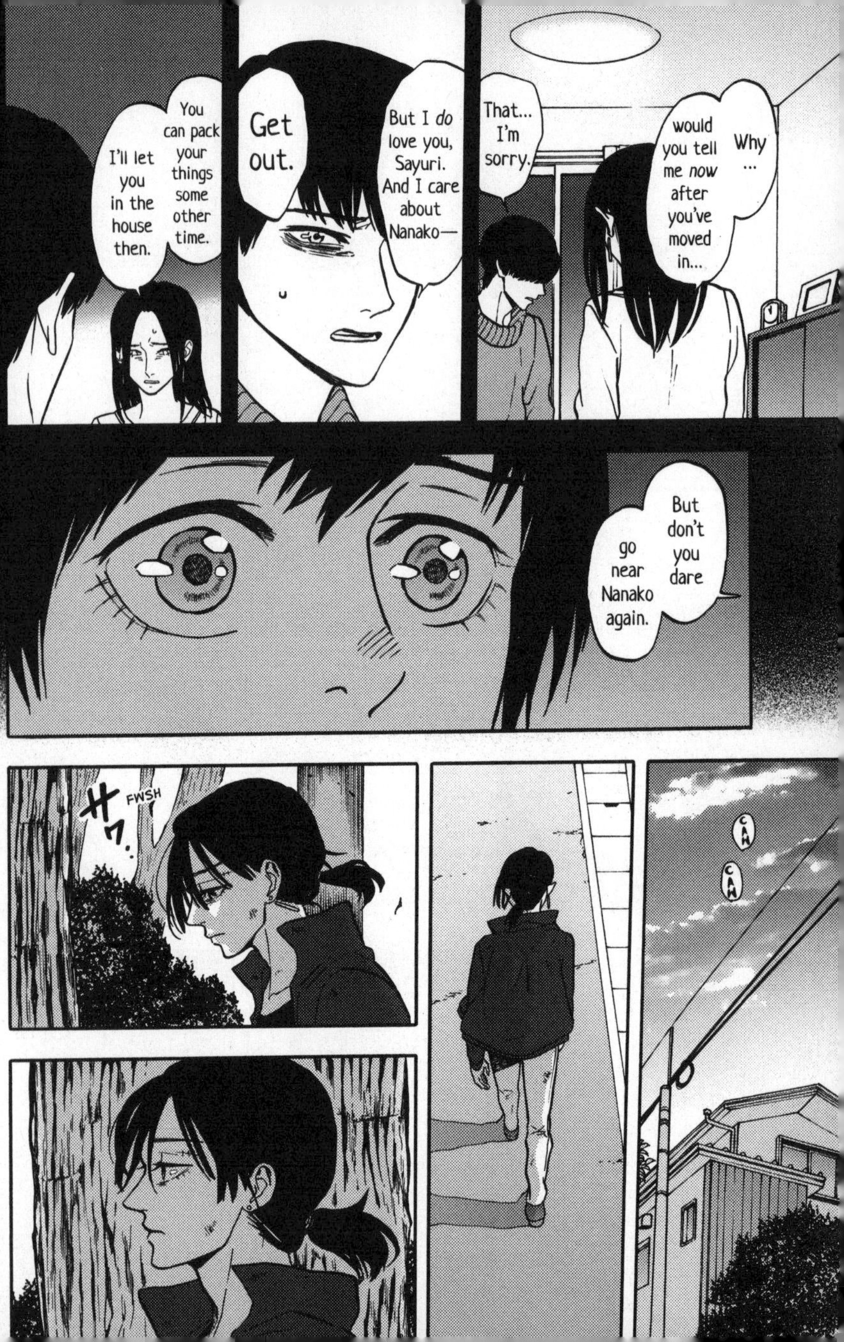
Why …
would you tell me *now* after you've moved in…
That… I'm sorry.
But I *do* love you, Sayuri. And I care about Nanako—
Get out.
You can pack your things some other time.
I'll let you in the house then.
But don't you dare go near Nanako again.
CAW
CAW
FWSH

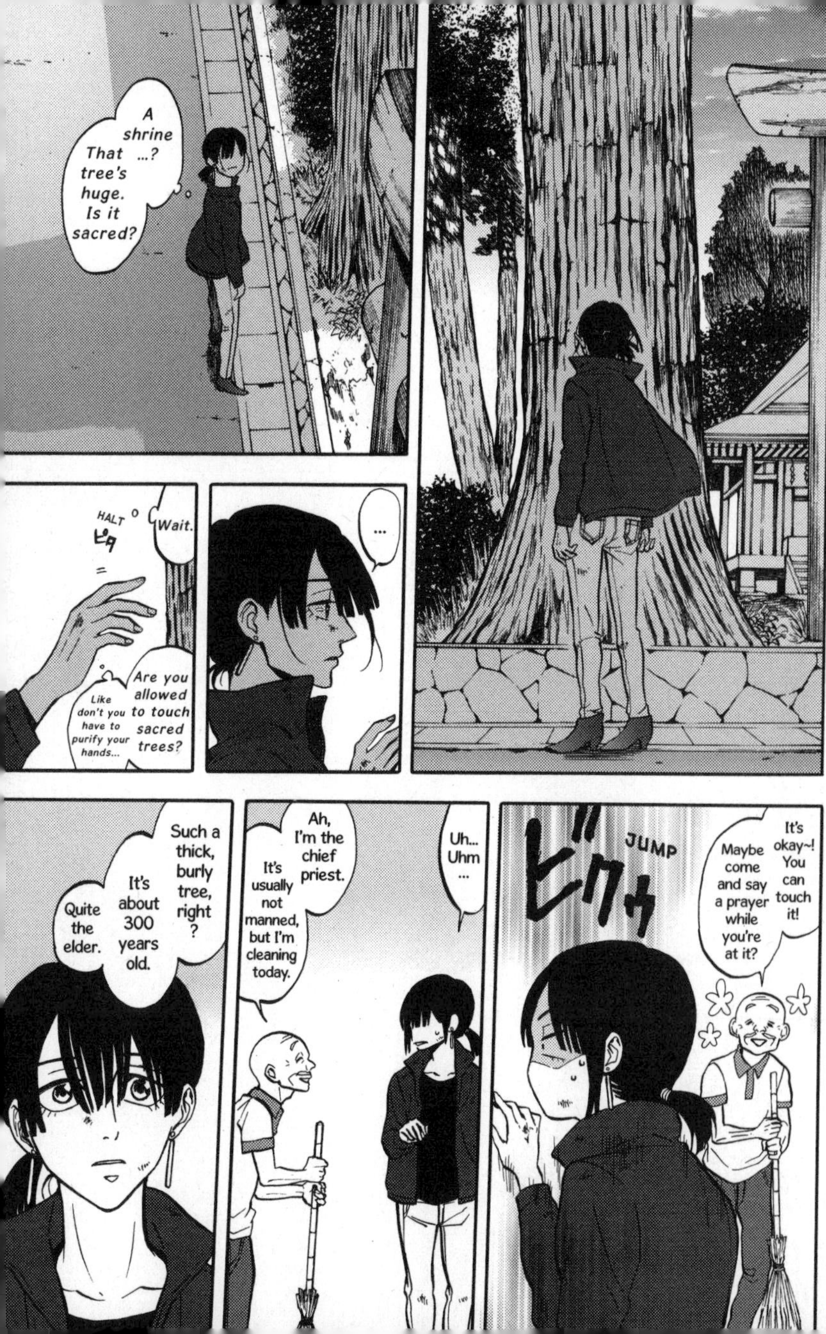
A shrine ...?
That tree's huge. Is it sacred?
...
HALT
ピタ
Wait.
Are you allowed to touch sacred trees?
Like don't you have to purify your hands...
JUMP
ビクゥ
It's okay~! You can touch it!
Maybe come and say a prayer while you're at it?
Uh... Uhm ...
Ah, I'm the chief priest.
It's usually not manned, but I'm cleaning today.
Such a thick, burly tree, right?
It's about 300 years old.
Quite the elder.

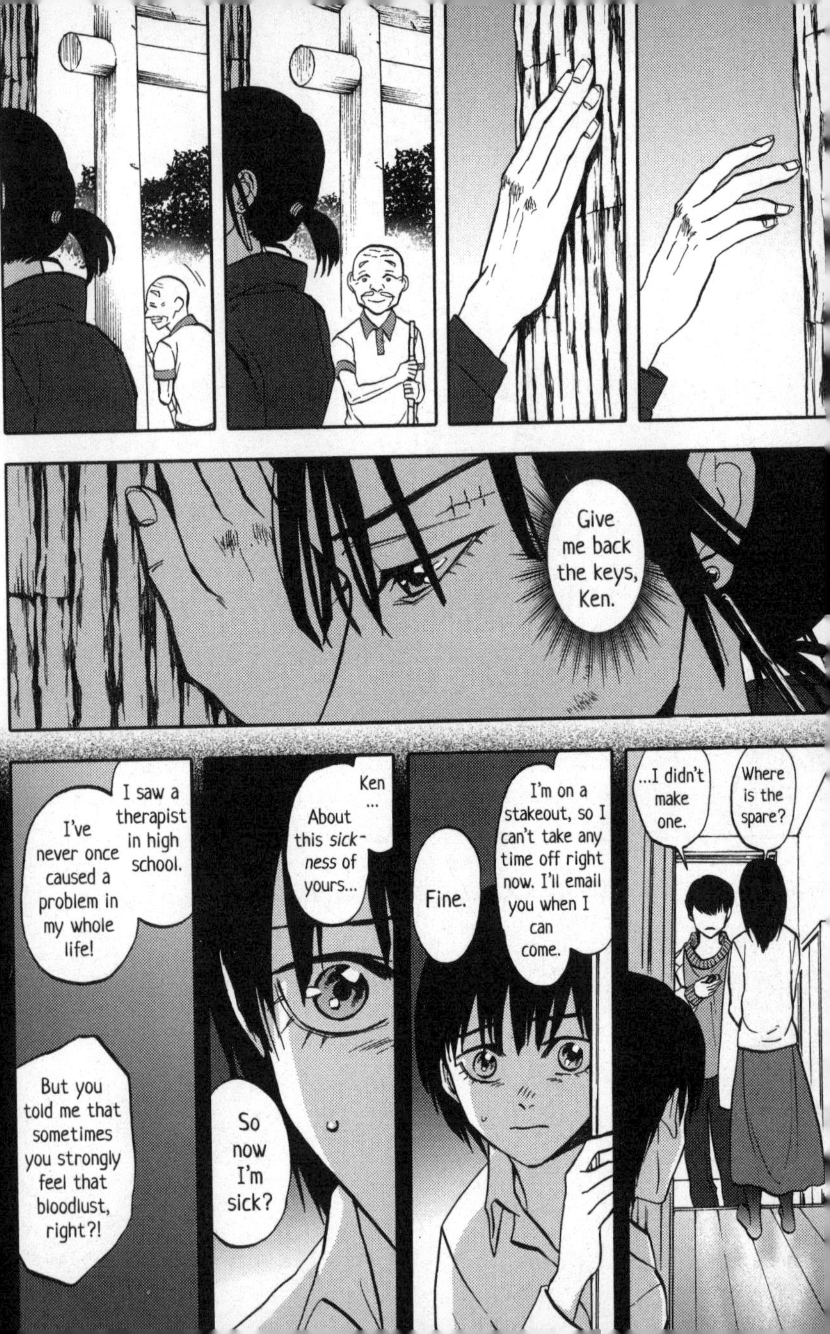
Give me back the keys, Ken.
Where is the spare?
...I didn't make one.
I'm on a stakeout, so I can't take any time off right now. I'll email you when I can come.
Fine.
Ken ...
About this *sickness* of yours...
So now I'm sick?
I saw a therapist in high school.
I've never once caused a problem in my whole life!
But you told me that sometimes you strongly feel that bloodlust, right?!

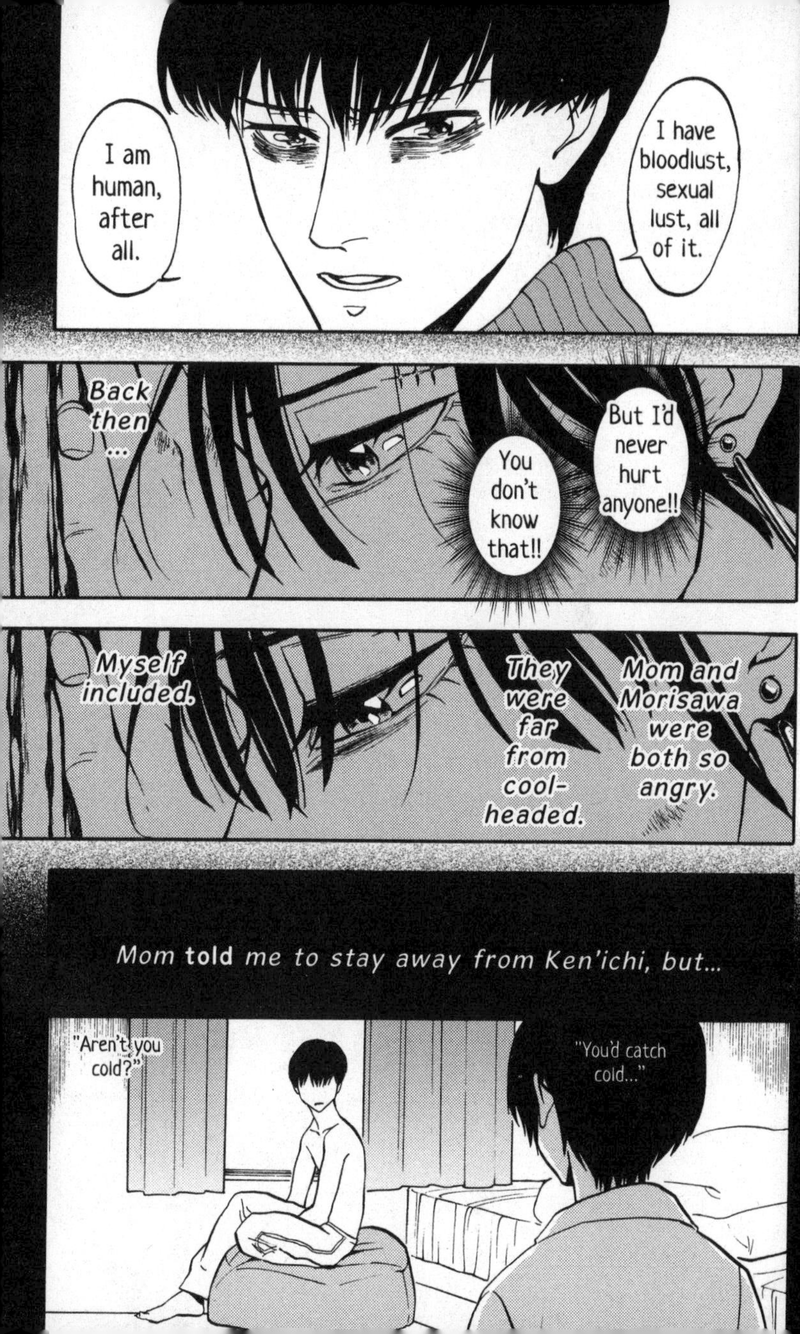
I have bloodlust, sexual lust, all of it.
I am human, after all.
But I'd never hurt anyone!!
You don't know that!!
Back then...
Mom and Morisawa were both so angry.
They were far from cool-headed.
Myself included.
Mom told me to stay away from Ken'ichi, but...
"You'd catch cold..."
"Aren't you cold?"

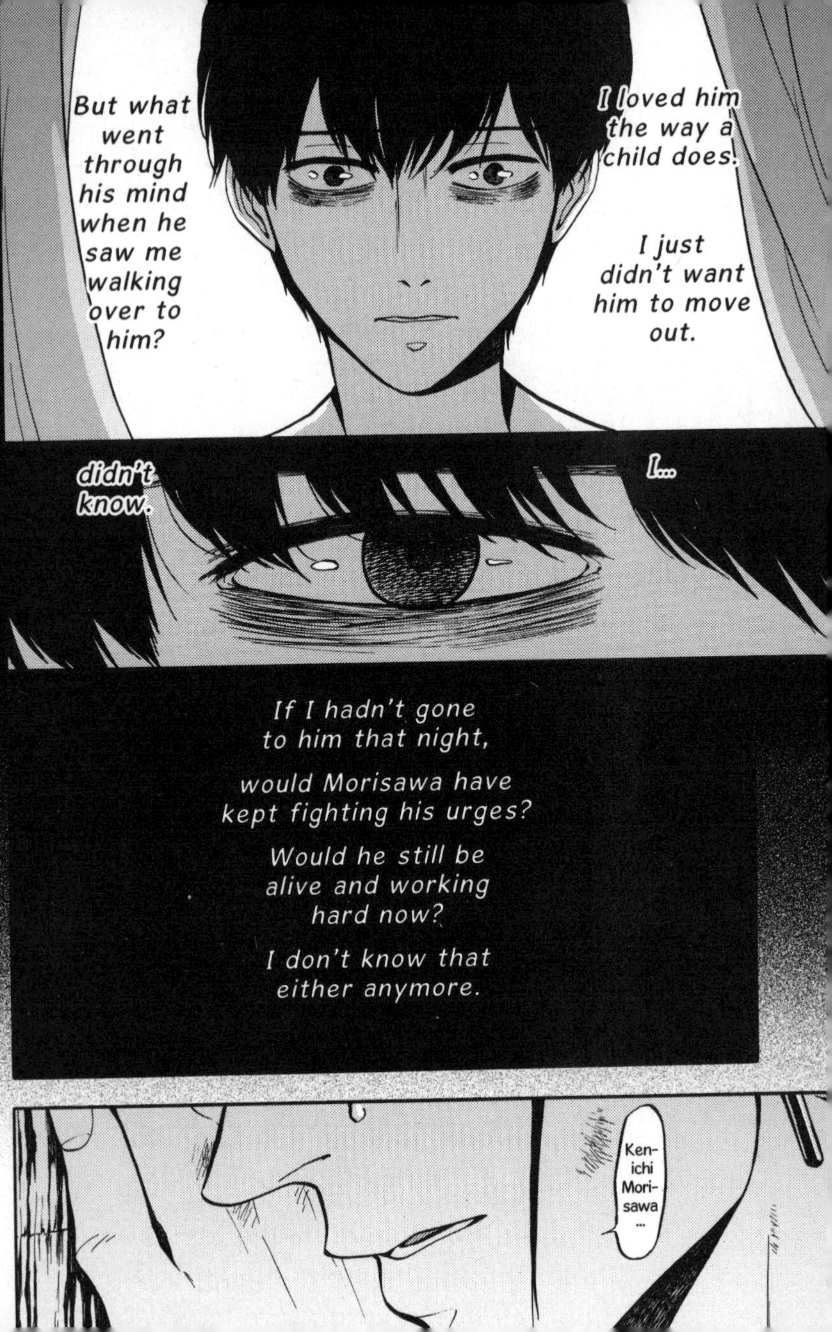
I loved him the way a child does.
I just didn't want him to move out.
But what went through his mind when he saw me walking over to him?
I...
didn't know.
If I hadn't gone to him that night,
would Morisawa have kept fighting his urges?
Would he still be alive and working hard now?
I don't know that either anymore.
Ken-ichi Mori-sawa...

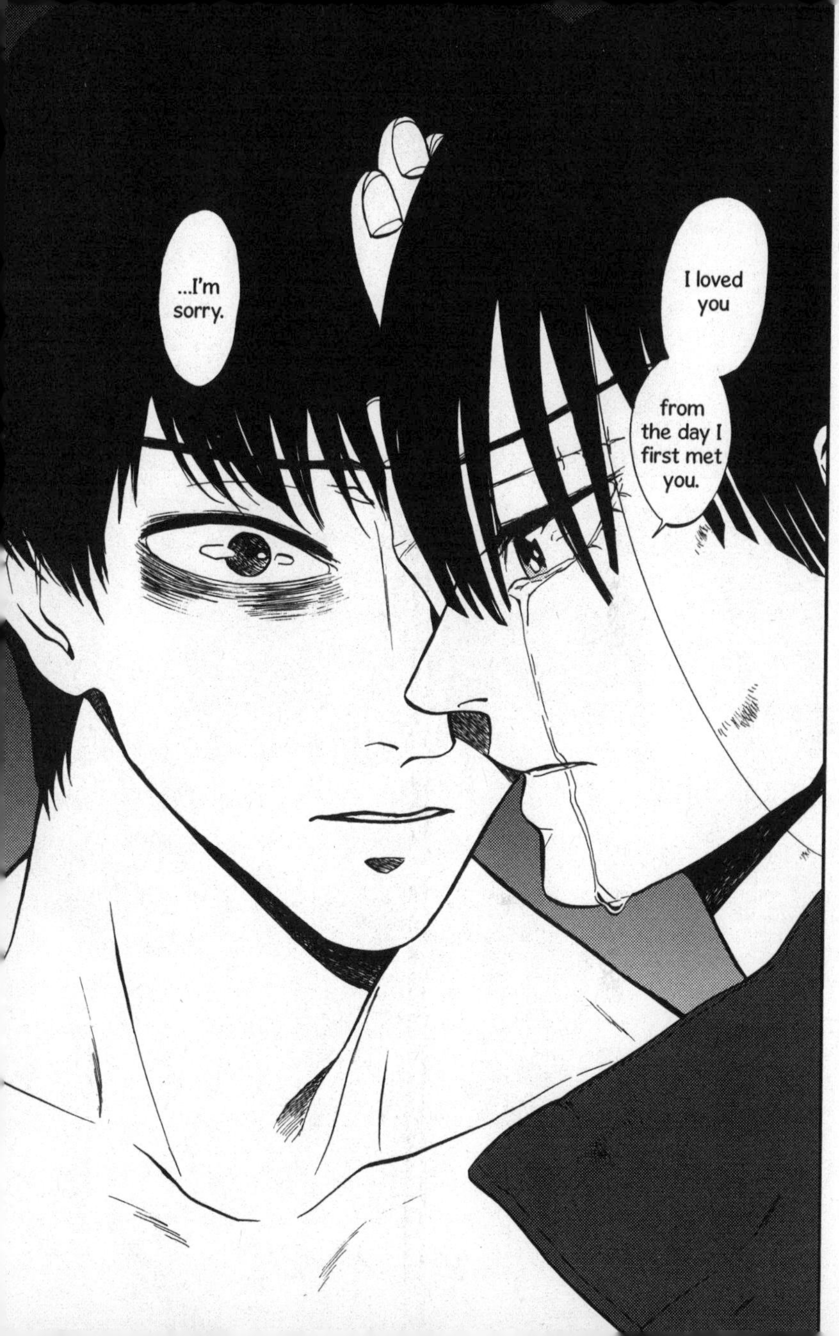
I loved you
from the day I first met you.
...I'm sorry.

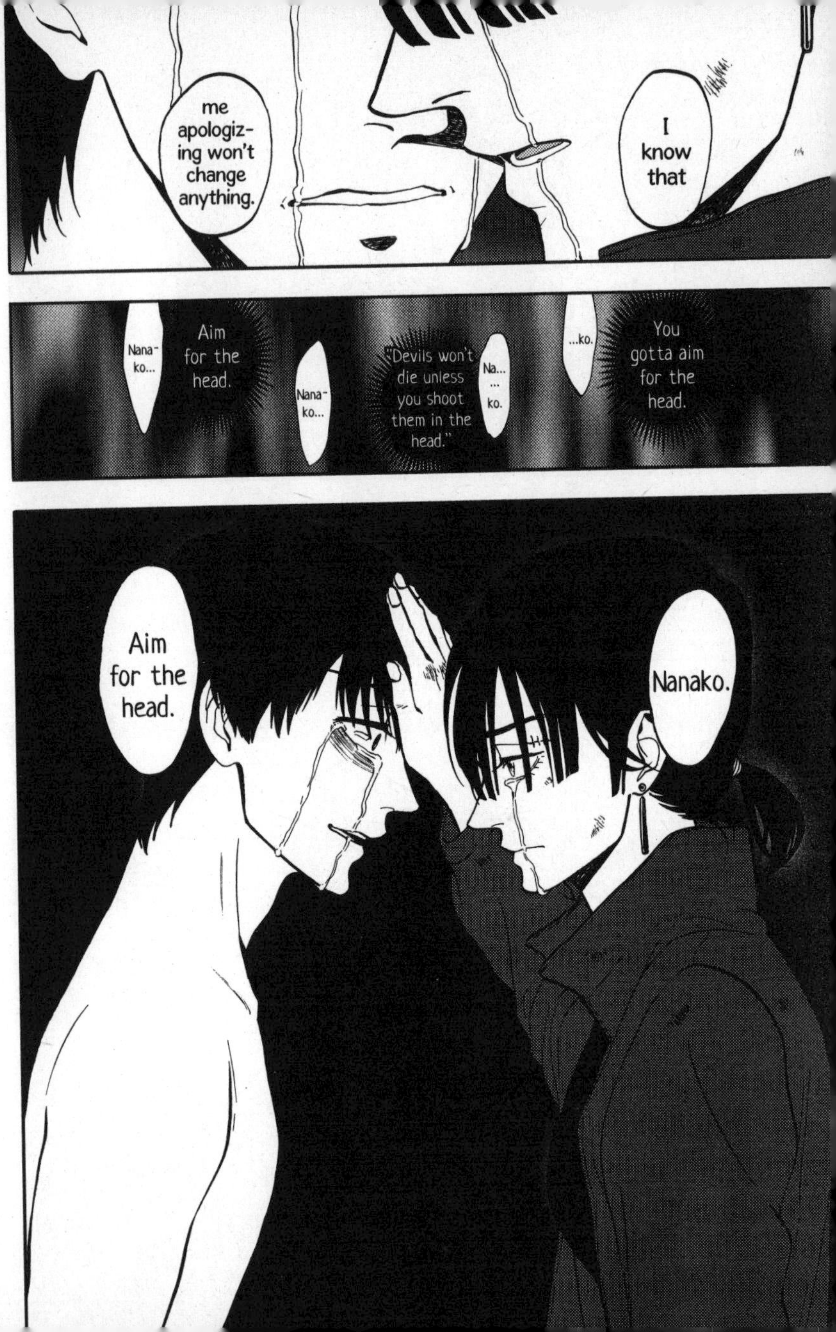
I know that
me apologizing won't change anything.
You gotta aim for the head.
...ko.
Na... ... ko.
"Devils won't die unless you shoot them in the head."
Nana-ko...
Aim for the head.
Nana-ko...
Nanako.
Aim for the head.

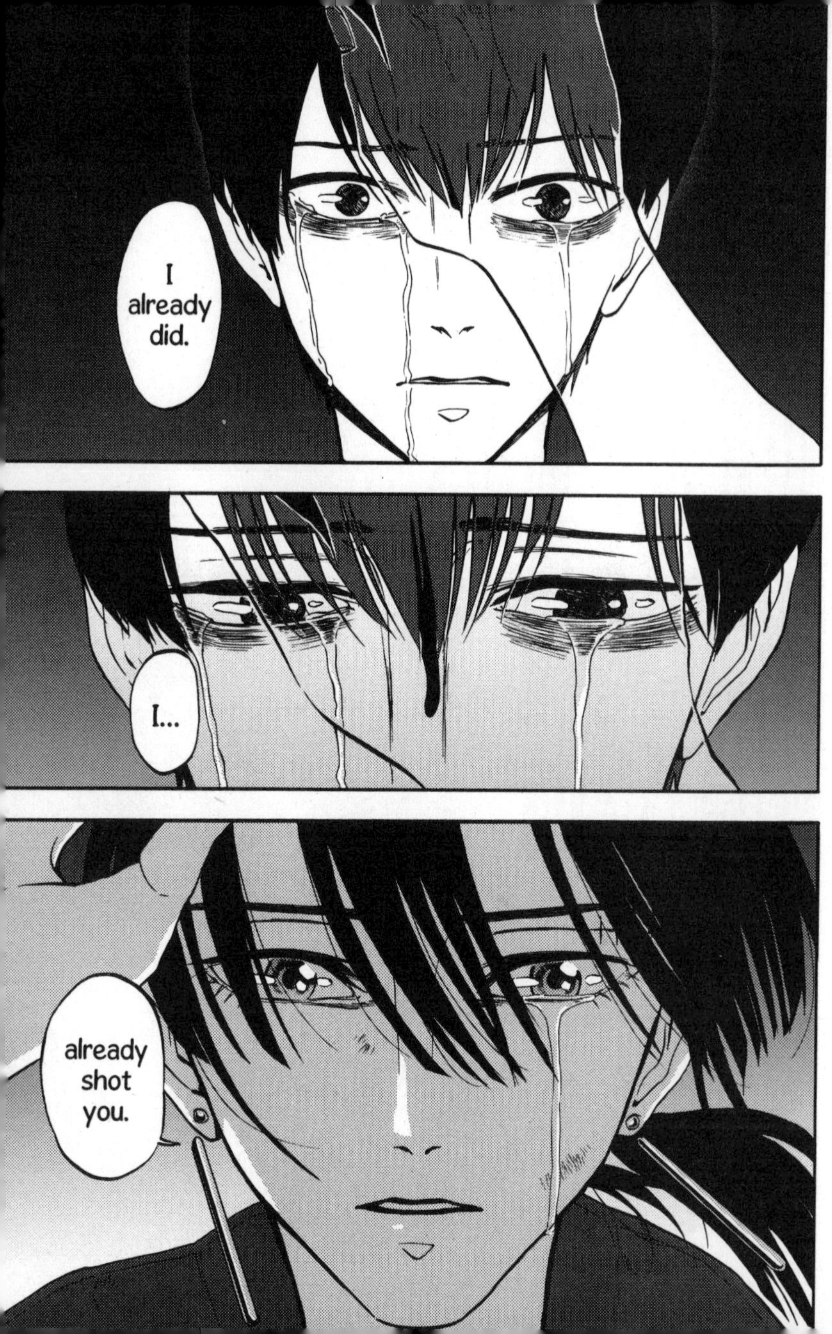
I already did.
I...
already shot you.

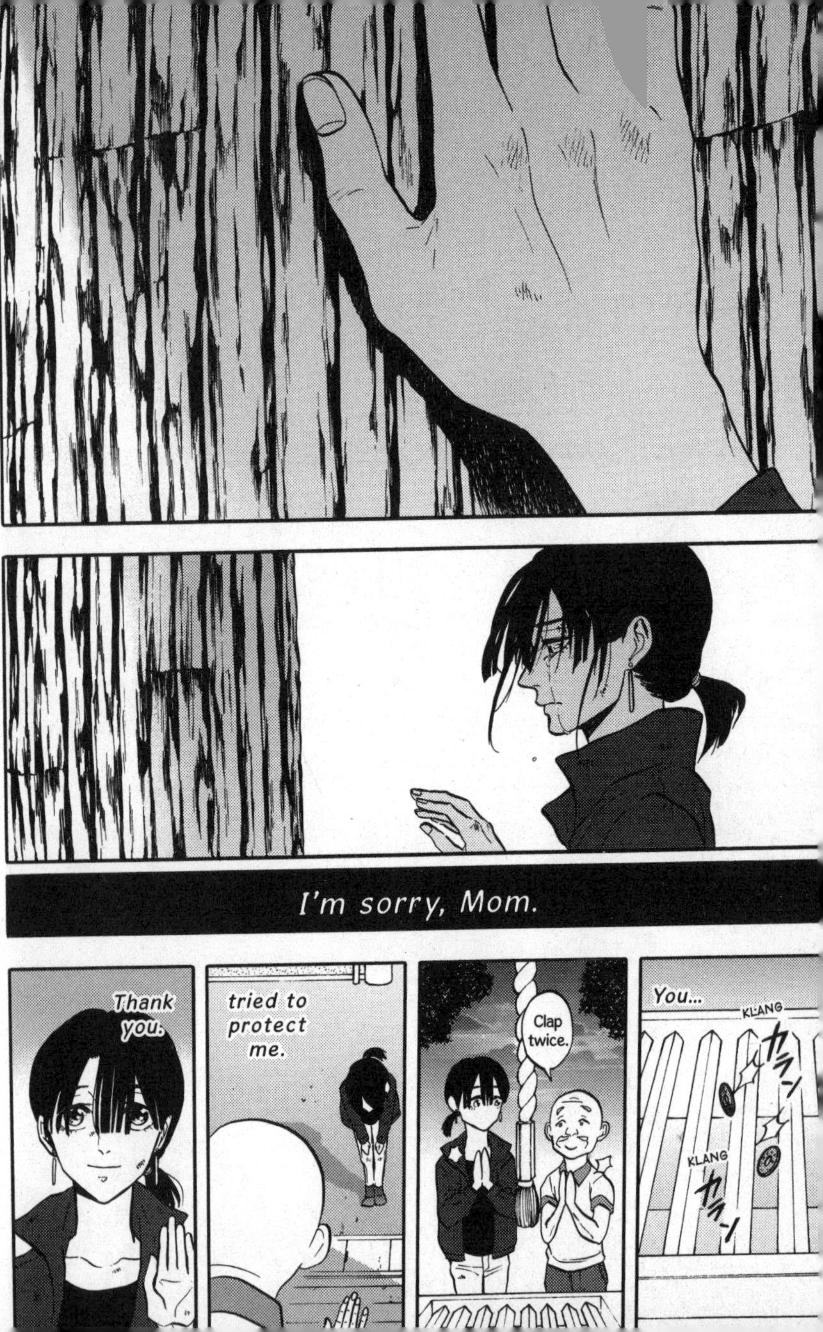
I'm sorry, Mom.
You...
KLANG
KLANG
Clap twice.
tried to protect me.
Thank you.

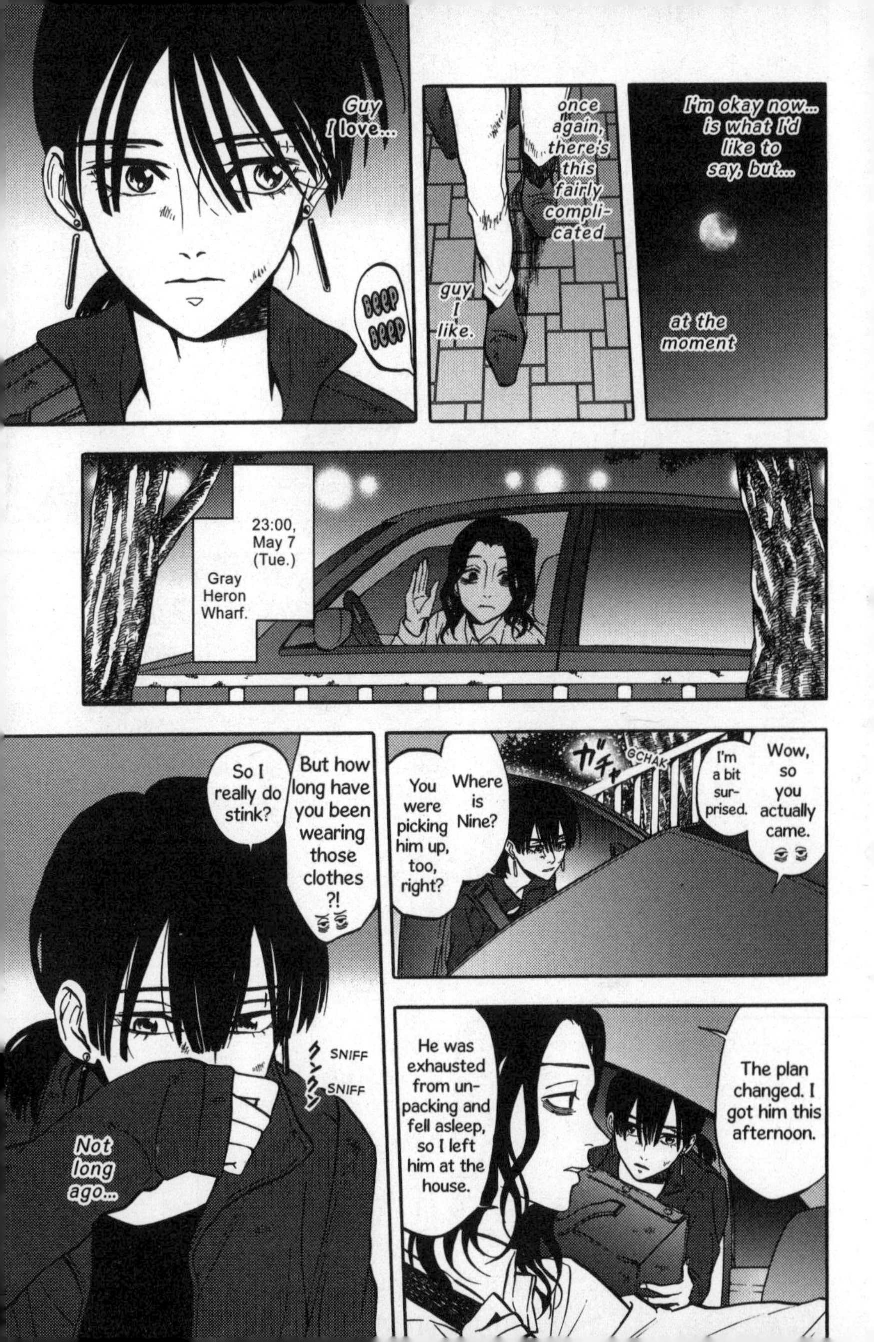
I'm okay now... is what I'd like to say, but...
at the moment
once again, there's this fairly compli-cated
guy I like.
Guy I love...
BEEP BEEP
23:00, May 7 (Tue.)
Gray Heron Wharf.
Wow, so you actually came.
I'm a bit sur-prised.
ガチャ GCHAK
Where is Nine?
You were picking him up, too, right?
The plan changed. I got him this afternoon.
He was exhausted from un-packing and fell asleep, so I left him at the house.
But how long have you been wearing those clothes ?!
So I really do stink?
クンクン SNIFF SNIFF
Not long ago...

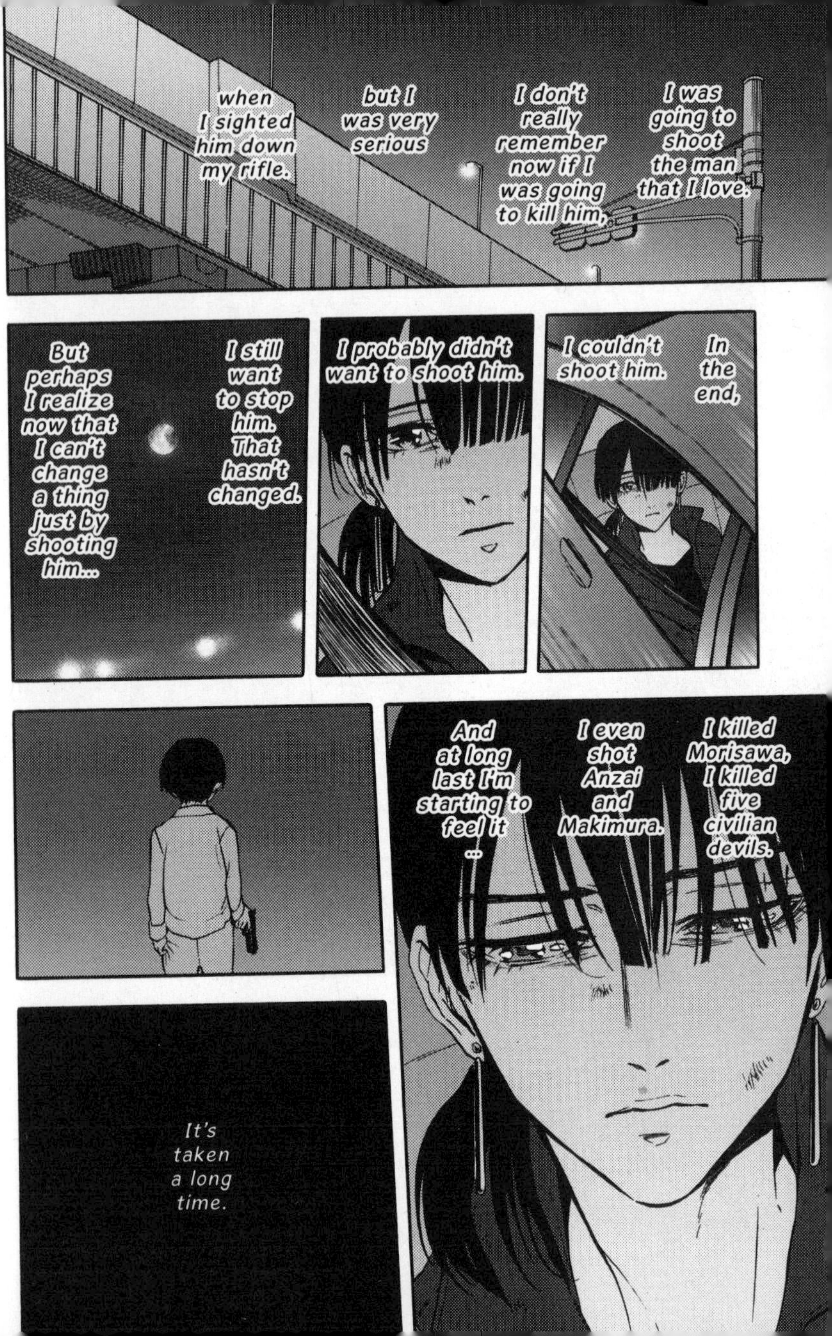
I was going to shoot the man that I love.
I don't really remember now if I was going to kill him,
but I was very serious
when I sighted him down my rifle.
In the end,
I couldn't shoot him.
I probably didn't want to shoot him.
I still want to stop him. That hasn't changed.
But perhaps I realize now that I can't change a thing just by shooting him...
I killed Morisawa, I killed five civilian devils.
I even shot Anzai and Makimura.
And at long last I'm starting to feel it ...
It's taken a long time.

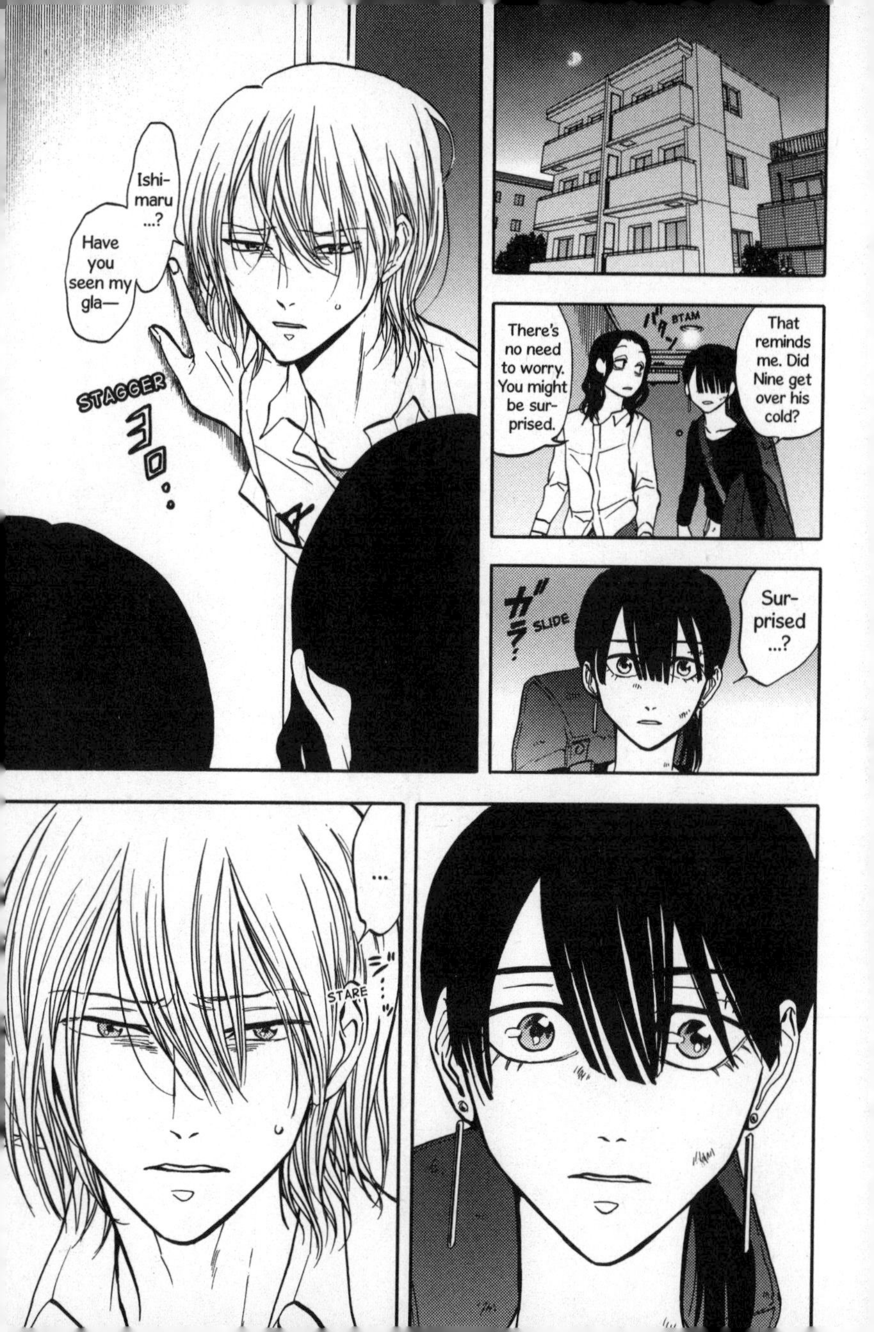
BTAM
That reminds me. Did Nine get over his cold?
There's no need to worry. You might be sur-prised.
SLIDE
Sur-prised ...?
Ishi-maru ...?
Have you seen my gla—
STAGGER
...
STARE

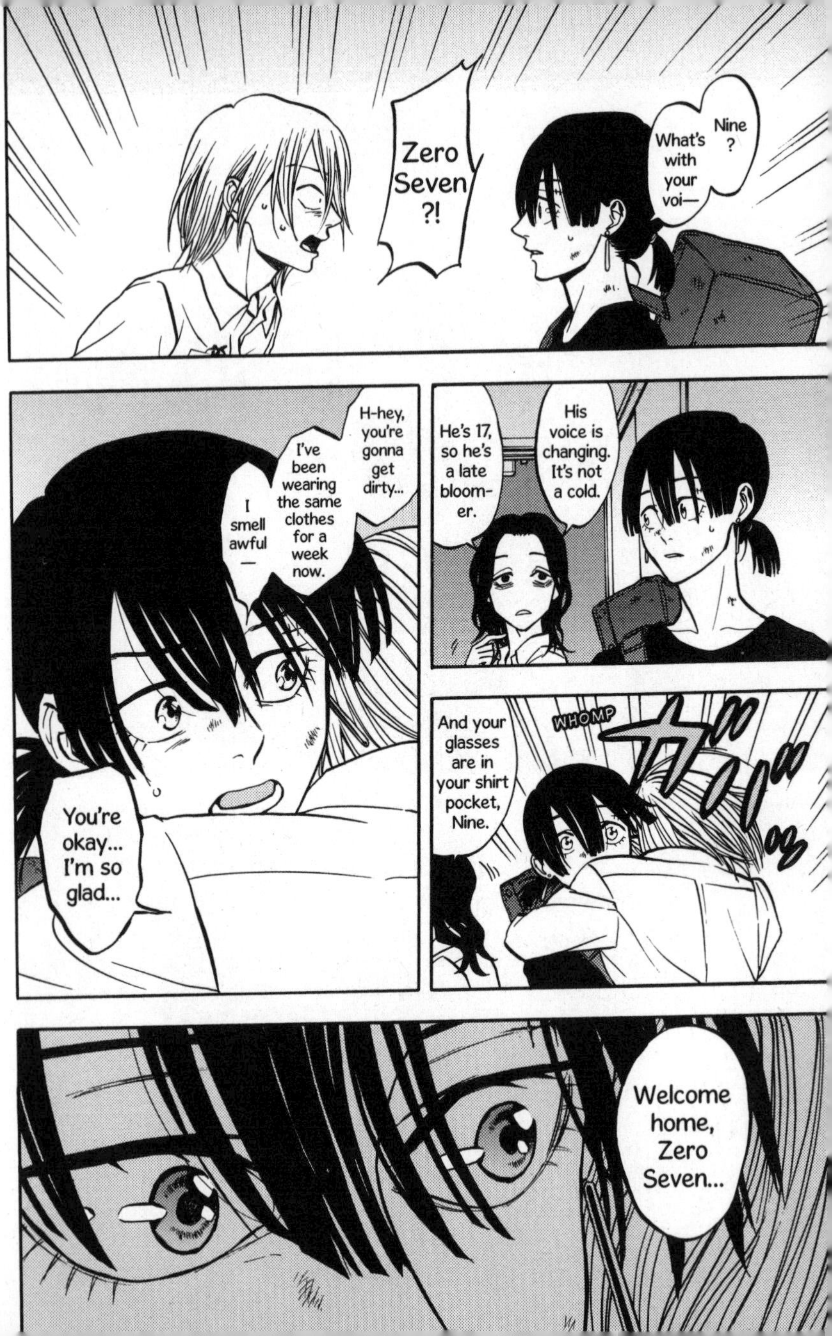
Nine? What's with your voi—
Zero Seven?!
His voice is changing. It's not a cold.
He's 17, so he's a late bloomer.
WHOMP
And your glasses are in your shirt pocket, Nine.
H-hey, you're gonna get dirty...
I've been wearing the same clothes for a week now.
I smell awful—
You're okay... I'm so glad...
Welcome home, Zero Seven...

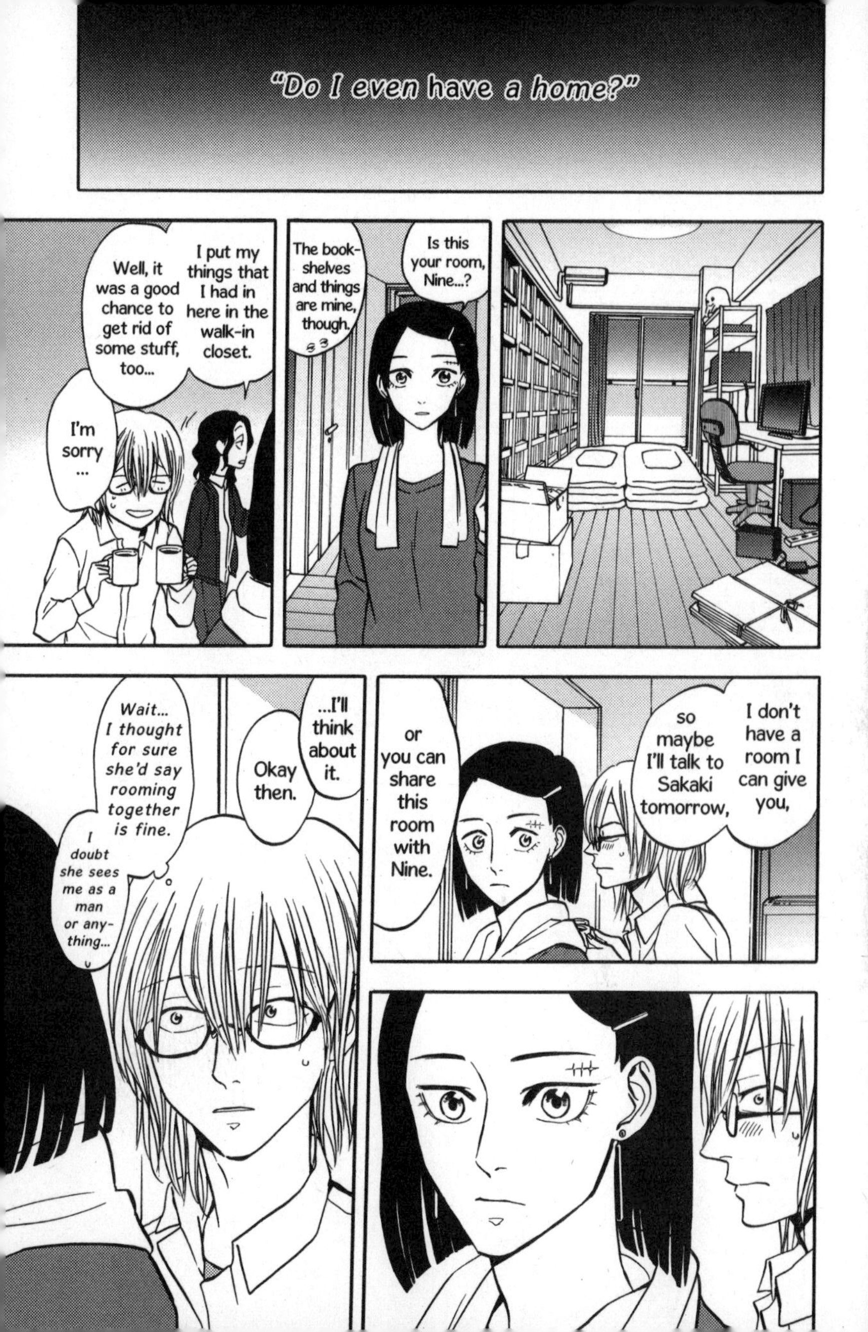
"Do I even have a home?"
Is this your room, Nine...?
The book-shelves and things are mine, though.
I put my things that I had in here in the walk-in closet.
Well, it was a good chance to get rid of some stuff, too...
I'm sorry ...
I don't have a room I can give you,
so maybe I'll talk to Sakaki tomorrow,
or you can share this room with Nine.
...I'll think about it.
Okay then.
Wait... I thought for sure she'd say rooming together is fine.
I doubt she sees me as a man or any-thing...

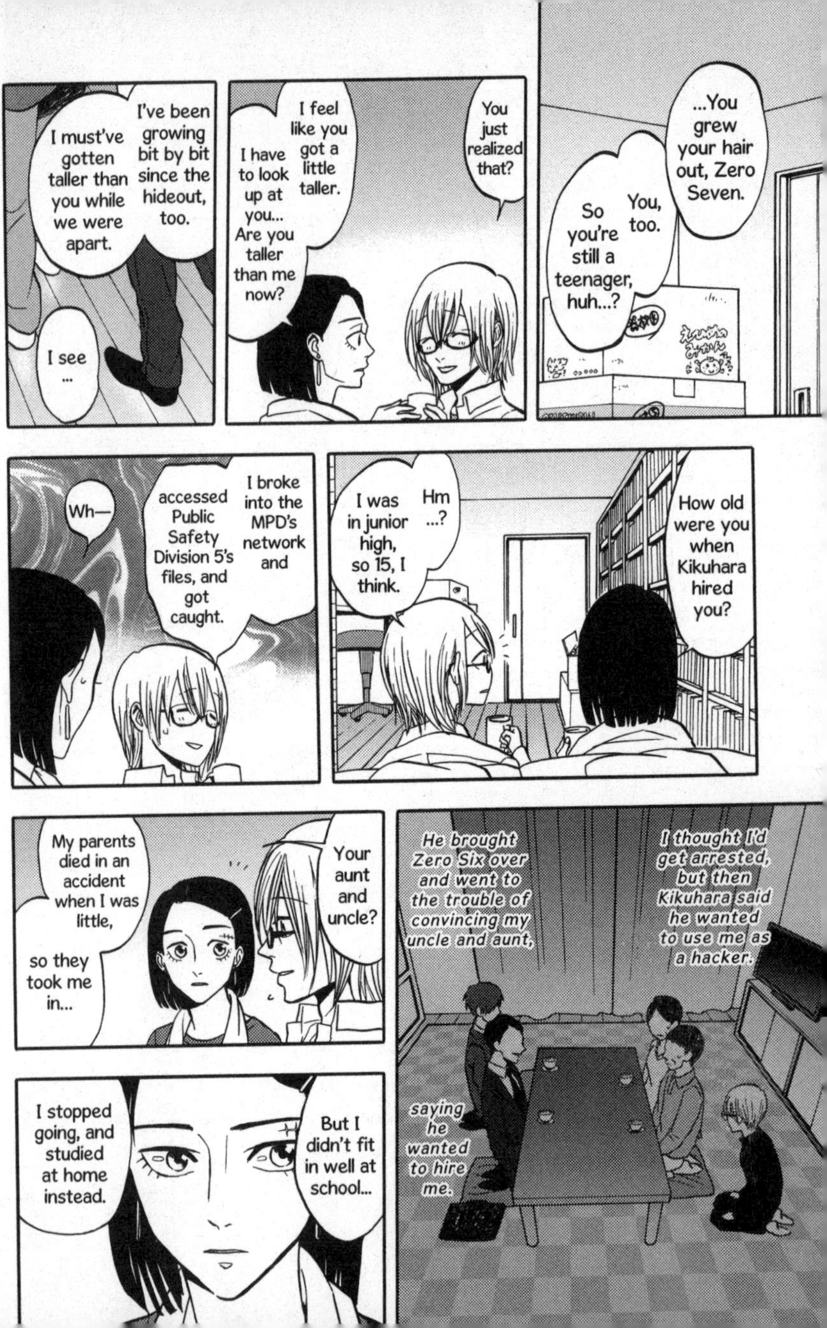
...You grew your hair out, Zero Seven.
You, too.
So you're still a teenager, huh...?
You just realized that?
I feel like you got a little taller.
I have to look up at you... Are you taller than me now?
I've been growing bit by bit since the hideout, too.
I must've gotten taller than you while we were apart.
I see...
How old were you when Kikuhara hired you?
Hm...?
I was in junior high, so 15, I think.
I broke into the MPD's network and
accessed Public Safety Division 5's files, and got caught.
Wh—
I thought I'd get arrested, but then Kikuhara said he wanted to use me as a hacker.
He brought Zero Six over and went to the trouble of convincing my uncle and aunt,
saying he wanted to hire me.
Your aunt and uncle?
My parents died in an accident when I was little,
so they took me in...
But I didn't fit in well at school...
I stopped going, and studied at home instead.

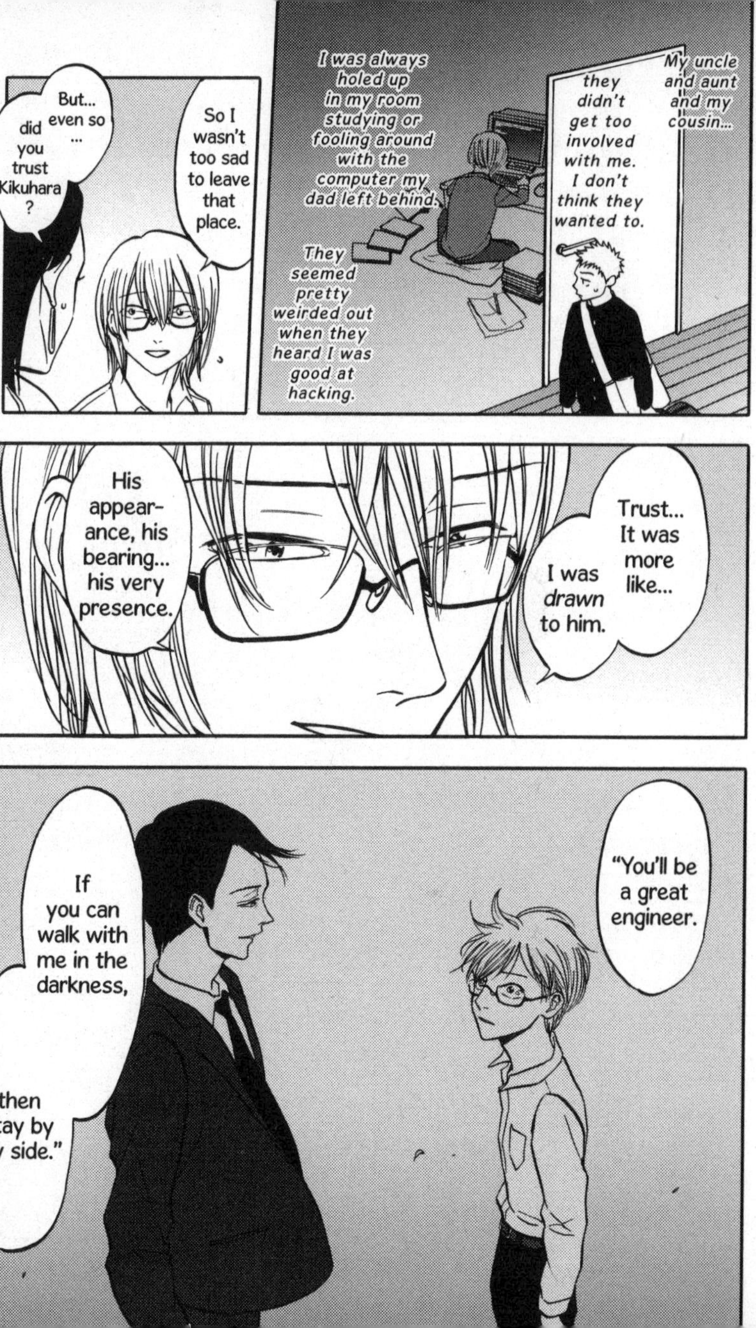
My uncle and aunt and my cousin...
they didn't get too involved with me. I don't think they wanted to.
I was always holed up in my room studying or fooling around with the computer my dad left behind.
They seemed pretty weirded out when they heard I was good at hacking.
So I wasn't too sad to leave that place.
But... even so ... did you trust Kikuhara ?
Trust... It was more like...
I was *drawn* to him.
His appearance, his bearing... his very presence.
"You'll be a great engineer.
If you can walk with me in the darkness,
then stay by my side."

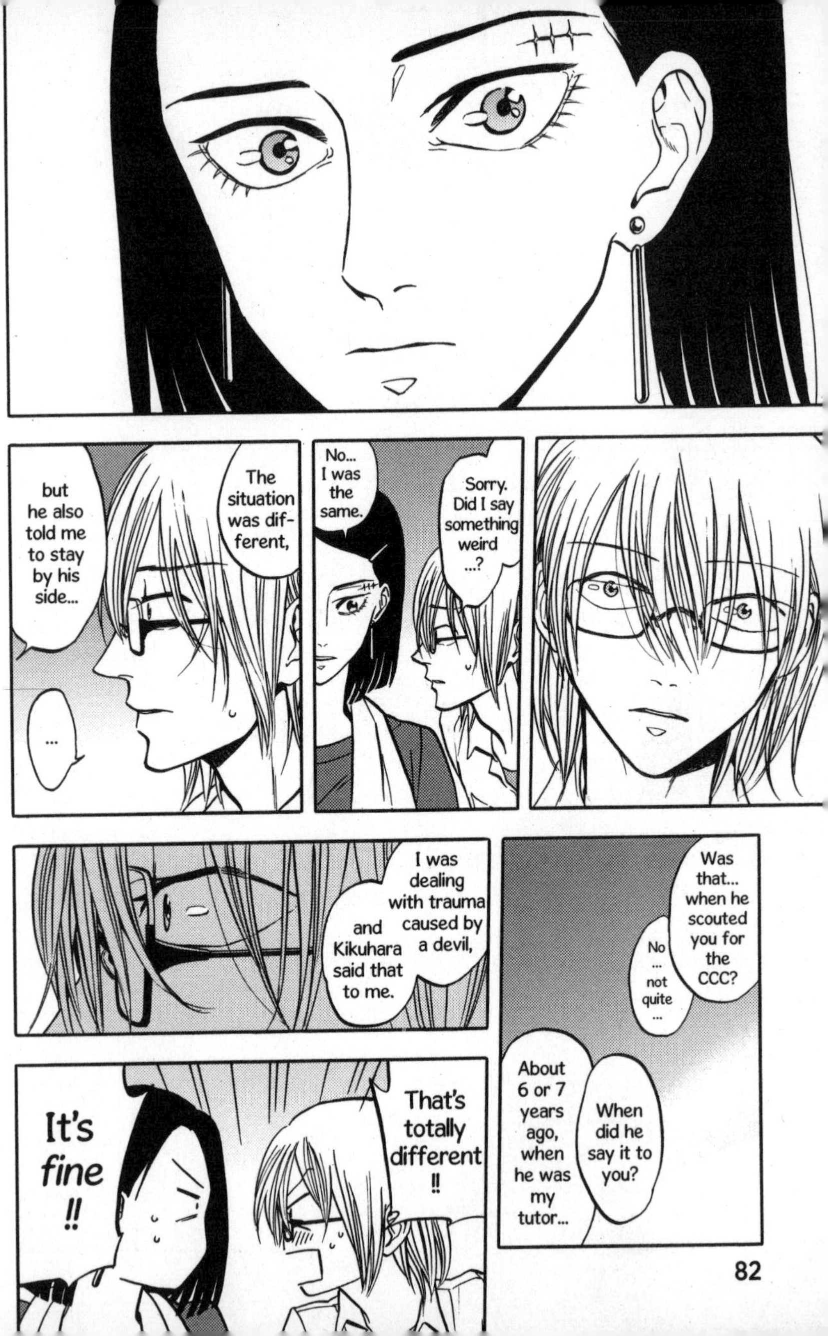

Sorry. Did I say something weird ...?
No... I was the same.
The situation was different,
but he also told me to stay by his side...
...
Was that... when he scouted you for the CCC?
No ... not quite ...
When did he say it to you?
About 6 or 7 years ago, when he was my tutor...
I was dealing with trauma caused by a devil,
and Kikuhara said that to me.
That's totally different !!
It's *fine* !!

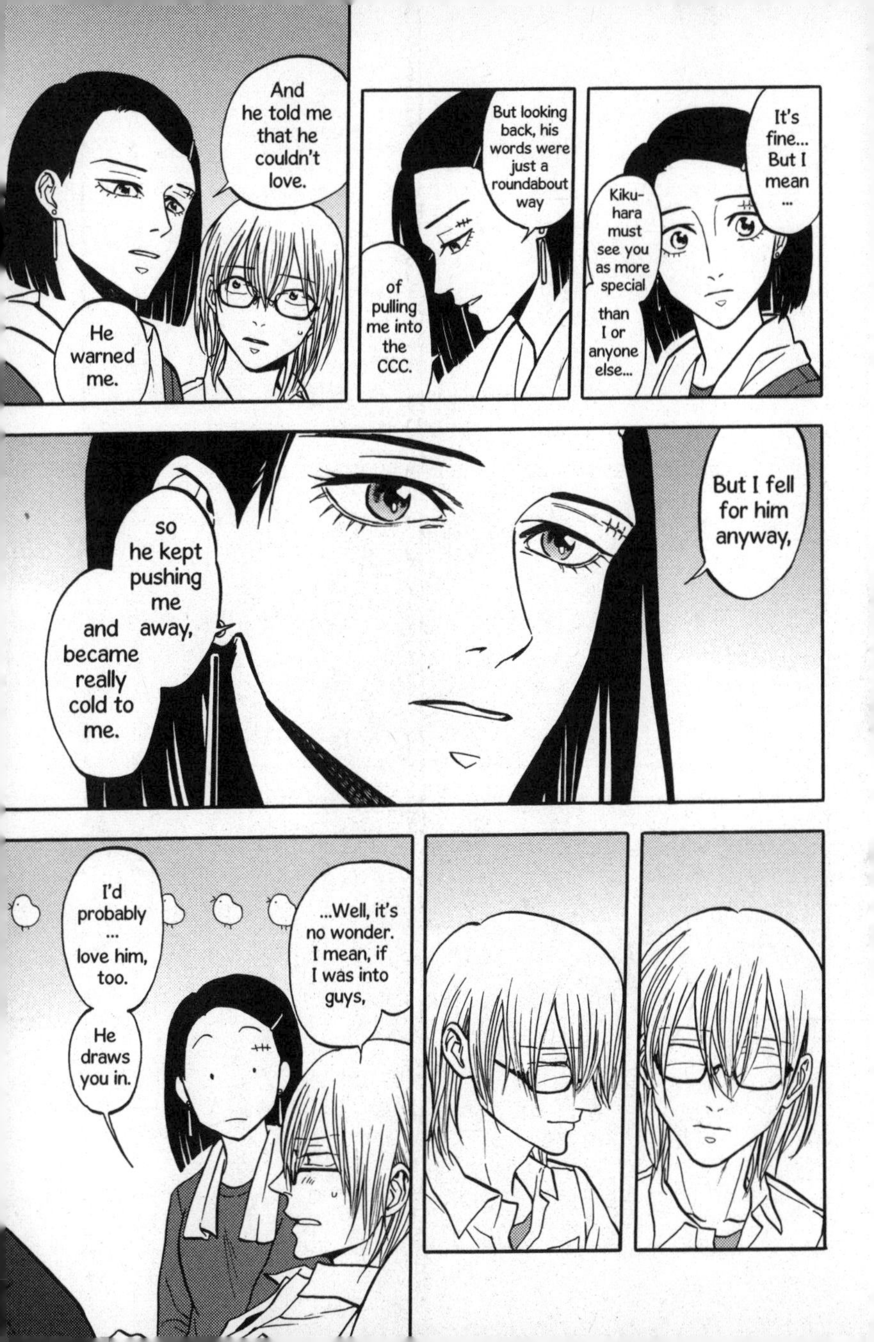
It's fine... But I mean ...
Kikuhara must see you as more special
than I or anyone else...
But looking back, his words were just a roundabout way
of pulling me into the CCC.
And he told me that he couldn't love.
He warned me.
But I fell for him anyway,
so he kept pushing me away,
and became really cold to me.
...Well, it's no wonder. I mean, if I was into guys,
I'd probably ... love him, too.
He draws you in.

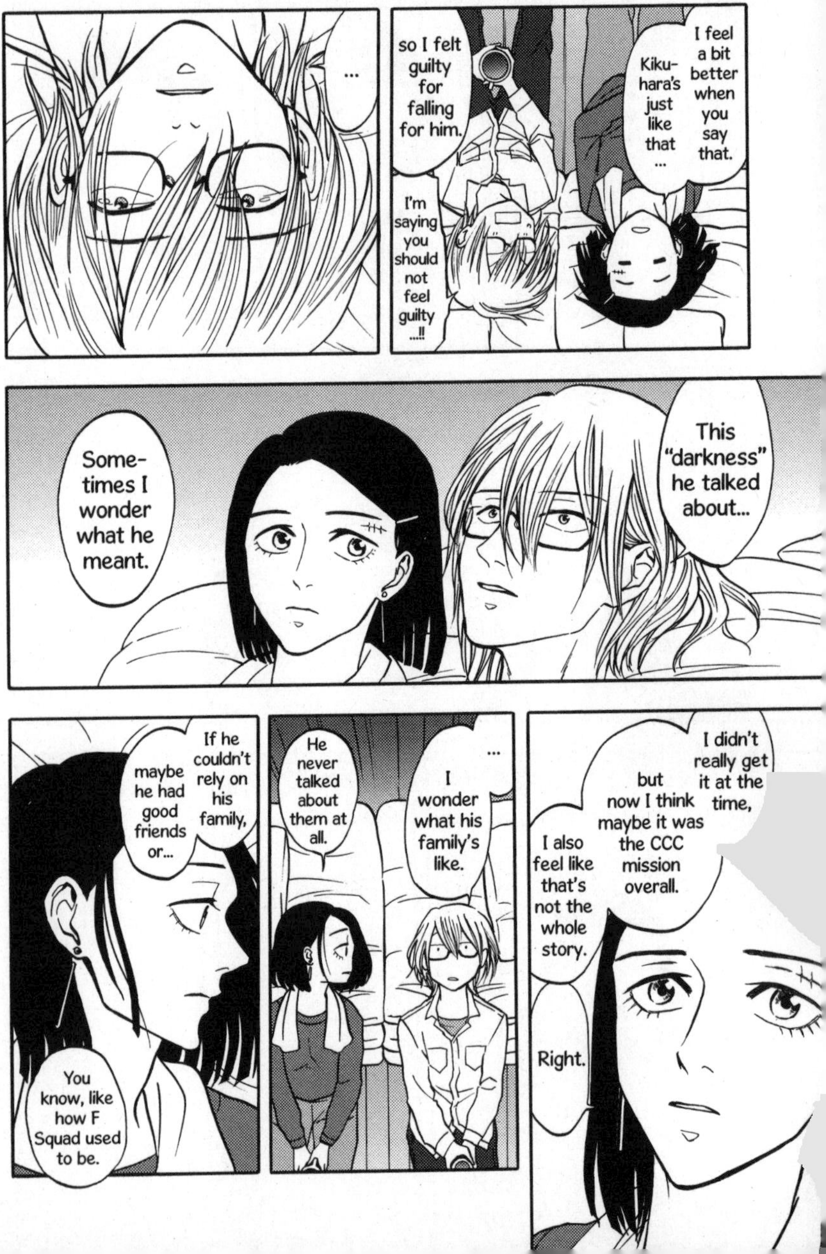

I feel a bit better when you say that.
Kiku-hara's just like that ...
so I felt guilty for falling for him.
I'm saying you should not feel guilty ...!!
...
This "darkness" he talked about...
Some-times I wonder what he meant.
I didn't really get it at the time,
but now I think maybe it was the CCC mission overall.
I also feel like that's not the whole story.
Right.
...
I wonder what his family's like.
He never talked about them at all.
If he couldn't rely on his family,
maybe he had good friends or...
You know, like how F Squad used to be.

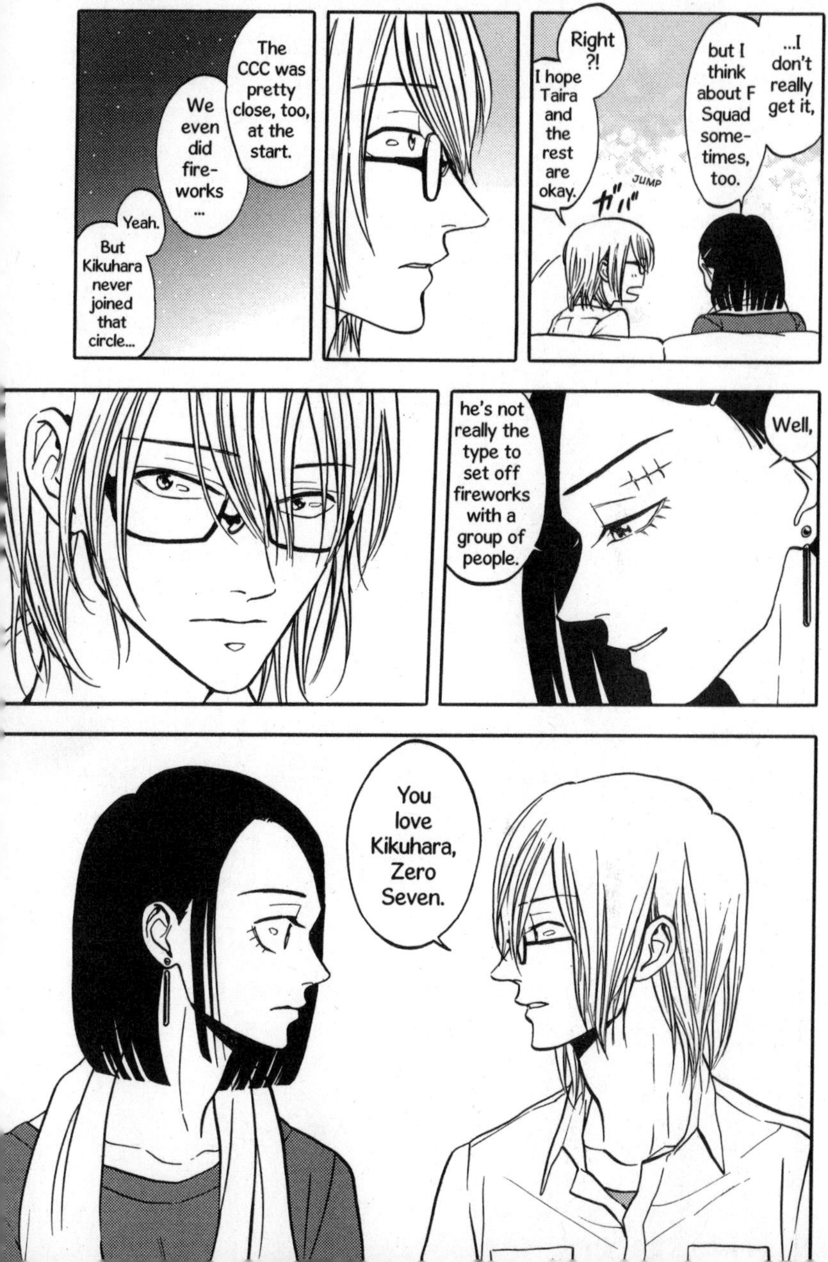
...I don't really get it,
but I think about F Squad some-times, too.
Right?!
I hope Taira and the rest are okay.
JUMP
The CCC was pretty close, too, at the start.
We even did fire-works...
Yeah.
But Kikuhara never joined that circle...
Well,
he's not really the type to set off fireworks with a group of people.
You love Kikuhara, Zero Seven.

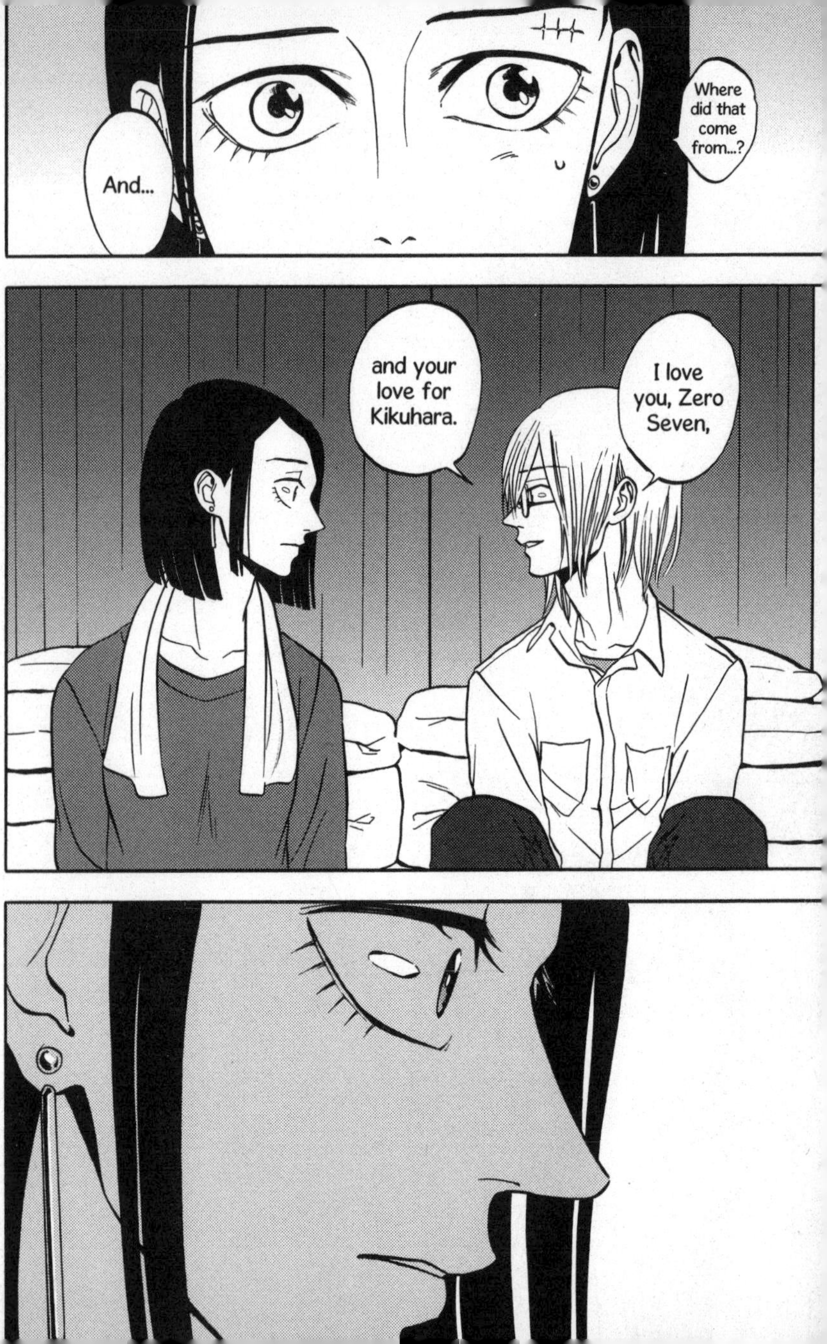
Where did that come from...?
And...
I love you, Zero Seven,
and your love for Kikuhara.

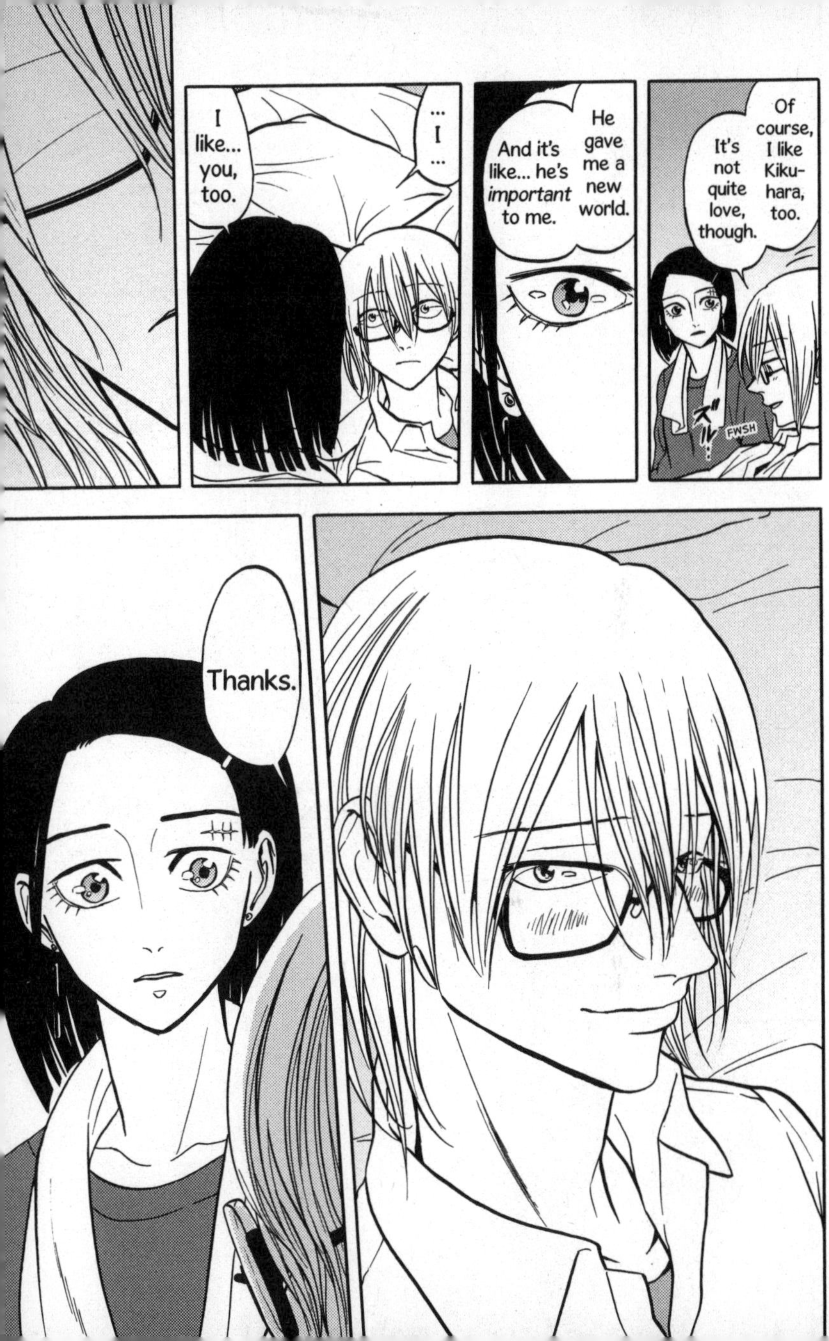
Of course, I like Kikuhara, too.
It's not quite love, though.
ズル…
FWSH
He gave me a new world.
And it's like... he's *important* to me.
... I ...
I like... you, too.
Thanks.

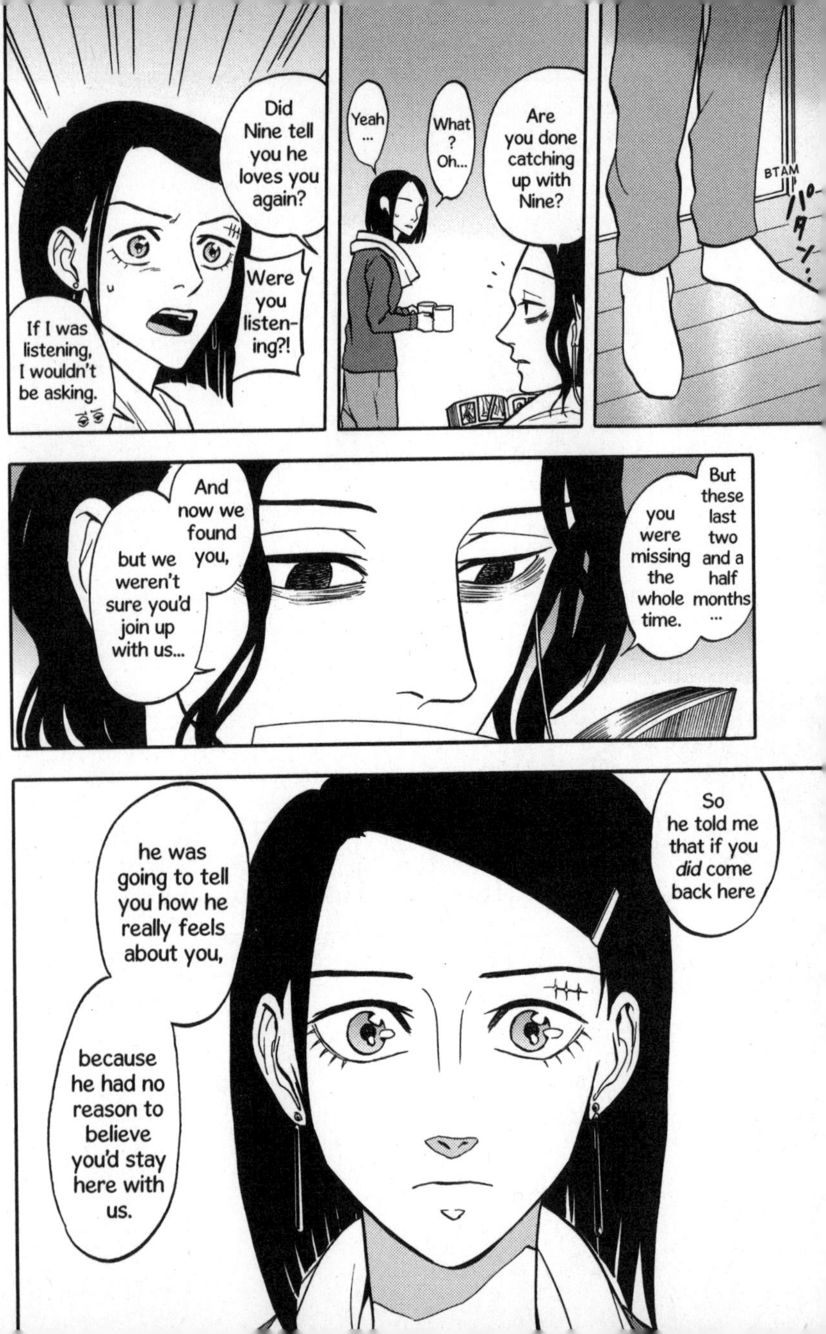
BTAM
Are you done catching up with Nine?
What? Oh...
Yeah ...
Did Nine tell you he loves you again?
Were you listen-ing?!
If I was listening, I wouldn't be asking.
But these last two and a half months ...
you were missing the whole time.
And now we found you,
but we weren't sure you'd join up with us...
So he told me that if you *did* come back here
he was going to tell you how he really feels about you,
because he had no reason to believe you'd stay here with us.

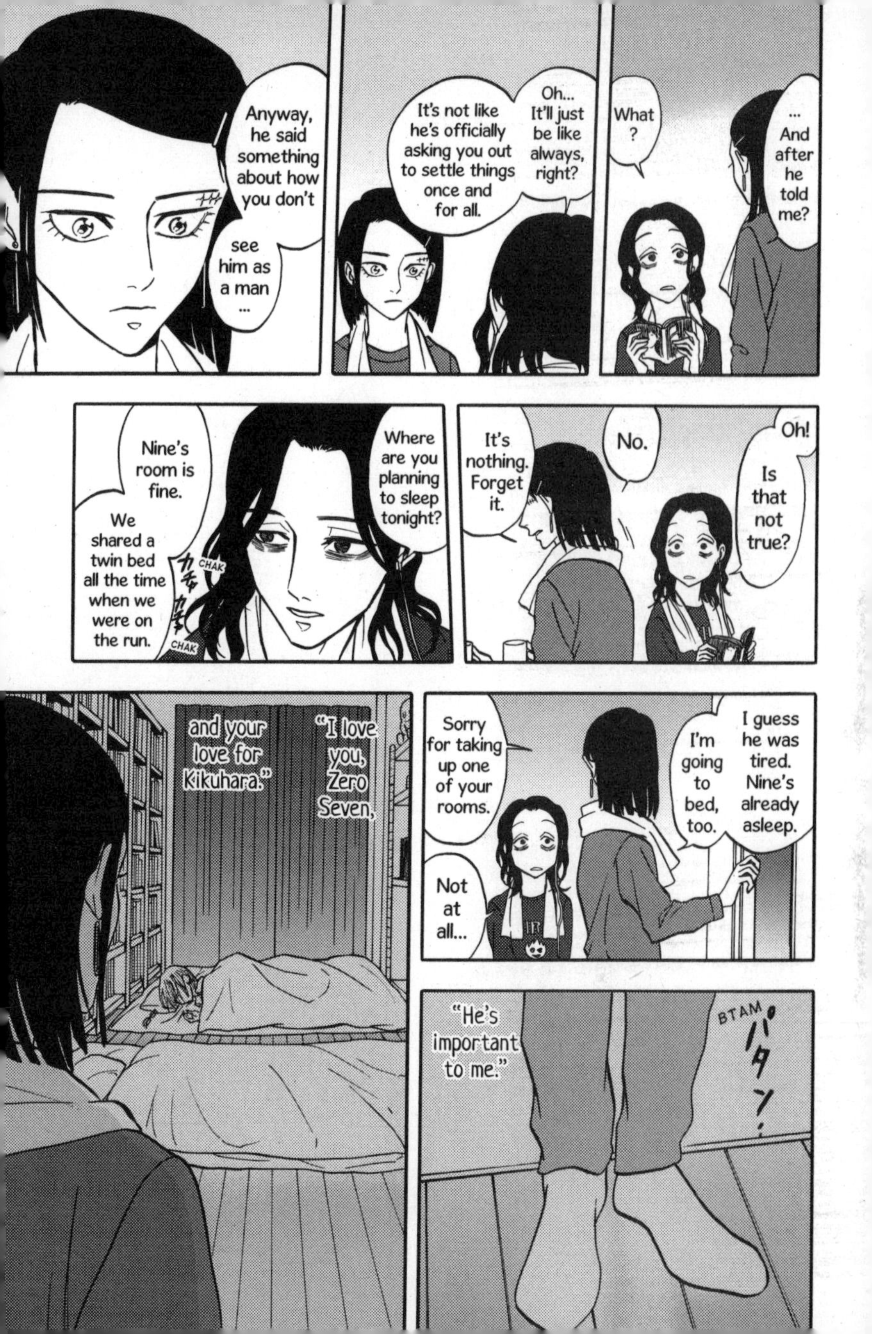
... And after he told me?
What ?
Oh... It'll just be like always, right?
It's not like he's officially asking you out to settle things once and for all.
Anyway, he said something about how you don't
see him as a man ...
Oh!
Is that not true?
No.
It's nothing. Forget it.
Where are you planning to sleep tonight?
Nine's room is fine.
We shared a twin bed all the time when we were on the run.
CHAK
CHAK
I guess he was tired. Nine's already asleep.
I'm going to bed, too.
Sorry for taking up one of your rooms.
Not at all...
BTAM
"He's important to me."
"I love you, Zero Seven,
and your love for Kikuhara."

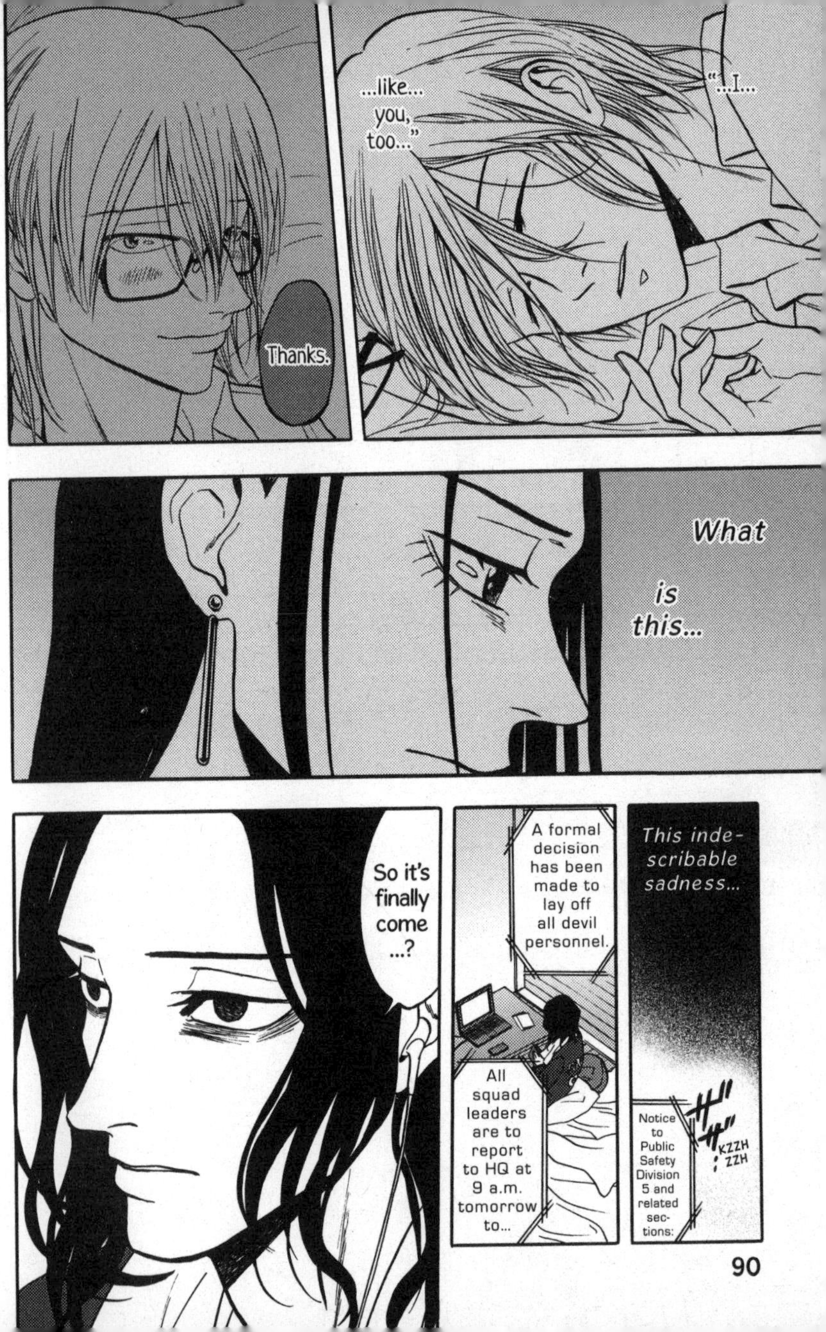
"…I…
…like… you, too…"
Thanks.
What is this…
This inde-scribable sadness…
Notice to Public Safety Division 5 and related sec-tions:
KZZH ZZH
A formal decision has been made to lay off all devil personnel.
All squad leaders are to report to HQ at 9 a.m. tomorrow to…
So it's finally come …?

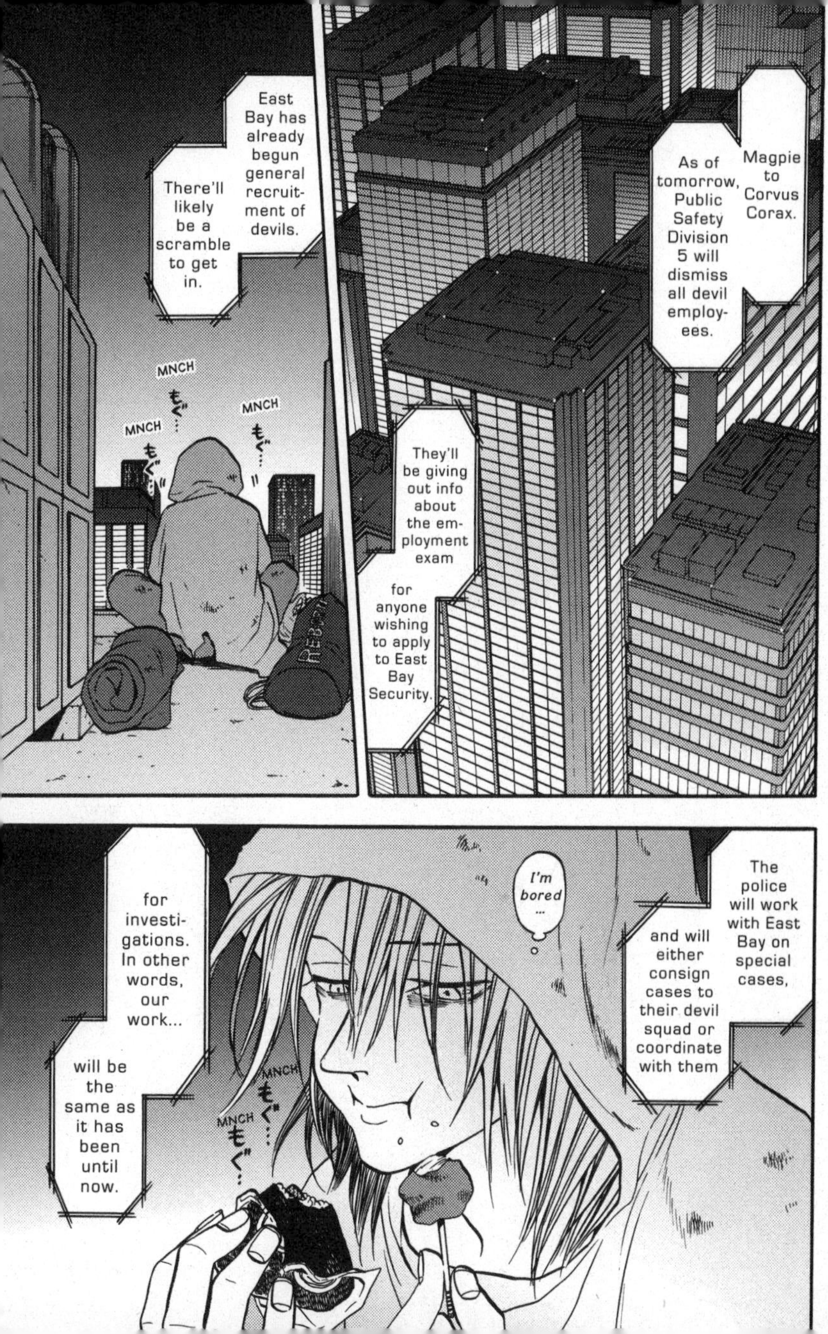

Magpie to Corvus Corax.
As of tomorrow, Public Safety Division 5 will dismiss all devil employees.
They'll be giving out info about the employment exam
for anyone wishing to apply to East Bay Security.
East Bay has already begun general recruitment of devils.
There'll likely be a scramble to get in.
MNCH
もぐ…
MNCH
もぐ…
MNCH
もぐ…
The police will work with East Bay on special cases,
and will either consign cases to their devil squad or coordinate with them
I'm bored…
for investigations. In other words, our work…
will be the same as it has been until now.
MNCH
もぐ…
MNCH
もぐ…

Line 55
Inter Nos

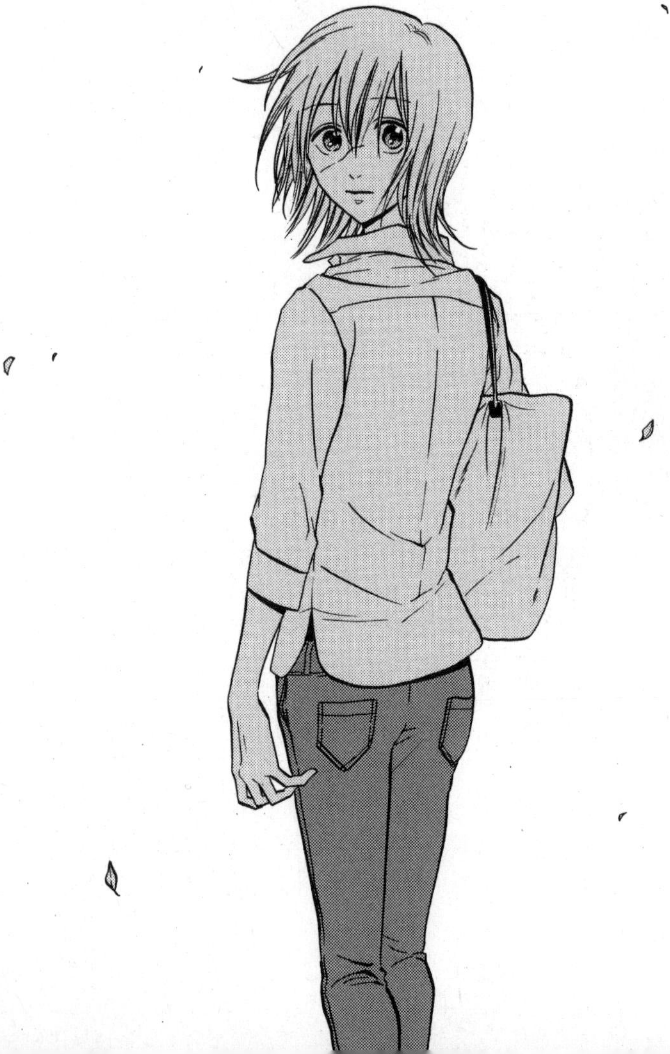

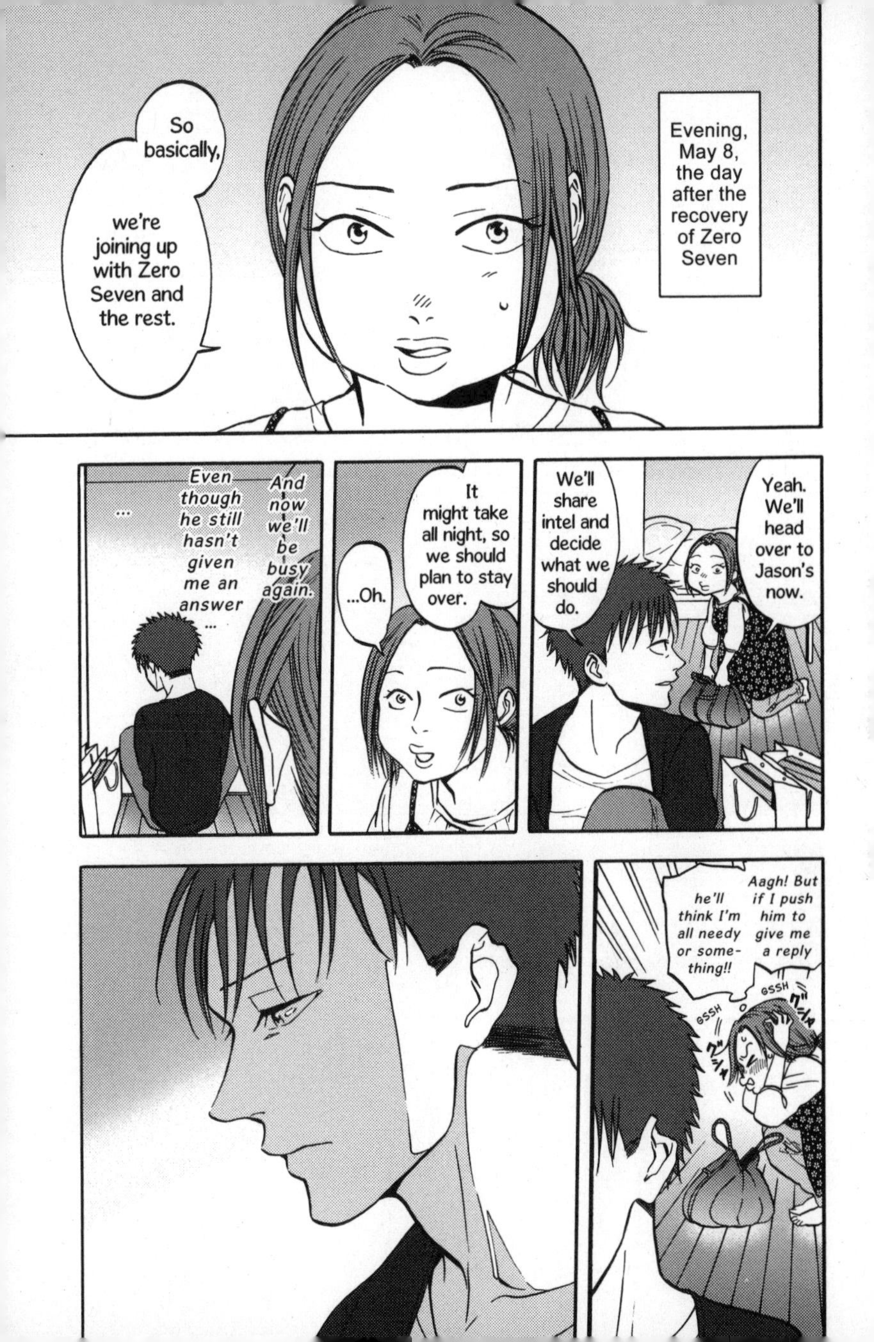
Evening, May 8, the day after the recovery of Zero Seven
So basically,
we're joining up with Zero Seven and the rest.
Yeah. We'll head over to Jason's now.
We'll share intel and decide what we should do.
It might take all night, so we should plan to stay over.
...Oh.
And now we'll be busy again.
Even though he still hasn't given me an answer ...
...
Aagh! But if I push him to give me a reply
he'll think I'm all needy or something!!
GSSH
GSSH

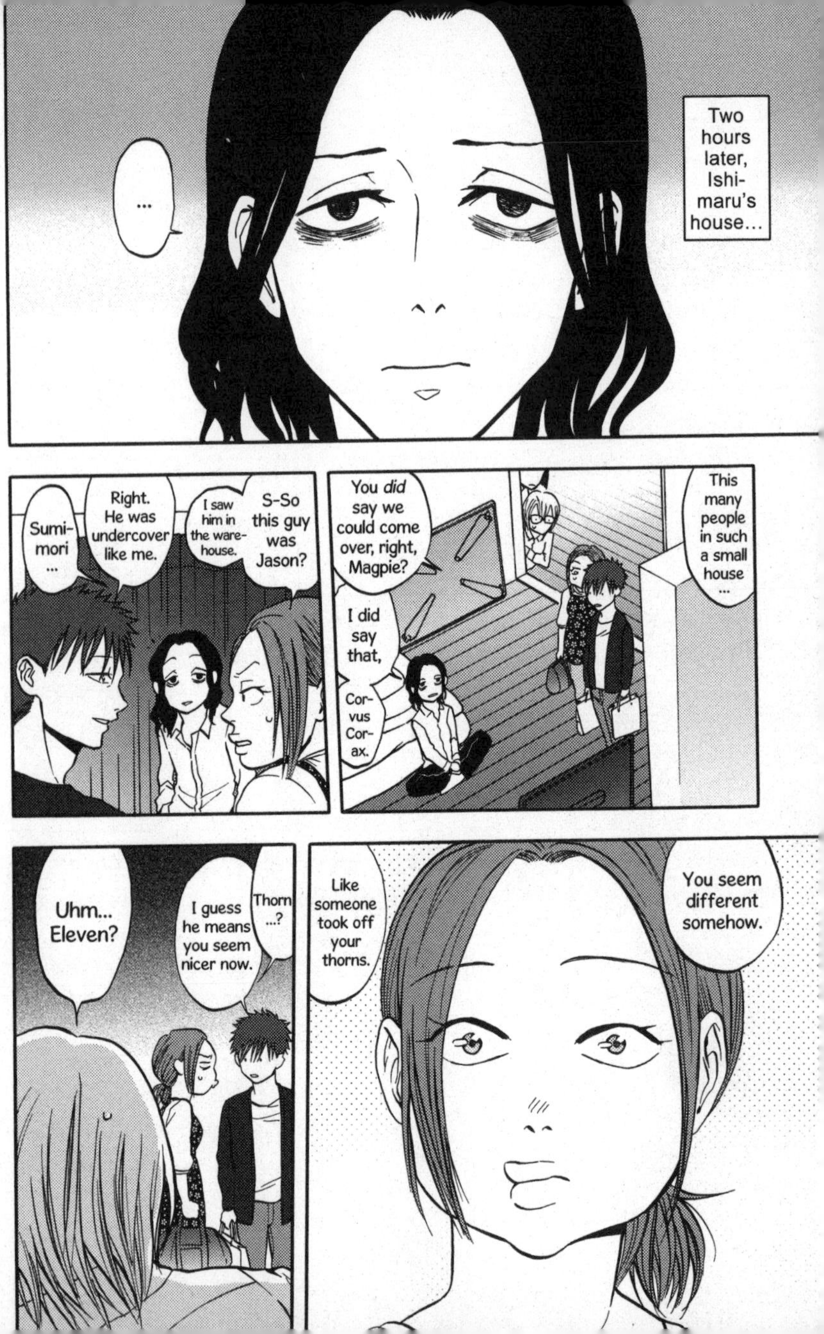
Two hours later, Ishi-maru's house…
…
This many people in such a small house …
You *did* say we could come over, right, Magpie?
I did say that,
Cor-vus Cor-ax.
S-So this guy was Jason?
I saw him in the ware-house.
Right. He was undercover like me.
Sumi-mori …
You seem different somehow.
Like someone took off your thorns.
Thorn …?
I guess he means you seem nicer now.
Uhm… Eleven?

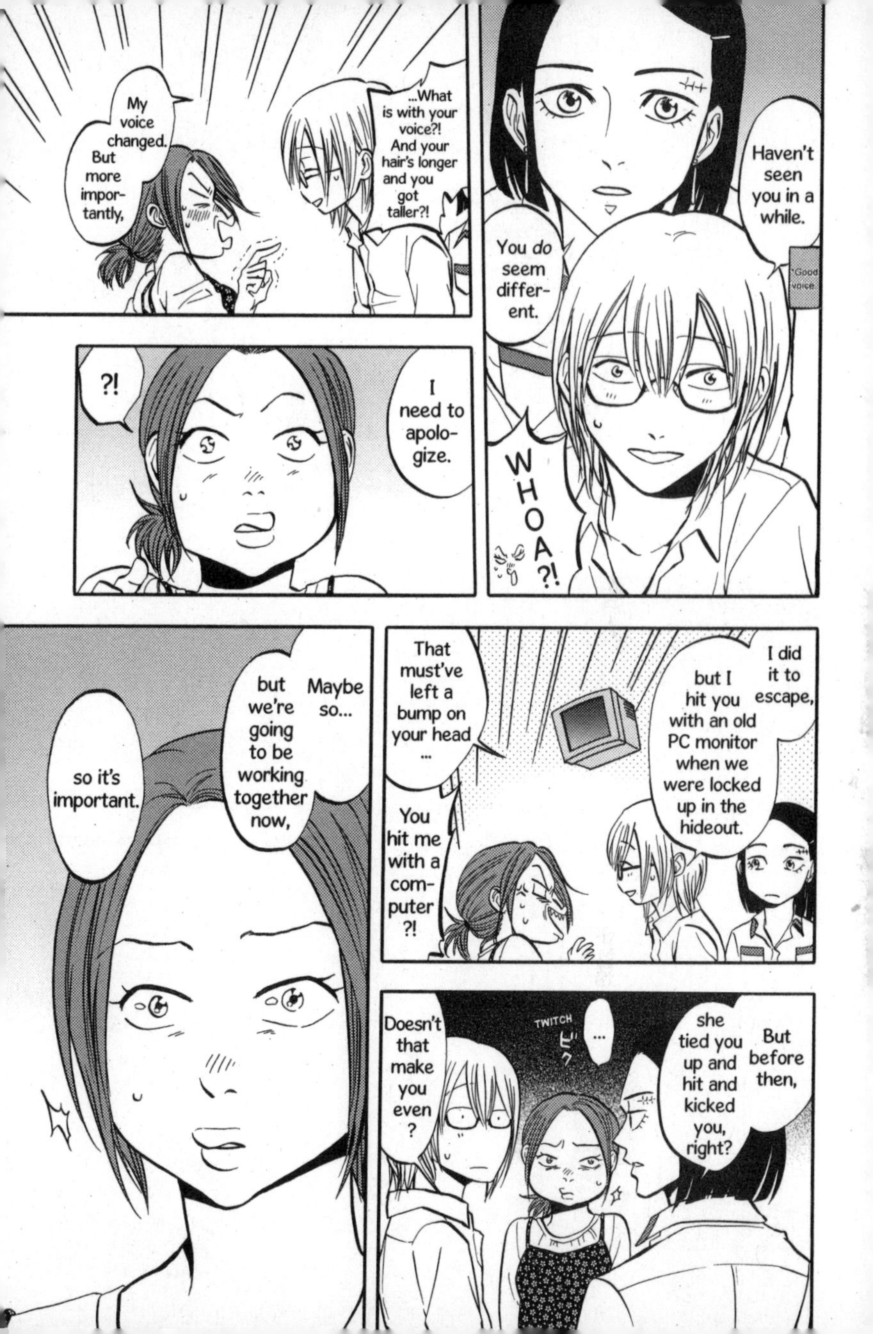

Haven't seen you in a while.
*Good voice
You *do* seem different.
WHOA?!
...What is with your voice?! And your hair's longer and you got taller?!
My voice changed. But more importantly,
I need to apologize.
?!
I did it to escape,
but I hit you with an old PC monitor when we were locked up in the hideout.
That must've left a bump on your head ...
You hit me with a computer?!
But before then,
she tied you up and hit and kicked you, right?
TWITCH
ビク
...
Doesn't that make you even ?
Maybe so...
but we're going to be working together now,
so it's important.

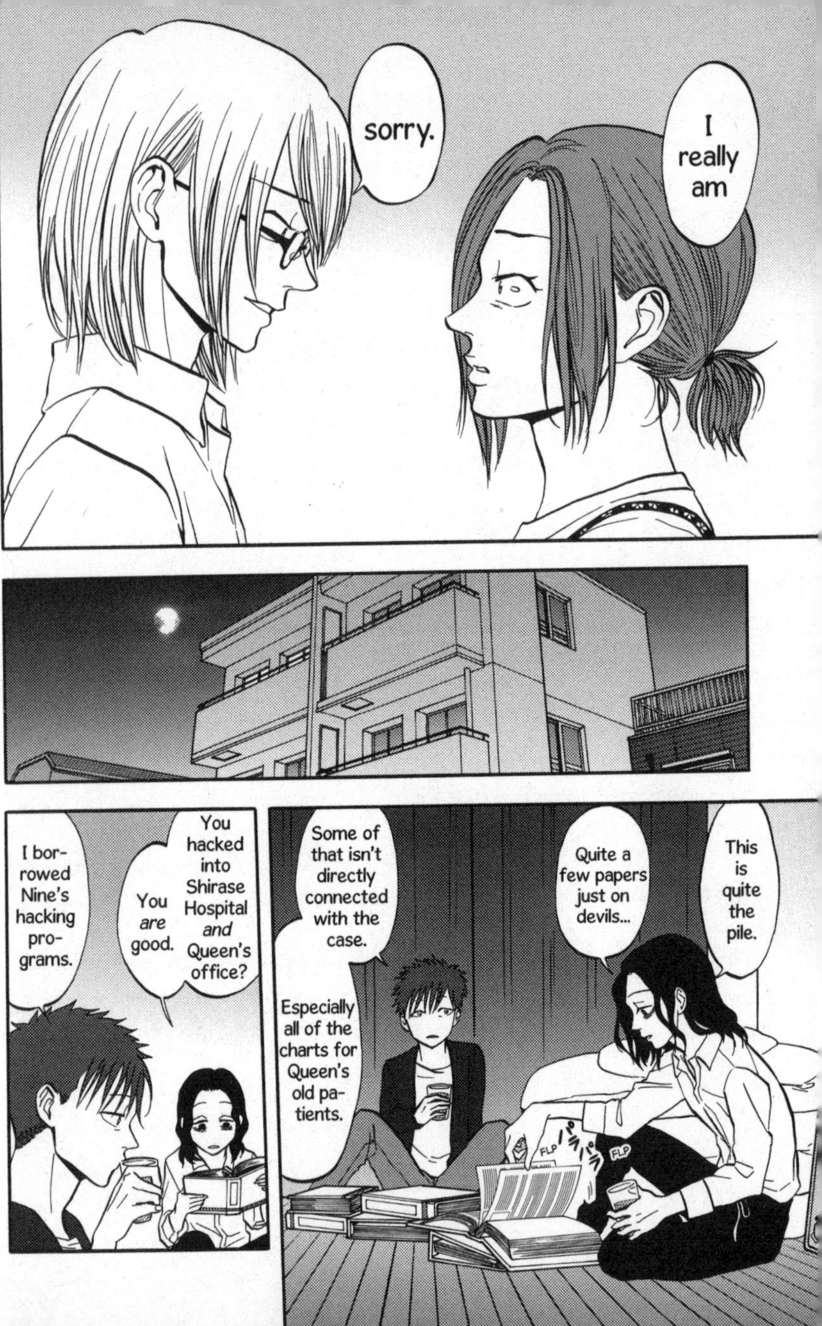
I really am
sorry.
This is quite the pile.
Quite a few papers just on devils...
Some of that isn't directly connected with the case.
Especially all of the charts for Queen's old patients.
FLP
FLP
You hacked into Shirase Hospital *and* Queen's office?
You *are* good.
I borrowed Nine's hacking programs.

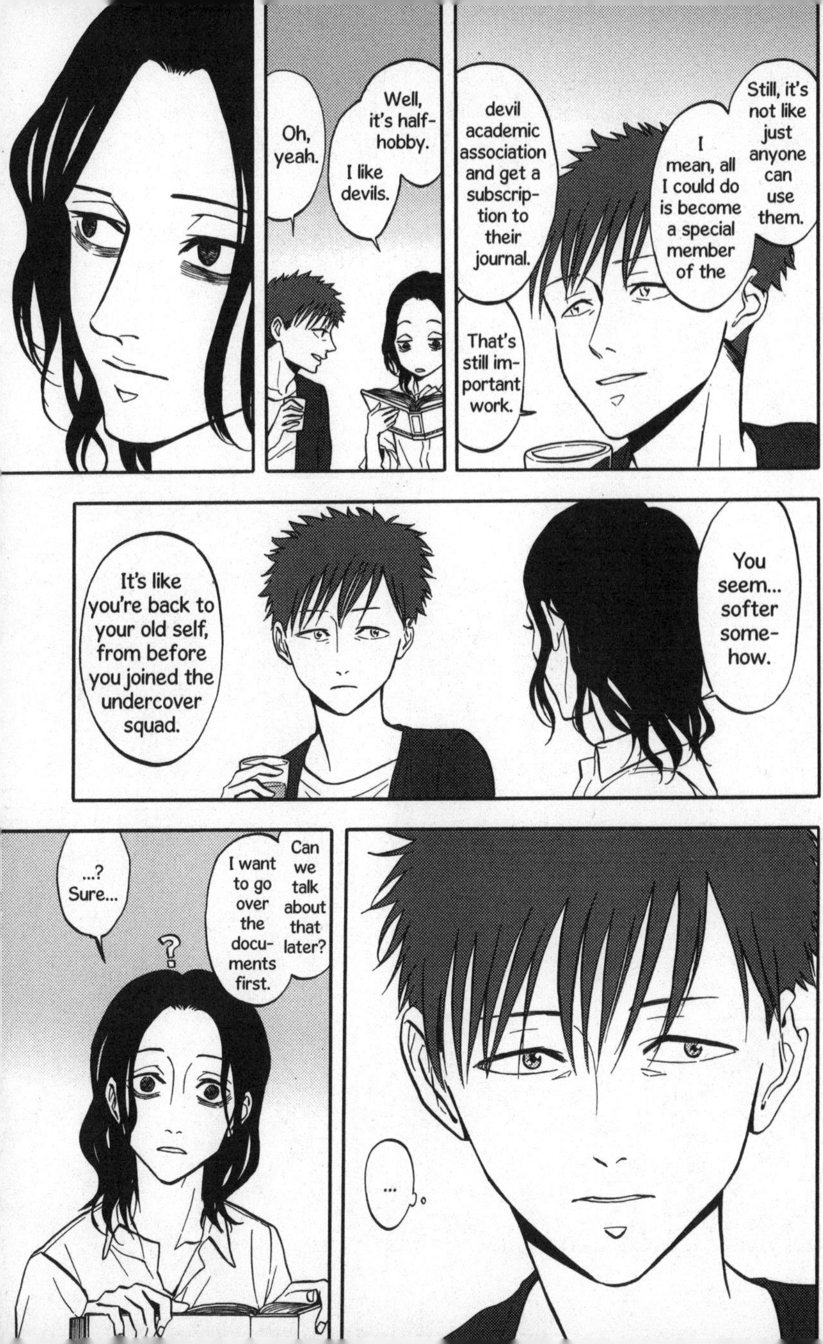
Still, it's not like just anyone can use them.
I mean, all I could do is become a special member of the
devil academic association and get a subscription to their journal.
That's still important work.
Well, it's half-hobby. I like devils.
Oh, yeah.
You seem... softer somehow.
It's like you're back to your old self, from before you joined the undercover squad.
...
Can we talk about that later?
I want to go over the documents first.
...? Sure...

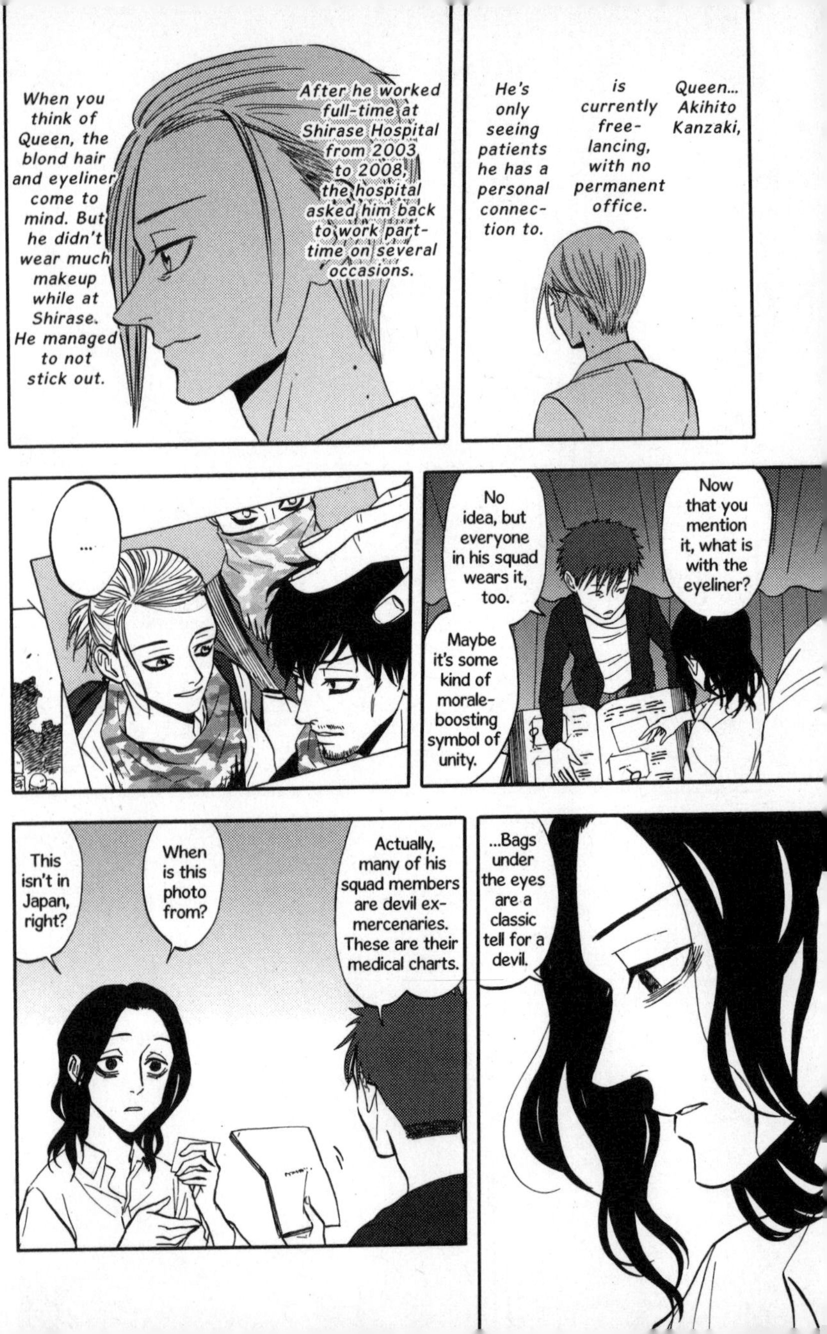
Queen... Akihito Kanzaki,
is currently free-lancing, with no permanent office.
He's only seeing patients he has a personal connection to.
After he worked full-time at Shirase Hospital from 2003 to 2008, the hospital asked him back to work part-time on several occasions.
When you think of Queen, the blond hair and eyeliner come to mind. But he didn't wear much makeup while at Shirase. He managed to not stick out.
Now that you mention it, what is with the eyeliner?
No idea, but everyone in his squad wears it, too.
Maybe it's some kind of morale-boosting symbol of unity.
...
...Bags under the eyes are a classic tell for a devil.
Actually, many of his squad members are devil ex-mercenaries. These are their medical charts.
When is this photo from?
This isn't in Japan, right?

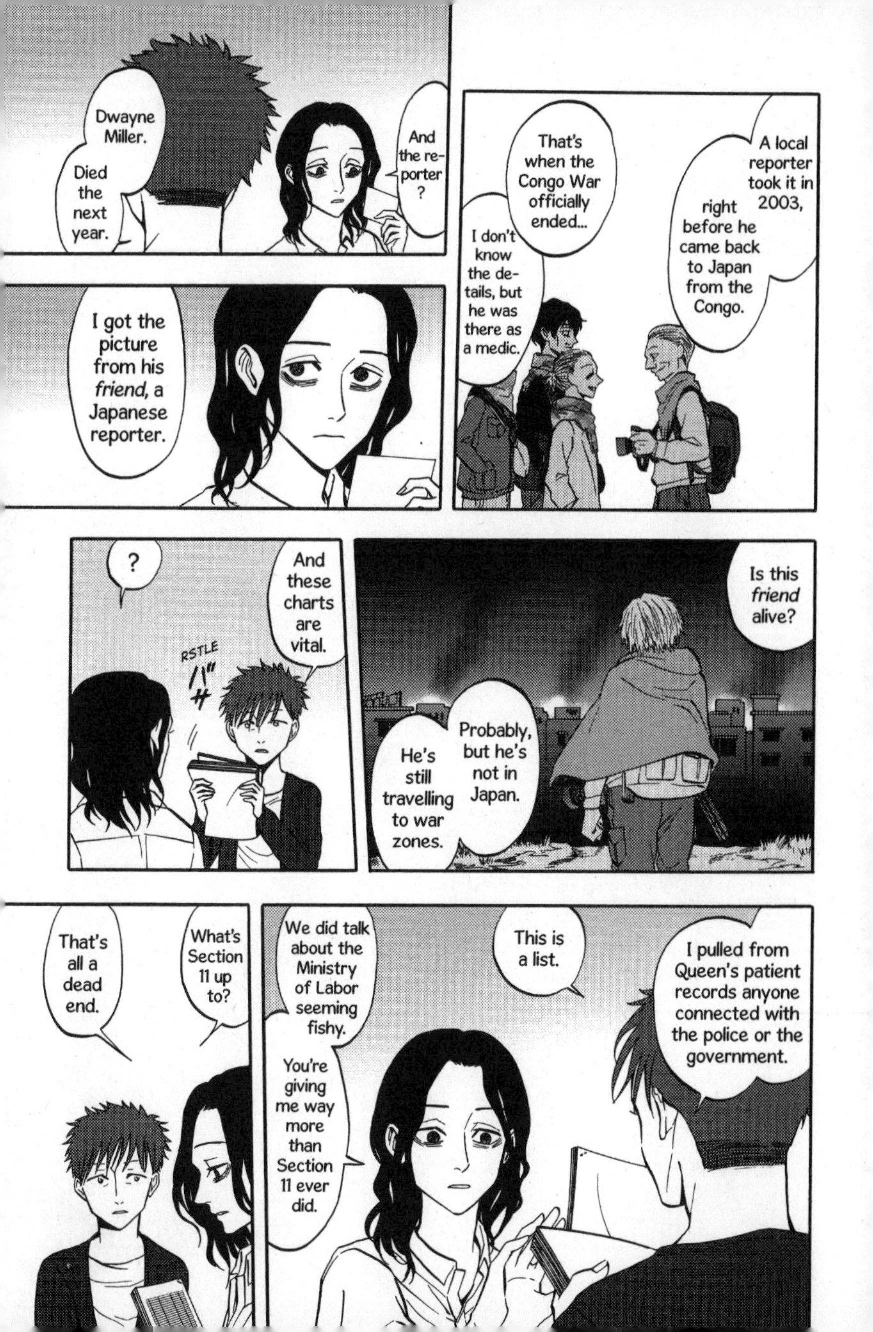

A local reporter took it in 2003,
right before he came back to Japan from the Congo.
That's when the Congo War officially ended...
I don't know the details, but he was there as a medic.
And the reporter?
Dwayne Miller.
Died the next year.
I got the picture from his *friend*, a Japanese reporter.
Is this *friend* alive?
Probably, but he's not in Japan.
He's still travelling to war zones.
And these charts are vital.
RSTLE
?
I pulled from Queen's patient records anyone connected with the police or the government.
This is a list.
We did talk about the Ministry of Labor seeming fishy.
You're giving me way more than Section 11 ever did.
What's Section 11 up to?
That's all a dead end.

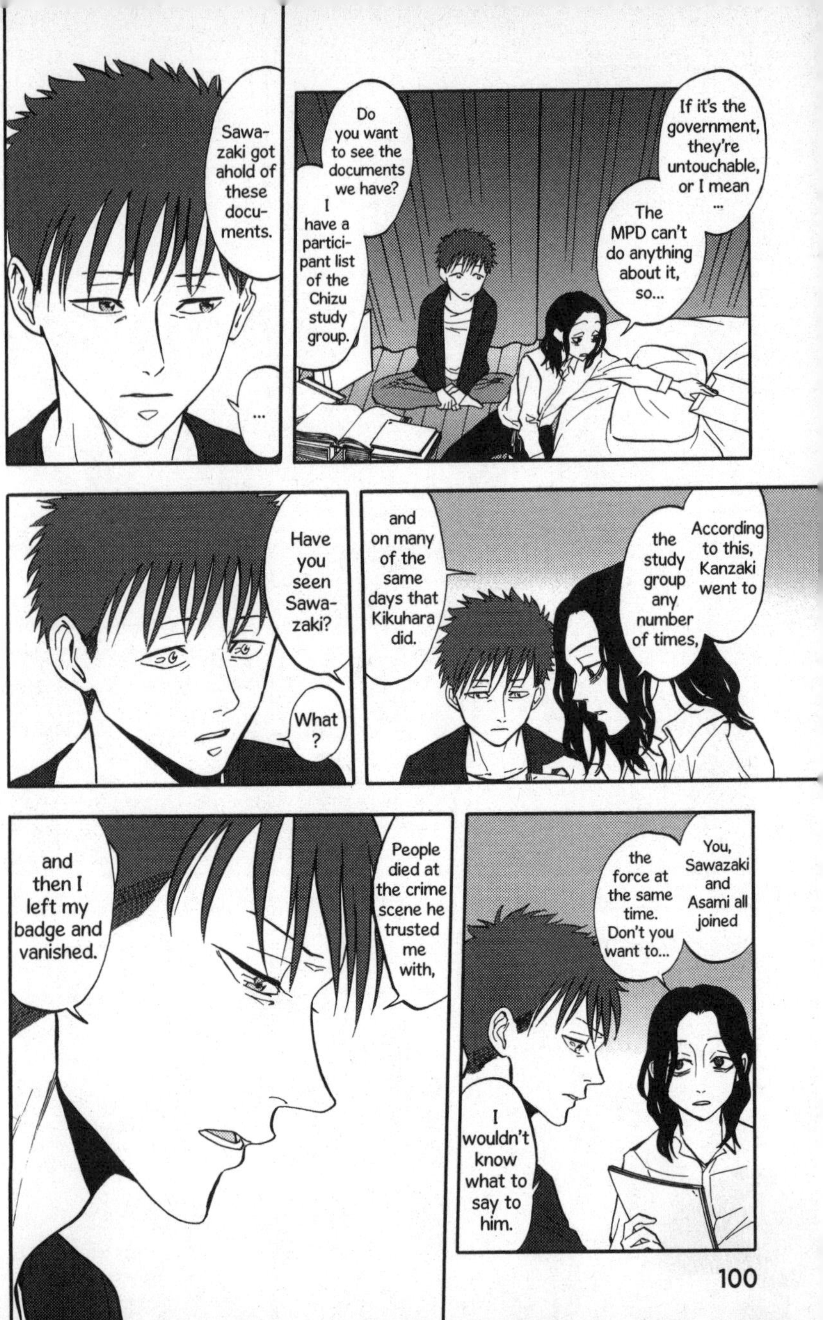

If it's the government, they're untouchable, or I mean ...
The MPD can't do anything about it, so...
Do you want to see the documents we have?
I have a partici-pant list of the Chizu study group.
Sawa-zaki got ahold of these docu-ments.
...
According to this, Kanzaki went to
the study group any number of times,
and on many of the same days that Kikuhara did.
Have you seen Sawa-zaki?
What?
You, Sawazaki and Asami all joined
the force at the same time. Don't you want to...
I wouldn't know what to say to him.
People died at the crime scene he trusted me with,
and then I left my badge and vanished.

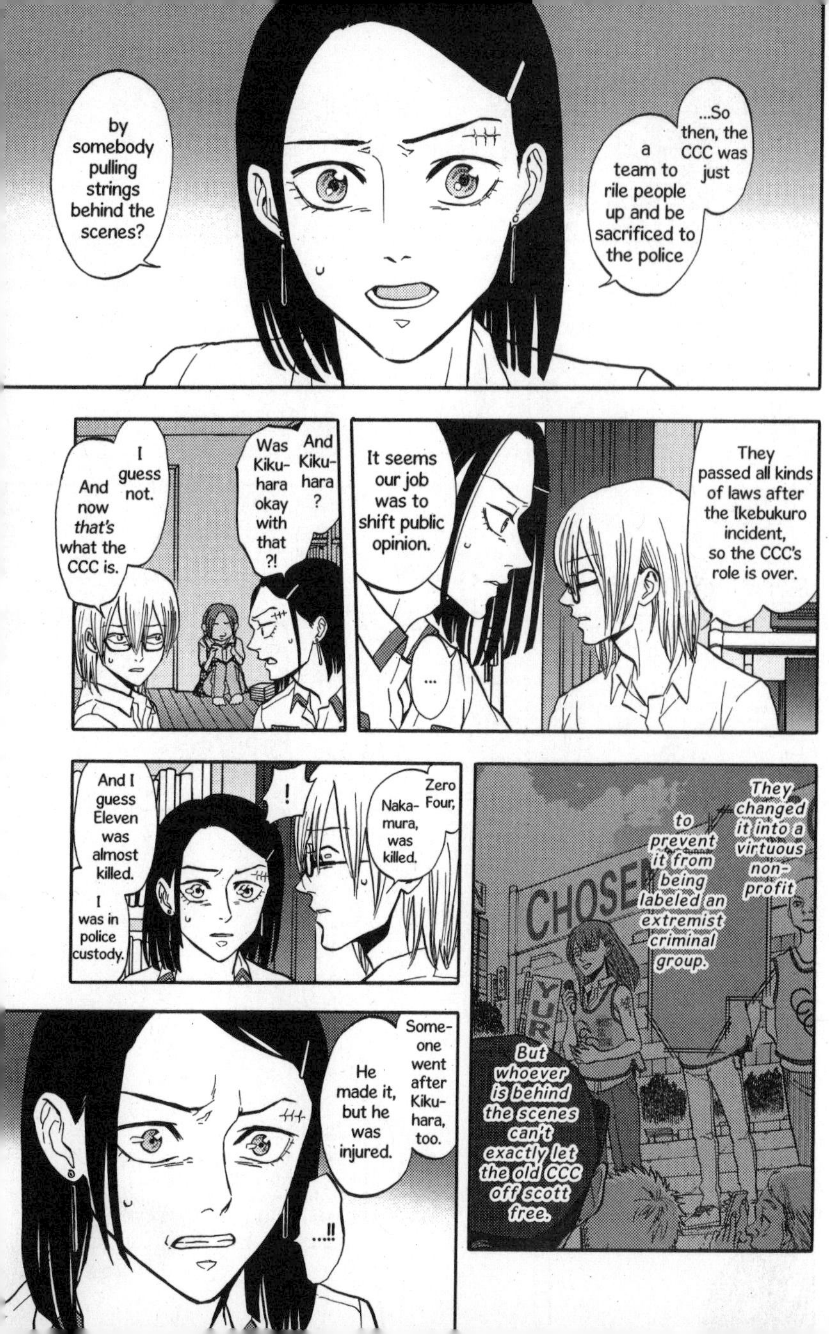
...So then, the CCC was just a team to rile people up and be sacrificed to the police
by somebody pulling strings behind the scenes?
They passed all kinds of laws after the Ikebukuro incident, so the CCC's role is over.
It seems our job was to shift public opinion.
...
And Kikuhara?
Was Kikuhara okay with that?!
I guess not.
And now *that's* what the CCC is.
They changed it into a virtuous non-profit
to prevent it from being labeled an extremist criminal group.
CHOSE
YUR
But whoever is behind the scenes can't exactly let the old CCC off scott free.
Zero Four, Nakamura, was killed.
!
And I guess Eleven was almost killed.
I was in police custody.
Someone went after Kikuhara, too.
He made it, but he was injured.
...!!

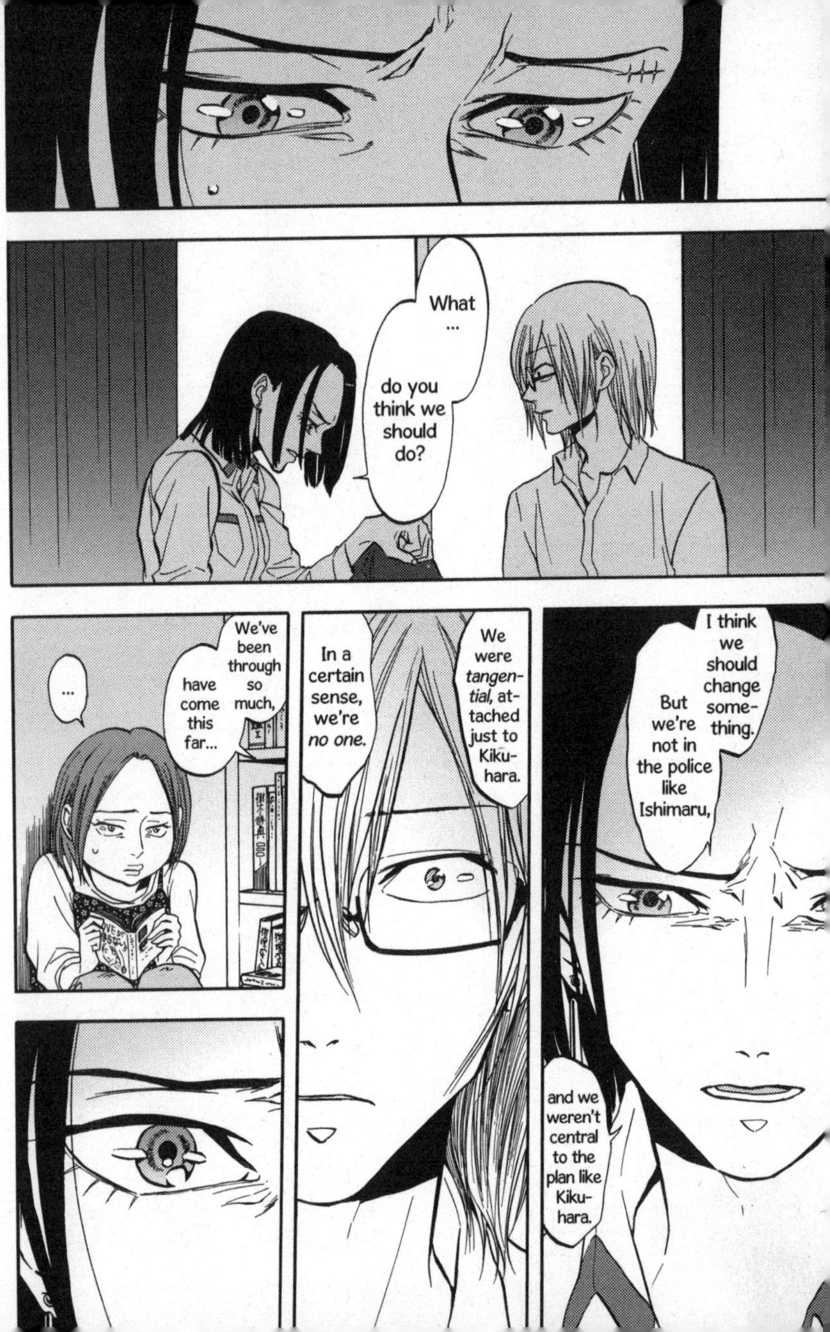
What ... do you think we should do?
I think we should change something.
But we're not in the police like Ishimaru,
and we weren't central to the plan like Kikuhara.
We were *tangential*, attached just to Kikuhara.
In a certain sense, we're *no one.*
We've been through so much,
have come this far...
...

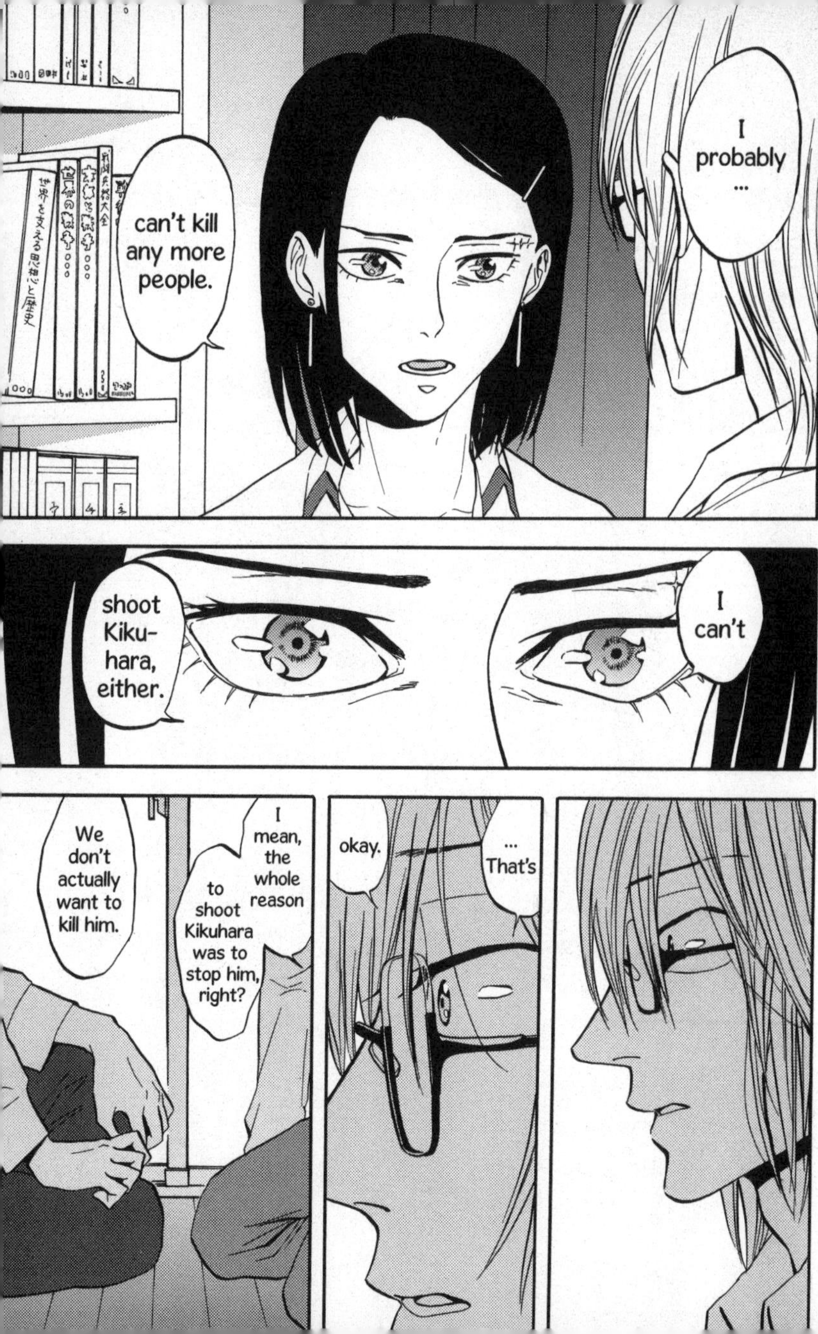
I probably ...
can't kill any more people.
I can't
shoot Kiku-hara, either.
... That's
okay.
I mean, the whole reason to shoot Kikuhara was to stop him, right?
We don't actually want to kill him.

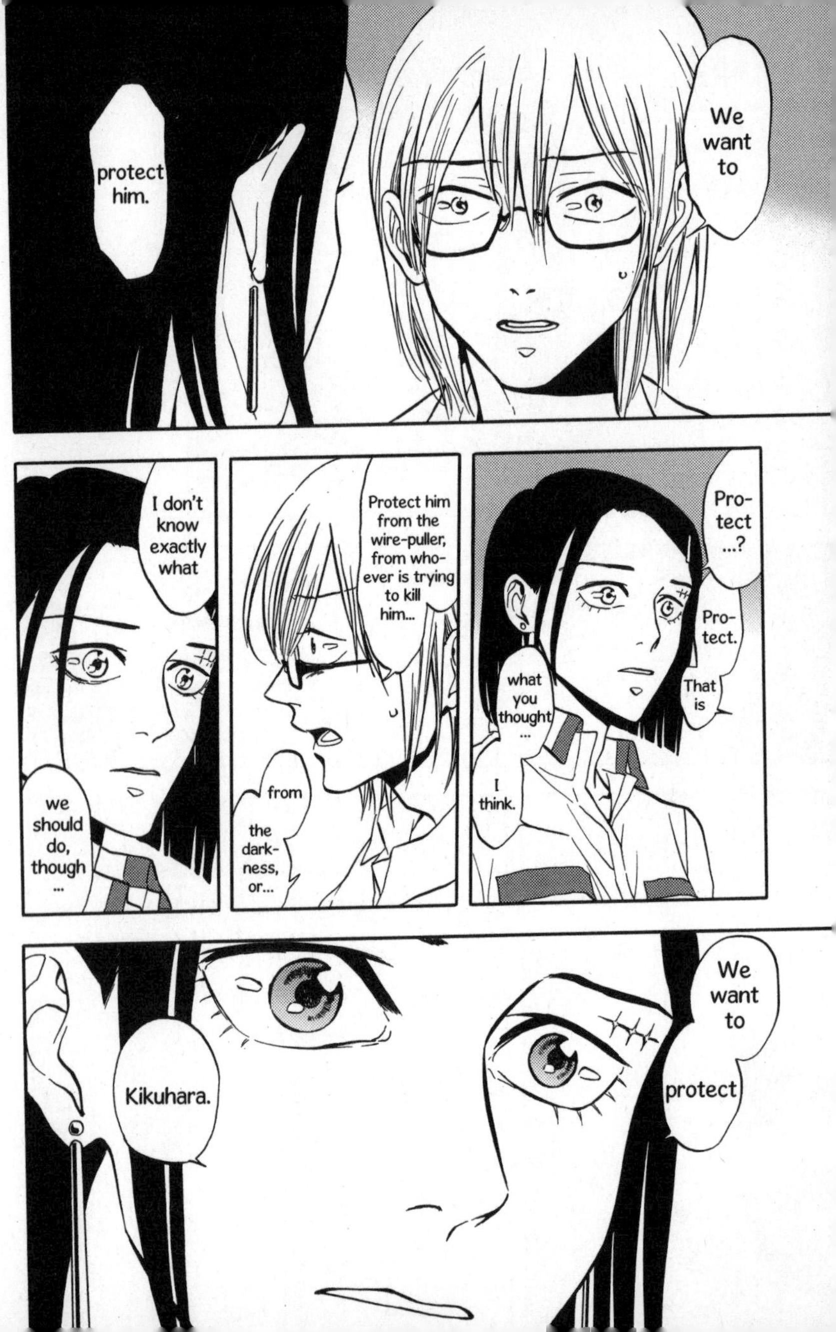
We want to
protect him.
Pro-tect ...?
Pro-tect.
That is
what you thought ...
I think.
Protect him from the wire-puller, from who-ever is trying to kill him...
from
the dark-ness, or...
I don't know exactly what
we should do, though ...
We want to
protect
Kikuhara.

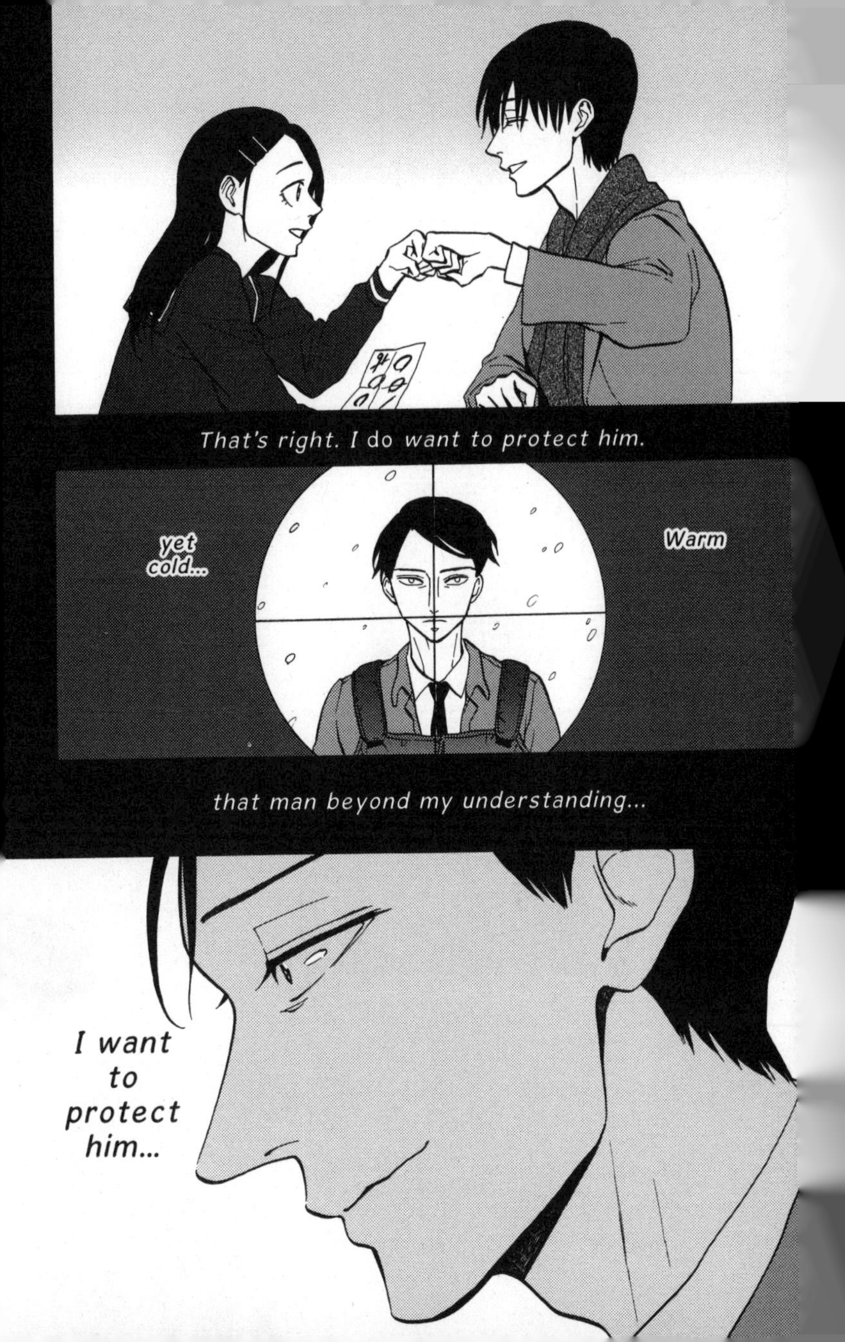
That's right. I do want to protect him.
Warm
yet cold...
that man beyond my understanding...
I want to protect him...

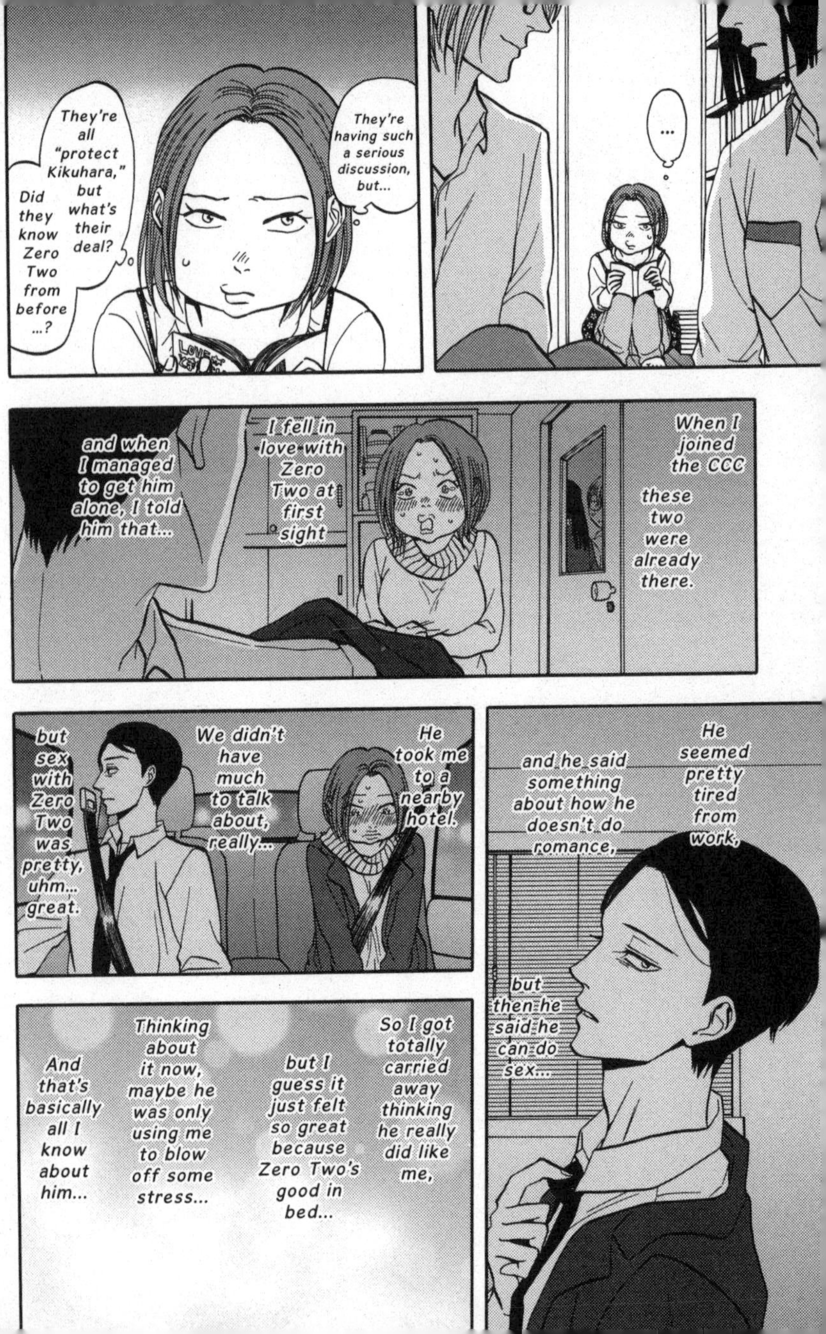
...
They're having such a serious discussion, but...
They're all "protect Kikuhara," but what's their deal? Did they know Zero Two from before ...?
When I joined the CCC
these two were already there.
I fell in love with Zero Two at first sight
and when I managed to get him alone, I told him that...
He seemed pretty tired from work,
and he said something about how he doesn't do romance,
but then he said he can do sex...
He took me to a nearby hotel.
We didn't have much to talk about, really...
but sex with Zero Two was pretty, uhm... great.
So I got totally carried away thinking he really did like me,
but I guess it just felt so great because Zero Two's good in bed...
Thinking about it now, maybe he was only using me to blow off some stress...
And that's basically all I know about him...

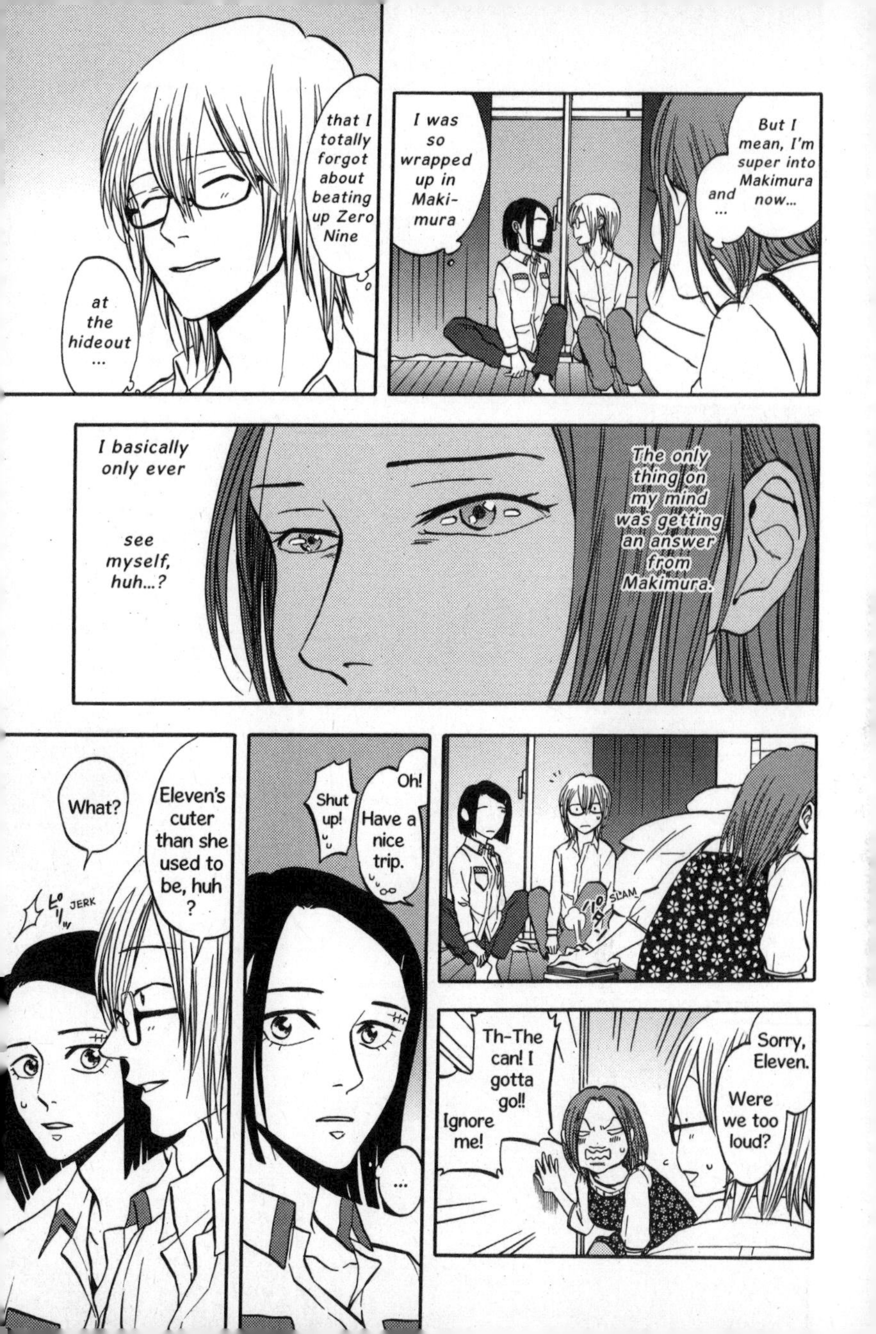
But I mean, I'm super into Makimura now...
and ...
I was so wrapped up in Makimura
that I totally forgot about beating up Zero Nine
at the hideout ...
The only thing on my mind was getting an answer from Makimura.
I basically only ever
see myself, huh...?
SLAM
Sorry, Eleven.
Were we too loud?
Th-The can! I gotta go!!
Ignore me!
Oh!
Have a nice trip.
Shut up!
...
Eleven's cuter than she used to be, huh?
What?
JERK

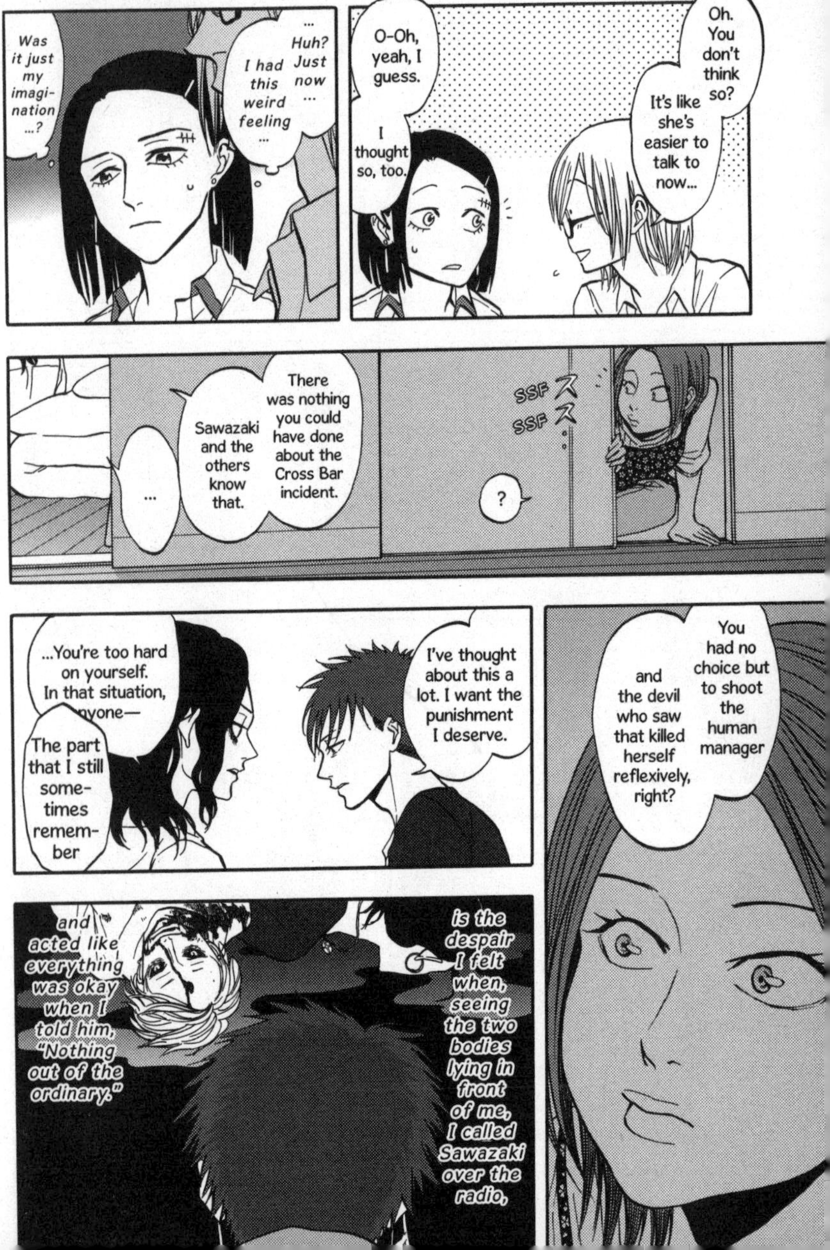
Oh. You don't think so?
It's like she's easier to talk to now...
O-Oh, yeah, I guess.
I thought so, too.
... Huh? Just now ...
I had this weird feeling ...
Was it just my imagination ...?
SSF ス
SSF ス
?
There was nothing you could have done about the Cross Bar incident.
Sawazaki and the others know that.
...
You had no choice but to shoot the human manager
and the devil who saw that killed herself reflexively, right?
I've thought about this a lot. I want the punishment I deserve.
...You're too hard on yourself. In that situation, nyone—
The part that I still sometimes remember
is the despair I felt when, seeing the two bodies lying in front of me, I called Sawazaki over the radio,
and acted like everything was okay when I told him, "Nothing out of the ordinary."

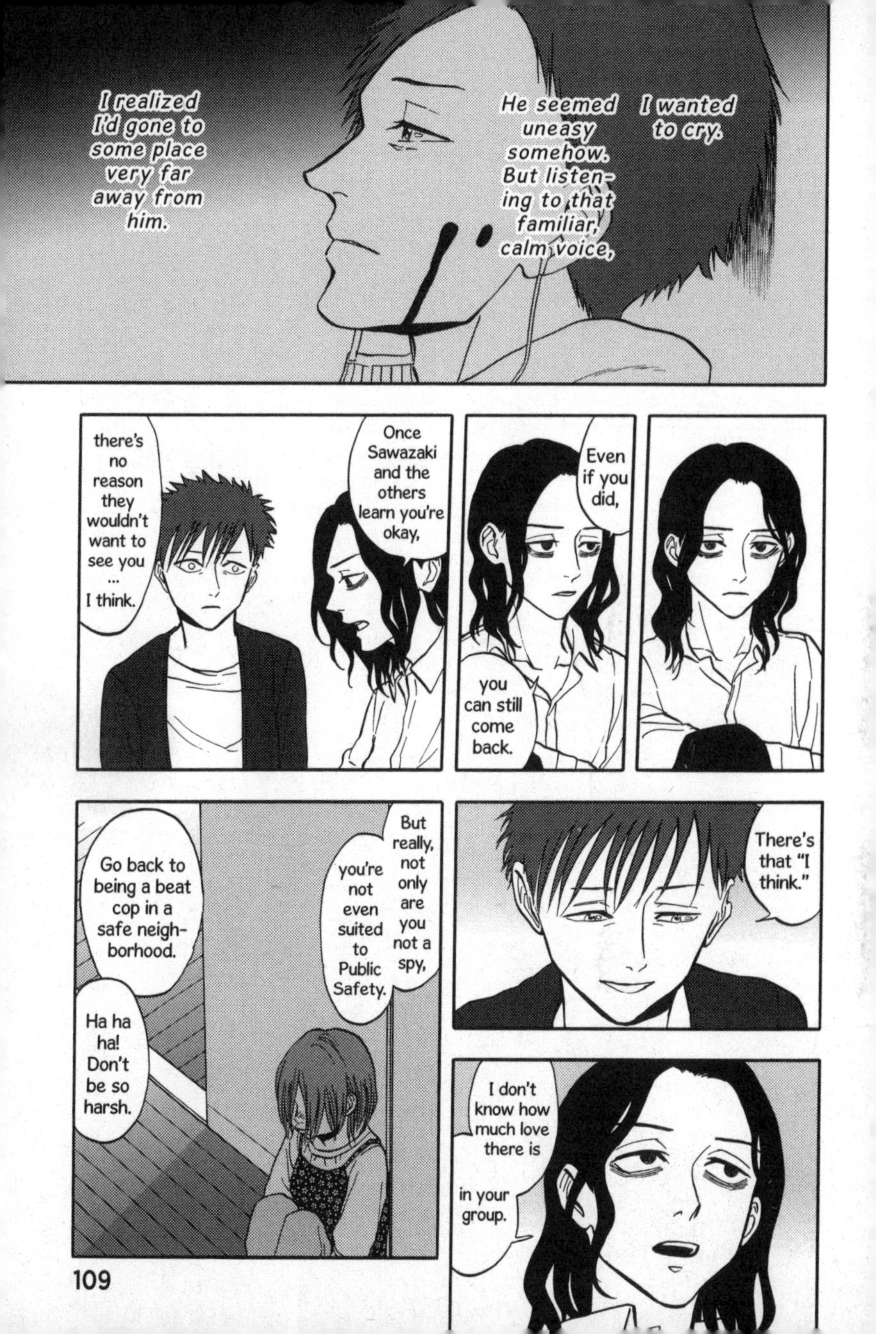
I wanted to cry.
He seemed uneasy somehow. But listening to that familiar, calm voice,
I realized I'd gone to some place very far away from him.
Even if you did,
you can still come back.
Once Sawazaki and the others learn you're okay,
there's no reason they wouldn't want to see you ... I think.
There's that "I think."
I don't know how much love there is
in your group.
But really, not only are you not a spy,
you're not even suited to Public Safety.
Go back to being a beat cop in a safe neighborhood.
Ha ha ha! Don't be so harsh.

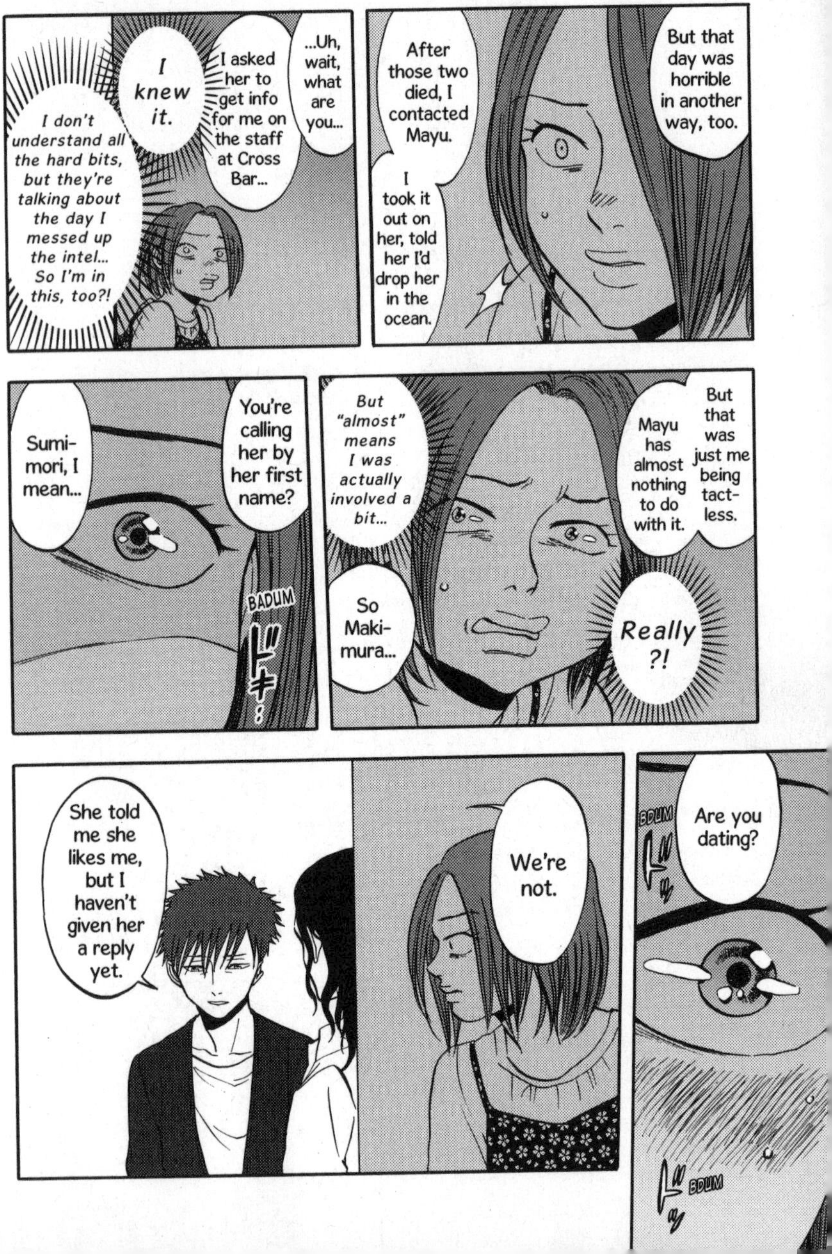
But that day was horrible in another way, too.
After those two died, I contacted Mayu.
I took it out on her, told her I'd drop her in the ocean.
...Uh, wait, what are you...
I asked her to get info for me on the staff at Cross Bar...
I knew it.
I don't understand all the hard bits, but they're talking about the day I messed up the intel... So I'm in this, too?!
But that was just me being tact-less.
Mayu has almost nothing to do with it.
But "almost" means I was actually involved a bit...
Really ?!
So Maki-mura...
You're calling her by her first name?
Sumi-mori, I mean...
BADUM
ドキ
Are you dating?
BDUM
BDUM
We're not.
She told me she likes me, but I haven't given her a reply yet.

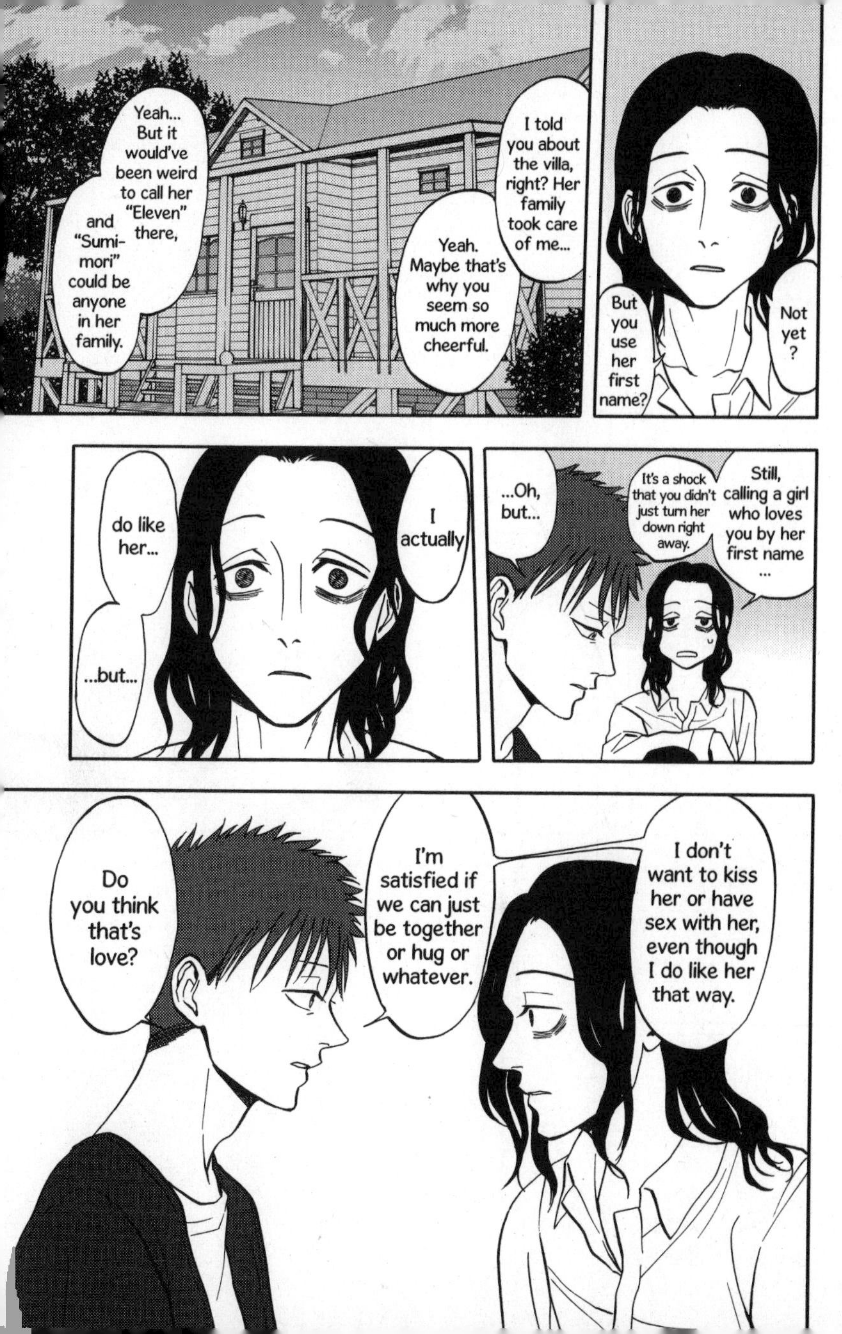
Not yet?
But you use her first name?
I told you about the villa, right? Her family took care of me...
Yeah. Maybe that's why you seem so much more cheerful.
Yeah... But it would've been weird to call her "Eleven" there,
and "Sumi-mori" could be anyone in her family.
Still, calling a girl who loves you by her first name ...
It's a shock that you didn't just turn her down right away.
...Oh, but...
I actually
do like her...
...but...
I don't want to kiss her or have sex with her, even though I do like her that way.
I'm satisfied if we can just be together or hug or whatever.
Do you think that's love?

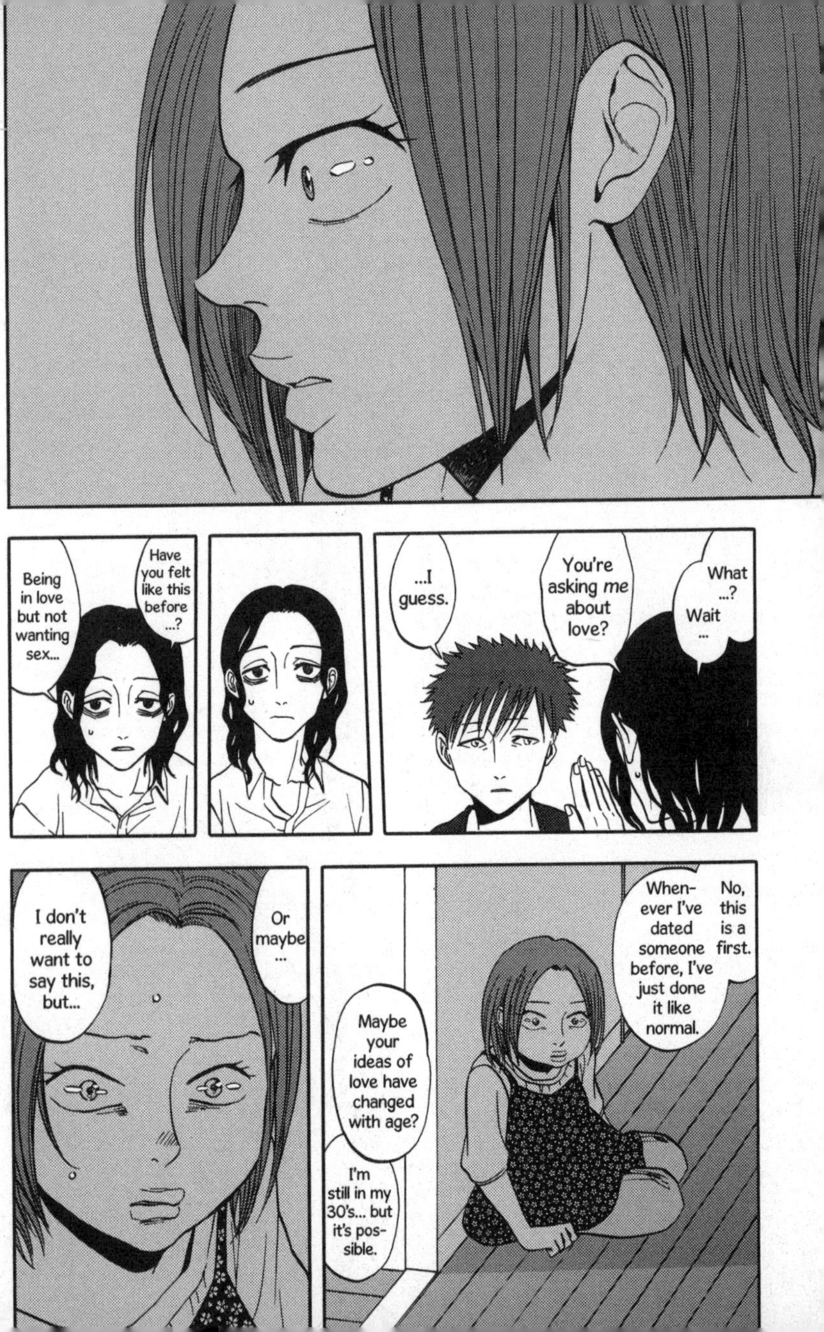
What ...? Wait ...
You're asking *me* about love?
...I guess.
Have you felt like this before ...?
Being in love but not wanting sex...
No, this is a first.
When-ever I've dated someone before, I've just done it like normal.
Maybe your ideas of love have changed with age?
I'm still in my 30's... but it's pos-sible.
Or maybe ...
I don't really want to say this, but...

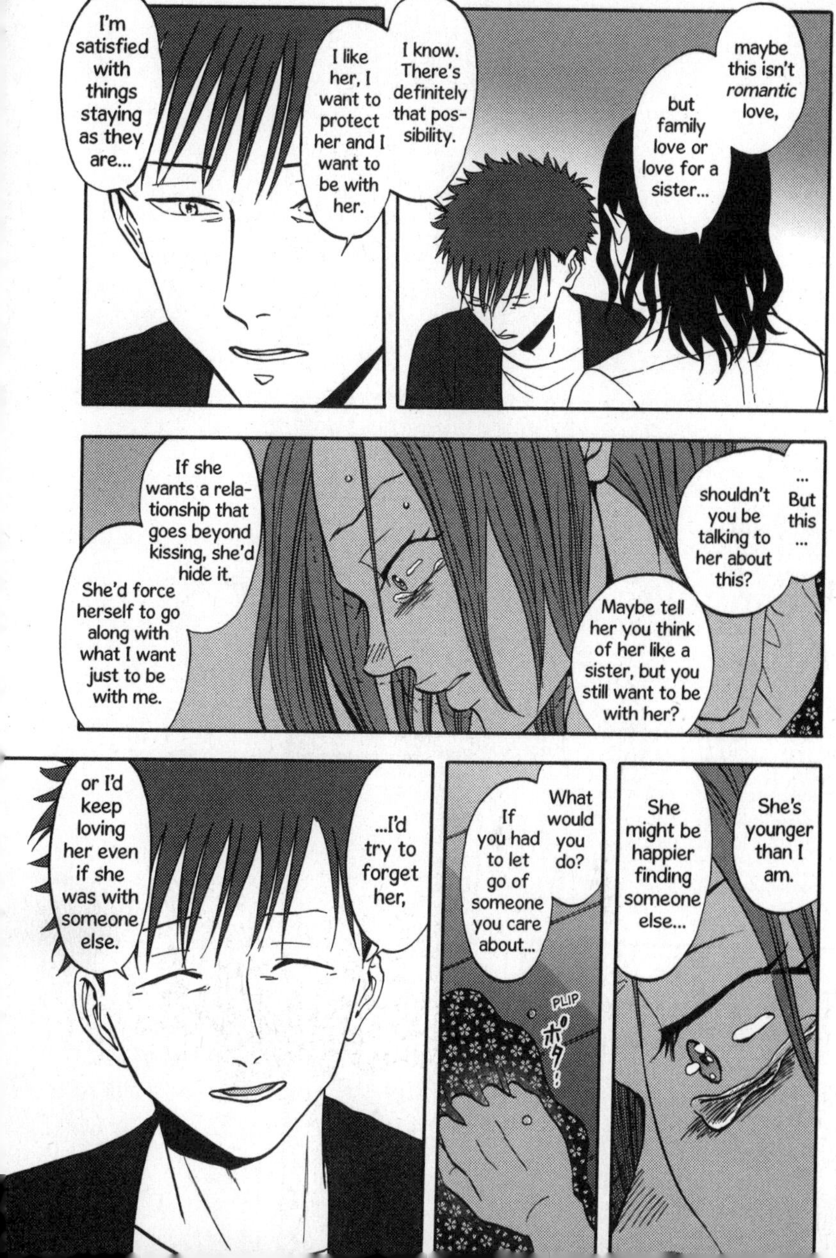
maybe this isn't *romantic* love,
but family love or love for a sister...
I know. There's definitely that possibility.
I like her, I want to protect her and I want to be with her.
I'm satisfied with things staying as they are...
... But this ...
shouldn't you be talking to her about this?
Maybe tell her you think of her like a sister, but you still want to be with her?
If she wants a relationship that goes beyond kissing, she'd hide it.
She'd force herself to go along with what I want just to be with me.
She's younger than I am.
She might be happier finding someone else...
What would you do?
If you had to let go of someone you care about...
PLIP
ポタ
...I'd try to forget her,
or I'd keep loving her even if she was with someone else.

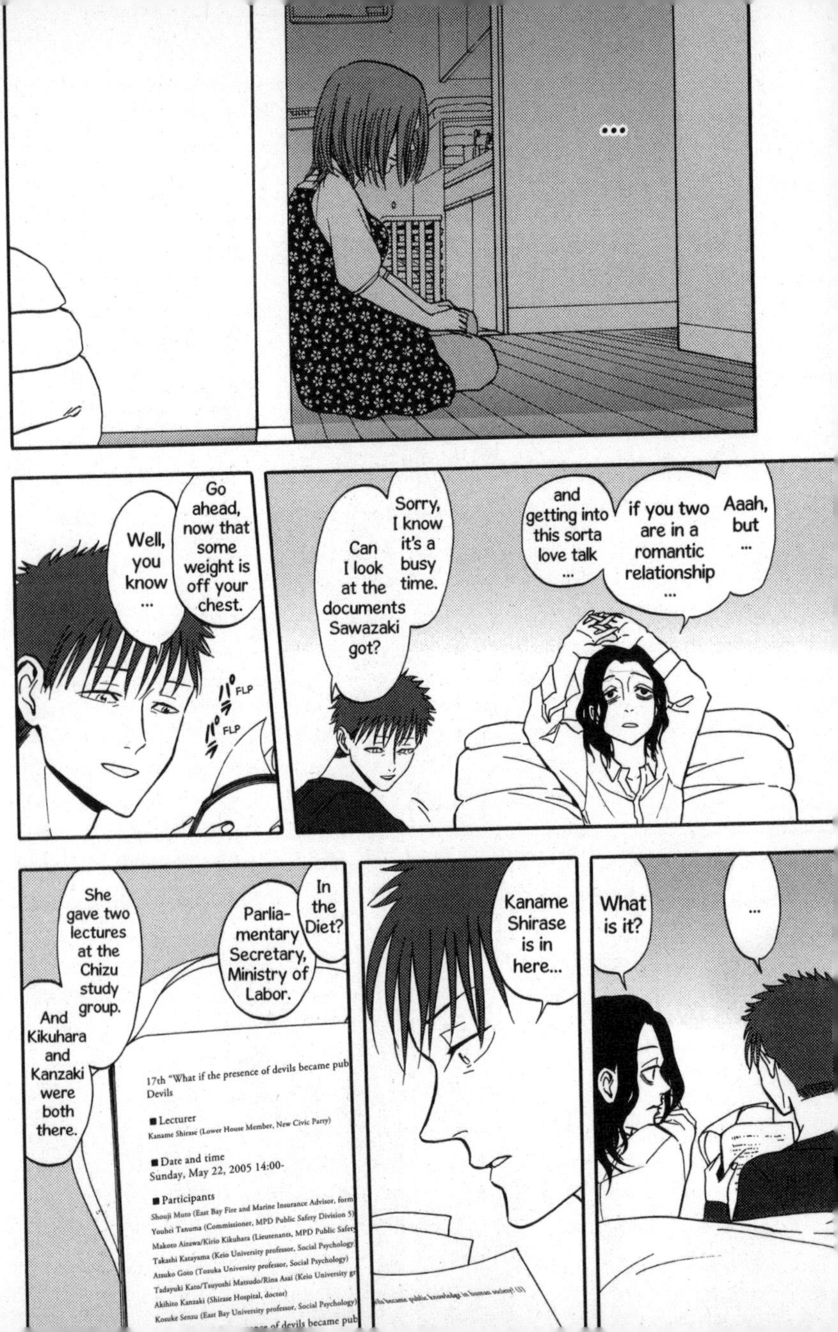
...
Aaah, but ...
if you two are in a romantic relationship ...
and getting into this sorta love talk ...
Sorry, I know it's a busy time.
Can I look at the documents Sawazaki got?
Go ahead, now that some weight is off your chest.
Well, you know ...
FLP
FLP
...
What is it?
Kaname Shirase is in here...
In the Diet?
Parliamentary Secretary, Ministry of Labor.
She gave two lectures at the Chizu study group.
And Kikuhara and Kanzaki were both there.
17th "What if the presence of devils became pub
Devils
■ Lecturer
Kaname Shirase (Lower House Member, New Civic Party)
■ Date and time
Sunday, May 22, 2005 14:00-
■ Participants
Shouji Muto (East Bay Fire and Marine Insurance Advisor, form
Youhei Tanuma (Commissioner, MPD Public Safety Division 5)
Makoto Aizawa/Kirio Kikuhara (Lieutenants, MPD Public Safety
Takashi Katayama (Keio University professor, Social Psychology)
Atsuko Goto (Tosuka University professor, Social Psychology)
Tadayuki Kato/Tsuyoshi Matsudo/Rina Asai (Keio University gr
Akihito Kanzaki (Shirase Hospital, doctor)
Kosuke Senzu (East Bay University professor, Social Psychology)

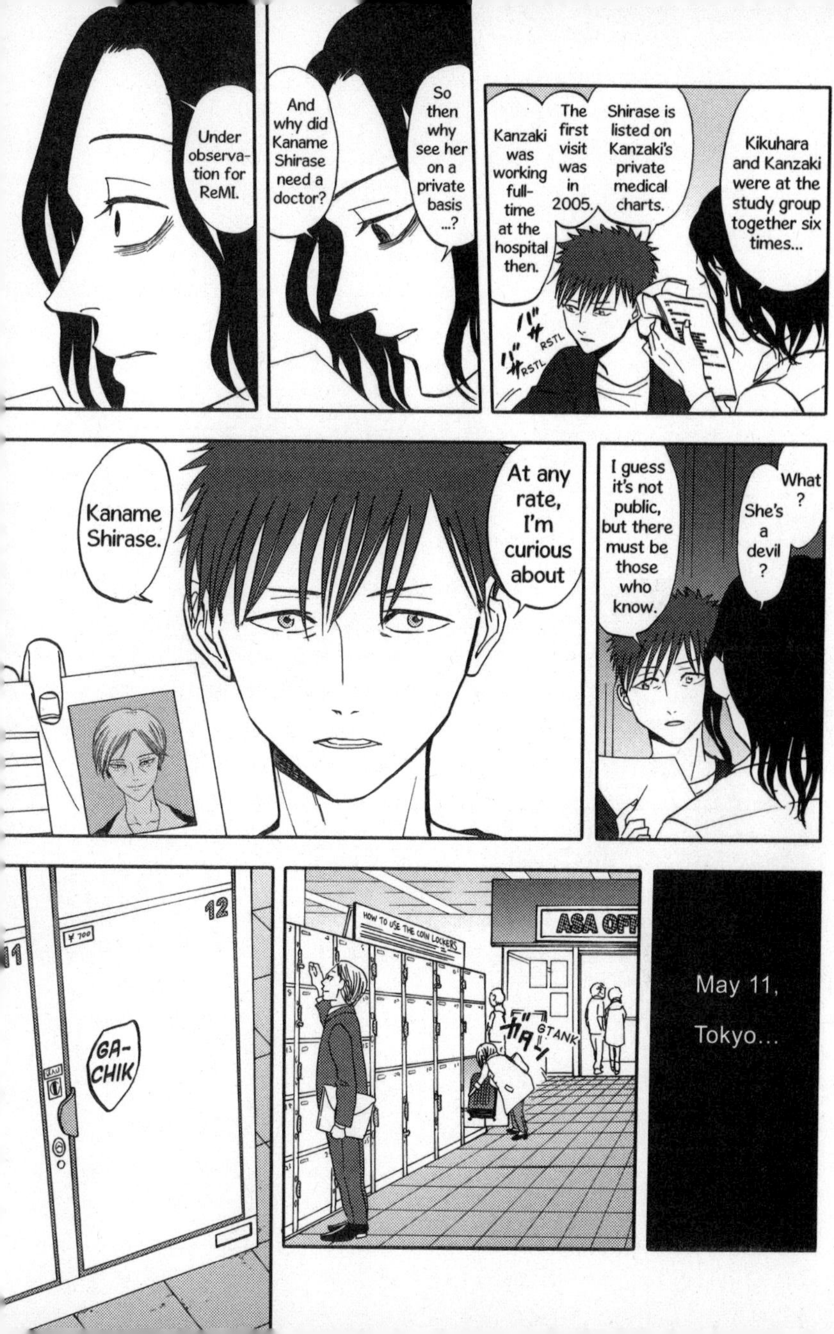
Kikuhara and Kanzaki were at the study group together six times...
Shirase is listed on Kanzaki's private medical charts.
The first visit was in 2005.
Kanzaki was working full-time at the hospital then.
RSTL
RSTL
So then why see her on a private basis ...?
And why did Kaname Shirase need a doctor?
Under observation for ReMI.
What? She's a devil?
I guess it's not public, but there must be those who know.
At any rate, I'm curious about
Kaname Shirase.
May 11, Tokyo...
HOW TO USE THE COIN LOCKERS
GTANK
12
¥700
11
GA-CHIK

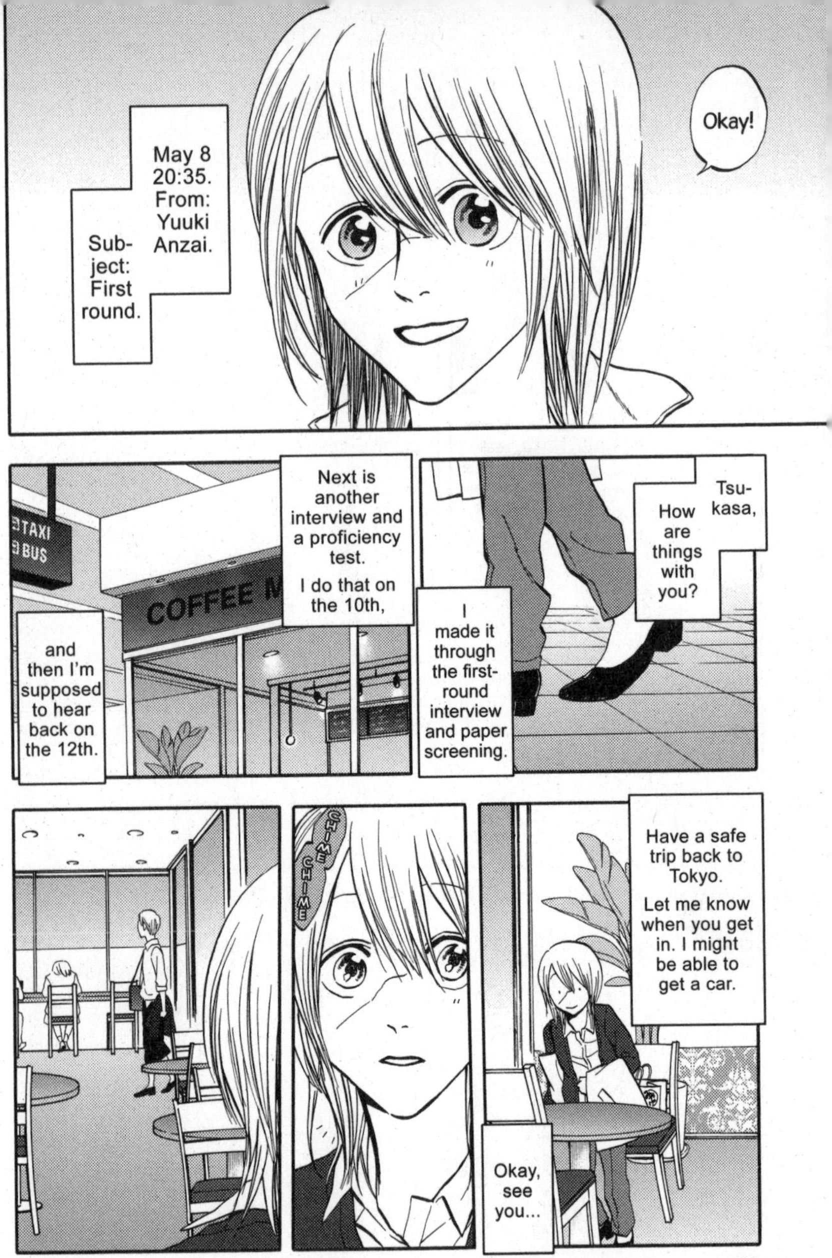

Okay!
May 8 20:35. From: Yuuki Anzai. Subject: First round.
Tsukasa, How are things with you?
I made it through the first-round interview and paper screening.
Next is another interview and a proficiency test. I do that on the 10th,
TAXI
BUS
COFFEE
and then I'm supposed to hear back on the 12th.
Have a safe trip back to Tokyo. Let me know when you get in. I might be able to get a car.
Okay, see you...
CHIME CHIME

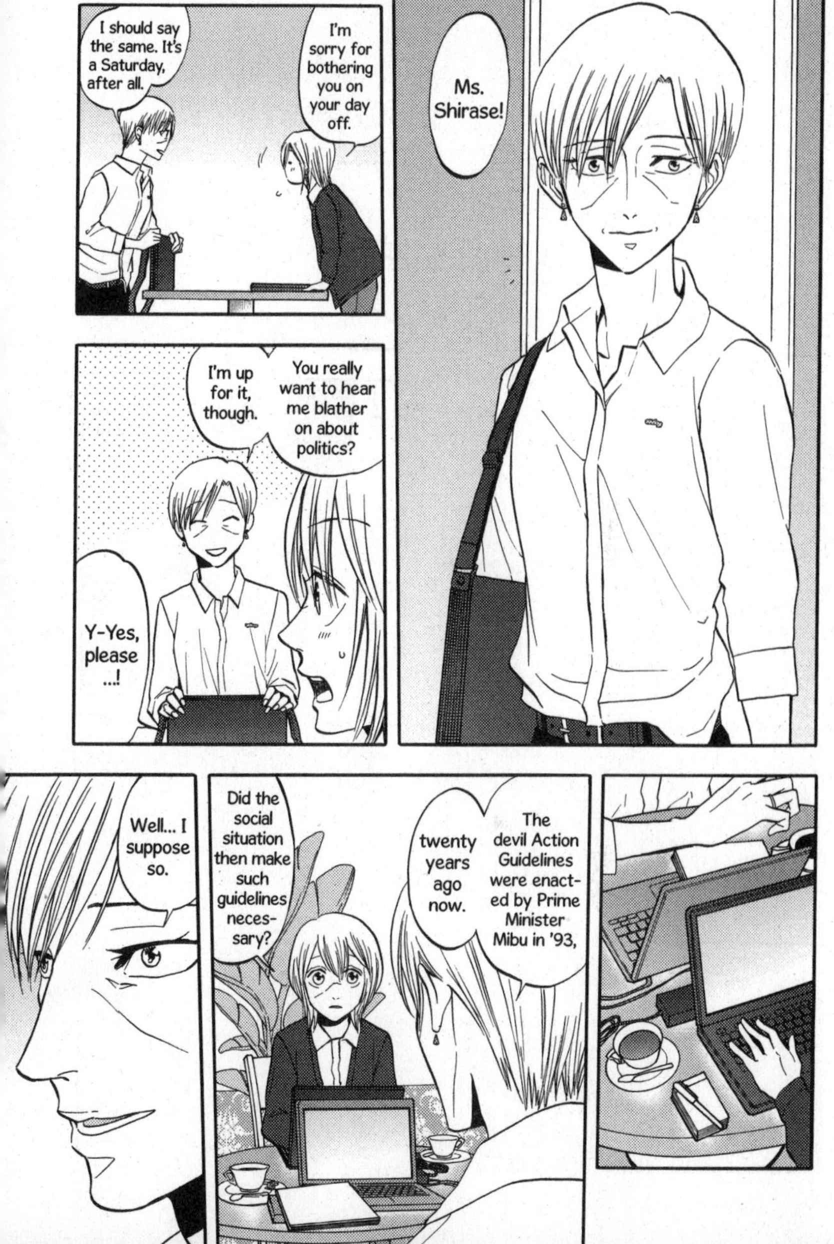
Ms. Shirase!
I'm sorry for bothering you on your day off.
I should say the same. It's a Saturday, after all.
You really want to hear me blather on about politics?
I'm up for it, though.
Y-Yes, please ...!
The devil Action Guidelines were enacted by Prime Minister Mibu in '93,
twenty years ago now.
Did the social situation then make such guidelines necessary?
Well... I suppose so.

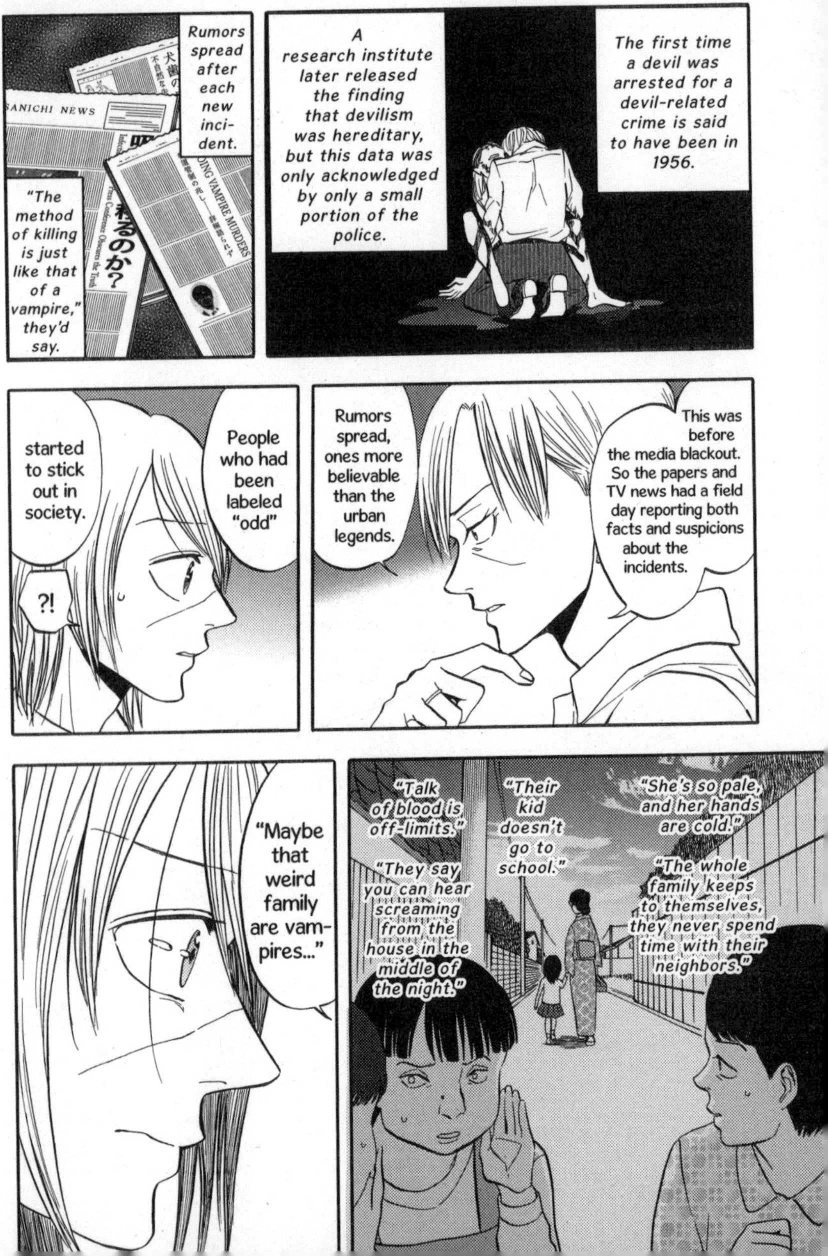
The first time a devil was arrested for a devil-related crime is said to have been in 1956.
A research institute later released the finding that devilism was hereditary, but this data was only acknowledged by only a small portion of the police.
Rumors spread after each new inci-dent.
SANICHI NEWS
VAMPIRE MURDERS
Press Conference Obscures the Truth
"The method of killing is just like that of a vampire," they'd say.
This was before the media blackout. So the papers and TV news had a field day reporting both facts and suspicions about the incidents.
Rumors spread, ones more believable than the urban legends.
People who had been labeled "odd"
started to stick out in society.
?!
"She's so pale, and her hands are cold."
"The whole family keeps to themselves, they never spend time with their neighbors."
"Their kid doesn't go to school."
"Talk of blood is off-limits."
"They say you can hear screaming from the house in the middle of the night."
"Maybe that weird family are vam-pires..."

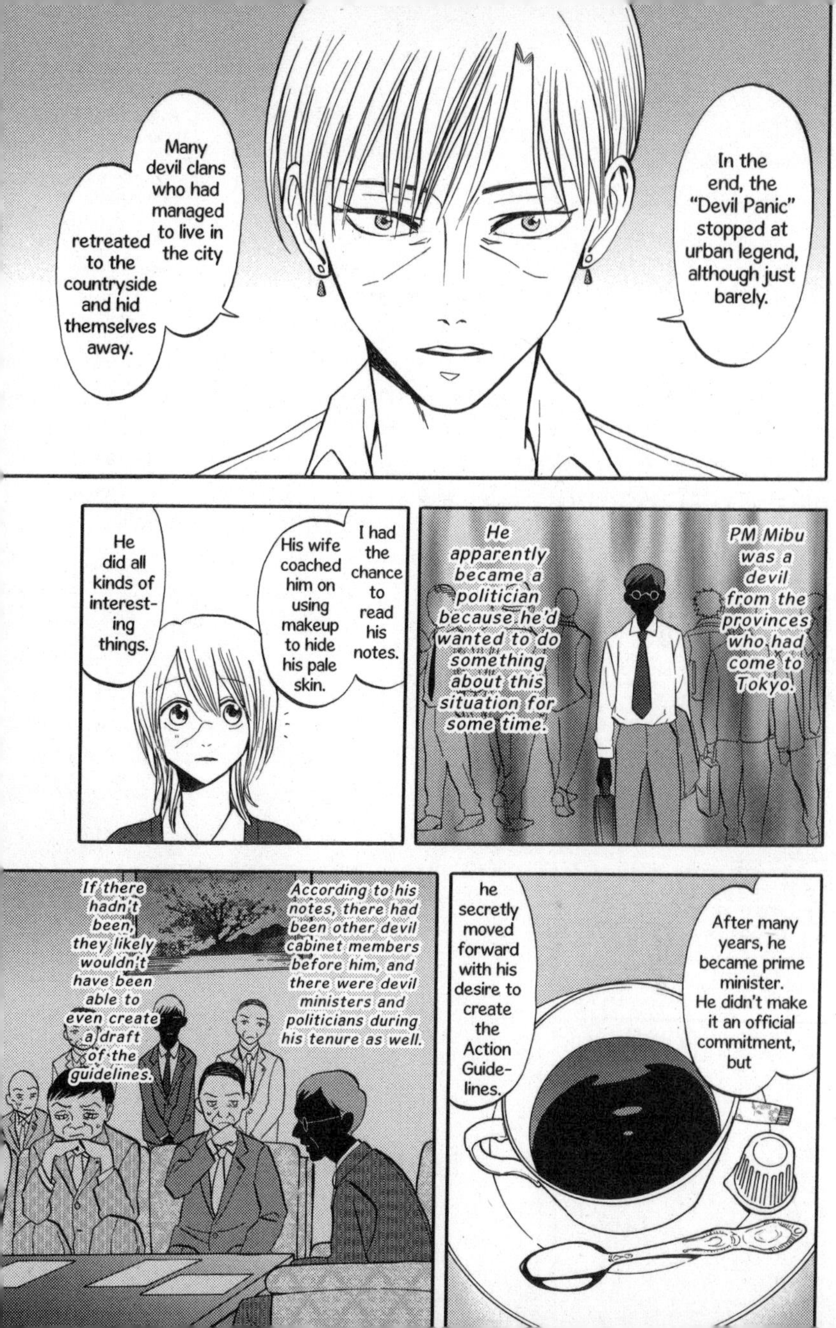
In the end, the "Devil Panic" stopped at urban legend, although just barely.
Many devil clans who had managed to live in the city retreated to the countryside and hid themselves away.
PM Mibu was a devil from the provinces who had come to Tokyo.
He apparently became a politician because he'd wanted to do something about this situation for some time.
I had the chance to read his notes.
His wife coached him on using makeup to hide his pale skin.
He did all kinds of interest-ing things.
After many years, he became prime minister. He didn't make it an official commitment, but
he secretly moved forward with his desire to create the Action Guide-lines.
According to his notes, there had been other devil cabinet members before him, and there were devil ministers and politicians during his tenure as well.
If there hadn't been, they likely wouldn't have been able to even create a draft of the guidelines.

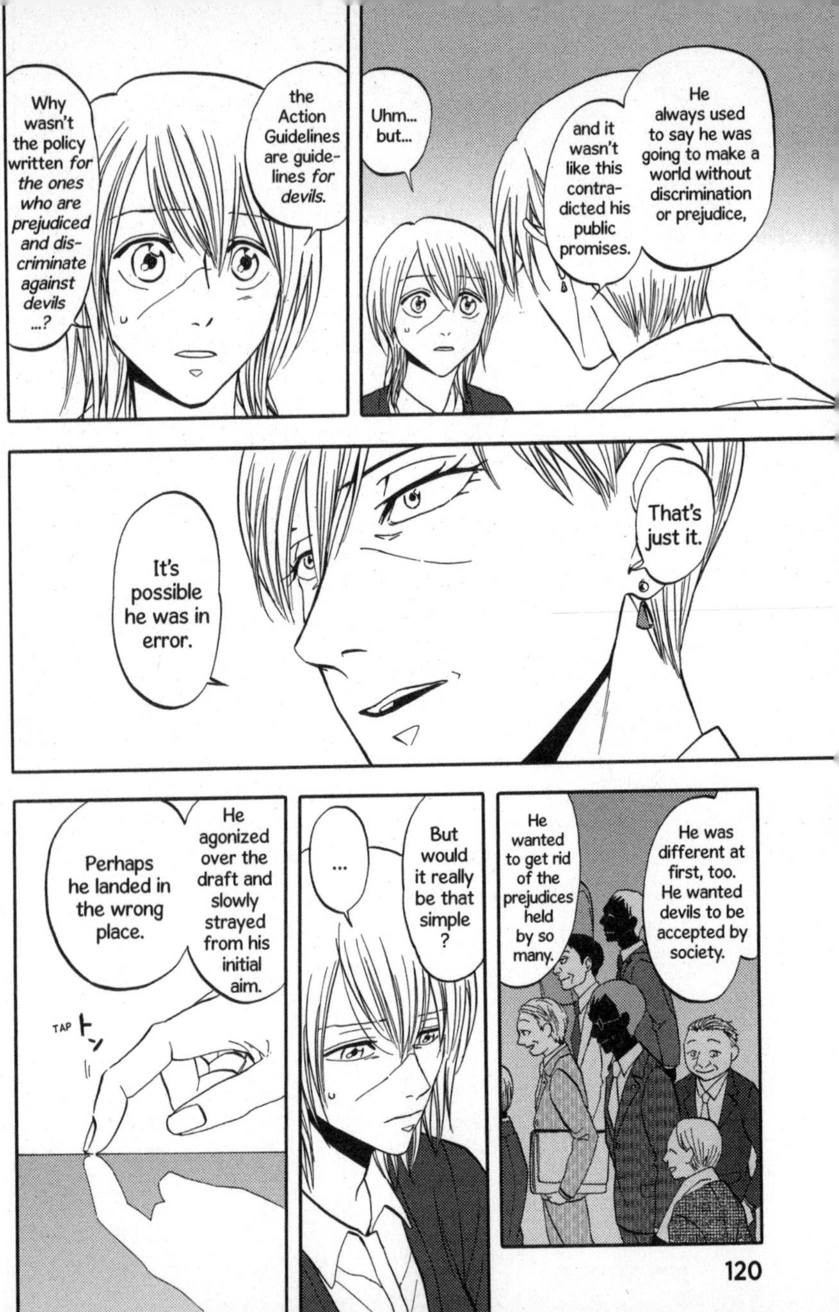
He always used to say he was going to make a world without discrimination or prejudice,
and it wasn't like this contradicted his public promises.
Uhm... but...
the Action Guidelines are guide-lines *for* devils.
Why wasn't the policy written *for the ones who are prejudiced and dis-criminate against devils ...?*
That's just it.
It's possible he was in error.
He was different at first, too. He wanted devils to be accepted by society.
He wanted to get rid of the prejudices held by so many.
But would it really be that simple?
...
He agonized over the draft and slowly strayed from his initial aim.
Perhaps he landed in the wrong place.
TAP
トン

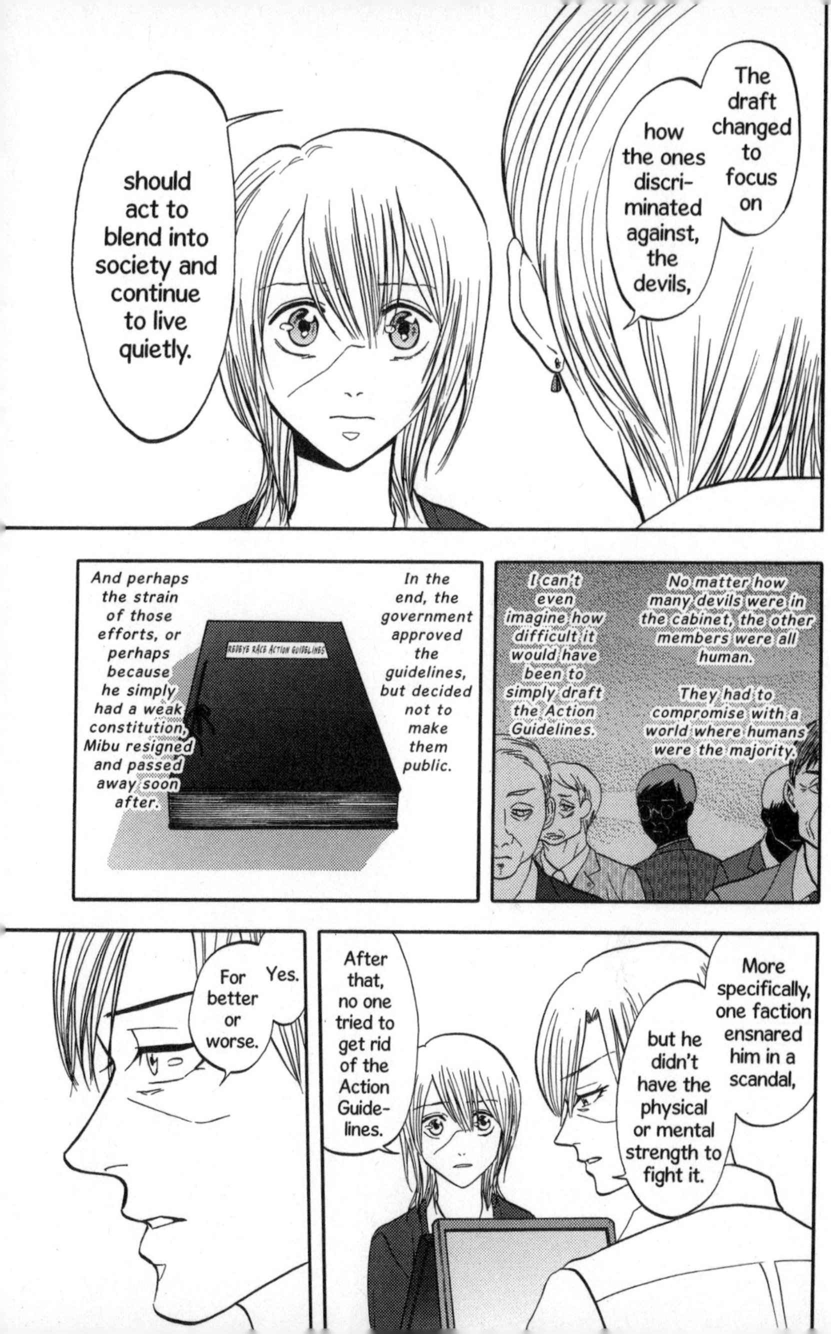

The draft changed to focus on how the ones discriminated against, the devils,
should act to blend into society and continue to live quietly.
No matter how many devils were in the cabinet, the other members were all human.
They had to compromise with a world where humans were the majority.
I can't even imagine how difficult it would have been to simply draft the Action Guidelines.
In the end, the government approved the guidelines, but decided not to make them public.
REDEYE RACE ACTION GUIDELINES
And perhaps the strain of those efforts, or perhaps because he simply had a weak constitution, Mibu resigned and passed away soon after.
More specifically, one faction ensnared him in a scandal,
but he didn't have the physical or mental strength to fight it.
After that, no one tried to get rid of the Action Guide-lines.
Yes.
For better or worse.

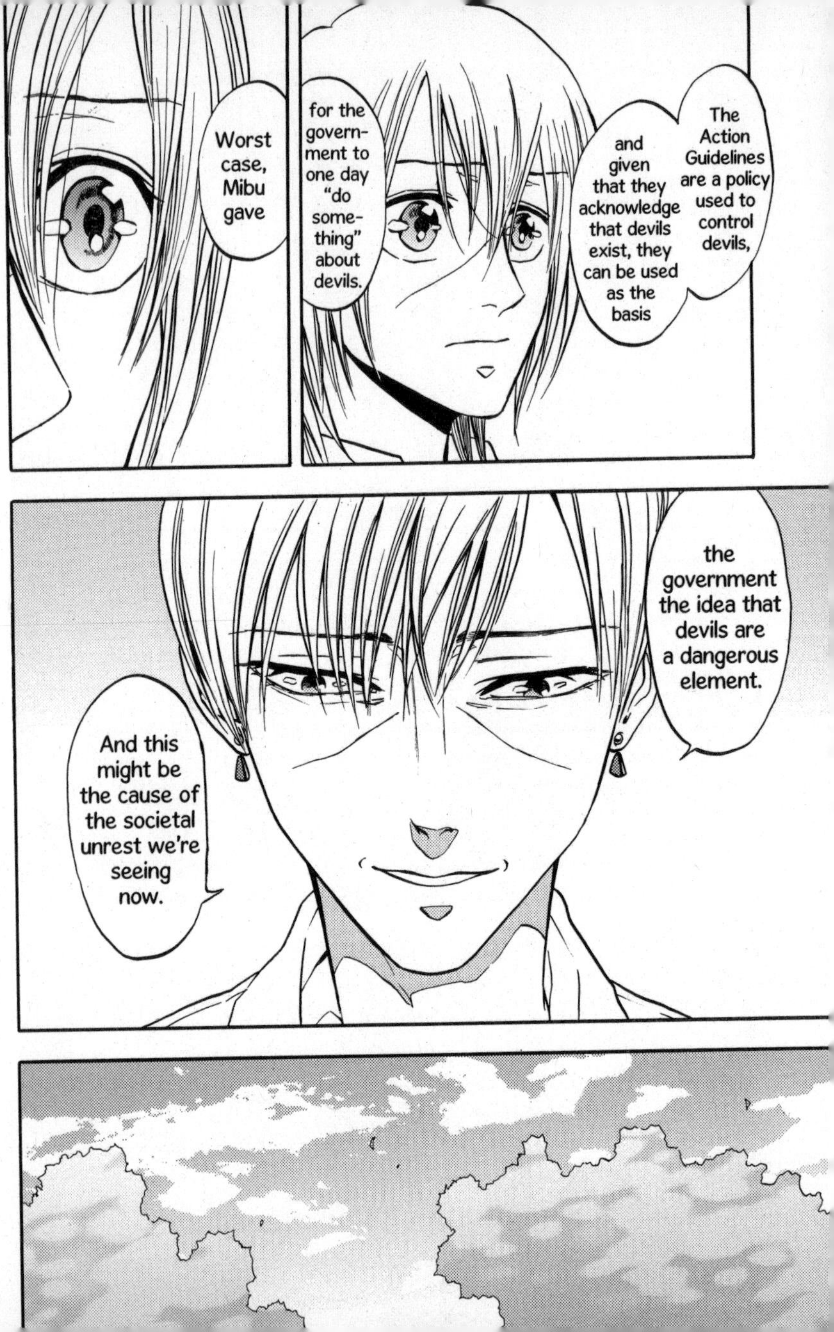
The Action Guidelines are a policy used to control devils,
and given that they acknowledge that devils exist, they can be used as the basis
for the government to one day "do something" about devils.
Worst case, Mibu gave
the government the idea that devils are a dangerous element.
And this might be the cause of the societal unrest we're seeing now.

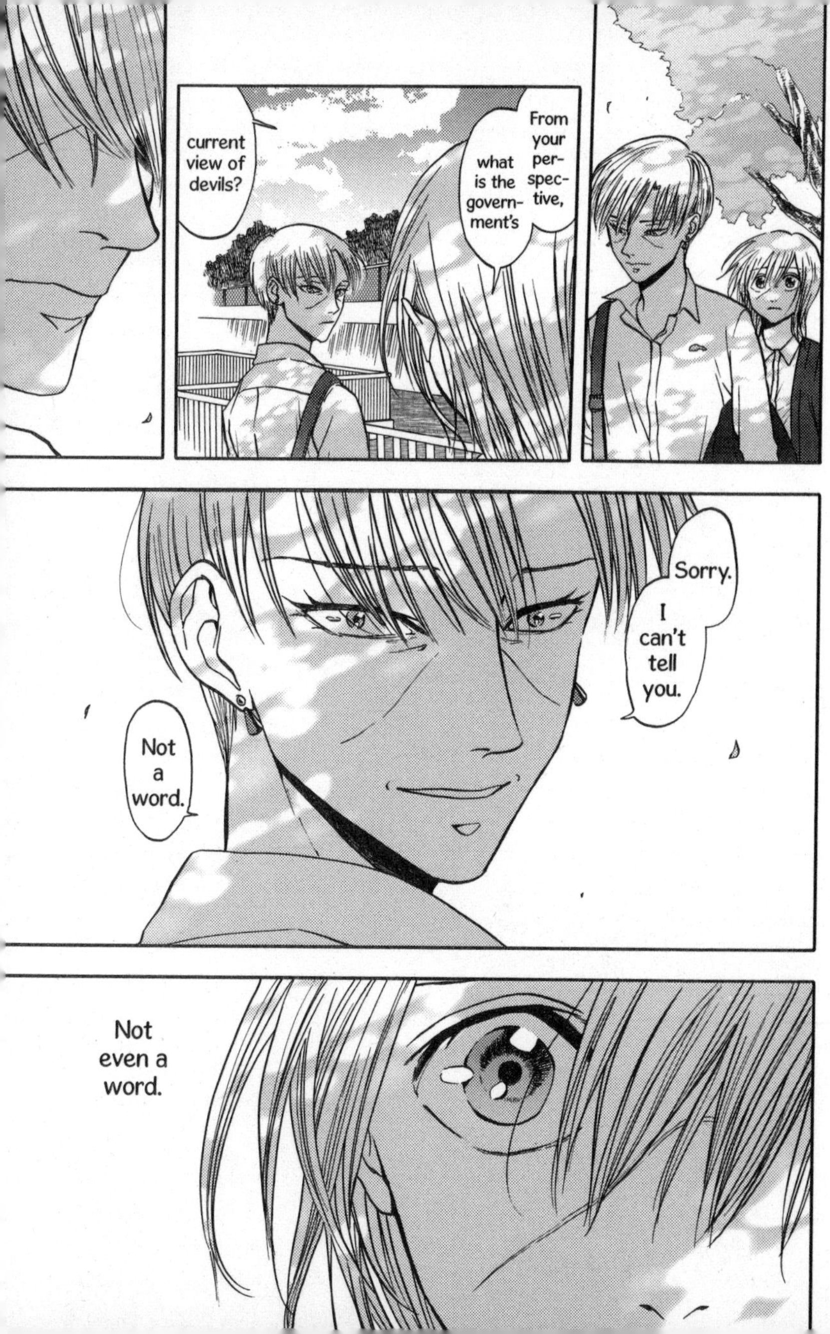
From your perspective, what is the government's
current view of devils?
Sorry.
I can't tell you.
Not a word.
Not even a word.

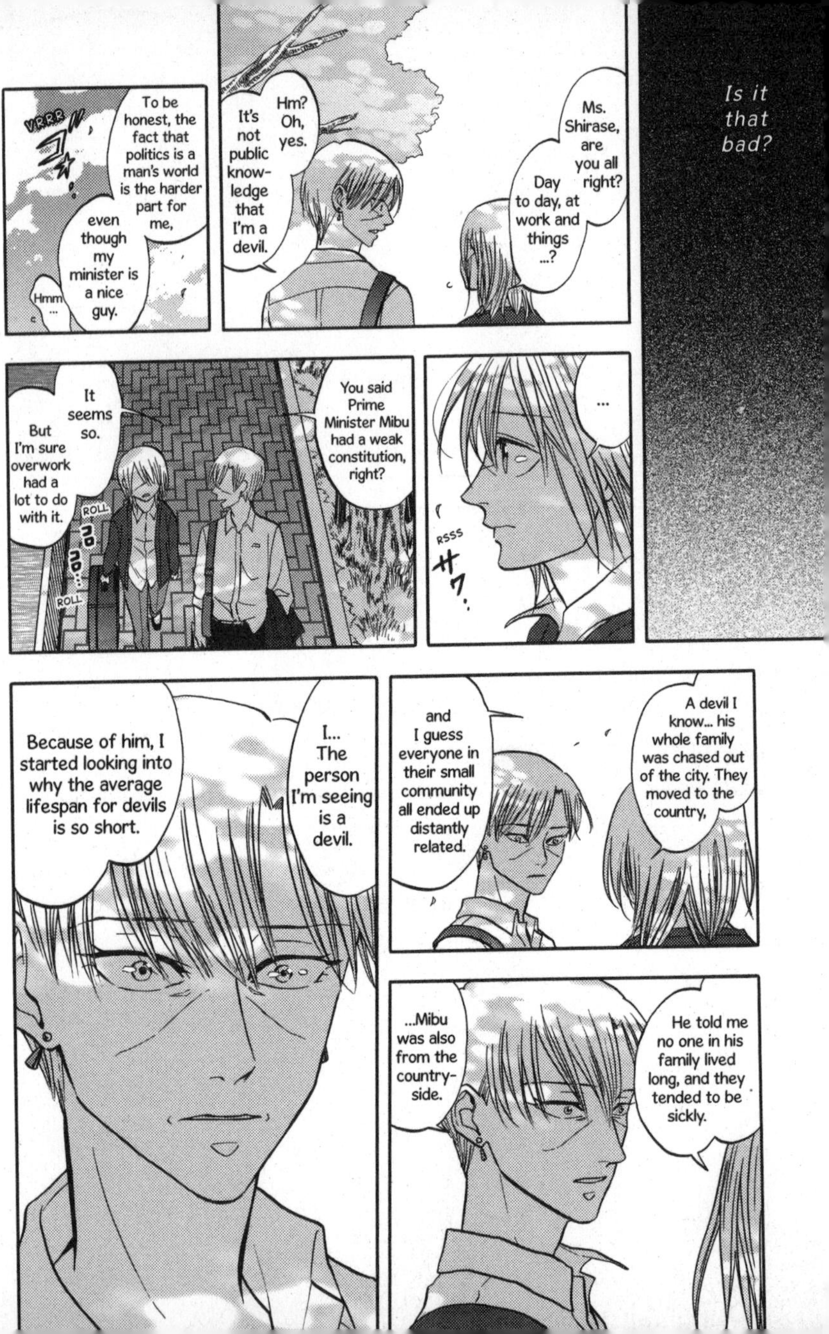
Is it that bad?
Ms. Shirase, are you all right?
Day to day, at work and things ...?
Hm? Oh, yes.
It's not public knowledge that I'm a devil.
To be honest, the fact that politics is a man's world is the harder part for me,
VRRR
even though my minister is a nice guy.
Hmm ...
...
RSSS
You said Prime Minister Mibu had a weak constitution, right?
It seems so.
But I'm sure overwork had a lot to do with it.
ROLL
ROLL
A devil I know... his whole family was chased out of the city. They moved to the country,
and I guess everyone in their small community all ended up distantly related.
He told me no one in his family lived long, and they tended to be sickly.
...Mibu was also from the country-side.
I... The person I'm seeing is a devil.
Because of him, I started looking into why the average lifespan for devils is so short.

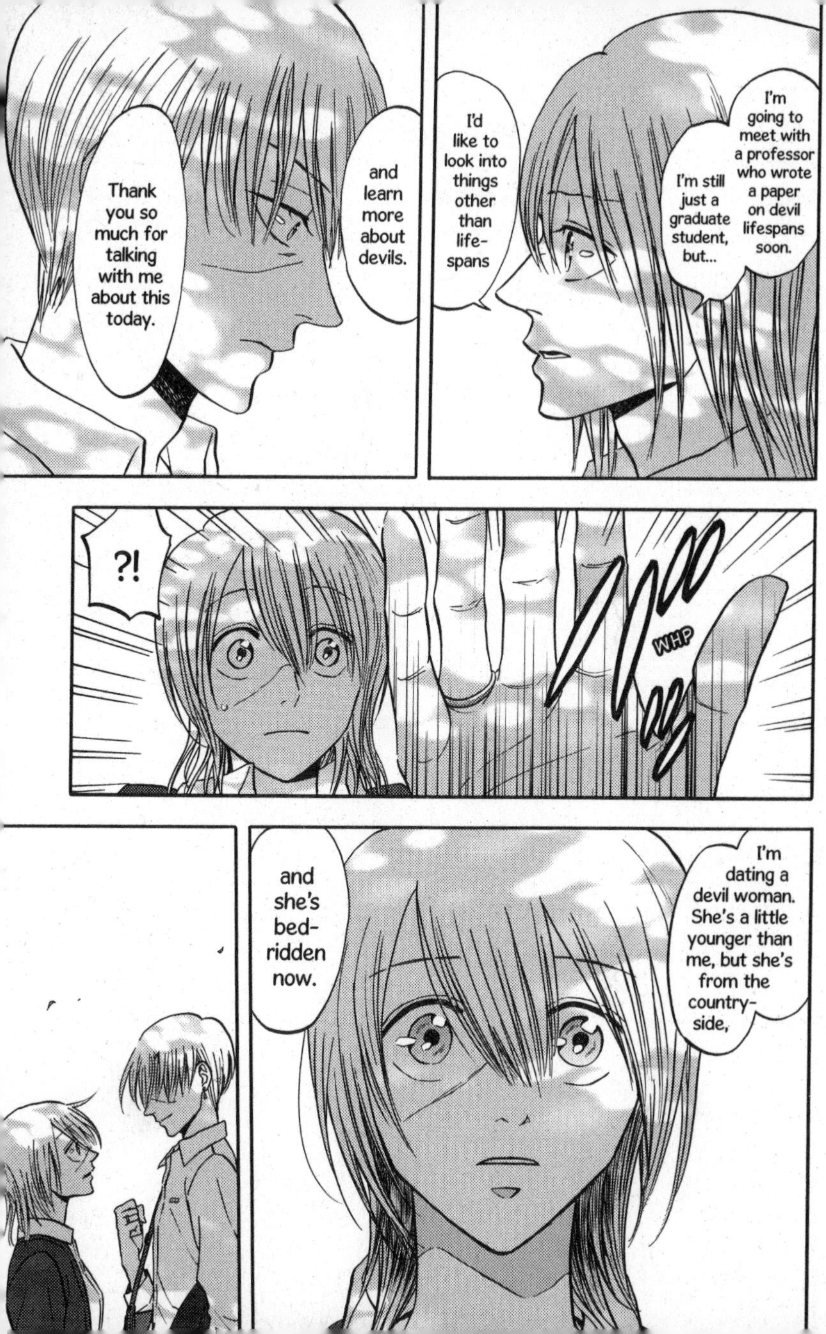
I'm going to meet with a professor who wrote a paper on devil lifespans soon.
I'm still just a graduate student, but...
I'd like to look into things other than life-spans
and learn more about devils.
Thank you so much for talking with me about this today.
?!
WHP
I'm dating a devil woman. She's a little younger than me, but she's from the country-side,
and she's bed-ridden now.

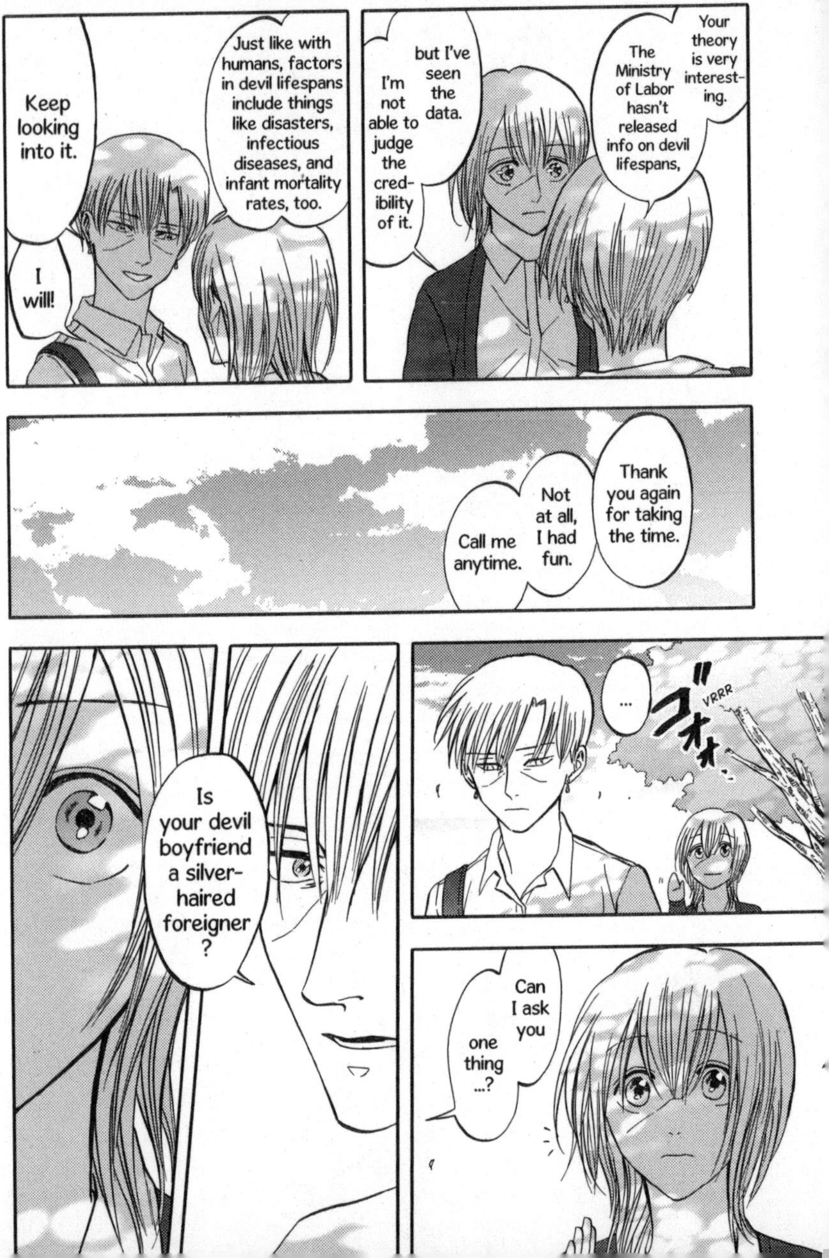
Your theory is very interest-ing.
The Ministry of Labor hasn't released info on devil lifespans,
but I've seen the data.
I'm not able to judge the cred-ibility of it.
Just like with humans, factors in devil lifespans include things like disasters, infectious diseases, and infant mortality rates, too.
Keep looking into it.
I will!
Thank you again for taking the time.
Not at all, I had fun.
Call me anytime.
...
ゴォォ
VRRR
Can I ask you one thing ...?
Is your devil boyfriend a silver-haired foreigner ?

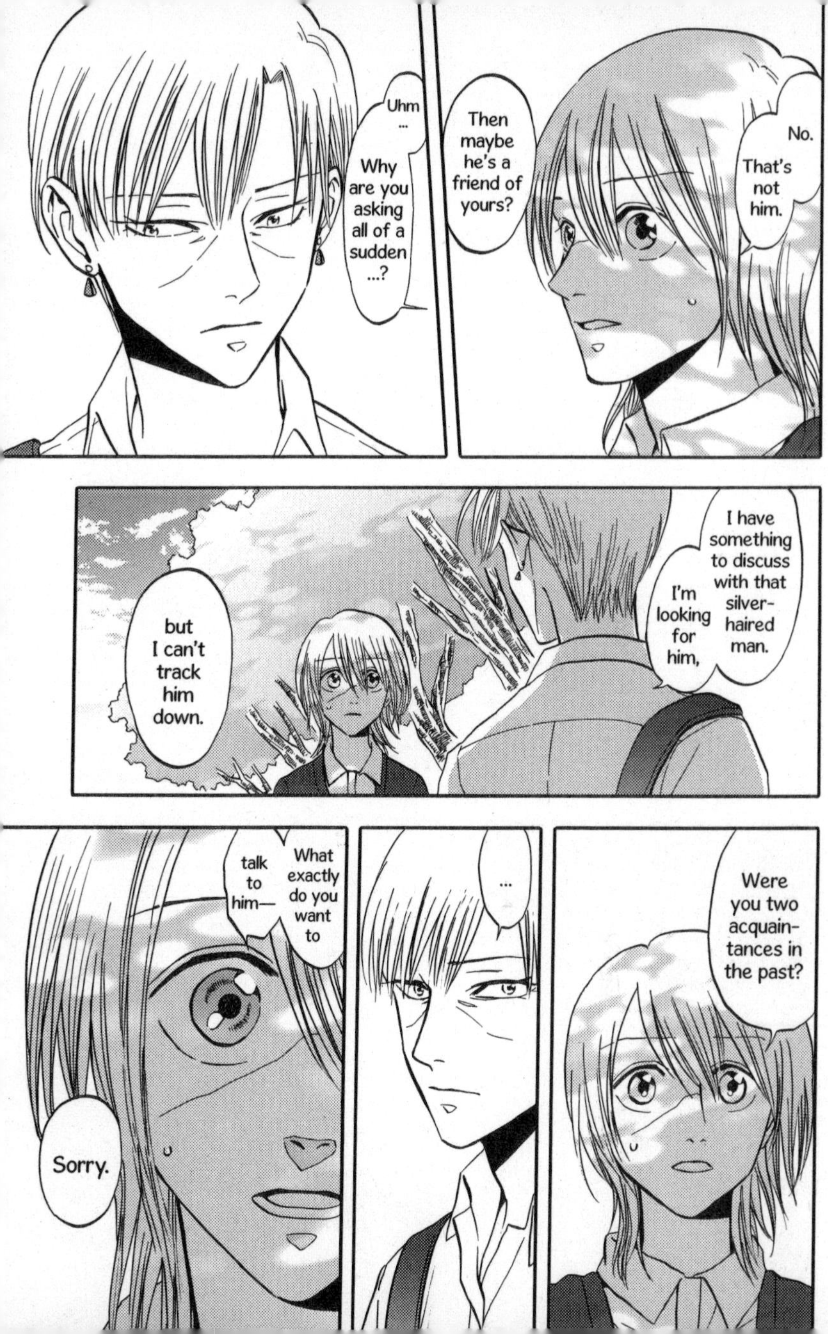
No.
That's not him.
Then maybe he's a friend of yours?
Uhm ...
Why are you asking all of a sudden ...?
I have something to discuss with that silver-haired man.
I'm looking for him,
but I can't track him down.
Were you two acquaintances in the past?
...
What exactly do you want to
talk to him—
Sorry.

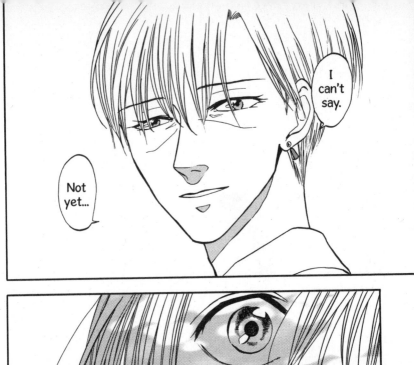

I can't say.

Not yet...

VRR

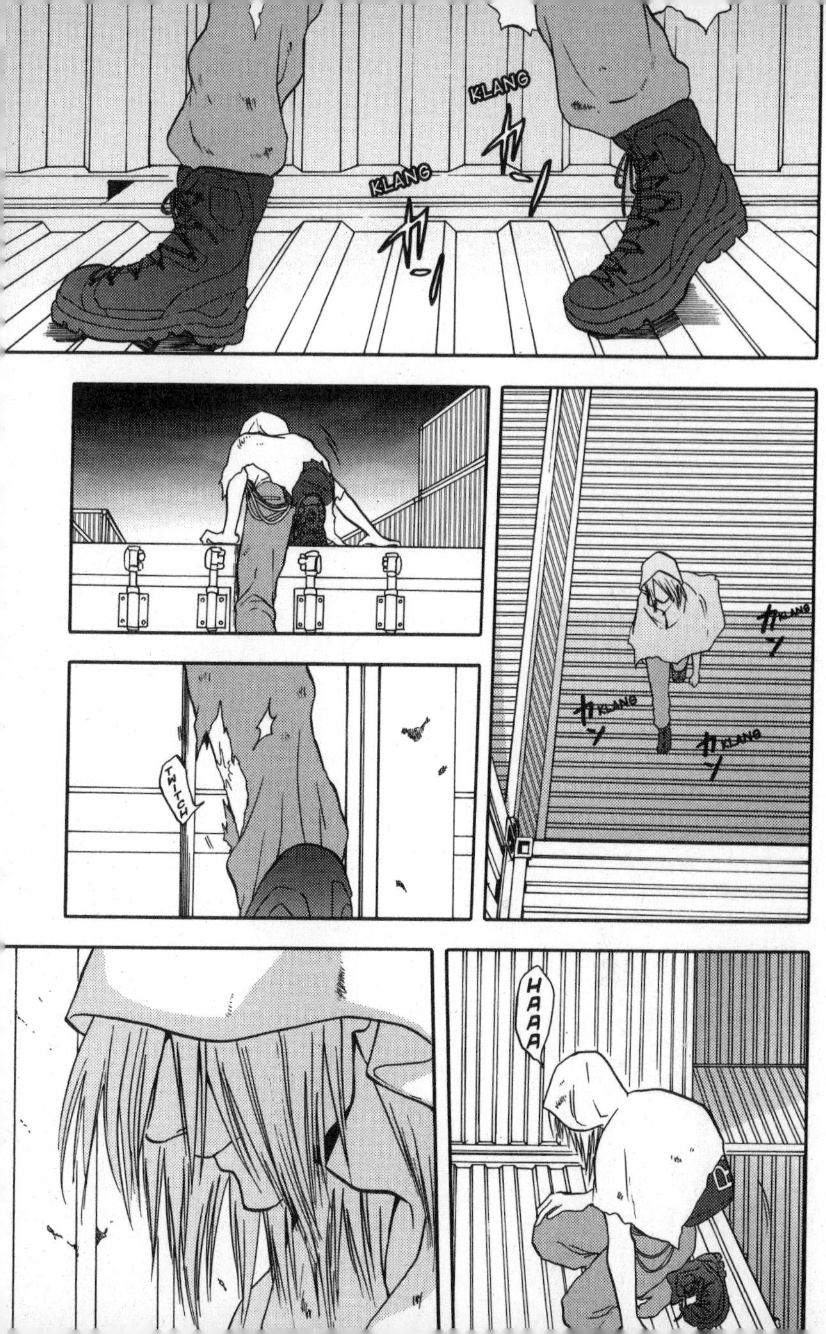
KLANG
KLANG
KLANG
KLANG
KLANG
TWITCH
HAAAA

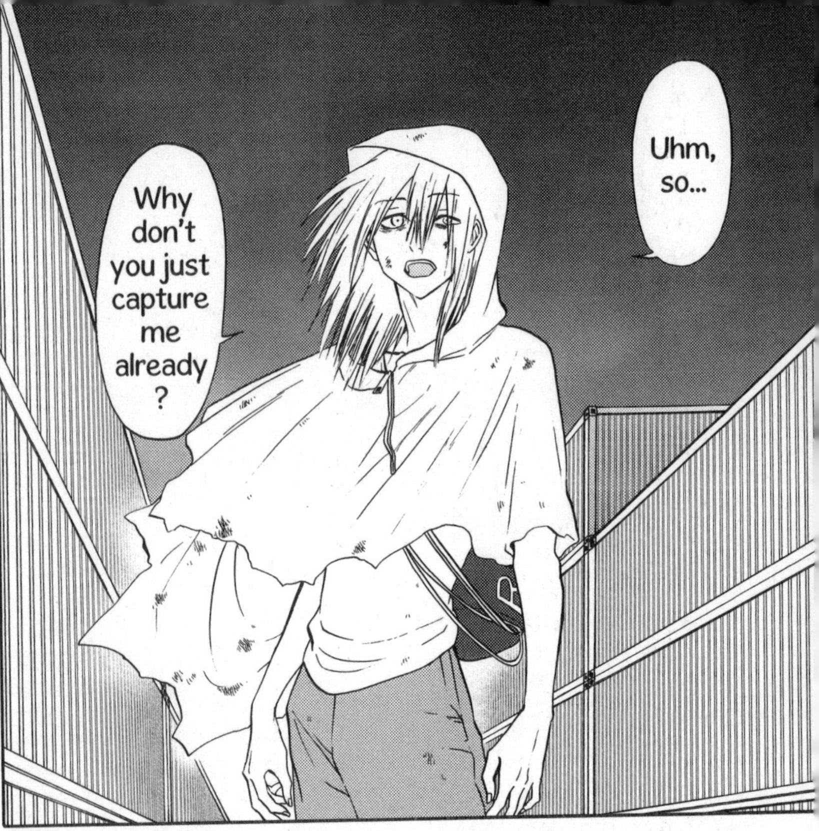
Uhm, so...
Why don't you just capture me already?

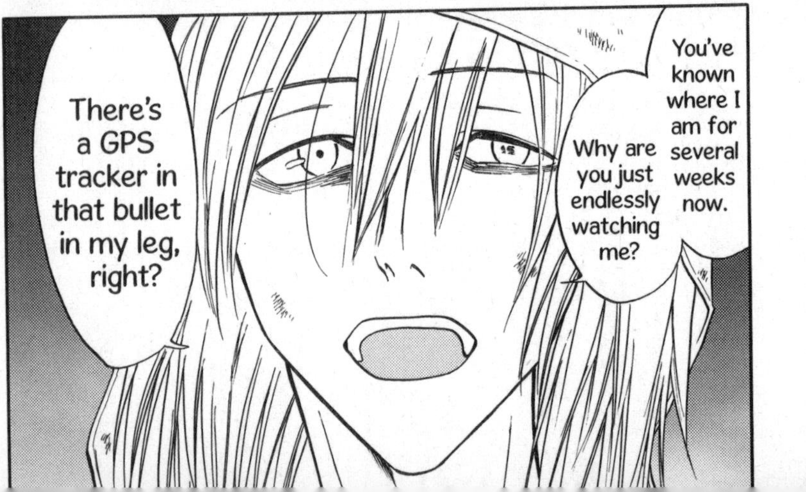
You've known where I am for several weeks now.
Why are you just endlessly watching me?
There's a GPS tracker in that bullet in my leg, right?

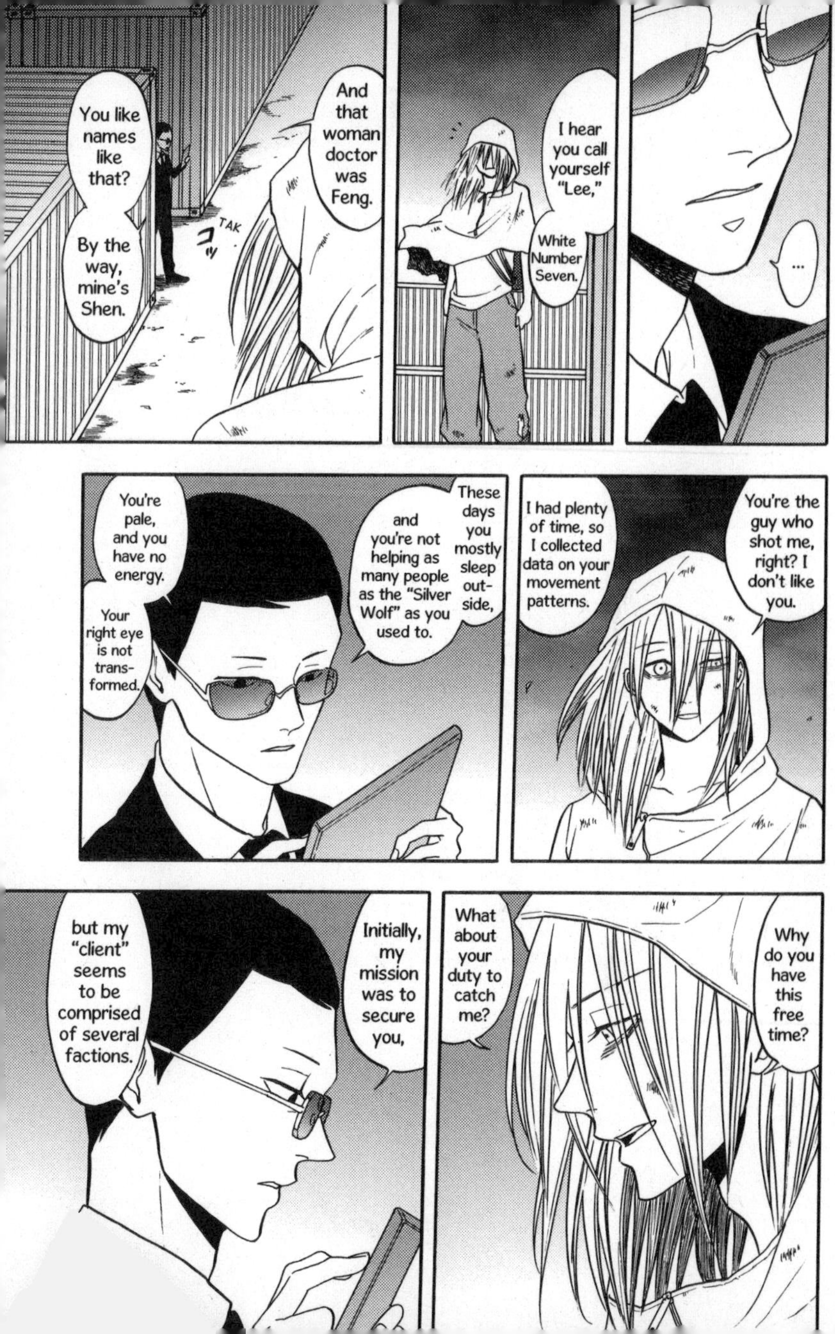
...
I hear you call yourself "Lee,"
White Number Seven.
And that woman doctor was Feng.
TAK
コツ
You like names like that?
By the way, mine's Shen.
You're the guy who shot me, right? I don't like you.
I had plenty of time, so I collected data on your movement patterns.
These days you mostly sleep out-side,
and you're not helping as many people as the "Silver Wolf" as you used to.
You're pale, and you have no energy.
Your right eye is not trans-formed.
Why do you have this free time?
What about your duty to catch me?
Initially, my mission was to secure you,
but my "client" seems to be comprised of several factions.

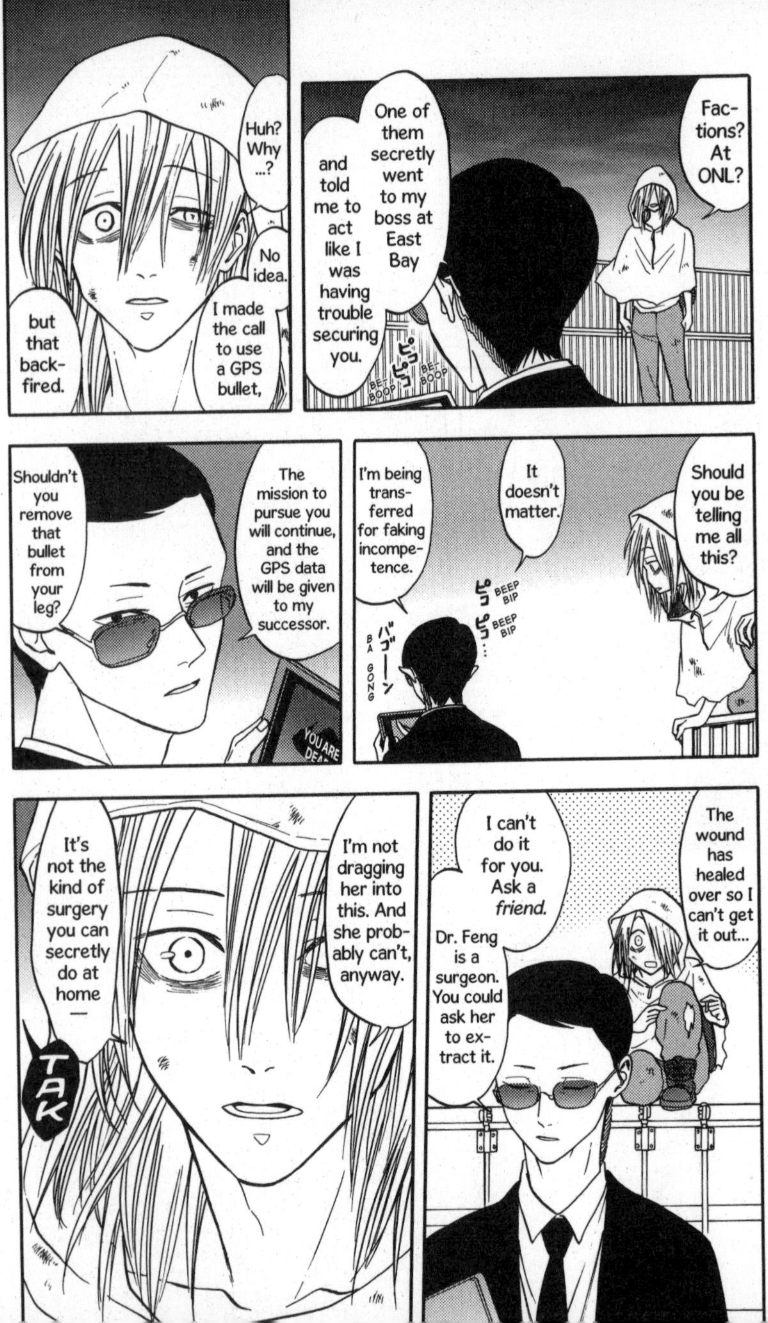
Fac-tions? At ONL?
One of them secretly went to my boss at East Bay
and told me to act like I was having trouble securing you.
BE-BOOP BE-BOOP
Huh? Why ...?
No idea.
I made the call to use a GPS bullet,
but that back-fired.
Should you be telling me all this?
It doesn't matter.
BEEP BIP BEEP BIP
I'm being trans-ferred for faking incompe-tence.
BA GONG
The mission to pursue you will continue, and the GPS data will be given to my successor.
Shouldn't you remove that bullet from your leg?
The wound has healed over so I can't get it out...
I can't do it for you. Ask a *friend.*
Dr. Feng is a surgeon. You could ask her to extract it.
I'm not dragging her into this. And she prob-ably can't, anyway.
It's not the kind of surgery you can secretly do at home—
TAK

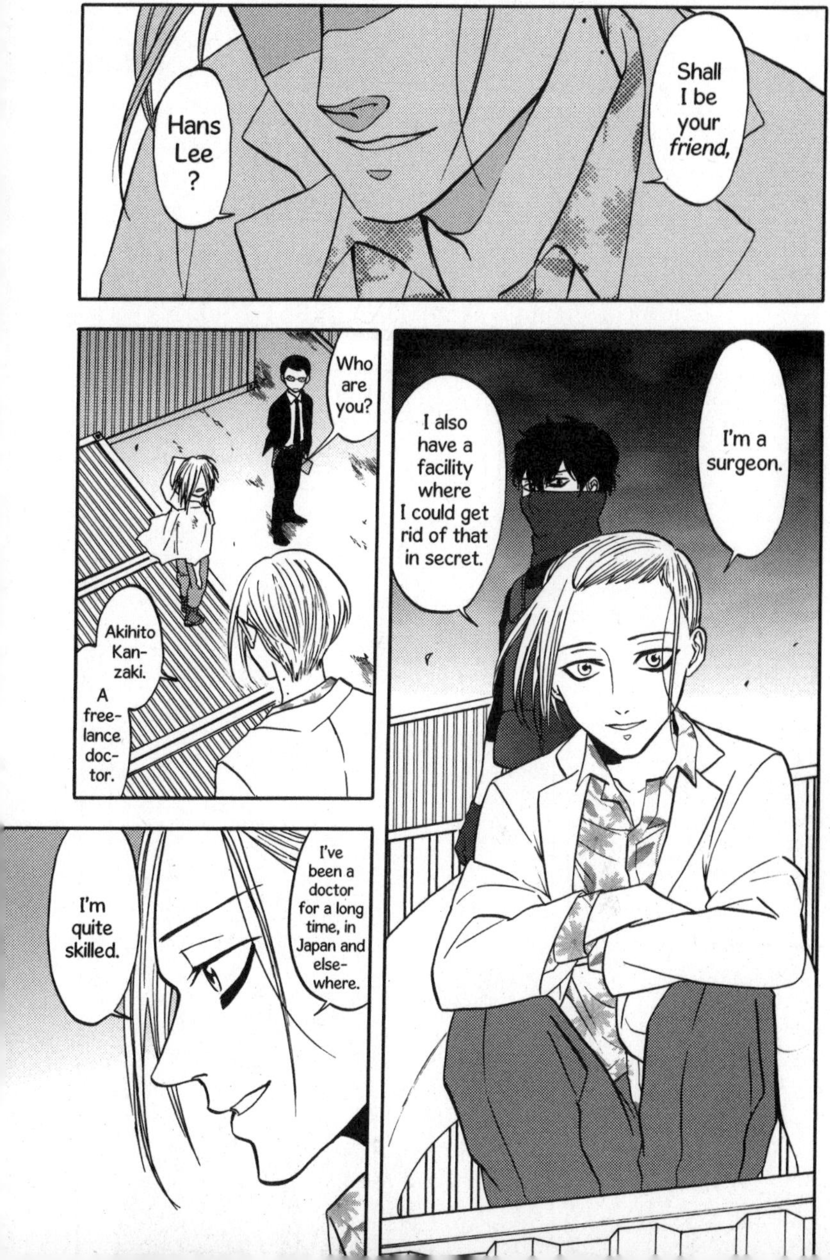
Shall I be your *friend,*
Hans Lee?
I'm a surgeon.
I also have a facility where I could get rid of that in secret.
Who are you?
Akihito Kan-zaki. A free-lance doc-tor.
I've been a doctor for a long time, in Japan and else-where.
I'm quite skilled.

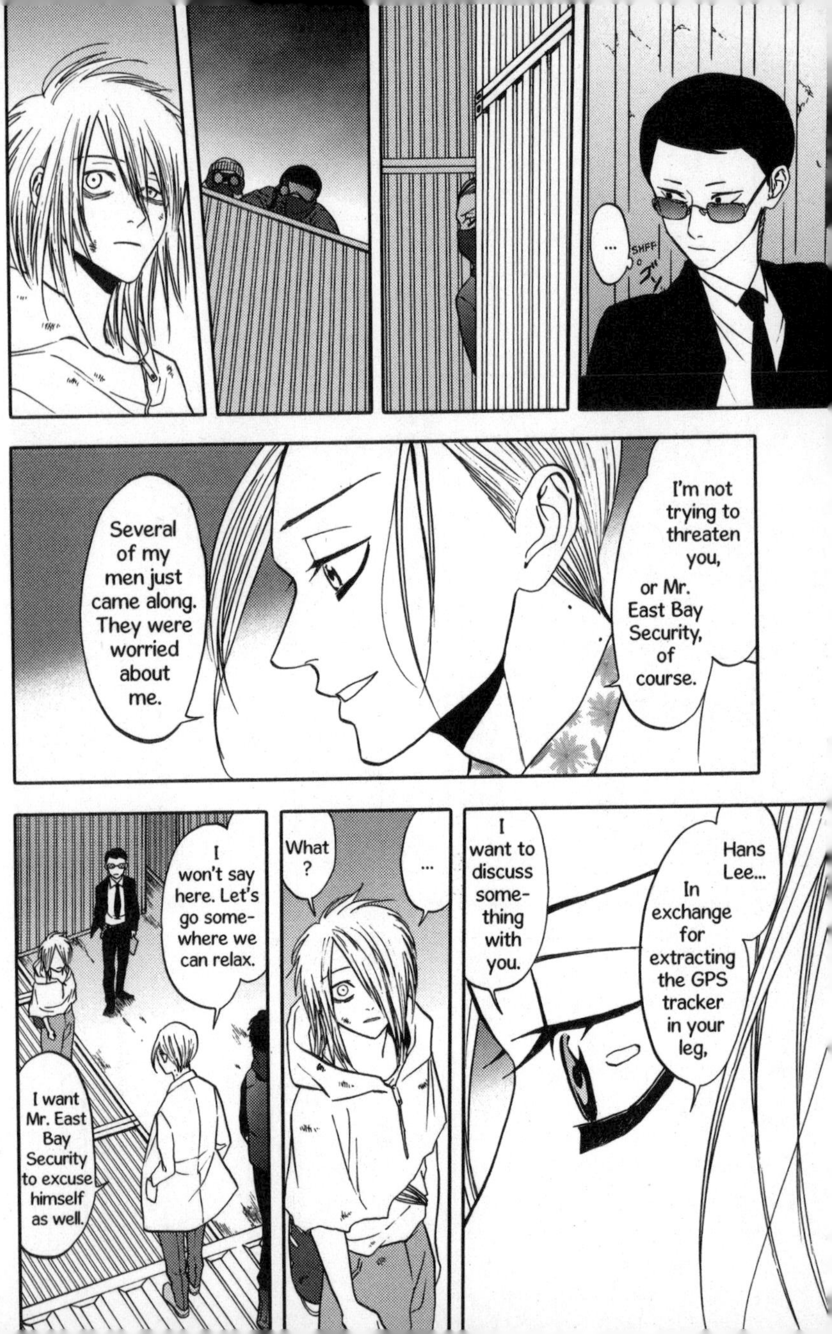
...
SHFF
ズッ
I'm not trying to threaten you, or Mr. East Bay Security, of course.
Several of my men just came along. They were worried about me.
Hans Lee... In exchange for extracting the GPS tracker in your leg,
I want to discuss something with you.
...
What?
I won't say here. Let's go somewhere we can relax.
I want Mr. East Bay Security to excuse himself as well.

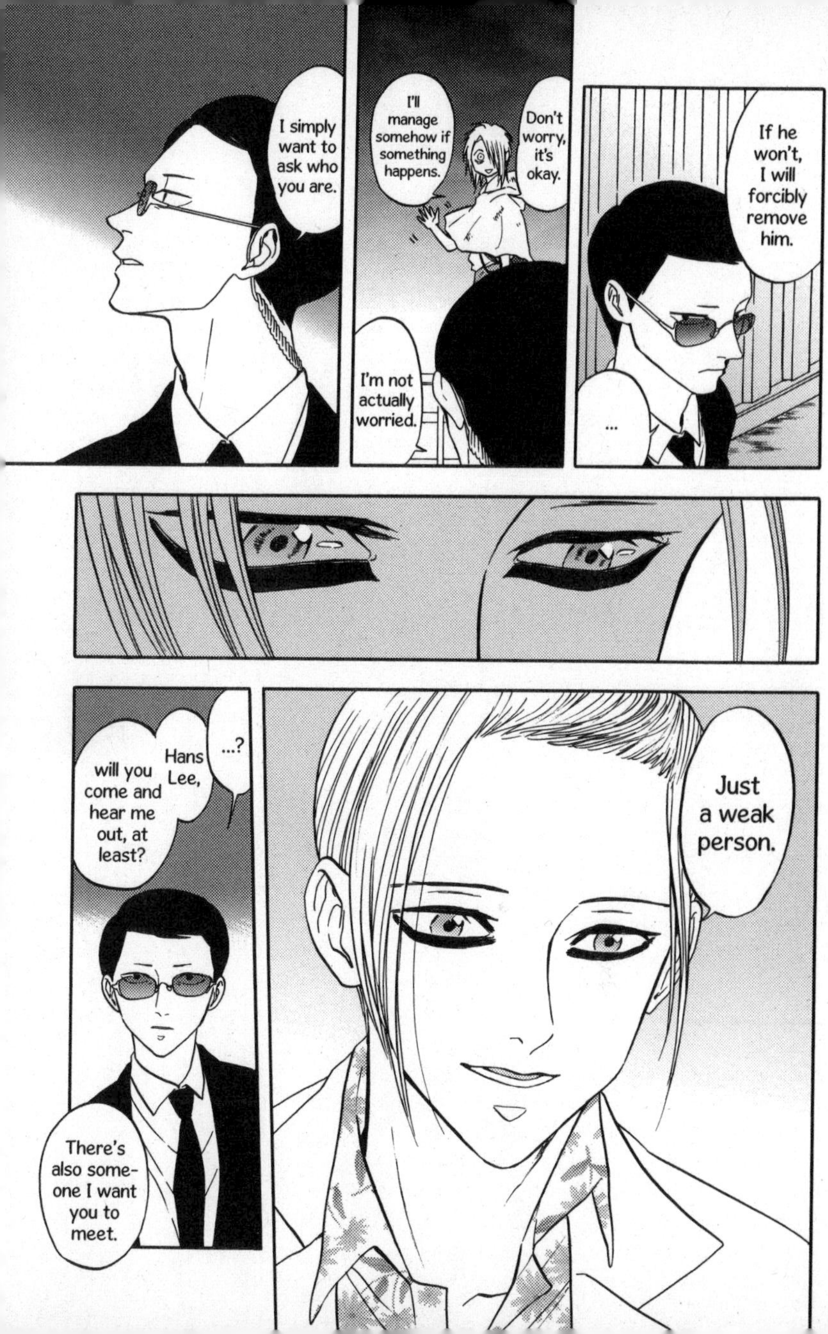
If he won't, I will forcibly remove him.
...
Don't worry, it's okay.
I'll manage somehow if something happens.
I'm not actually worried.
I simply want to ask who you are.
Just a weak person.
...?
Hans Lee, will you come and hear me out, at least?
There's also some-one I want you to meet.

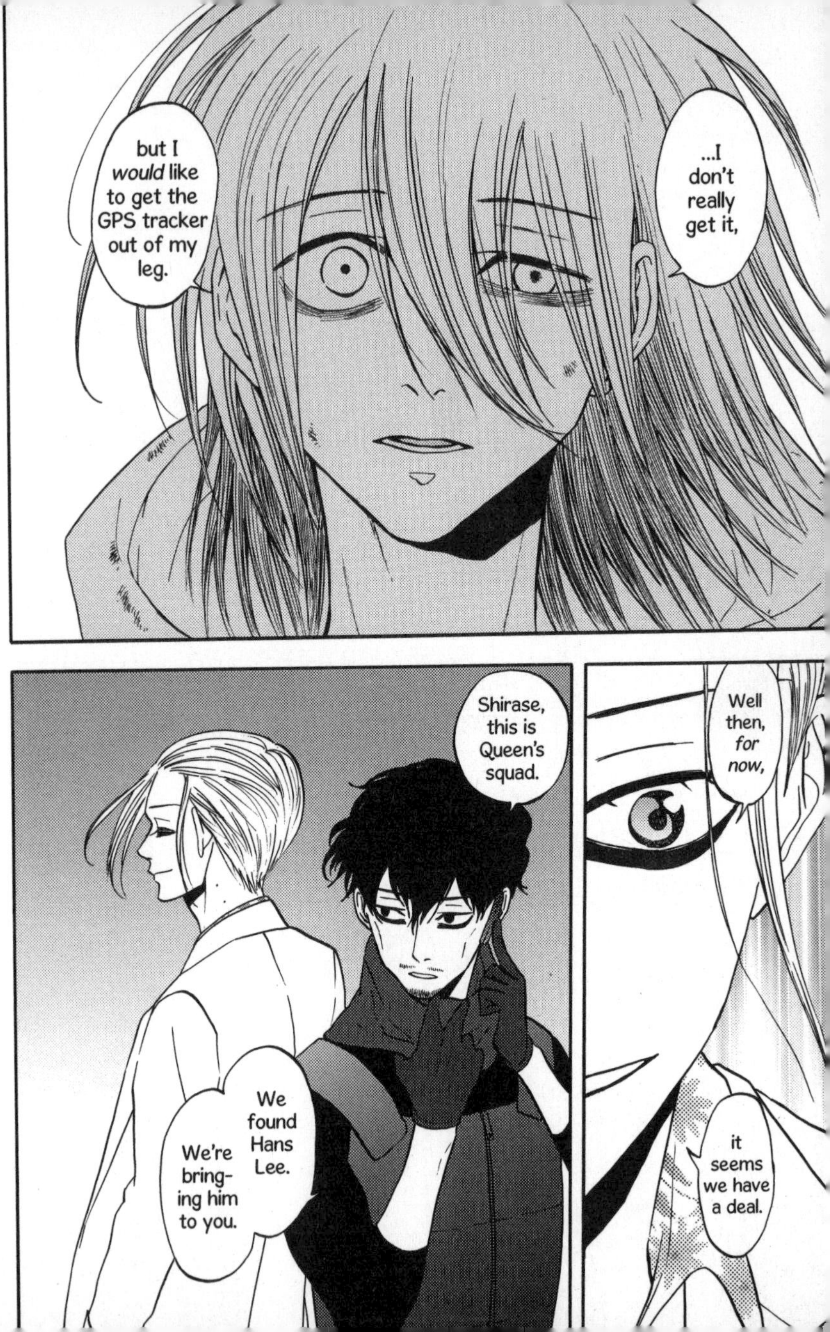
...I don't really get it,
but I *would* like to get the GPS tracker out of my leg.
Well then, *for now,*
it seems we have a deal.
Shirase, this is Queen's squad.
We found Hans Lee.
We're bring-ing him to you.

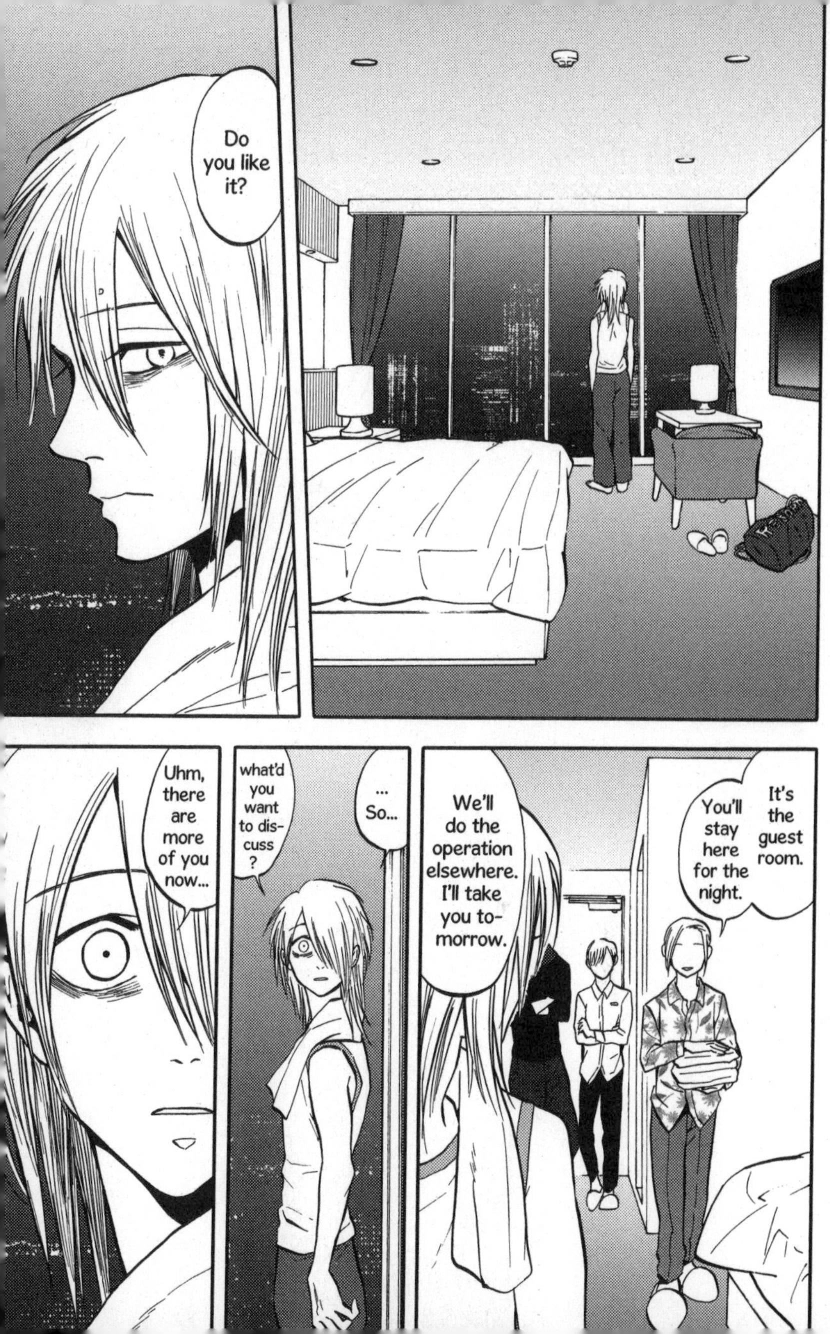
Do you like it?
It's the guest room.
You'll stay here for the night.
We'll do the operation elsewhere. I'll take you to-morrow.
... So...
what'd you want to discuss?
Uhm, there are more of you now...

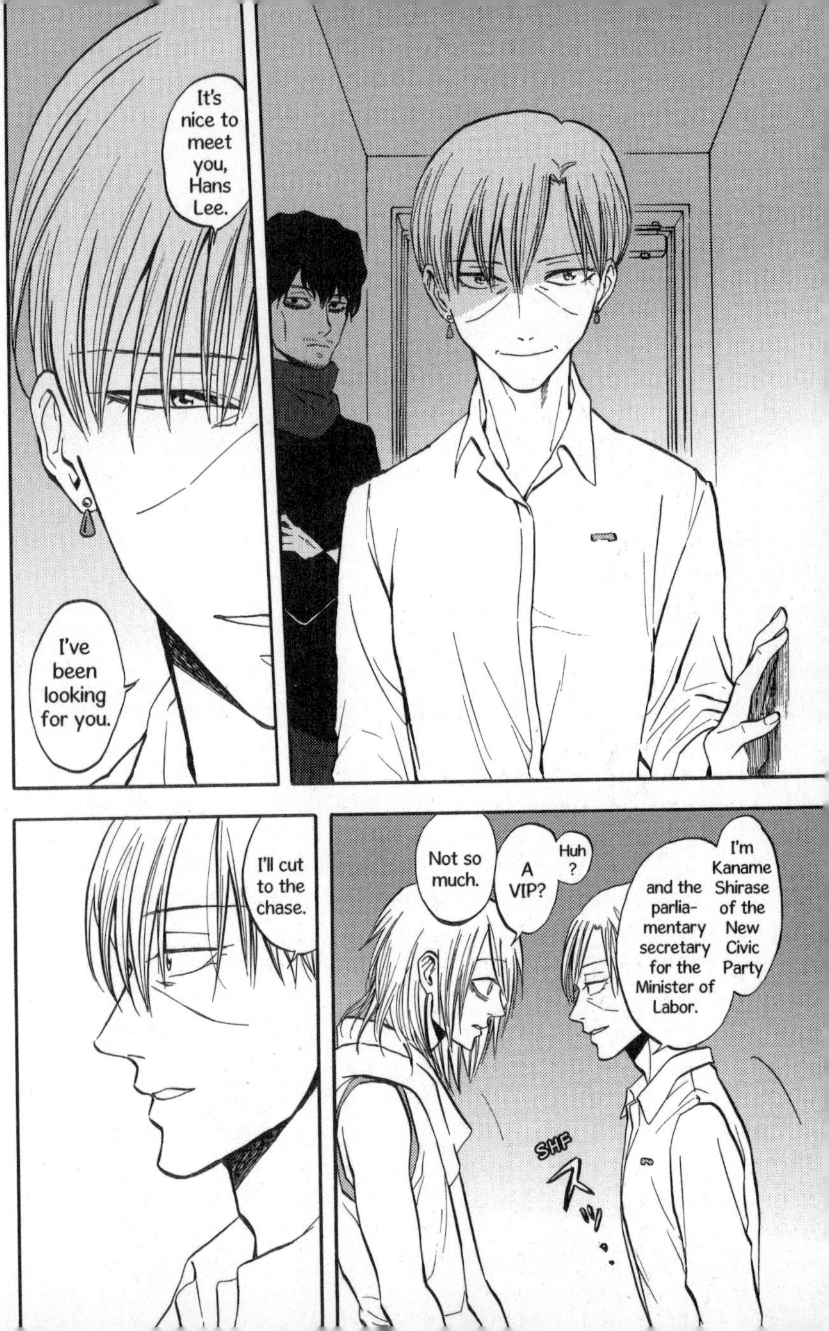
It's nice to meet you, Hans Lee.
I've been looking for you.
I'm Kaname Shirase of the New Civic Party
and the parliamentary secretary for the Minister of Labor.
Huh?
A VIP?
Not so much.
SHF
I'll cut to the chase.

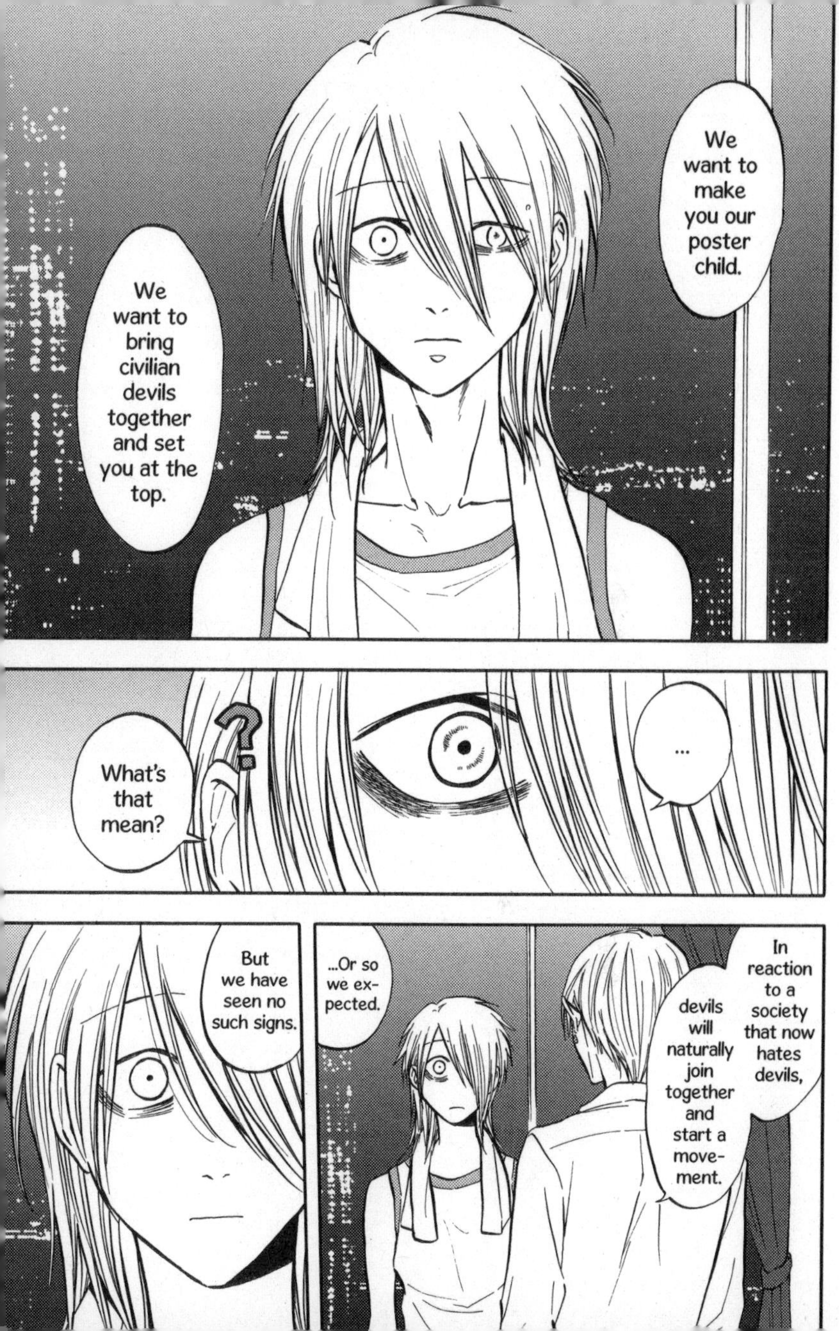
We want to make you our poster child.
We want to bring civilian devils together and set you at the top.
...
What's that mean?
In reaction to a society that now hates devils,
devils will naturally join together and start a movement.
...Or so we expected.
But we have seen no such signs.

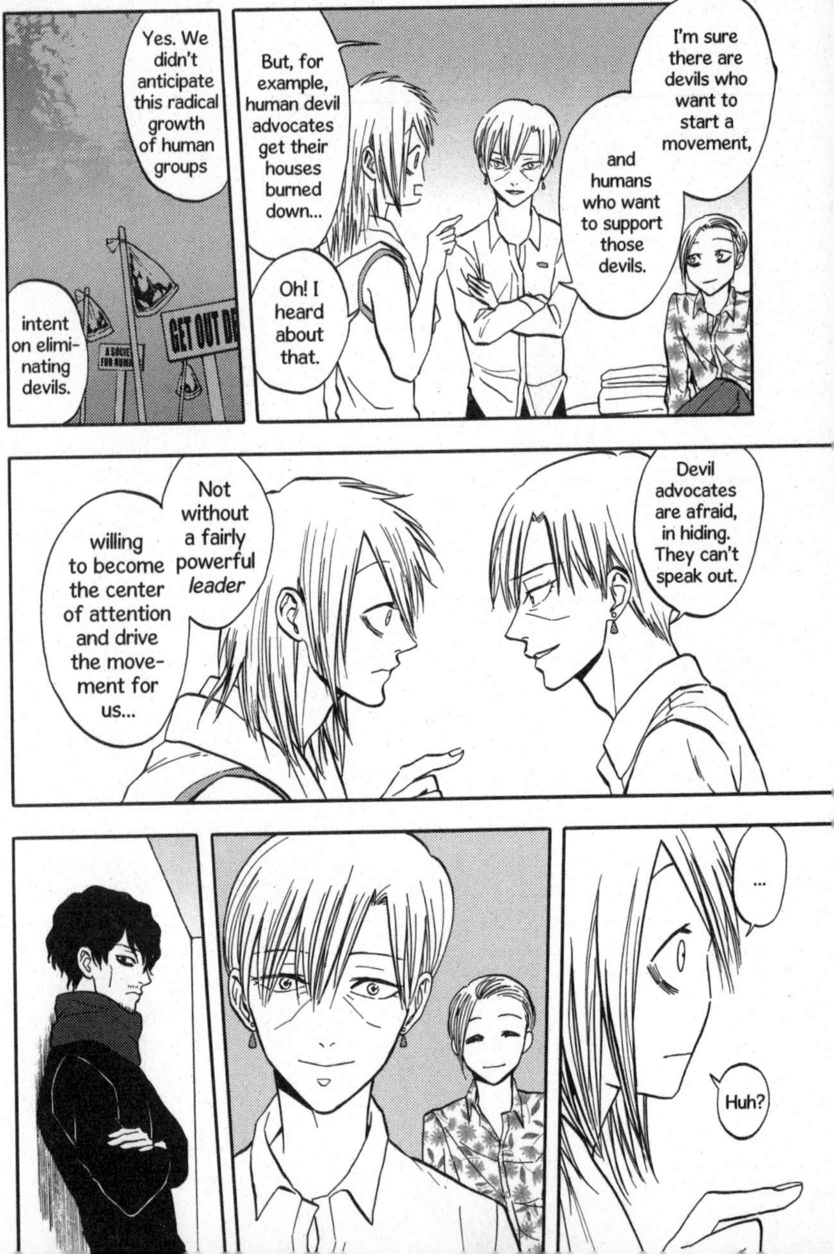
I'm sure there are devils who want to start a movement,
and humans who want to support those devils.
But, for example, human devil advocates get their houses burned down...
Oh! I heard about that.
Yes. We didn't anticipate this radical growth of human groups
GET OUT DE
intent on eliminating devils.
Devil advocates are afraid, in hiding. They can't speak out.
Not without a fairly powerful *leader*
willing to become the center of attention and drive the movement for us...
...
Huh?

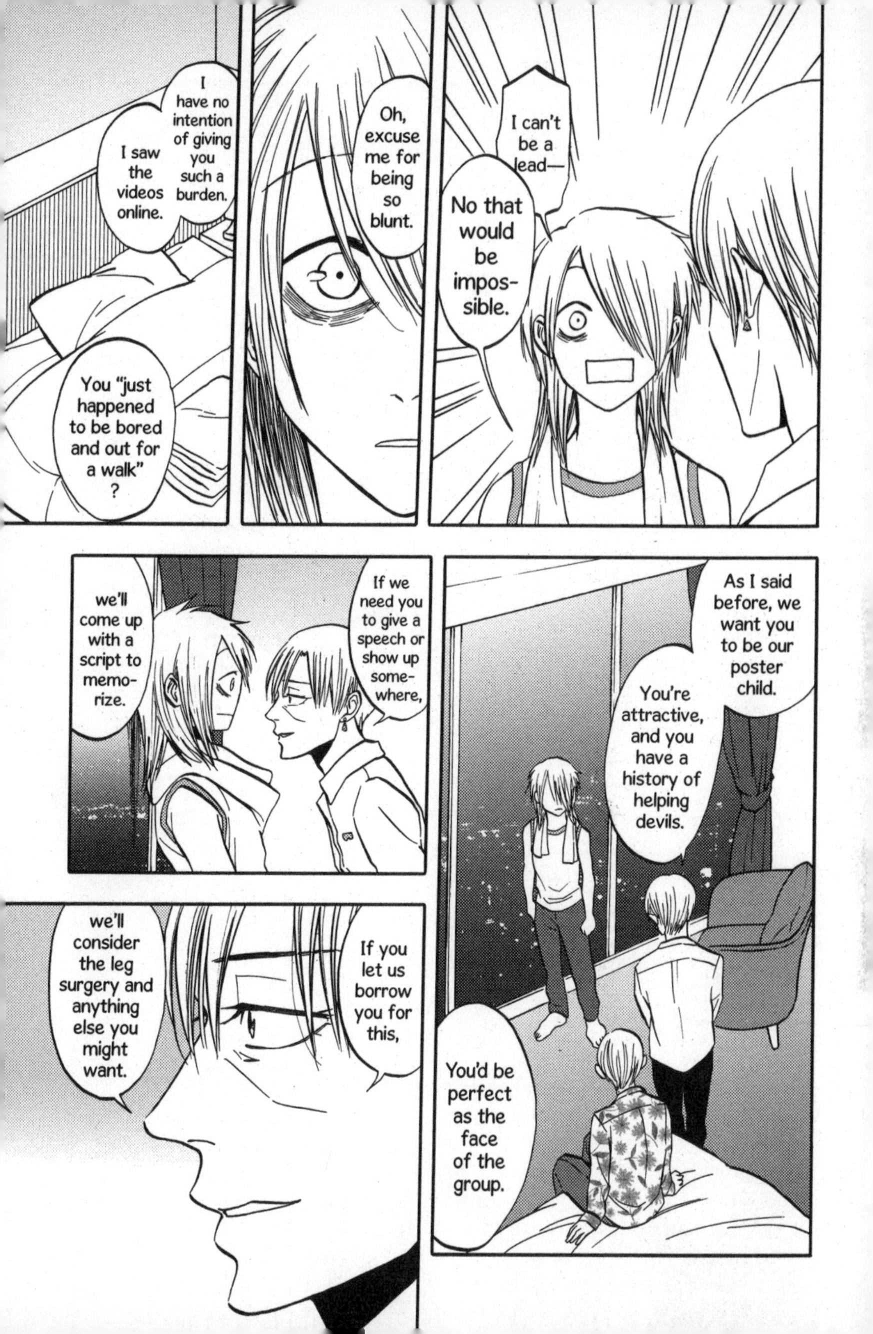
I can't be a lead—
No that would be impossible.
Oh, excuse me for being so blunt.
I have no intention of giving you such a burden.
I saw the videos online.
You "just happened to be bored and out for a walk"?
As I said before, we want you to be our poster child.
You're attractive, and you have a history of helping devils.
You'd be perfect as the face of the group.
If we need you to give a speech or show up somewhere,
we'll come up with a script to memorize.
If you let us borrow you for this,
we'll consider the leg surgery and anything else you might want.

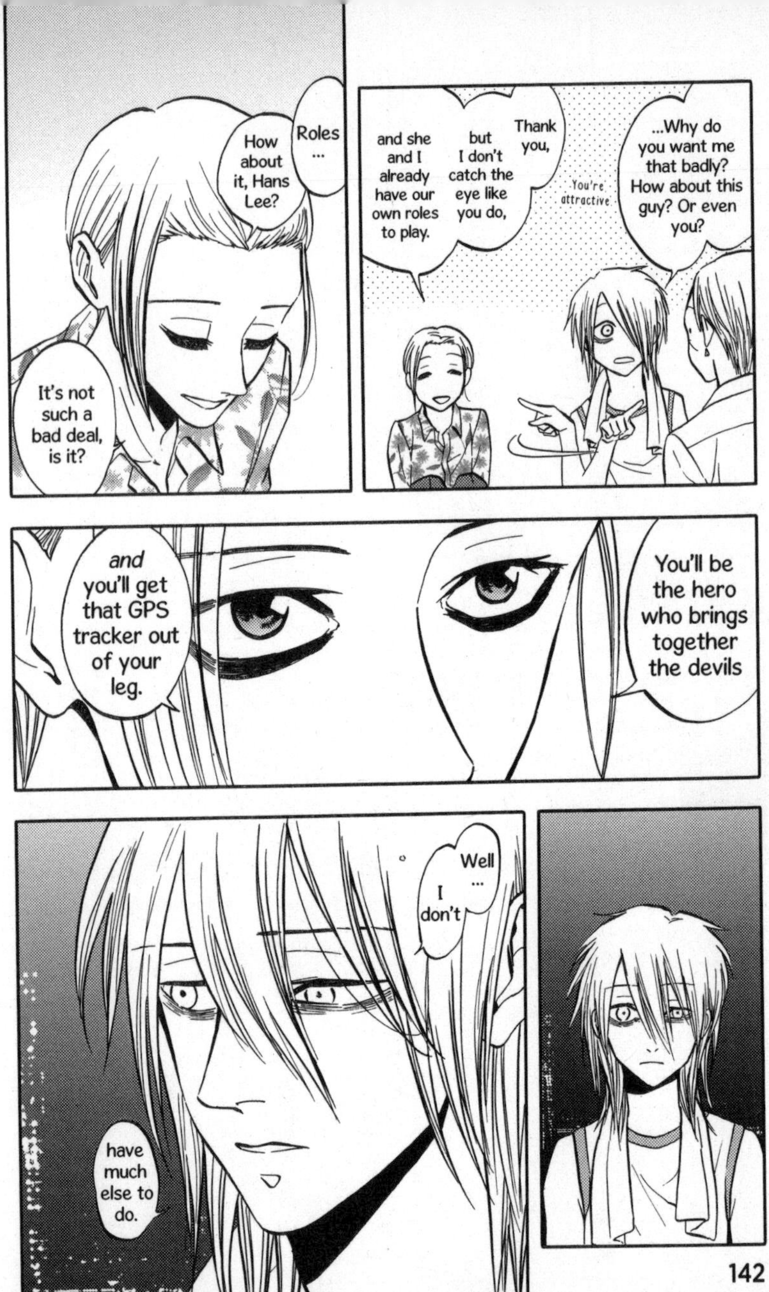
...Why do you want me that badly? How about this guy? Or even you?
You're attractive
Thank you,
but I don't catch the eye like you do,
and she and I already have our own roles to play.
Roles ...
How about it, Hans Lee?
It's not such a bad deal, is it?
You'll be the hero who brings together the devils
and you'll get that GPS tracker out of your leg.
Well ...
I don't
have much else to do.

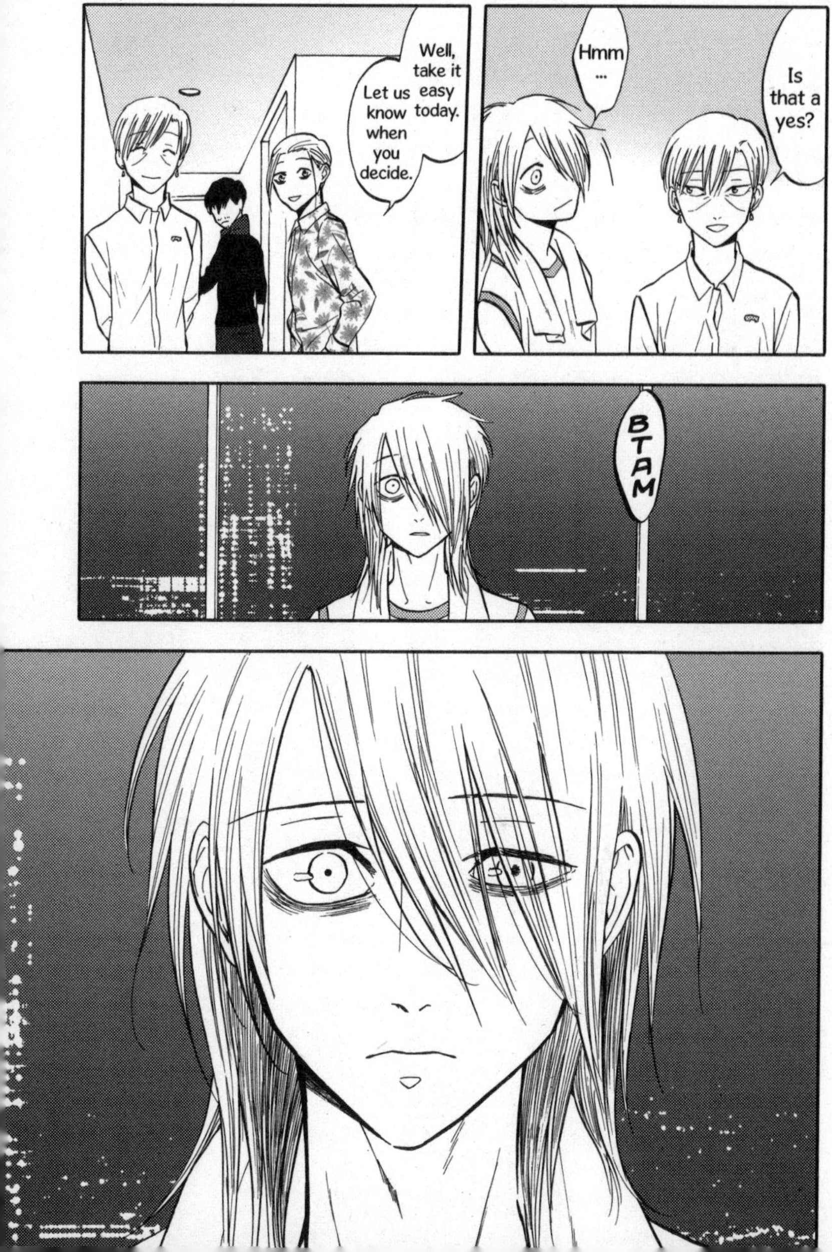
Is that a yes?
Hmm ...
Well, take it easy today.
Let us know when you decide.
BTAM

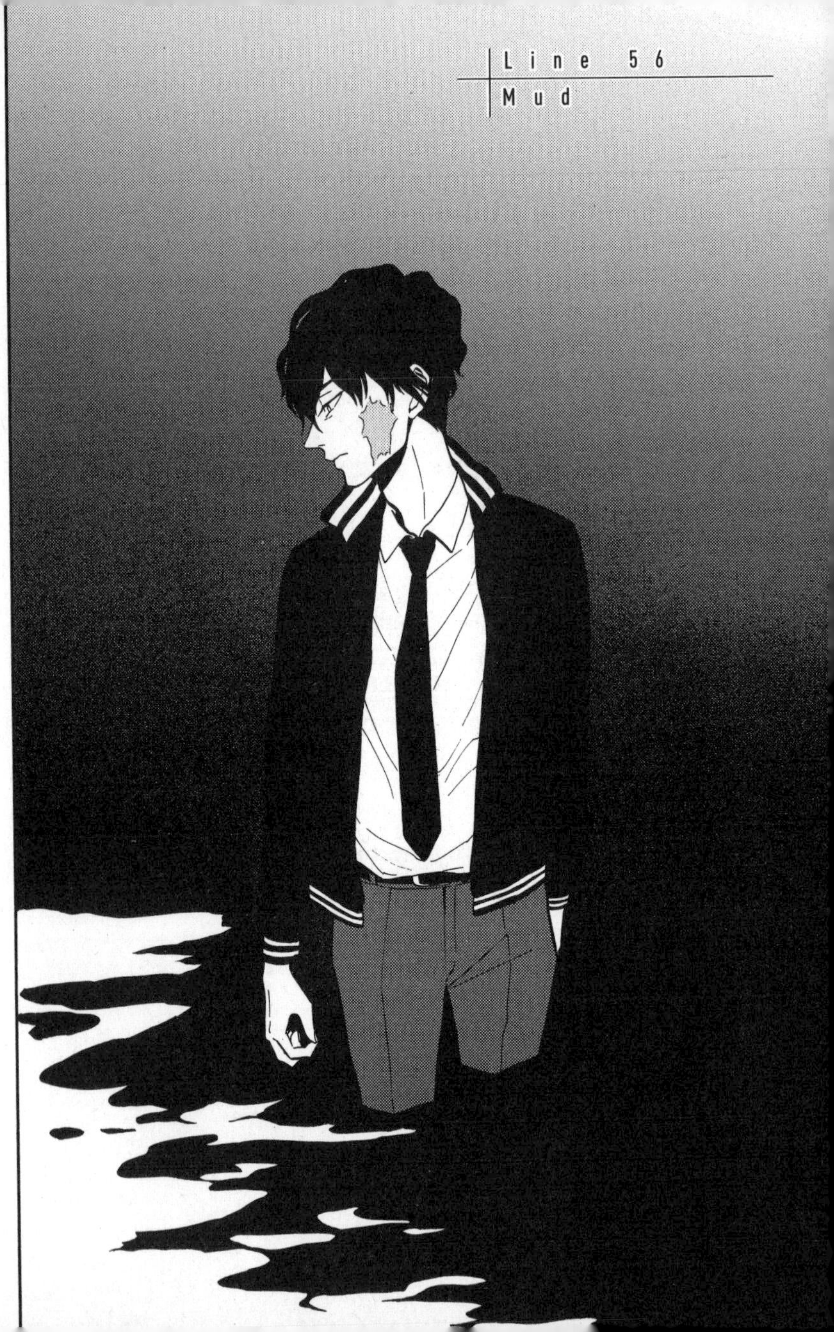
Line 56
Mud

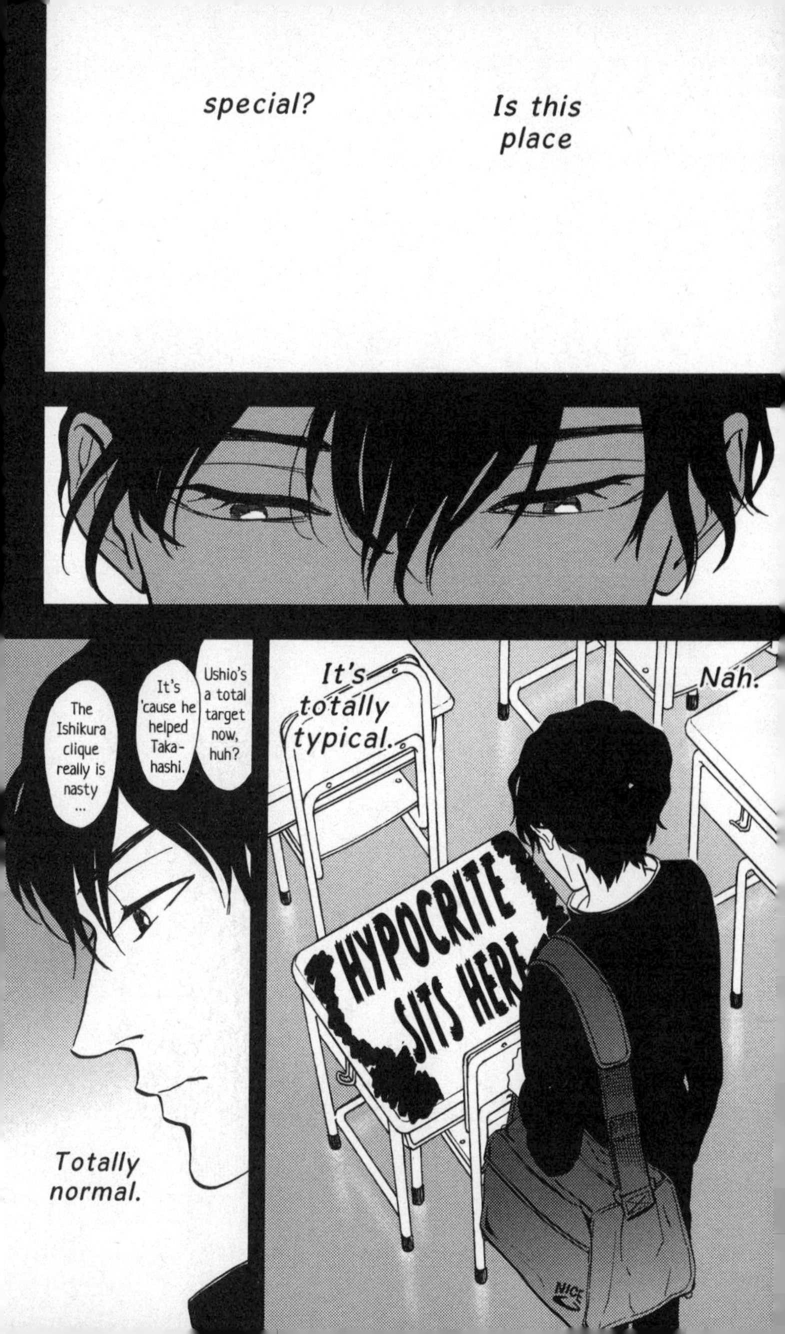
Is this place
special?
Nah.
It's totally typical.
HYPOCRITE SITS HERE
Ushio's a total target now, huh?
It's 'cause he helped Taka-hashi.
The Ishikura clique really is nasty ...
Totally normal.

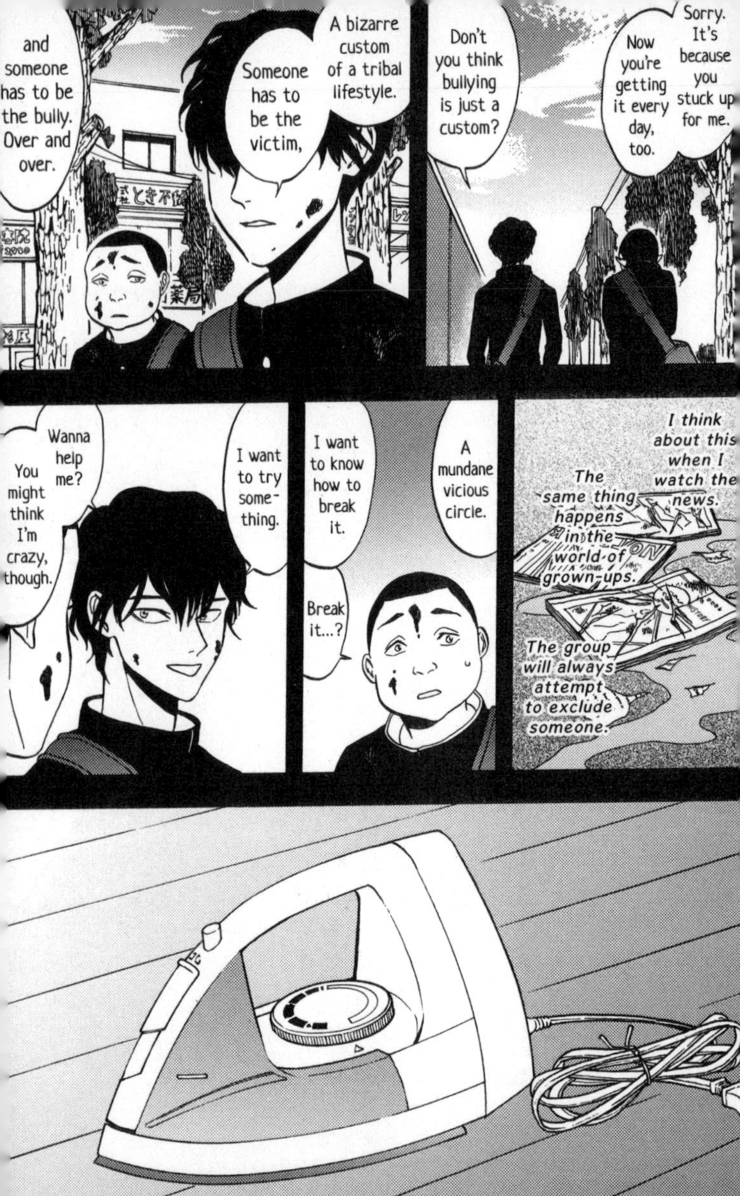
Sorry. It's because you stuck up for me.
Now you're getting it every day, too.
Don't you think bullying is just a custom?
A bizarre custom of a tribal lifestyle.
Someone has to be the victim,
and someone has to be the bully. Over and over.
I think about this when I watch the news.
The same thing happens in the world of grown-ups.
The group will always attempt to exclude someone.
A mundane vicious circle.
I want to know how to break it.
Break it...?
I want to try some-thing.
Wanna help me?
You might think I'm crazy, though.

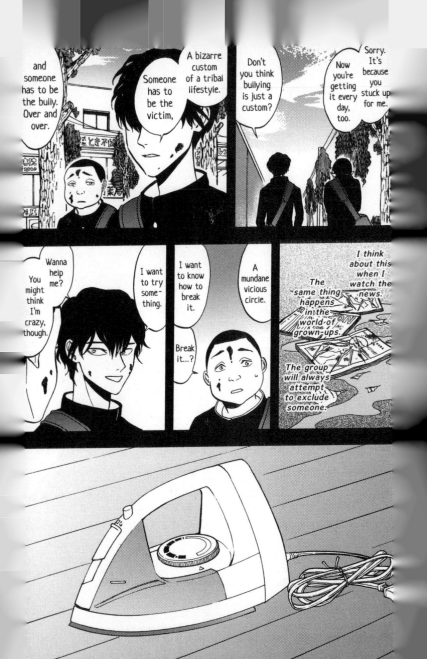

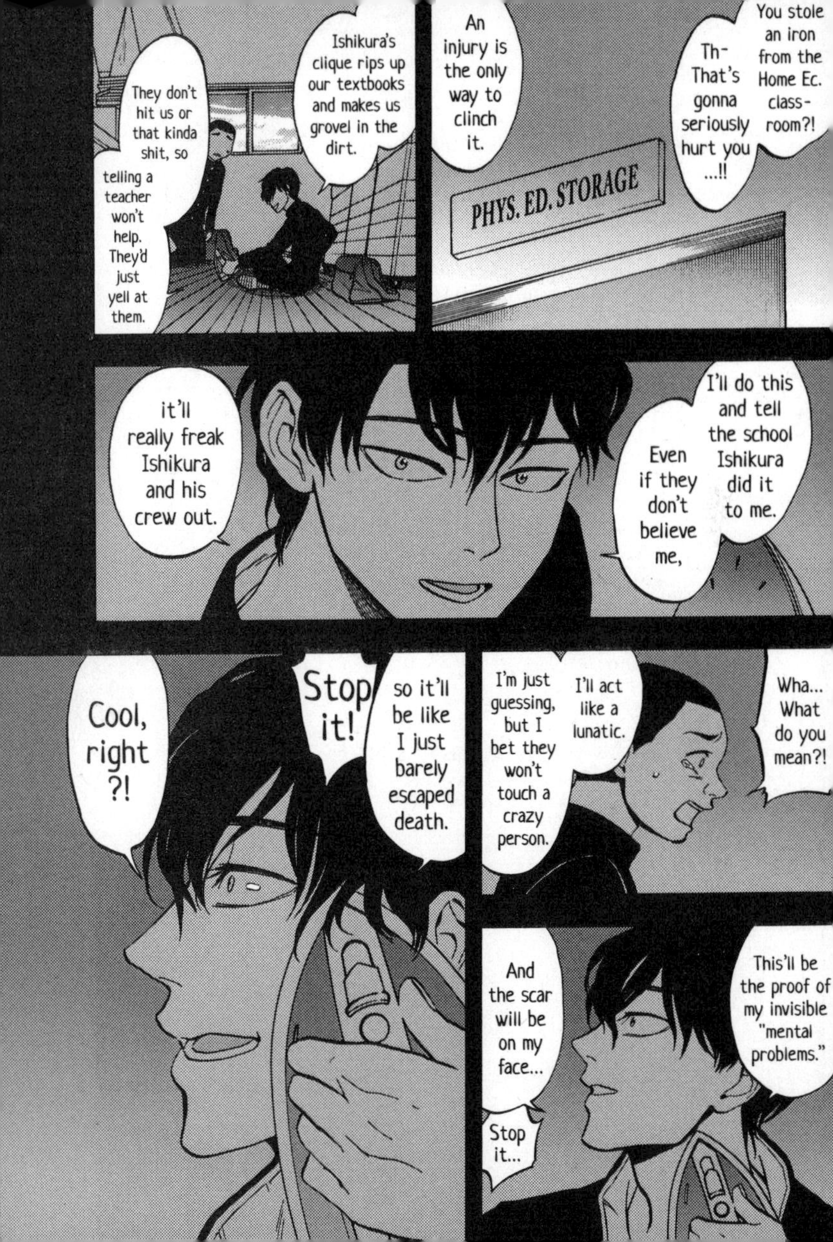
You stole an iron from the Home Ec. class-room?!
Th- That's gonna seriously hurt you ...!!
An injury is the only way to clinch it.
PHYS. ED. STORAGE
Ishikura's clique rips up our textbooks and makes us grovel in the dirt.
They don't hit us or that kinda shit, so
telling a teacher won't help. They'd just yell at them.
I'll do this and tell the school Ishikura did it to me.
Even if they don't believe me,
it'll really freak Ishikura and his crew out.
Wha... What do you mean?!
I'll act like a lunatic.
I'm just guessing, but I bet they won't touch a crazy person.
This'll be the proof of my invisible "mental problems."
And the scar will be on my face...
Stop it...
so it'll be like I just barely escaped death.
Stop it!
Cool, right ?!

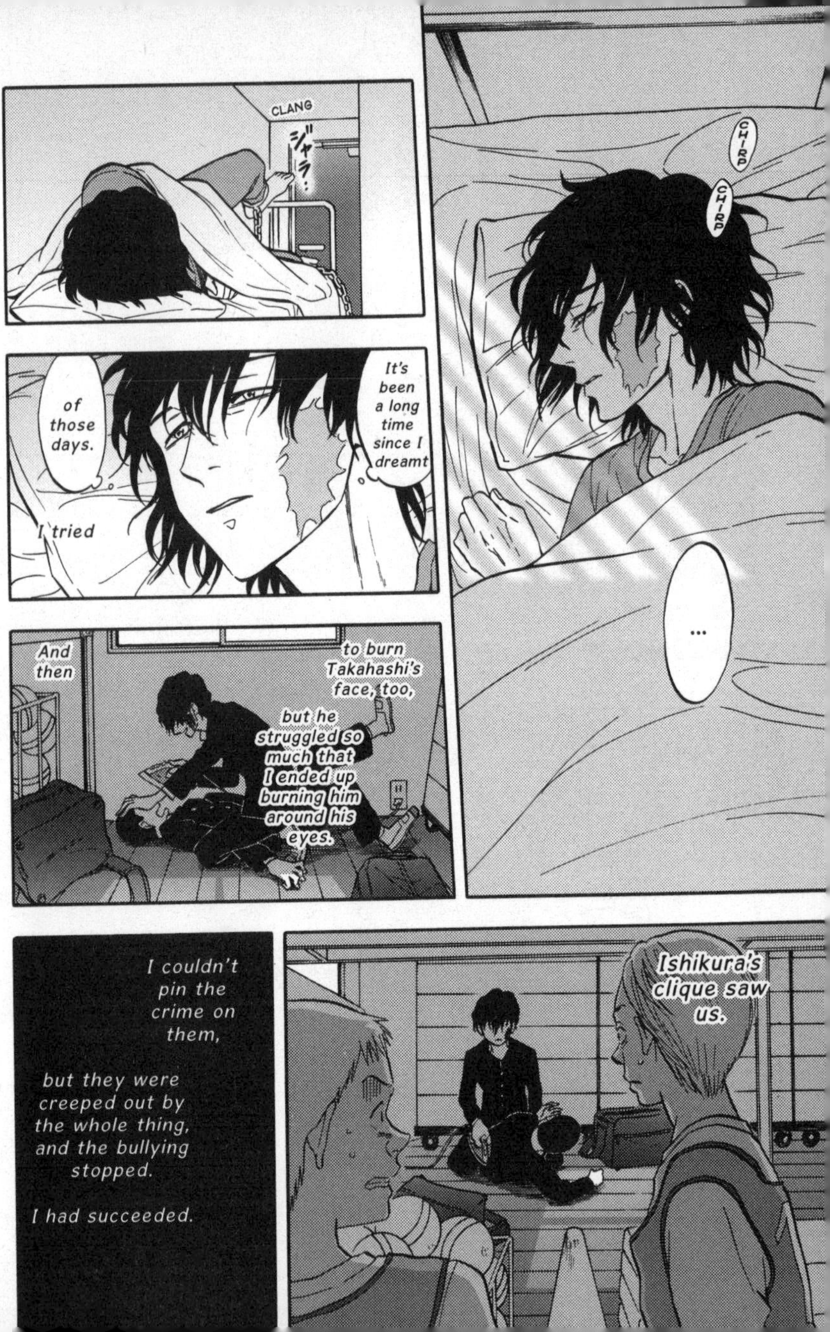
CHIRP
CHIRP
...
CLANG
ジャラ…
It's been a long time since I dreamt
of those days.
I tried
to burn Takahashi's face, too,
but he struggled so much that I ended up burning him around his eyes.
And then
Ishikura's clique saw us.
I couldn't pin the crime on them,
but they were creeped out by the whole thing, and the bullying stopped.
I had succeeded.

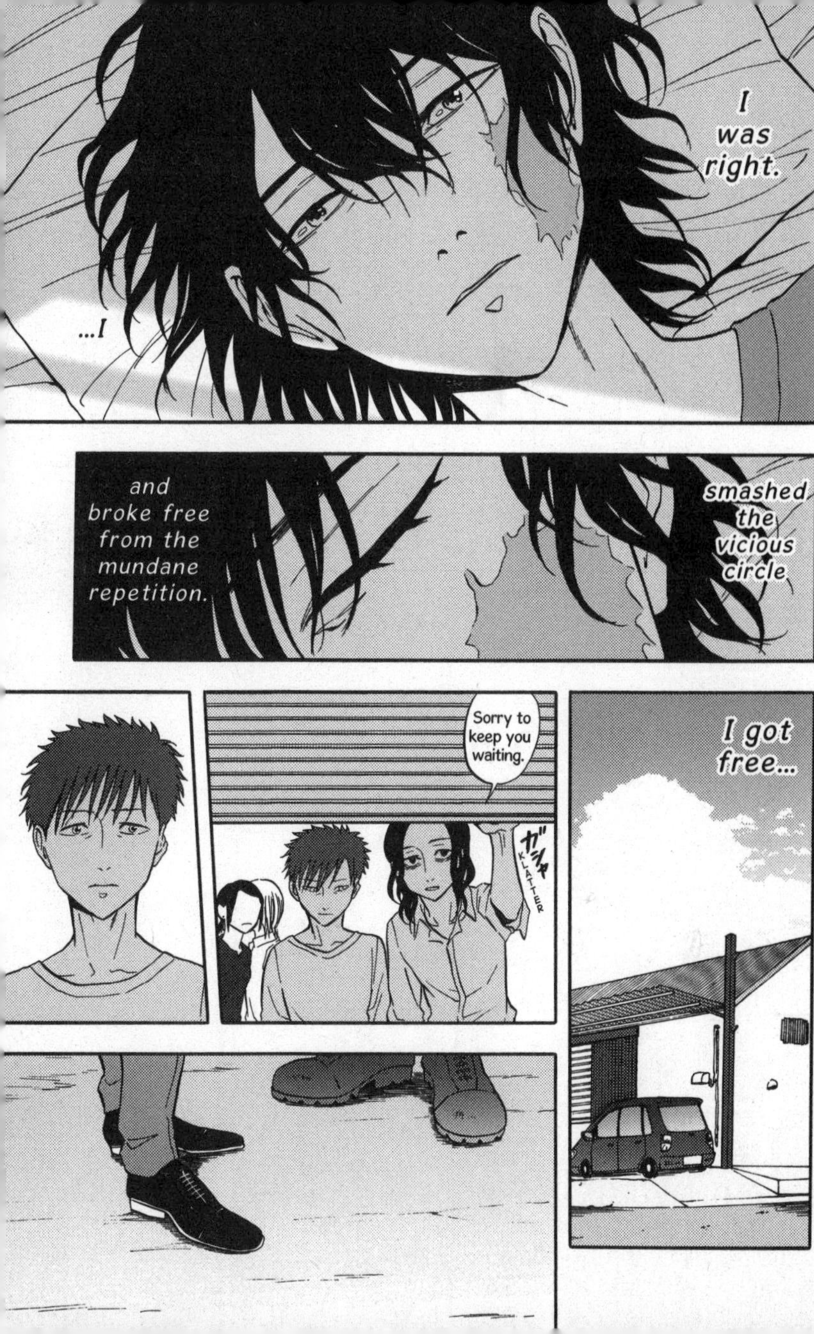
I was right.
...I
smashed the vicious circle
and broke free from the mundane repetition.
I got free...
Sorry to keep you waiting.
ガシャ KLATTER

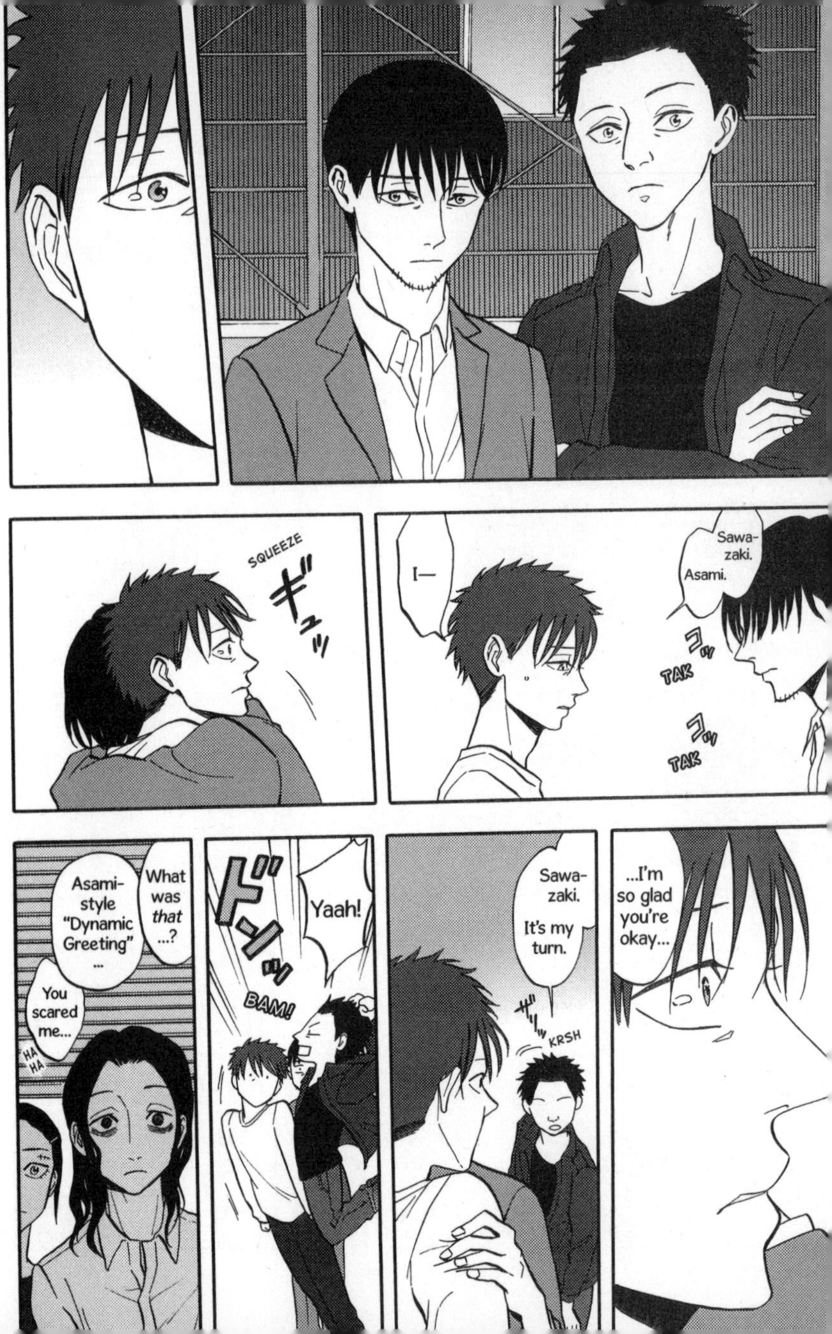
Sawa-
zaki.
Asami.
TAK
TAK
I—
SQUEEZE
...I'm so glad you're okay...
Sawa-
zaki.
It's my turn.
KRSH
Yaah!
BAM!
What was *that* ...?
Asami-style "Dynamic Greeting" ...
You scared me...
HA HA

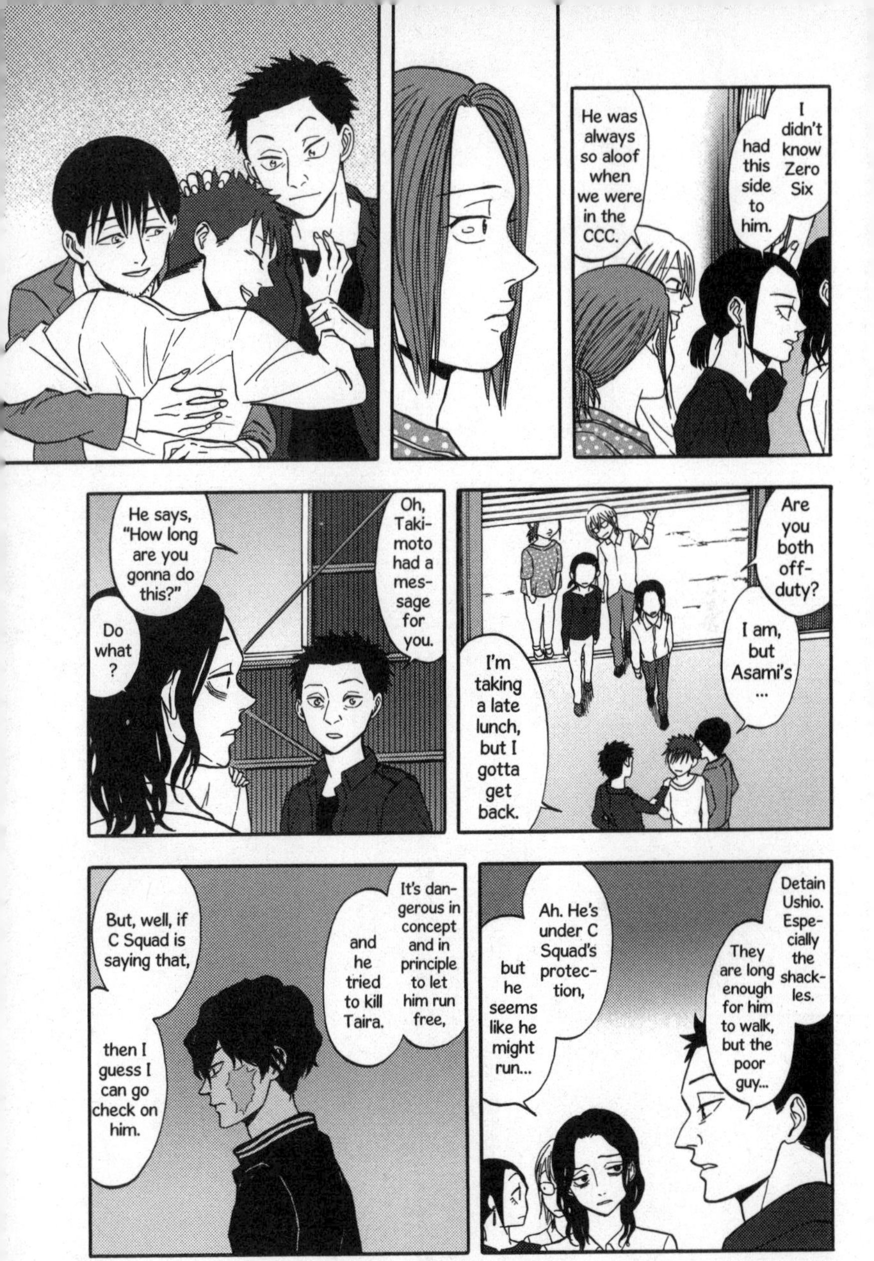
I didn't know Zero Six had this side to him.
He was always so aloof when we were in the CCC.
Are you both off-duty?
I am, but Asami's...
I'm taking a late lunch, but I gotta get back.
Oh, Takimoto had a message for you.
He says, "How long are you gonna do this?"
Do what?
Detain Ushio. Especially the shackles.
They are long enough for him to walk, but the poor guy...
Ah. He's under C Squad's protection,
but he seems like he might run...
It's dangerous in concept and in principle to let him run free,
and he tried to kill Taira.
But, well, if C Squad is saying that,
then I guess I can go check on him.

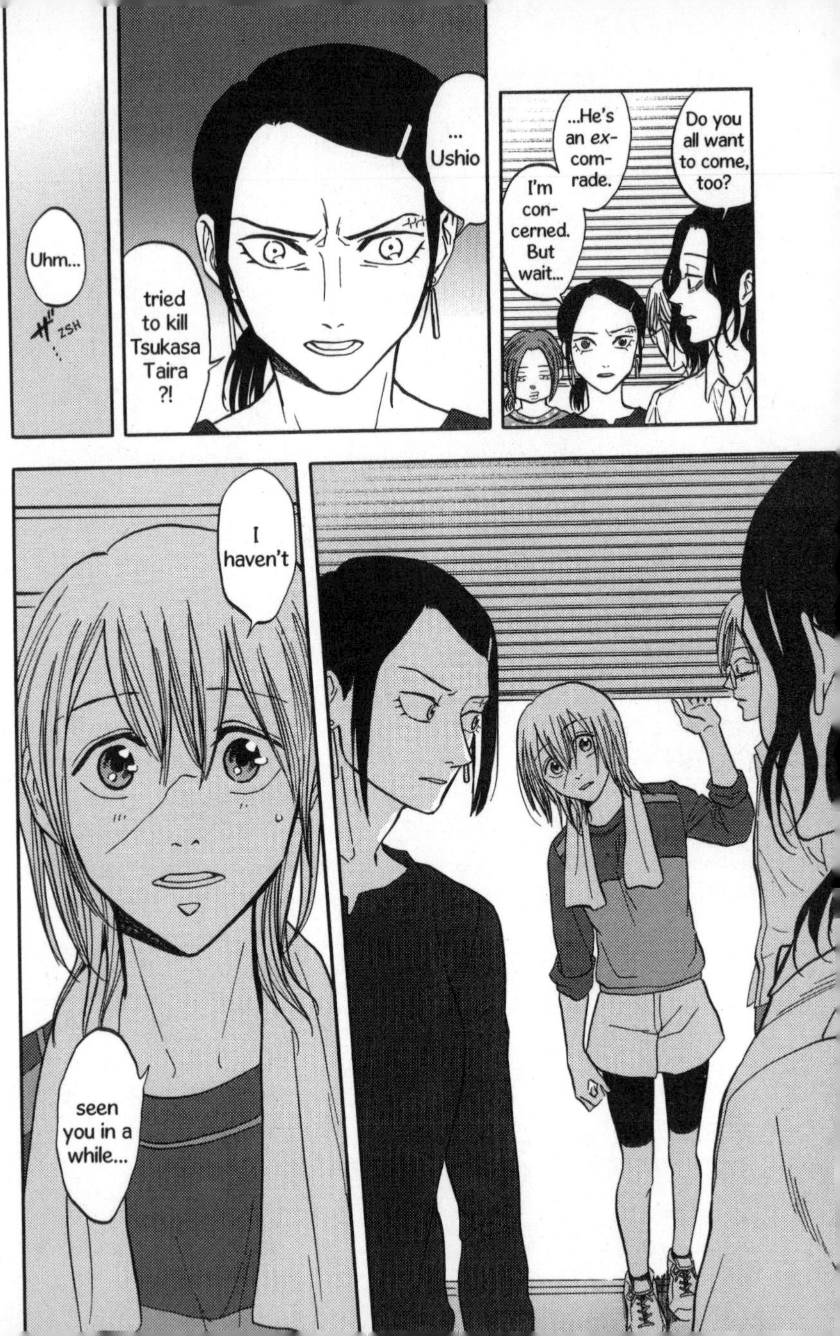
Do you all want to come, too?
...He's an *ex*-comrade.
I'm concerned. But wait...
... Ushio
tried to kill Tsukasa Taira ?!
Uhm...
ZSH
I haven't
seen you in a while...

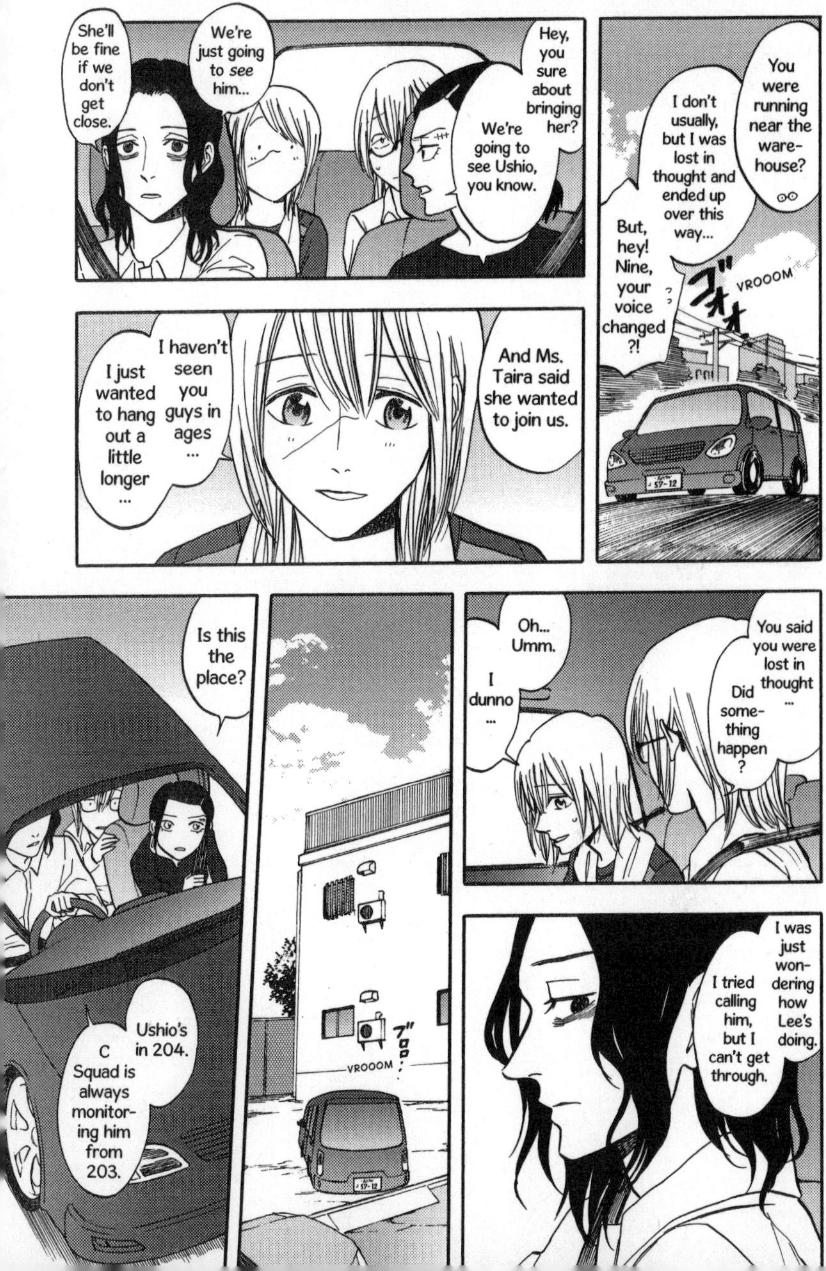
You were running near the warehouse?
I don't usually, but I was lost in thought and ended up over this way...
But, hey! Nine, your voice changed?!
VROOOM
Hey, you sure about bringing her?
We're going to see Ushio, you know.
We're just going to *see* him...
She'll be fine if we don't get close.
And Ms. Taira said she wanted to join us.
I haven't seen you guys in ages...
I just wanted to hang out a little longer...
You said you were lost in thought...
Did something happen?
Oh... Umm.
I dunno...
I was just wondering how Lee's doing.
I tried calling him, but I can't get through.
VROOOM
Is this the place?
Ushio's in 204.
C Squad is always monitoring him from 203.

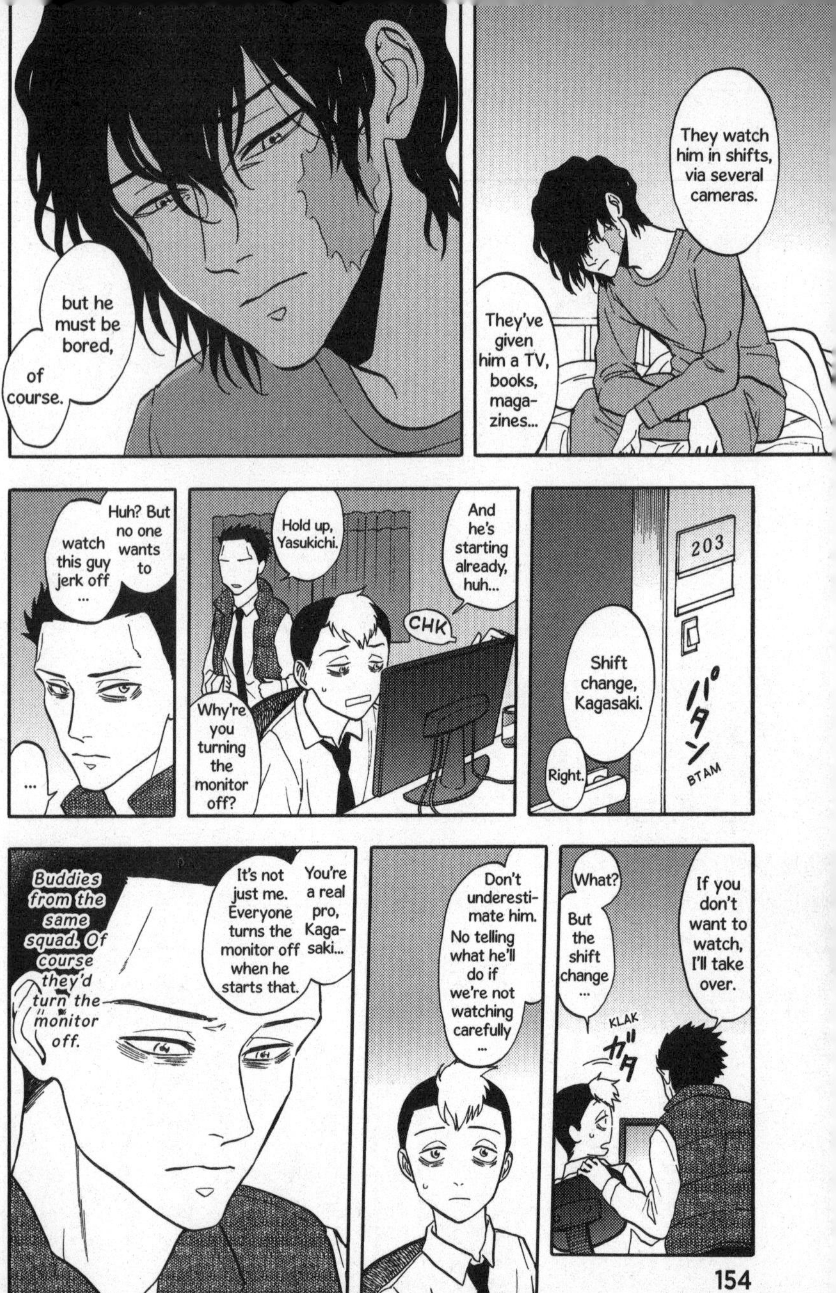
They watch him in shifts, via several cameras.
They've given him a TV, books, magazines...
but he must be bored,
of course.
Shift change, Kagasaki.
Right.
パタン
BTAM
And he's starting already, huh...
CHK
Hold up, Yasukichi.
Why're you turning the monitor off?
Huh? But no one wants to watch this guy jerk off...
...
If you don't want to watch, I'll take over.
What?
But the shift change...
KLAK
ガタ
Don't underestimate him. No telling what he'll do if we're not watching carefully...
You're a real pro, Kagasaki...
It's not just me. Everyone turns the monitor off when he starts that.
Buddies from the same squad. Of course they'd turn the monitor off.

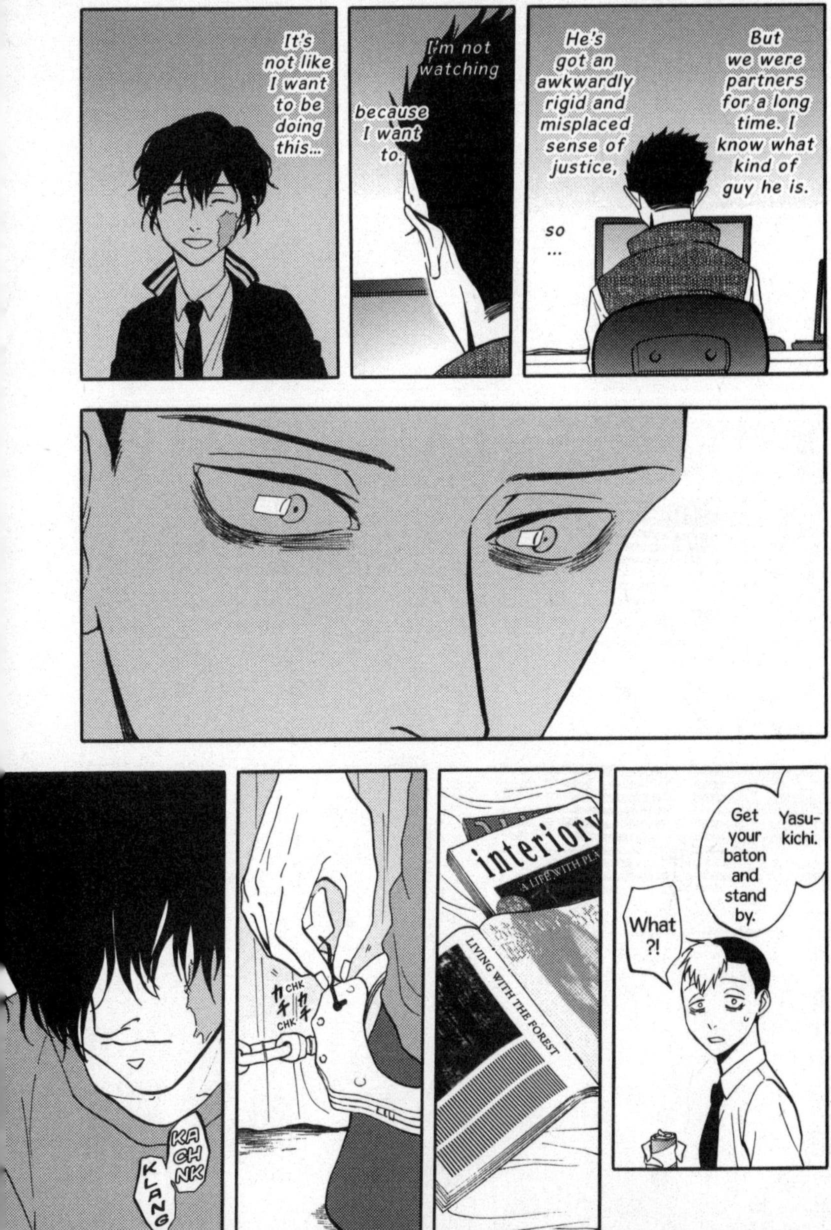
But we were partners for a long time. I know what kind of guy he is.
He's got an awkwardly rigid and misplaced sense of justice,
so ...
I'm not watching
because I want to.
It's not like I want to be doing this...
Yasu-kichi.
Get your baton and stand by.
What?!
interiory
LIVING WITH THE FOREST
カチ CHK
カチ CHK
KACHNK
KLANG

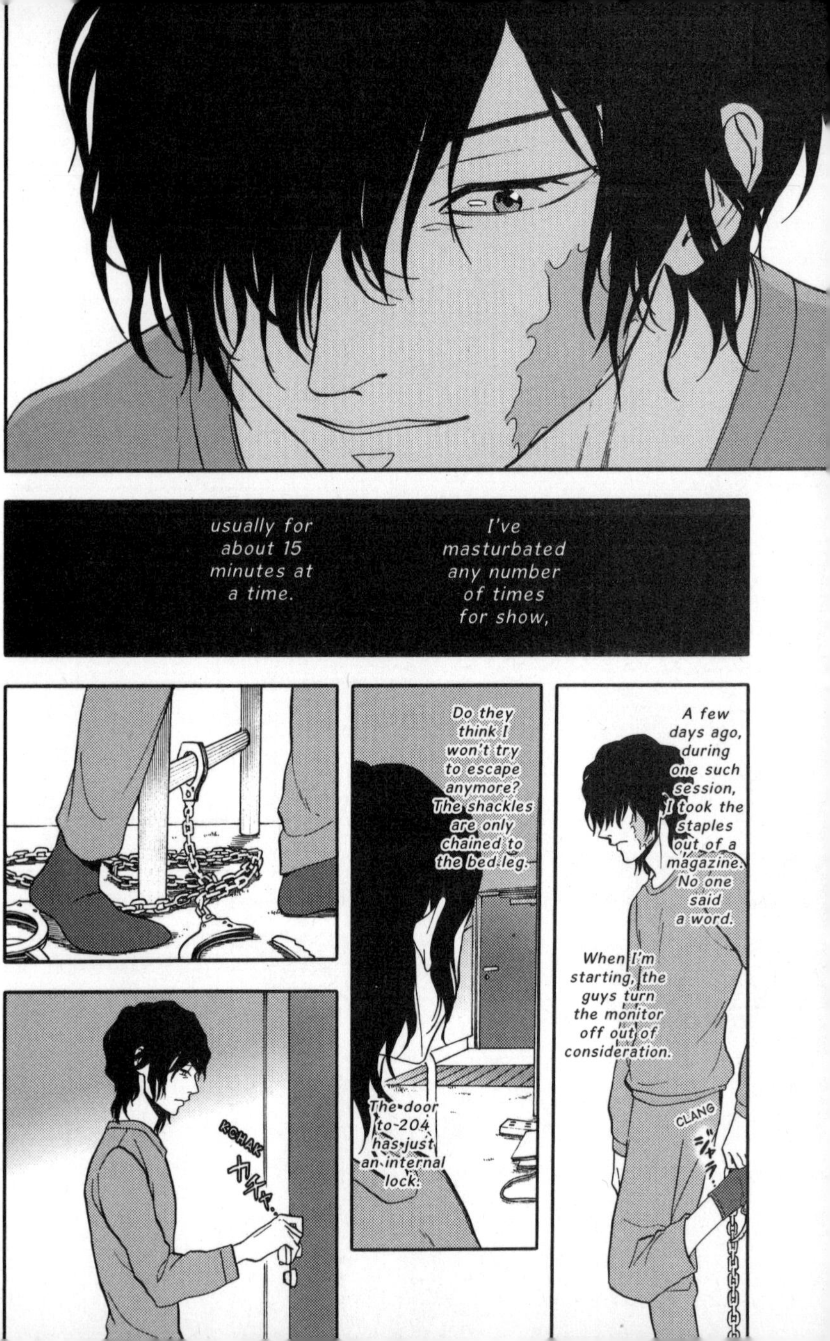
I've masturbated any number of times for show,
usually for about 15 minutes at a time.
A few days ago, during one such session, I took the staples out of a magazine. No one said a word.
When I'm starting, the guys turn the monitor off out of consideration.
CLANG
Do they think I won't try to escape anymore? The shackles are only chained to the bed leg.
The door to 204 has just an internal lock.
KCHAK

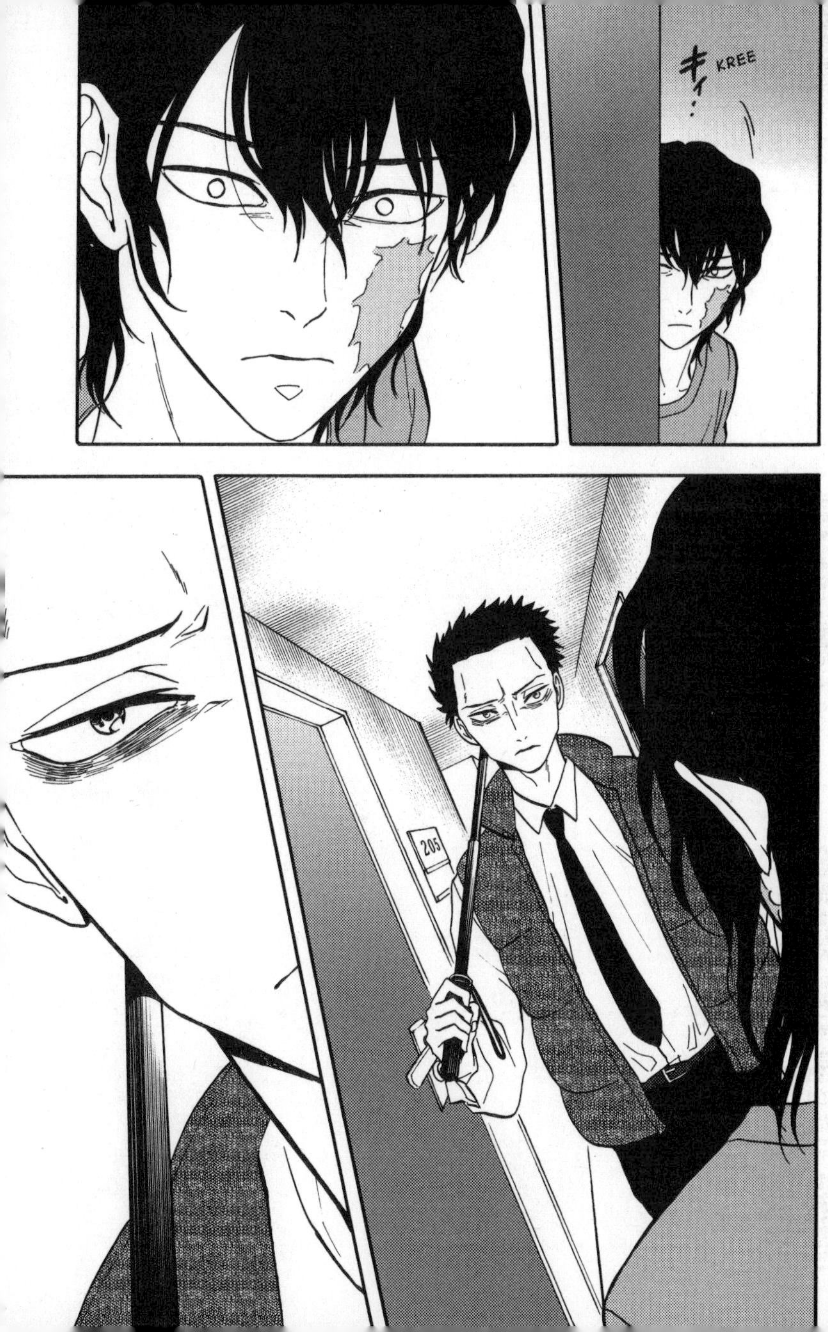
キィ…
KREE
205

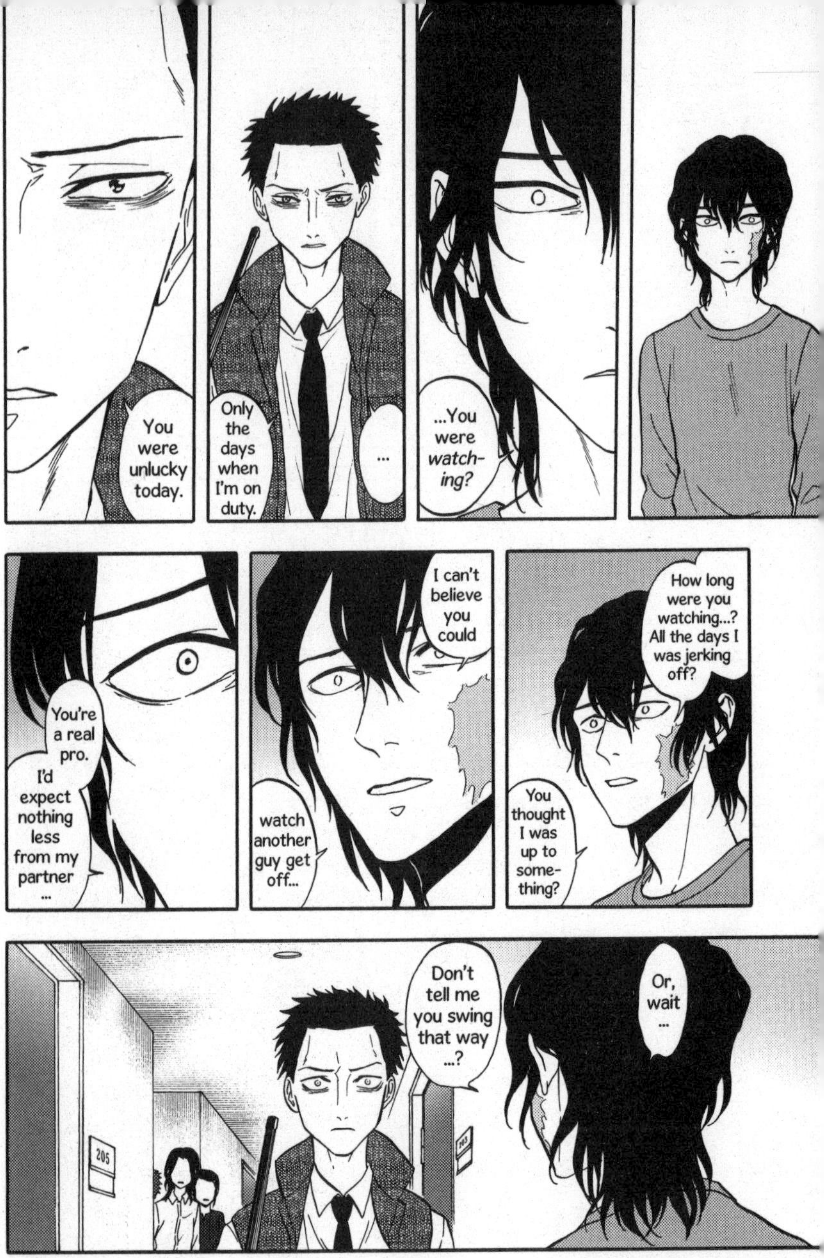
...You were watching?
...
Only the days when I'm on duty.
You were unlucky today.
How long were you watching...? All the days I was jerking off?
You thought I was up to something?
I can't believe you could
watch another guy get off...
You're a real pro.
I'd expect nothing less from my partner ...
Or, wait ...
Don't tell me you swing that way ...?
205

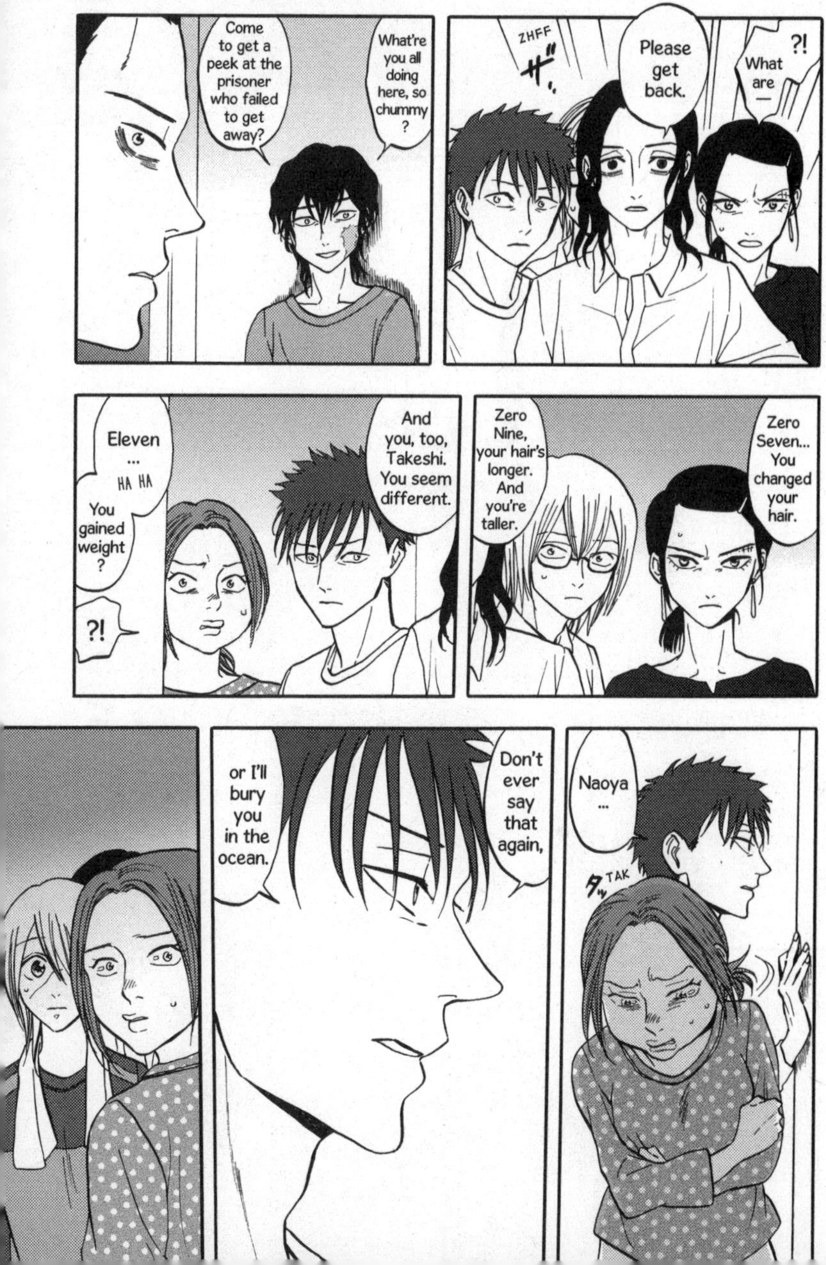
?!
What are —
Please get back.
ZHFF
What're you all doing here, so chummy?
Come to get a peek at the prisoner who failed to get away?
Zero Seven... You changed your hair.
Zero Nine, your hair's longer. And you're taller.
And you, too, Takeshi. You seem different.
Eleven...
HA HA
You gained weight?
?!
Naoya...
TAK
Don't ever say that again,
or I'll bury you in the ocean.

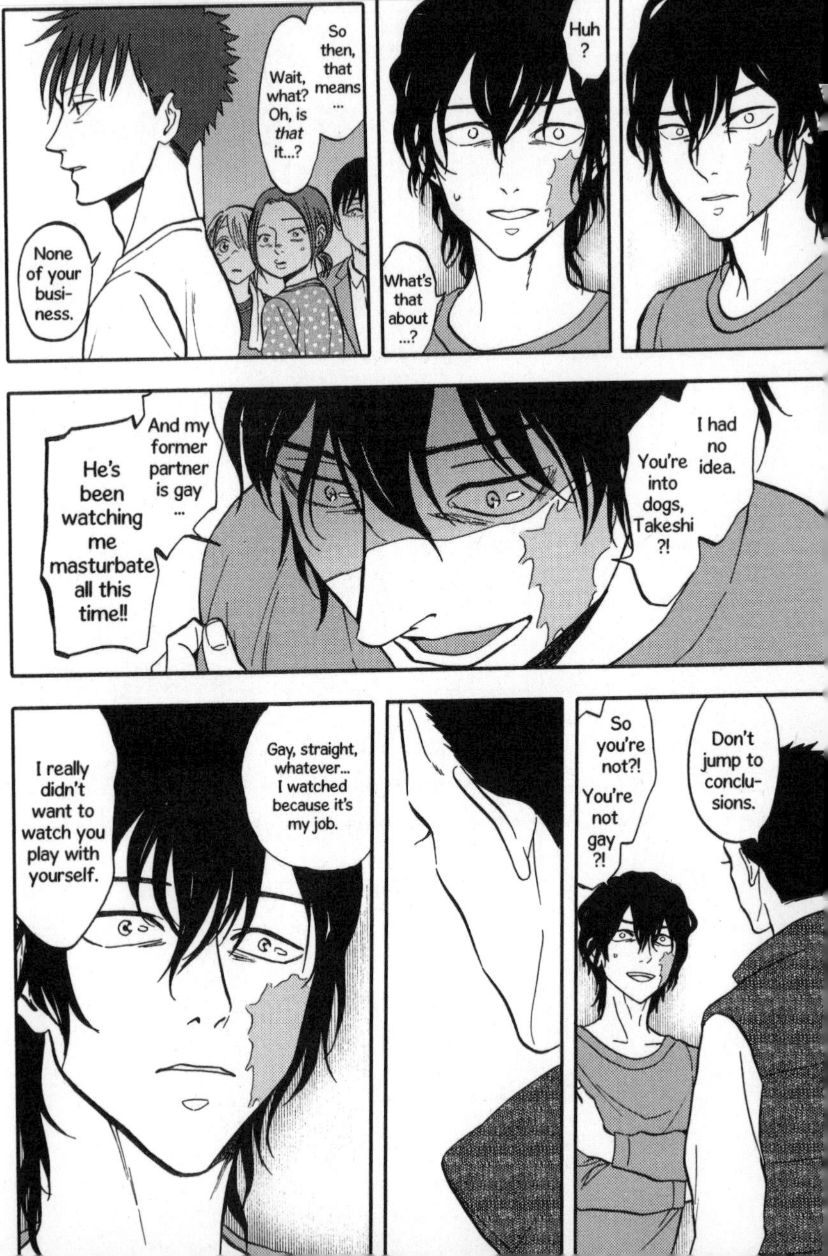
Huh?
What's that about...?
So then, that means...
Wait, what? Oh, is *that* it...?
None of your business.
I had no idea.
You're into dogs, Takeshi?!
And my former partner is gay...
He's been watching me masturbate all this time!!
Don't jump to conclusions.
So you're not?!
You're not gay?!
Gay, straight, whatever... I watched because it's my job.
I really didn't want to watch you play with yourself.

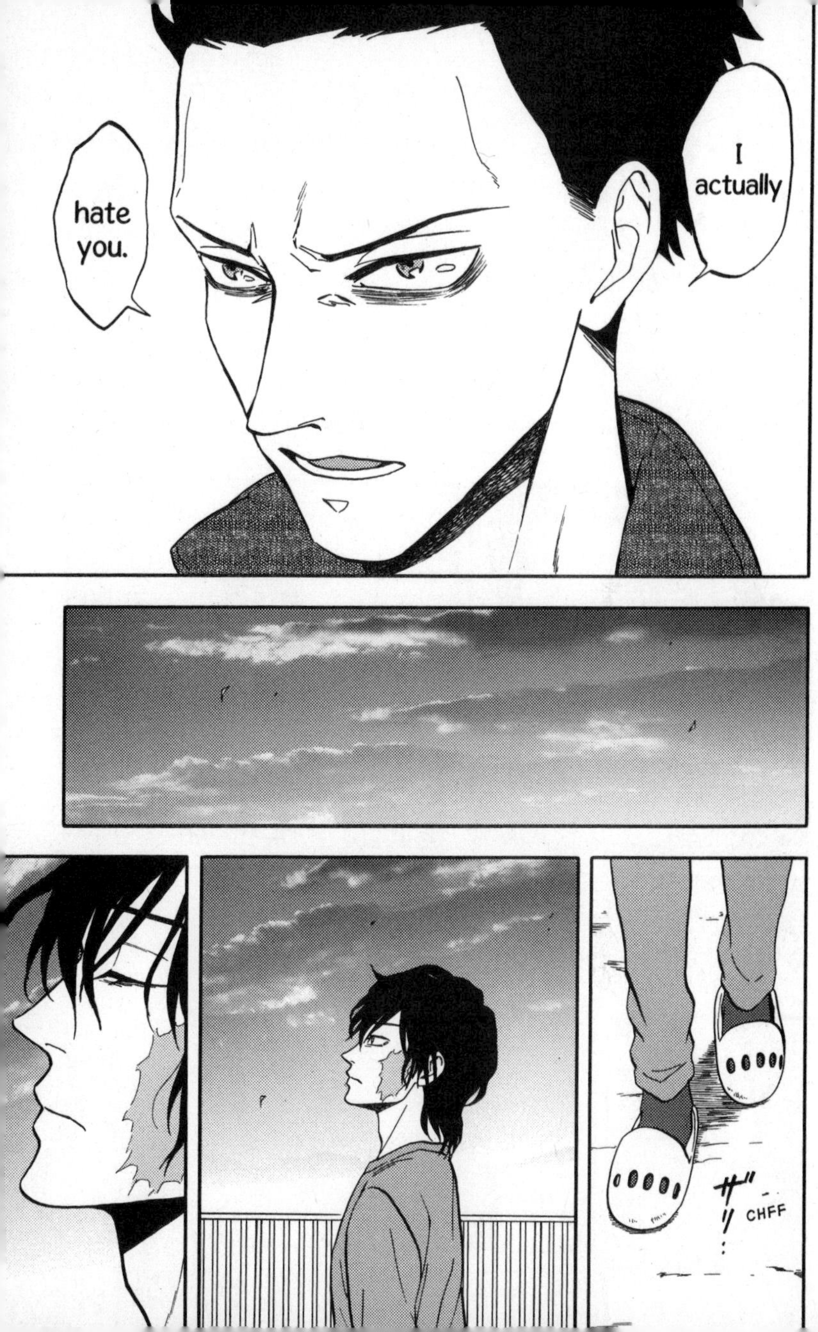
I actually
hate you.
CHFF

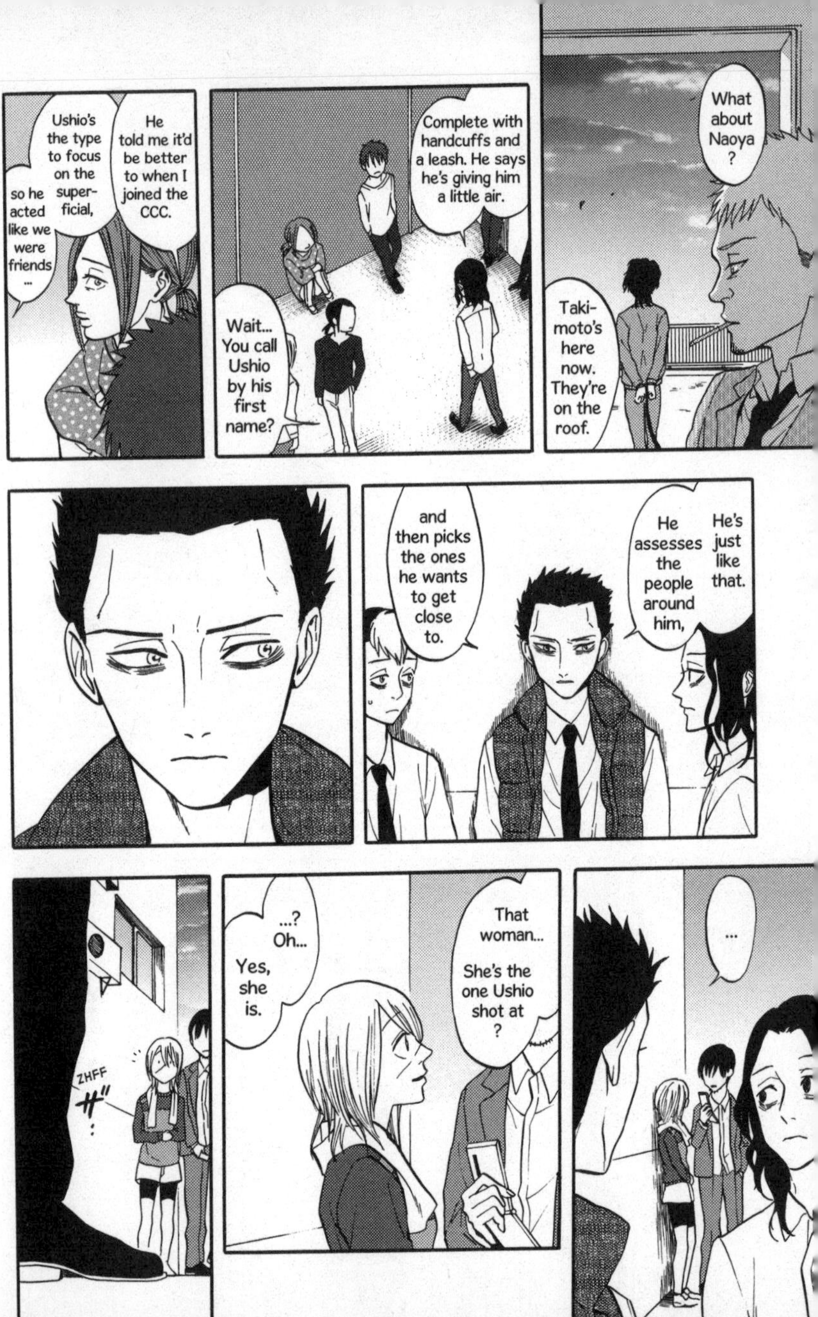
What about Naoya?
Taki-moto's here now. They're on the roof.
Complete with handcuffs and a leash. He says he's giving him a little air.
Wait... You call Ushio by his first name?
He told me it'd be better to when I joined the CCC.
Ushio's the type to focus on the super-ficial,
so he acted like we were friends ...
He's just like that.
He assesses the people around him,
and then picks the ones he wants to get close to.
...
That woman...
She's the one Ushio shot at?
...? Oh...
Yes, she is.
ZHFF

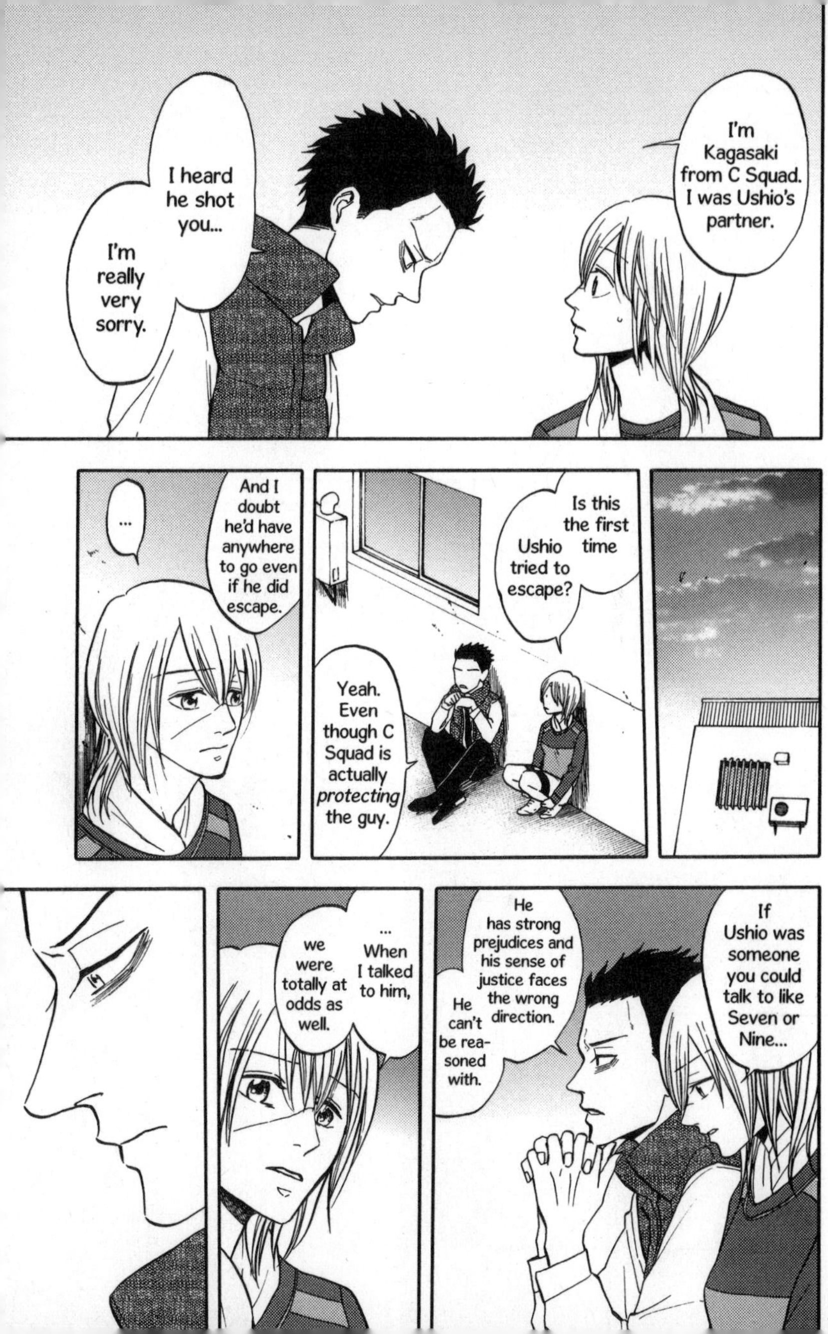
I'm Kagasaki from C Squad. I was Ushio's partner.
I heard he shot you...
I'm really very sorry.
Is this the first time Ushio tried to escape?
Yeah. Even though C Squad is actually *protecting* the guy.
And I doubt he'd have anywhere to go even if he did escape.
...
If Ushio was someone you could talk to like Seven or Nine...
He has strong prejudices and his sense of justice faces the wrong direction.
He can't be rea-soned with.
... When I talked to him,
we were totally at odds as well.

I just totally hate him...

THUP

?! Where ?!

Sawa-zaki?

it almost sounded like, "I love him."

...I'm sorry. Ushio really is...

I wonder why...

ZSH

When he said, "I hate him" just now...

He really...

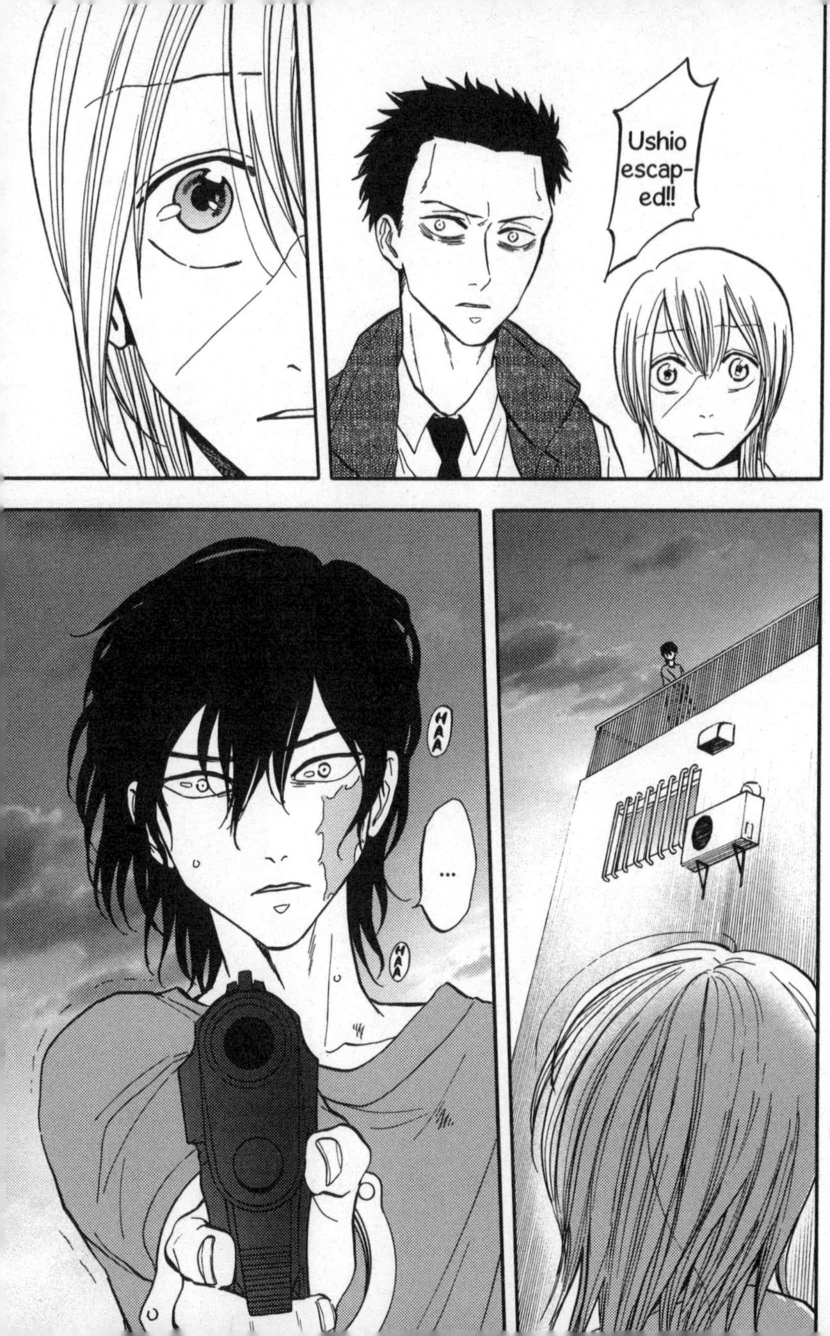

Ushio escap-ed!!
HAA
...
HAA

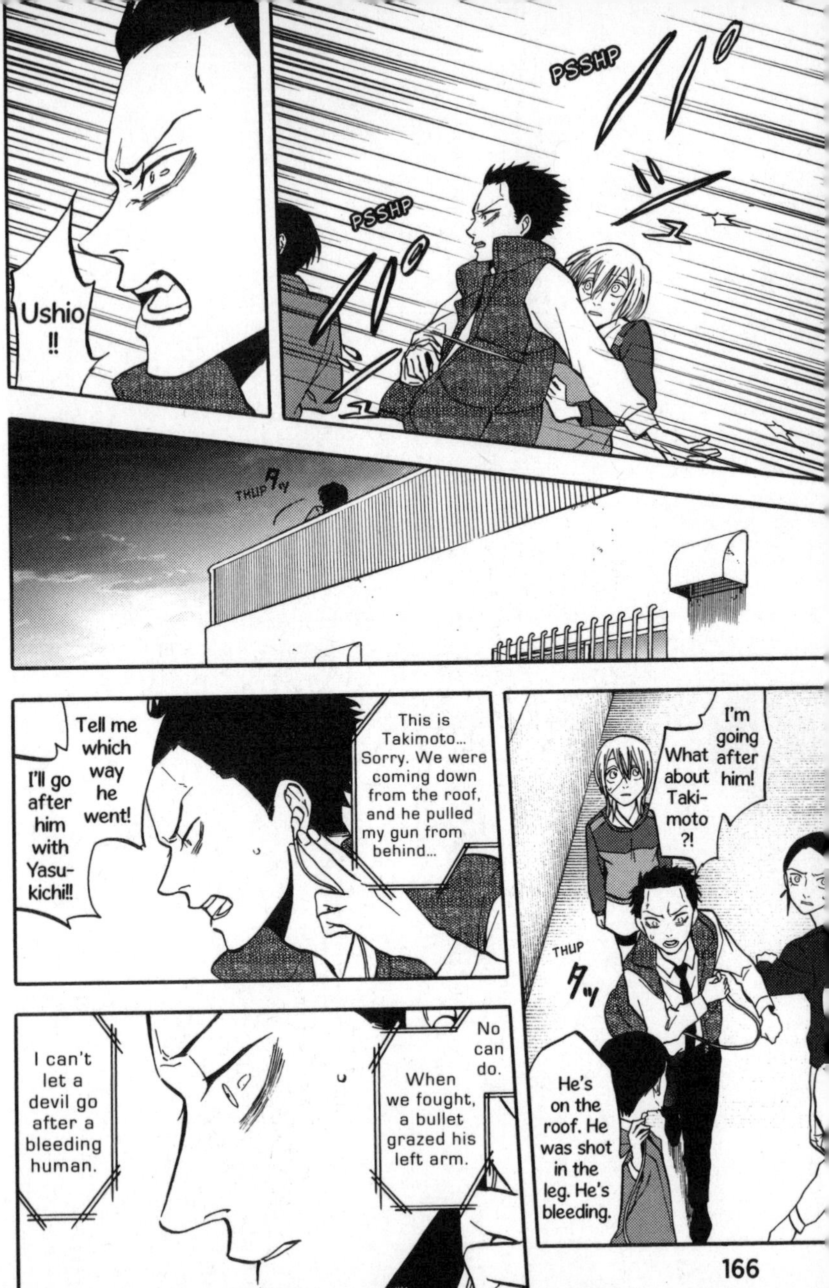

PSSHP
PSSHP
Ushio!!
THUP
I'm going after him!
What about Takimoto?!
THUP
He's on the roof. He was shot in the leg. He's bleeding.
This is Takimoto... Sorry. We were coming down from the roof, and he pulled my gun from behind...
Tell me which way he went!
I'll go after him with Yasukichi!!
No can do.
When we fought, a bullet grazed his left arm.
I can't let a devil go after a bleeding human.

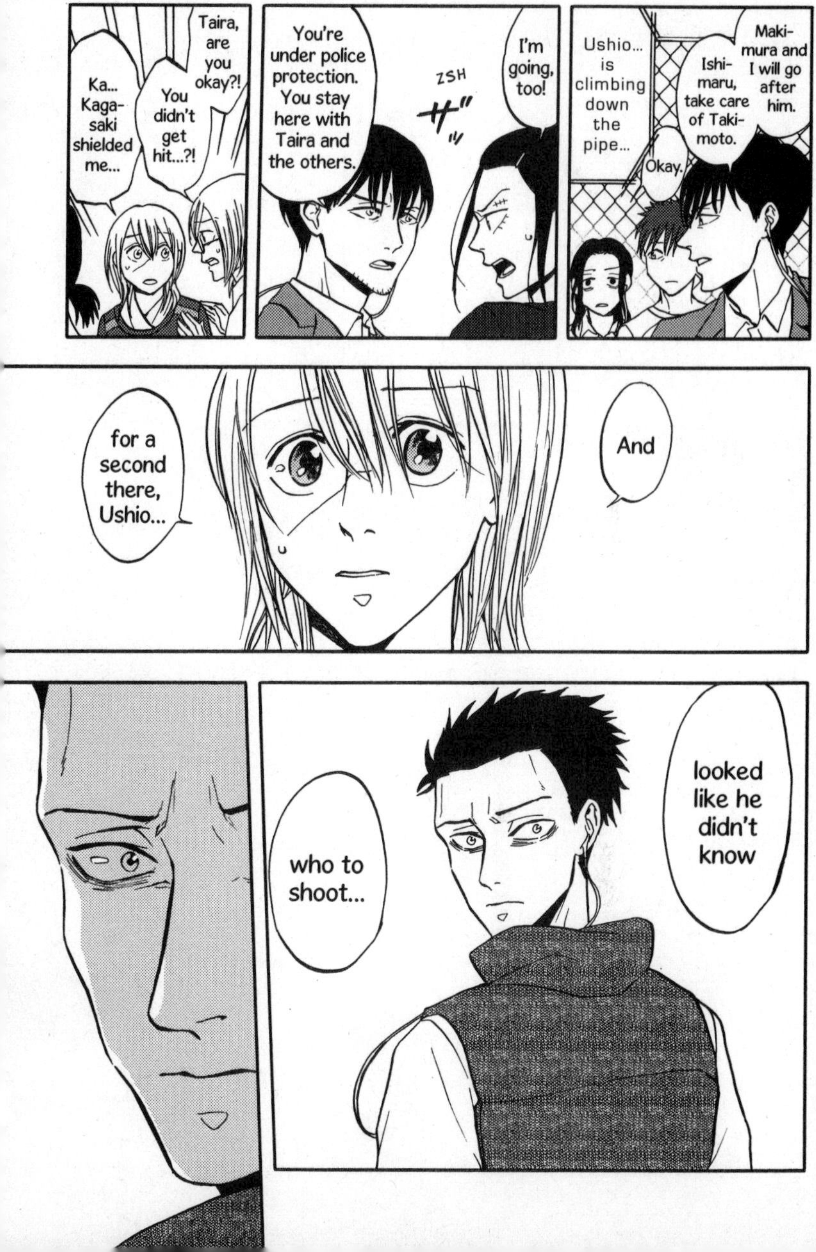
Maki-mura and I will go after him.
Ishi-maru, take care of Taki-moto.
Okay.
Ushio... is climbing down the pipe...
I'm going, too!
ZSH
ザッ
You're under police protection. You stay here with Taira and the others.
Taira, are you okay?!
You didn't get hit...?!
Ka... Kaga-saki shielded me...
And
for a second there, Ushio...
looked like he didn't know
who to shoot...

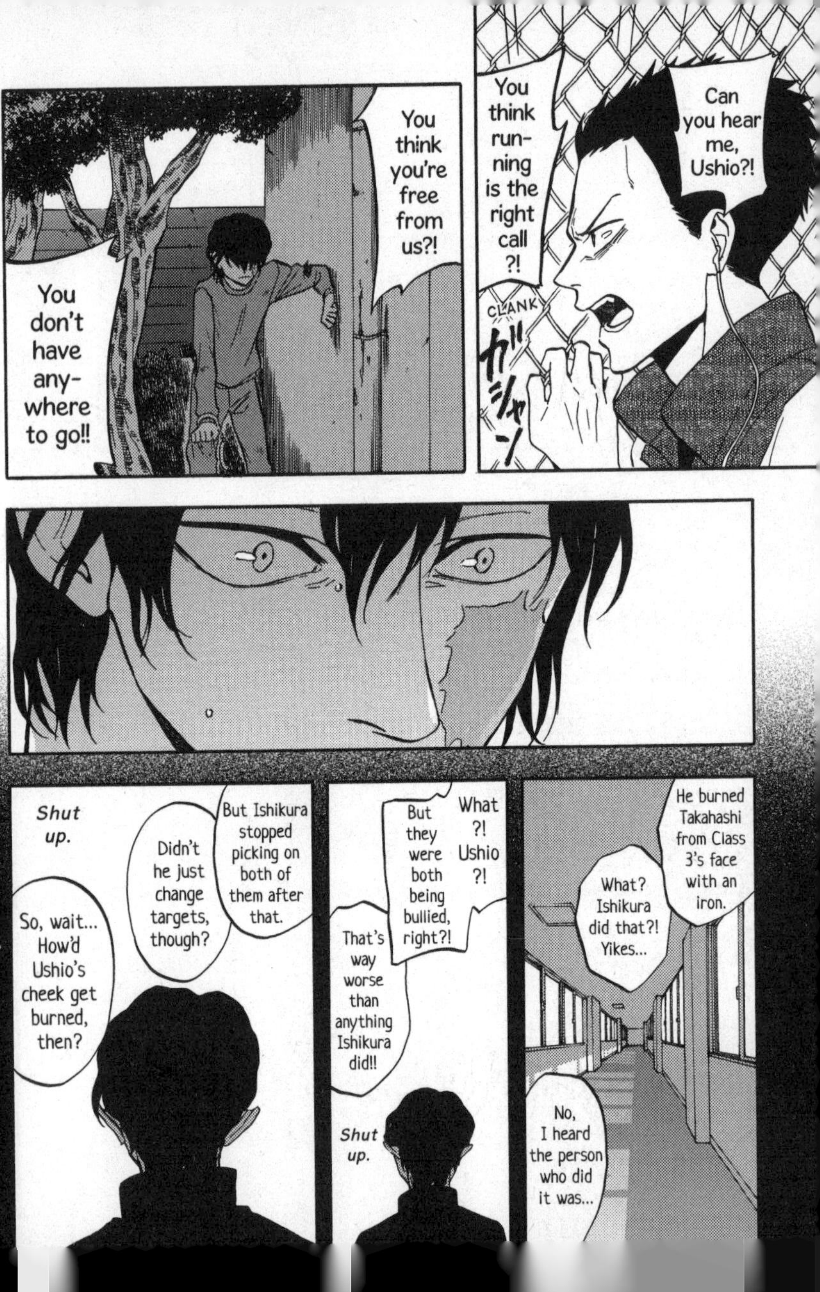

Can you hear me, Ushio?!
You think running is the right call?!
CLANK
ガシャーン
You think you're free from us?!
You don't have anywhere to go!!
He burned Takahashi from Class 3's face with an iron.
What? Ishikura did that?! Yikes...
No, I heard the person who did it was...
What?! Ushio?!
But they were both being bullied, right?!
That's way worse than anything Ishikura did!!
Shut up.
But Ishikura stopped picking on both of them after that.
Didn't he just change targets, though?
Shut up.
So, wait... How'd Ushio's cheek get burned, then?

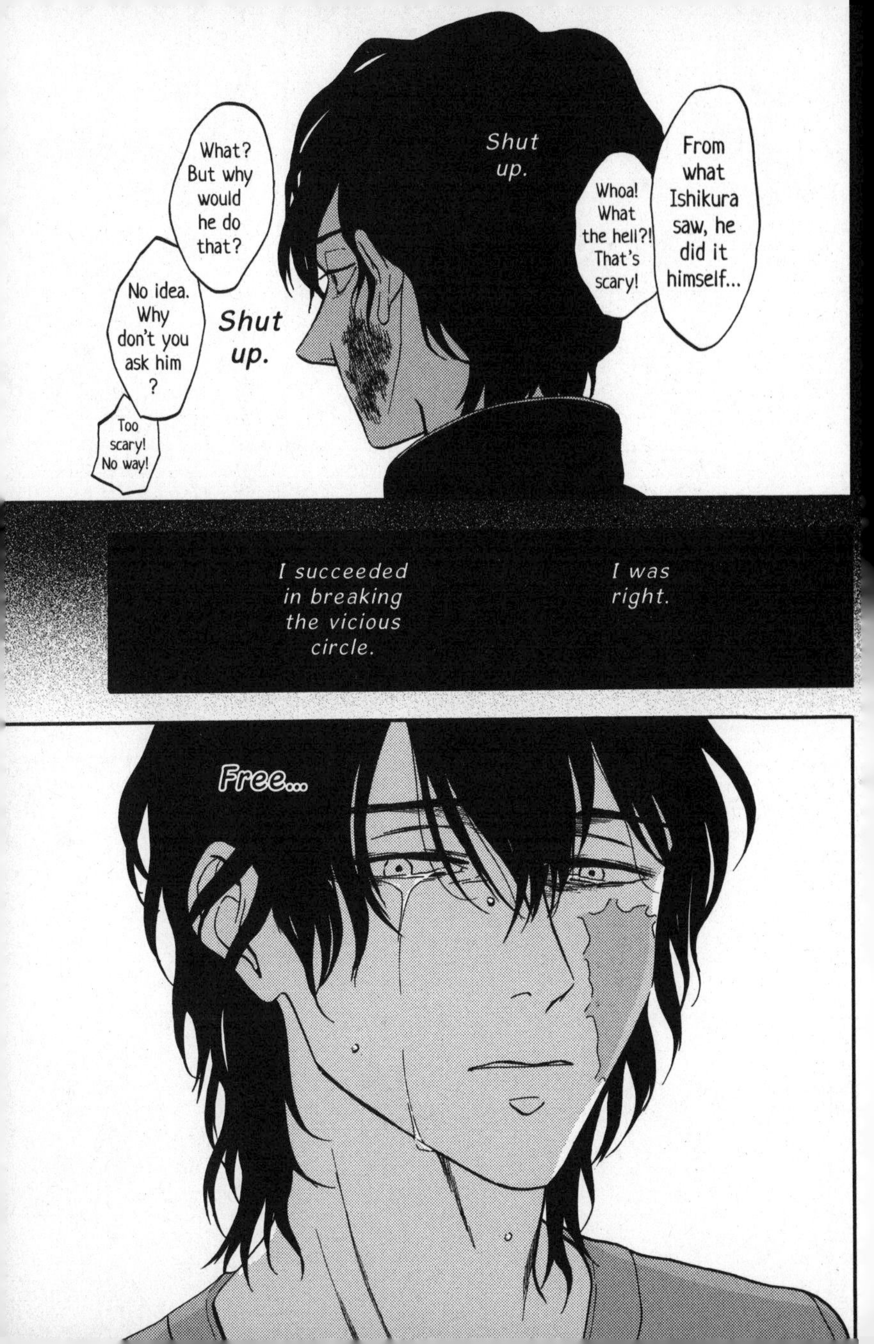
From what Ishikura saw, he did it himself...
Whoa! What the hell?! That's scary!
Shut up.
What? But why would he do that?
No idea. Why don't you ask him?
Shut up.
Too scary! No way!
I was right.
I succeeded in breaking the vicious circle.
Free...

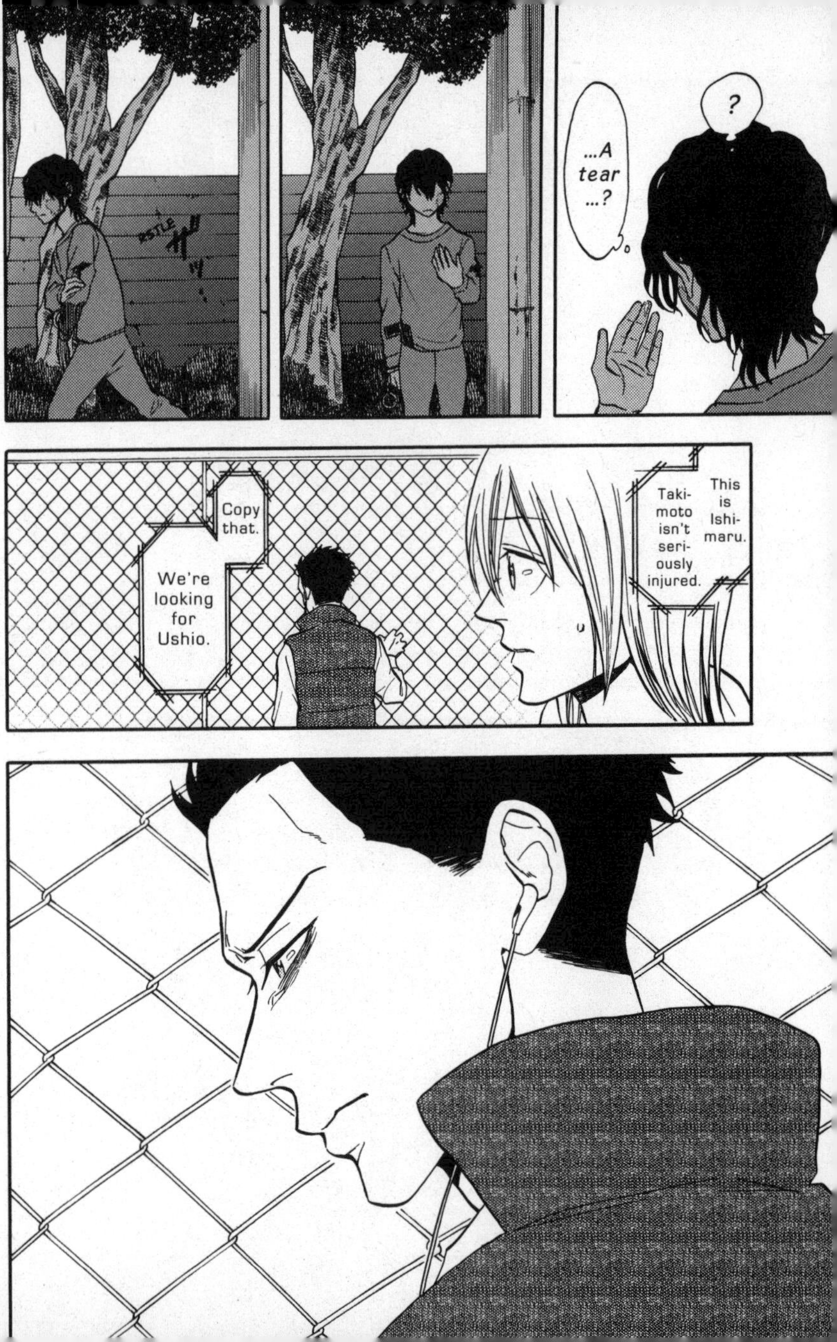
?
...A tear ...?
This is Ishimaru.
Takimoto isn't seriously injured.
Copy that.
We're looking for Ushio.

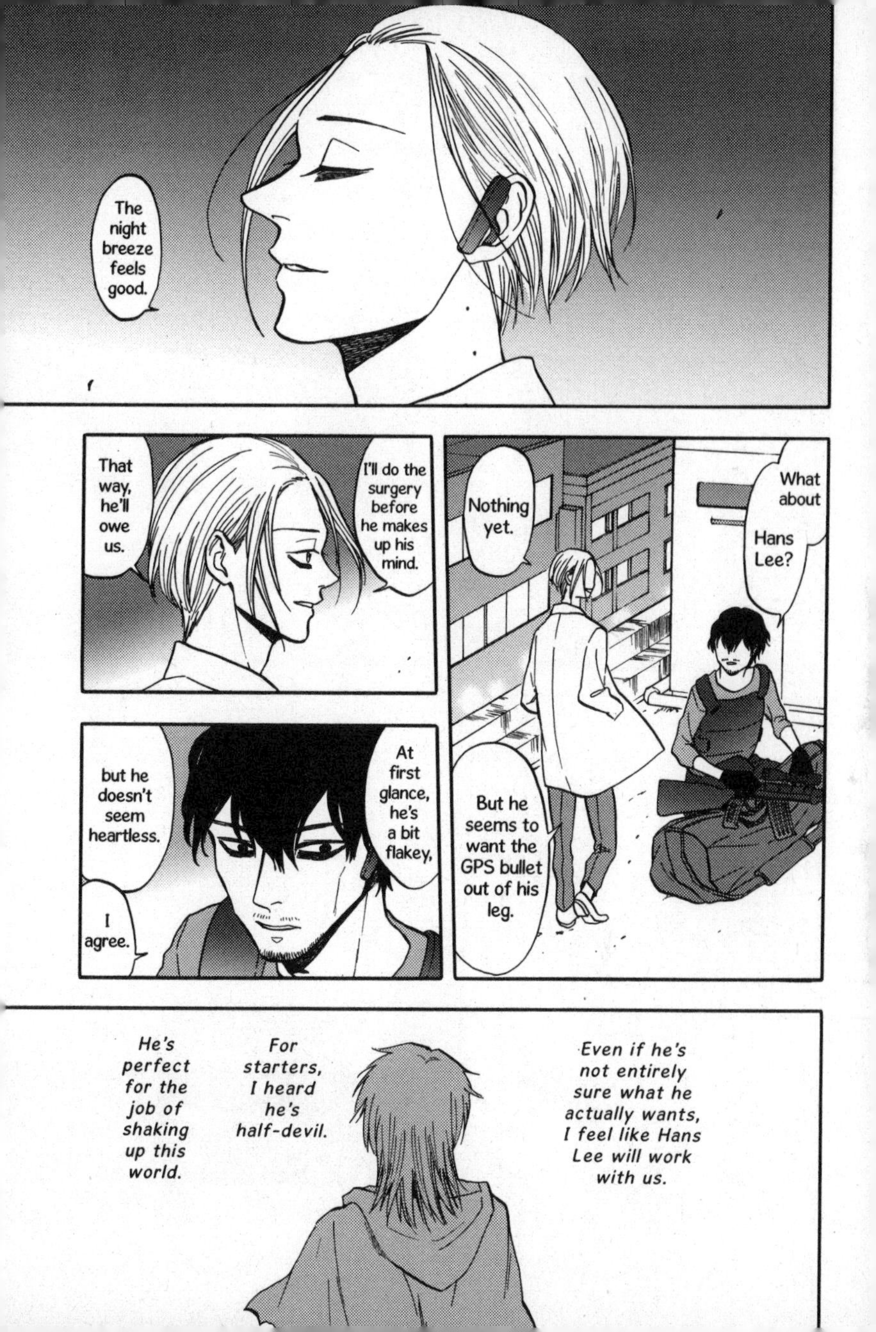
The night breeze feels good.
What about Hans Lee?
Nothing yet.
But he seems to want the GPS bullet out of his leg.
I'll do the surgery before he makes up his mind.
That way, he'll owe us.
At first glance, he's a bit flakey,
but he doesn't seem heartless.
I agree.
Even if he's not entirely sure what he actually wants, I feel like Hans Lee will work with us.
For starters, I heard he's half-devil.
He's perfect for the job of shaking up this world.

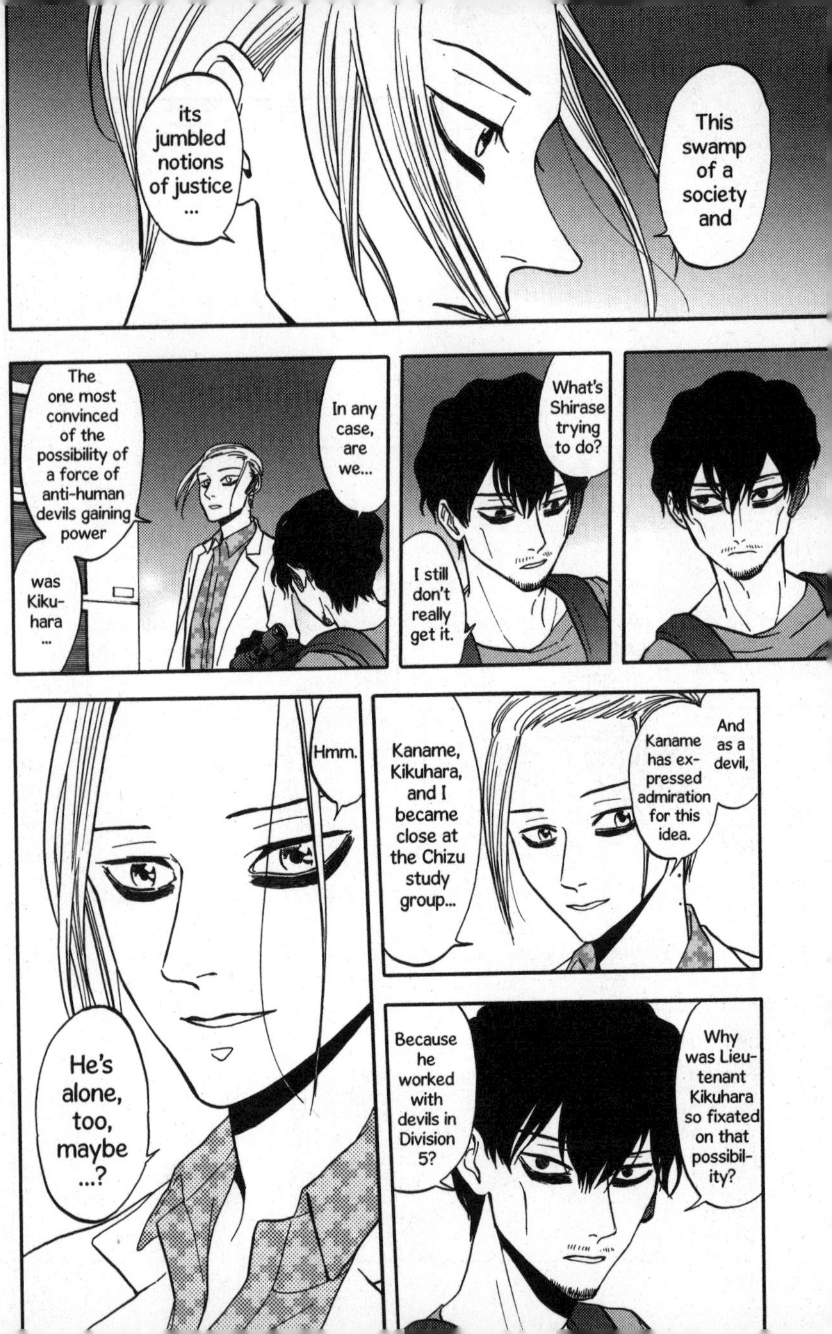
This swamp of a society and
its jumbled notions of justice ...
What's Shirase trying to do?
I still don't really get it.
In any case, are we...
The one most convinced of the possibility of a force of anti-human devils gaining power
was Kiku-hara ...
And as a devil,
Kaname has ex-pressed admiration for this idea.
Kaname, Kikuhara, and I became close at the Chizu study group...
Why was Lieu-tenant Kikuhara so fixated on that possibil-ity?
Because he worked with devils in Division 5?
Hmm.
He's alone, too, maybe ...?

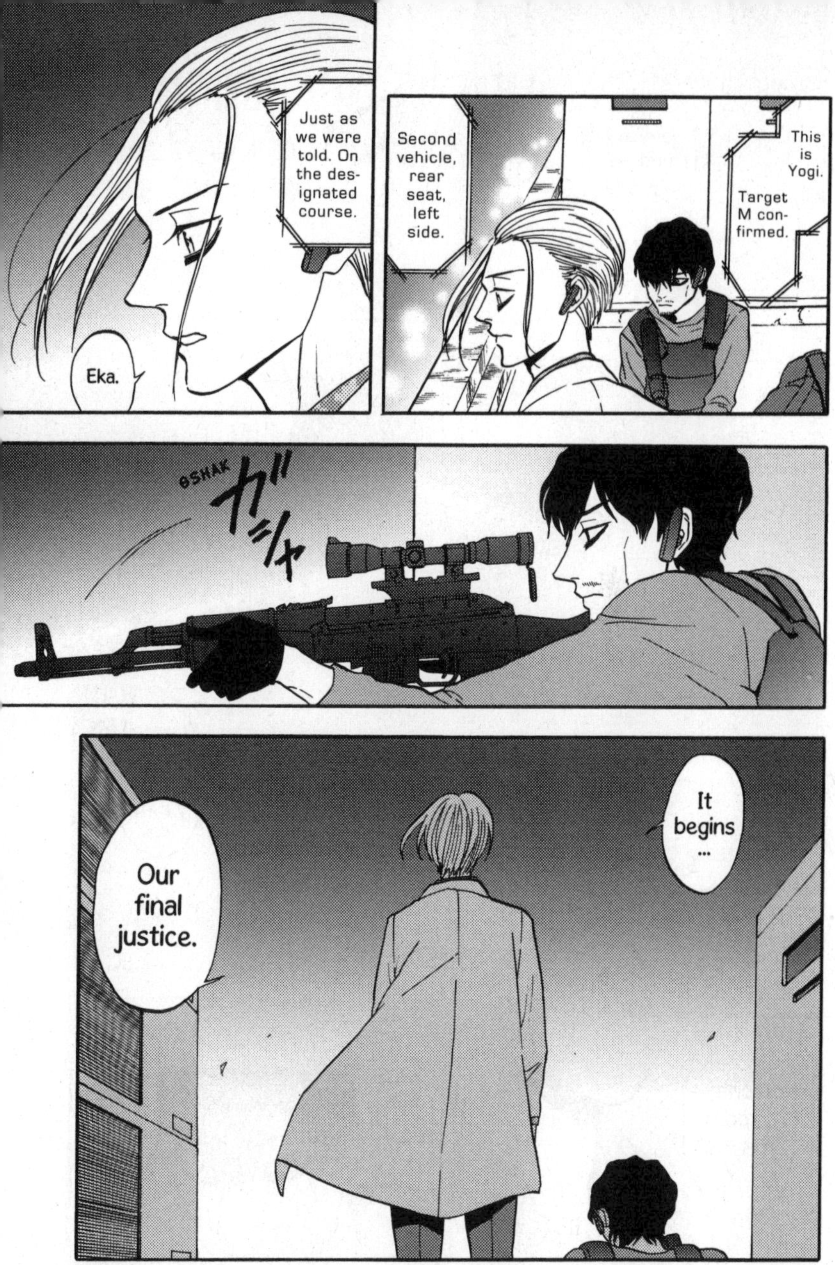
This is Yogi.
Target M confirmed.
Second vehicle, rear seat, left side.
Just as we were told. On the designated course.
Eka.
GSHAK
ガシャ
It begins...
Our final justice.

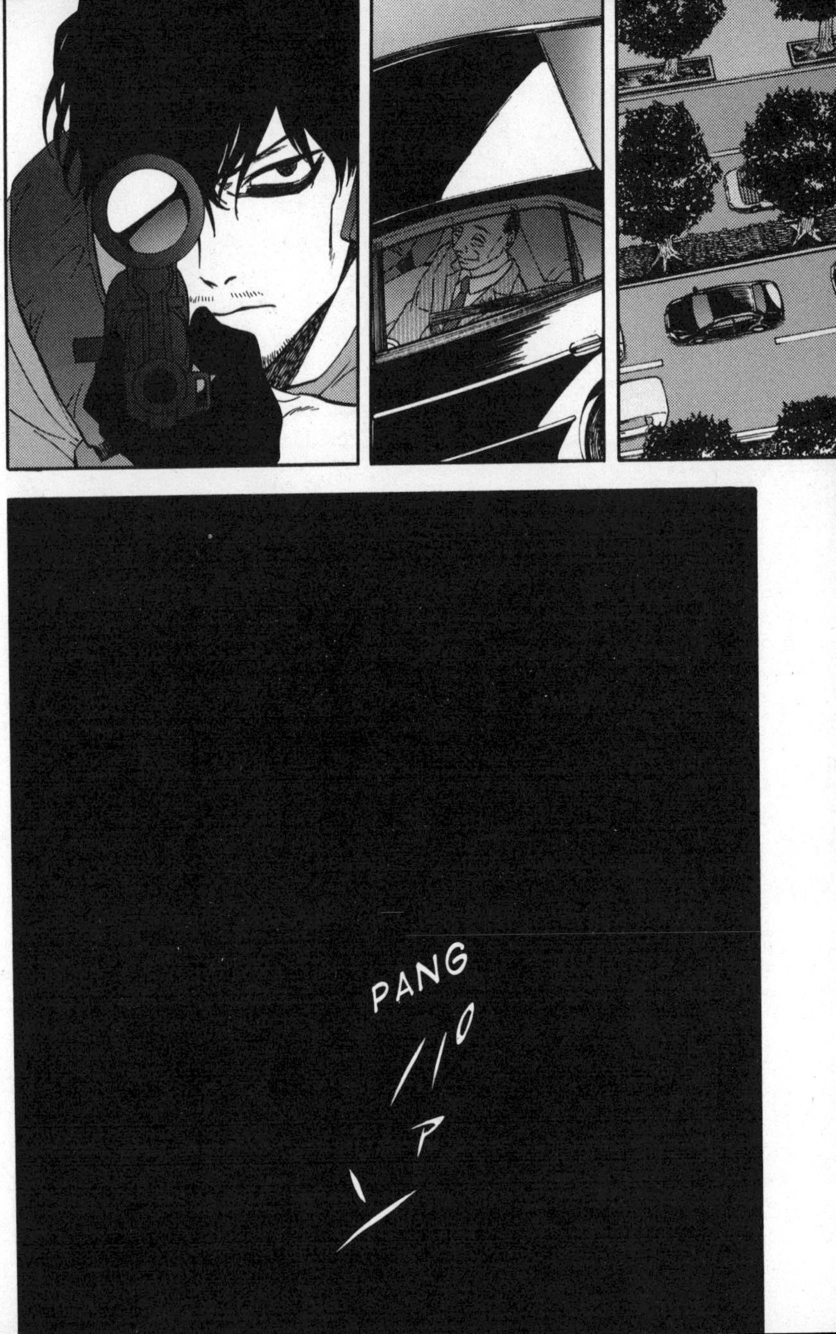
PANG

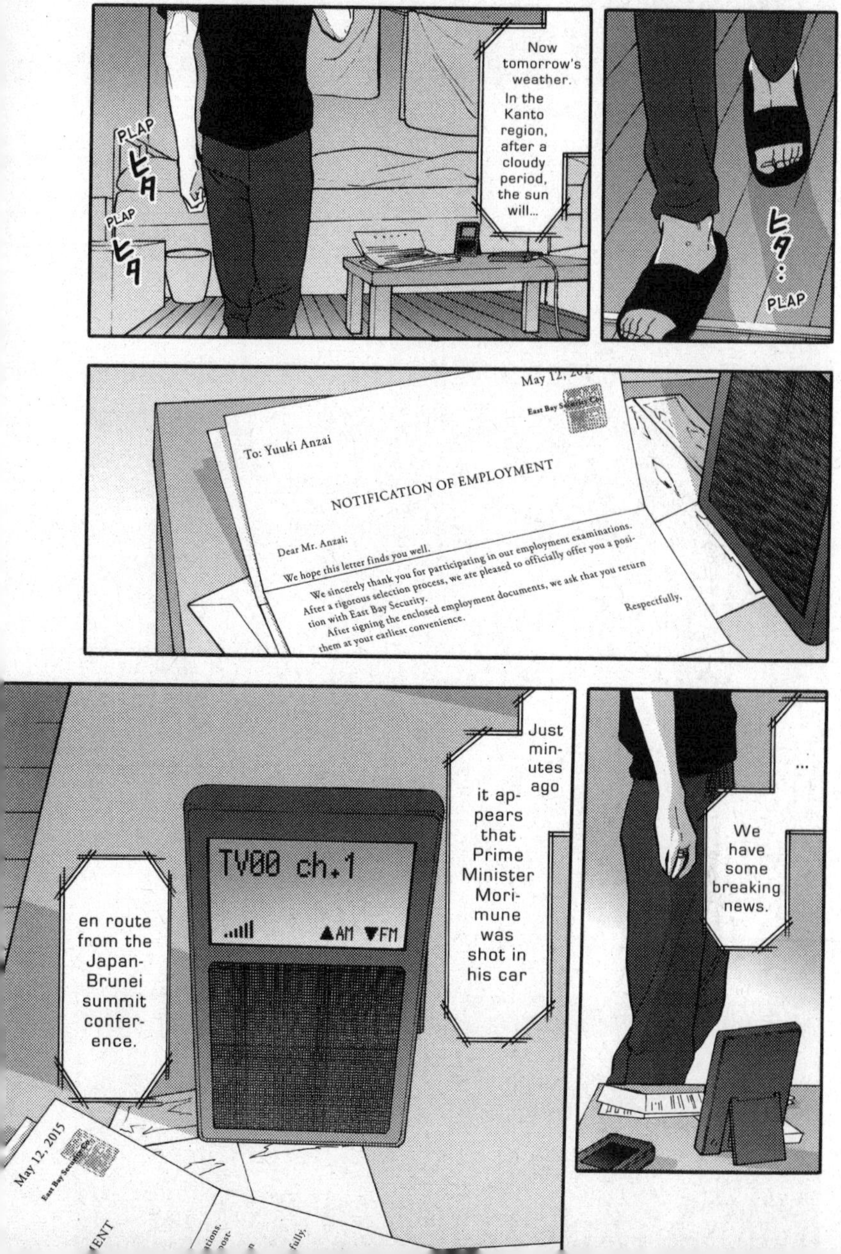
ヒタ…
PLAP
Now tomorrow's weather.
In the Kanto region, after a cloudy period, the sun will...
PLAP
ヒタ
PLAP
ヒタ
May 12, 2015
East Bay Security Co.
To: Yuuki Anzai
NOTIFICATION OF EMPLOYMENT
Dear Mr. Anzai;
We hope this letter finds you well.
We sincerely thank you for participating in our employment examinations. After a rigorous selection process, we are pleased to officially offer you a position with East Bay Security.
After signing the enclosed employment documents, we ask that you return them at your earliest convenience.
Respectfully,
...
We have some breaking news.
Just minutes ago
it appears that Prime Minister Morimune was shot in his car
en route from the Japan-Brunei summit conference.
TV00 ch.1
▲AM ▼FM
May 12, 2015
East Bay Security Co.

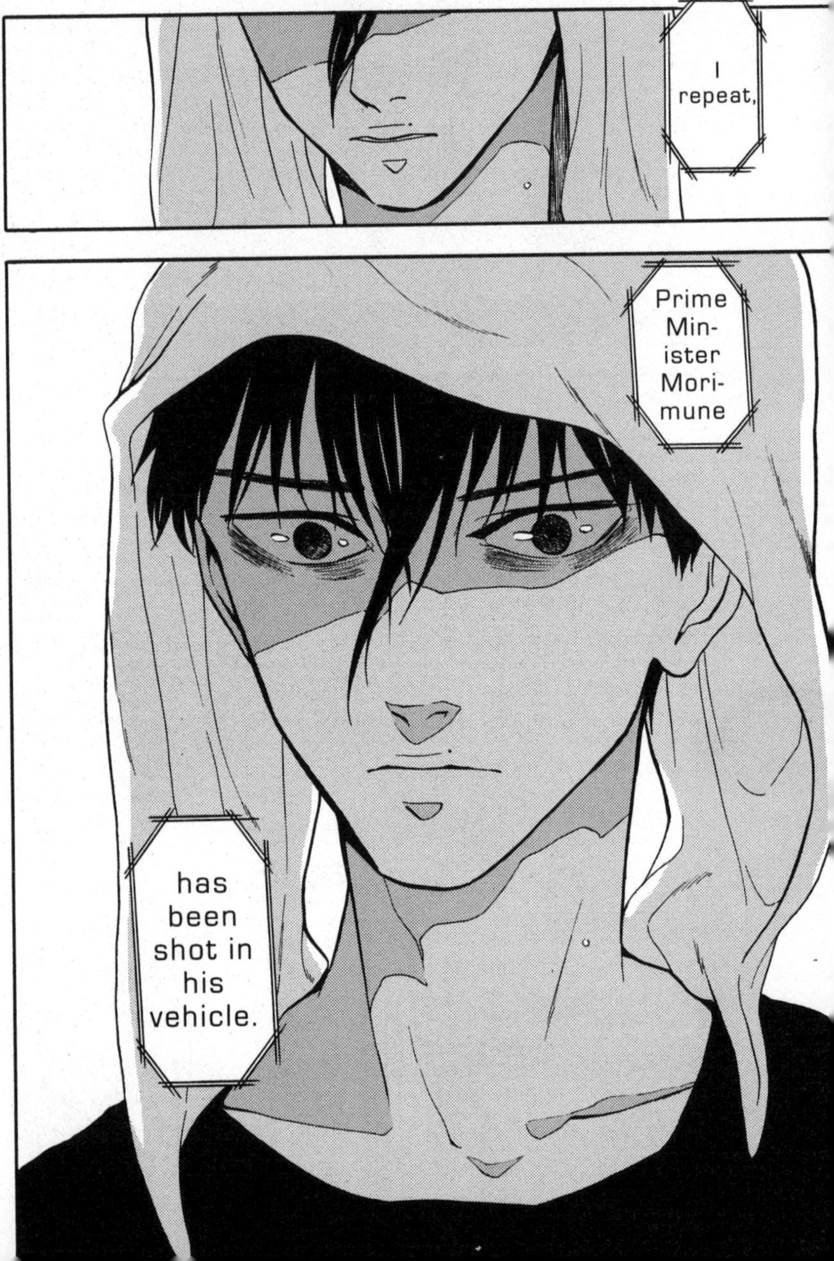
I repeat,
Prime Min-ister Mori-mune
has been shot in his vehicle.

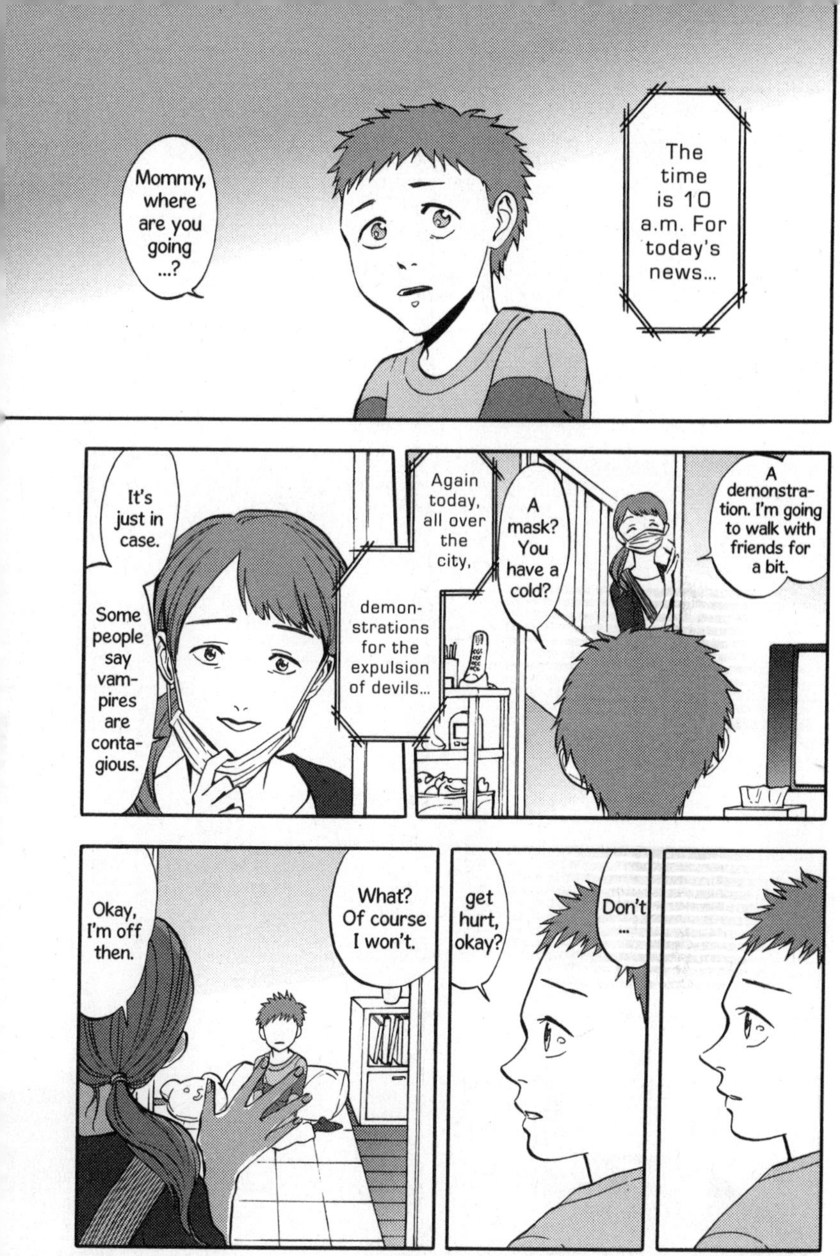
The time is 10 a.m. For today's news...
Mommy, where are you going ...?
A demonstration. I'm going to walk with friends for a bit.
A mask? You have a cold?
Again today, all over the city, demonstrations for the expulsion of devils...
It's just in case.
Some people say vampires are contagious.
Don't ...
get hurt, okay?
What? Of course I won't.
Okay, I'm off then.

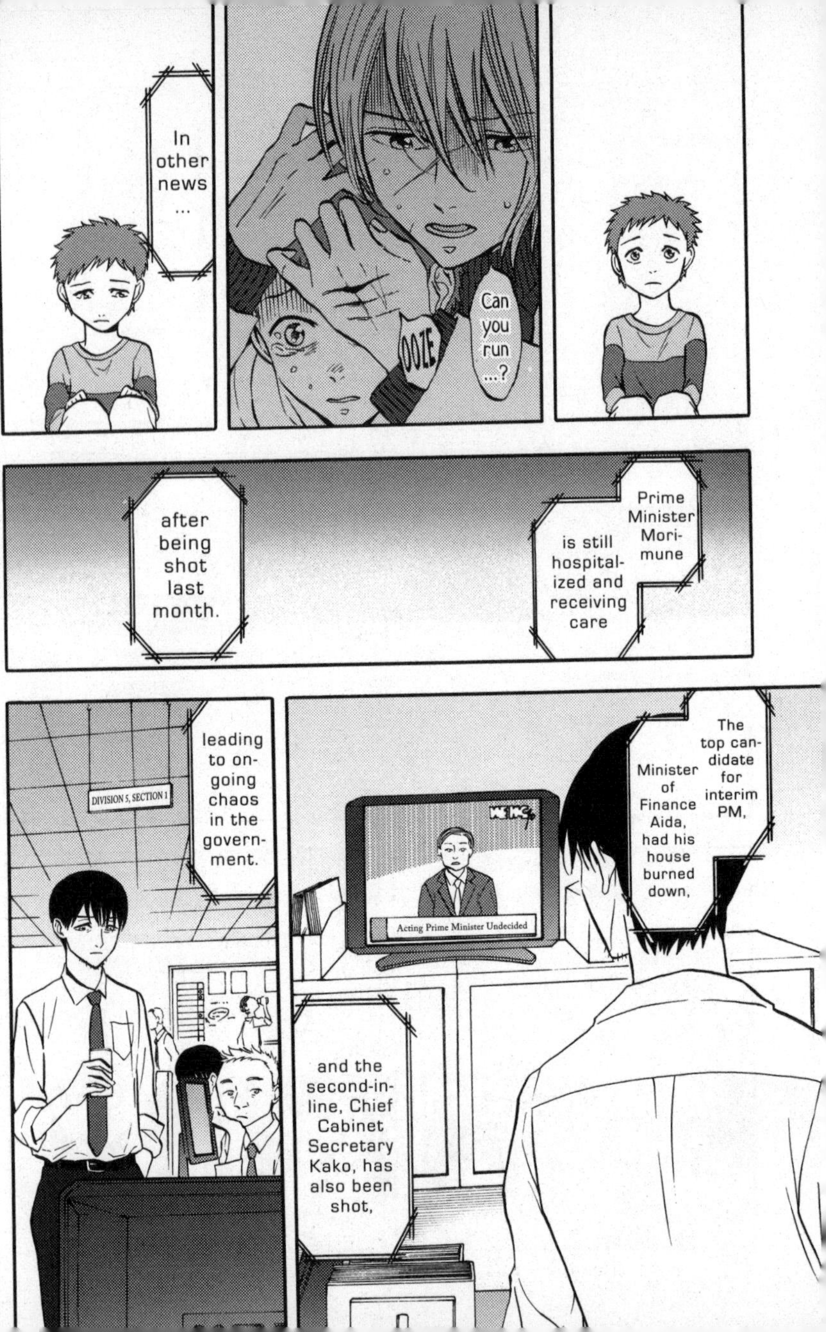
DOZE
Can you run ...?
In other news ...
Prime Minister Mori-mune is still hospital-ized and receiving care
after being shot last month.
The top can-didate for interim PM, Minister of Finance Aida, had his house burned down,
Acting Prime Minister Undecided
and the second-in-line, Chief Cabinet Secretary Kako, has also been shot,
DIVISION 5, SECTION 1
leading to on-going chaos in the govern-ment.

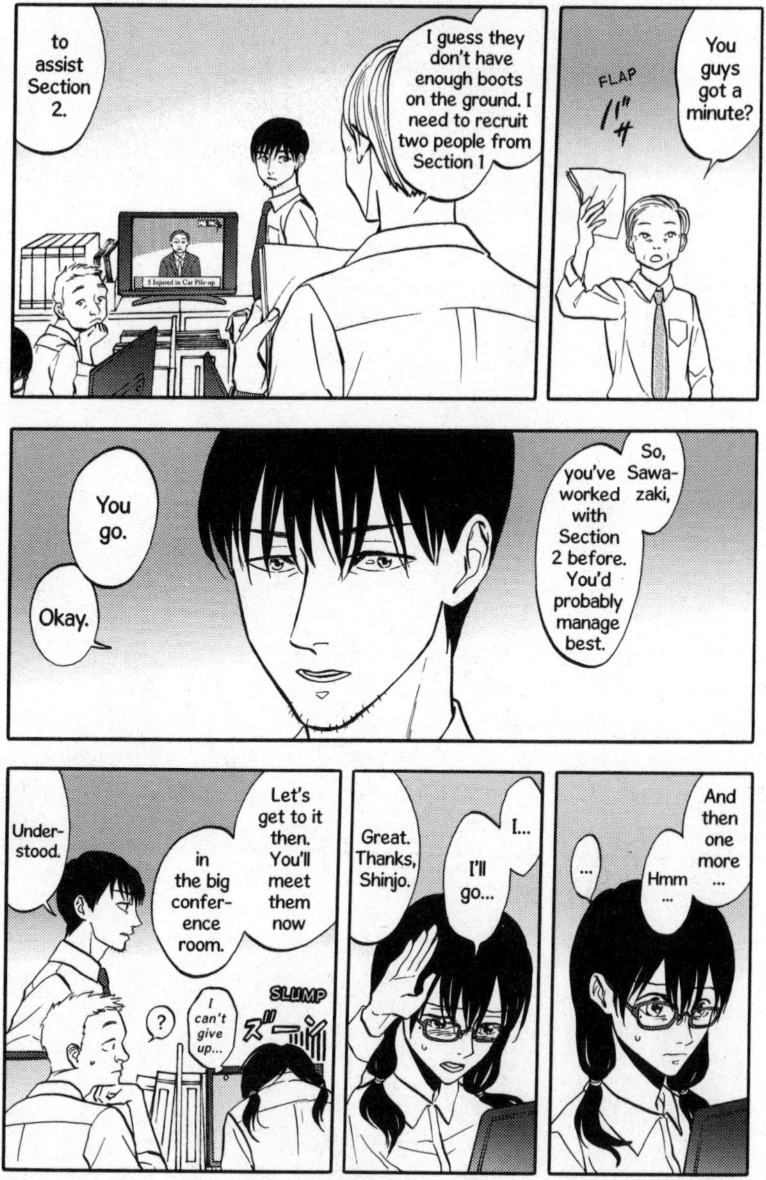
You guys got a minute?
FLAP
バッ
I guess they don't have enough boots on the ground. I need to recruit two people from Section 1
to assist Section 2.
5 Injured in Car Pile-up
So, Sawazaki, you've worked with Section 2 before. You'd probably manage best.
You go.
Okay.
And then one more ...
Hmm ...
...
I...
I'll go...
Great. Thanks, Shinjo.
Let's get to it then. You'll meet them now
in the big conference room.
Understood.
SLUMP
ズーン
I can't give up...
?

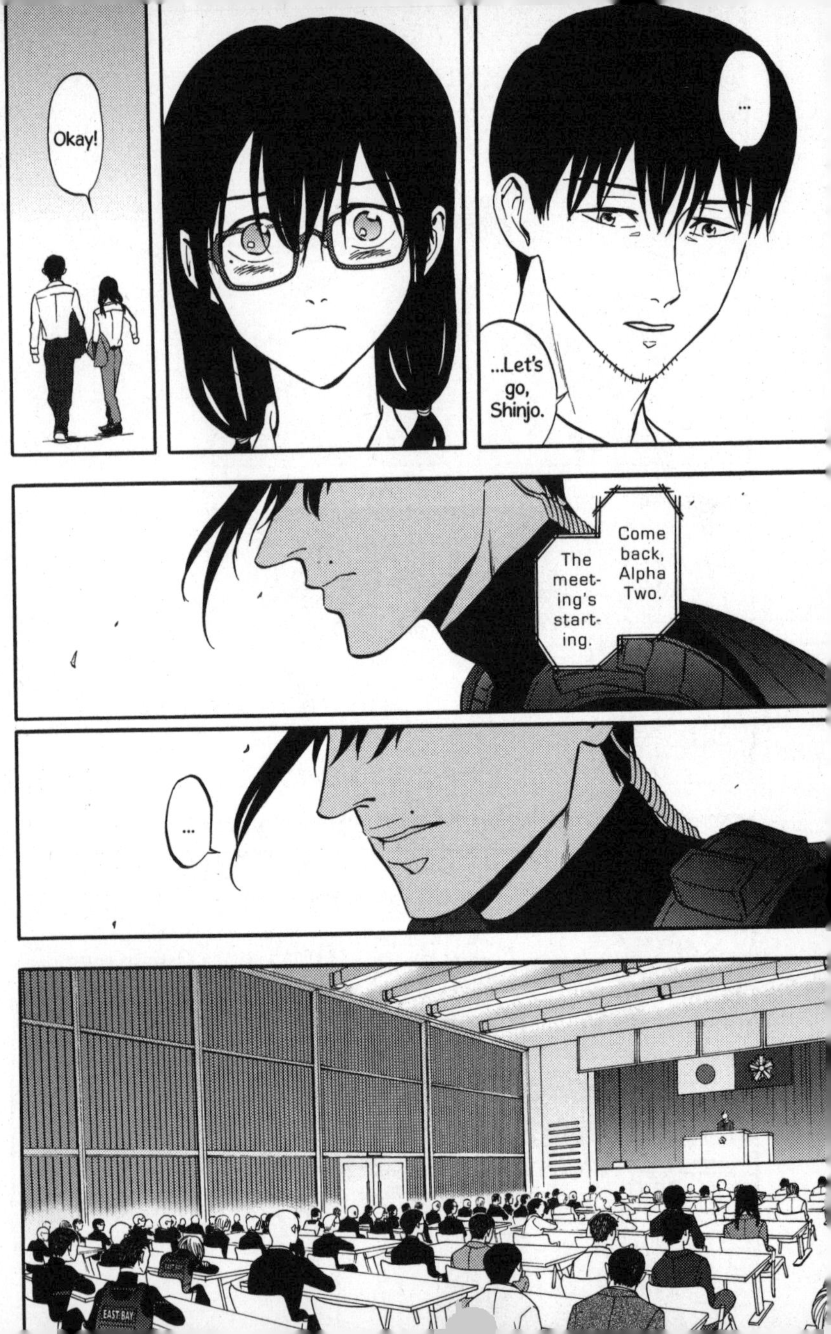
...
...Let's go, Shinjo.
Okay!
Come back, Alpha Two.
The meeting's starting.
...
EAST BAY
EAST BAY

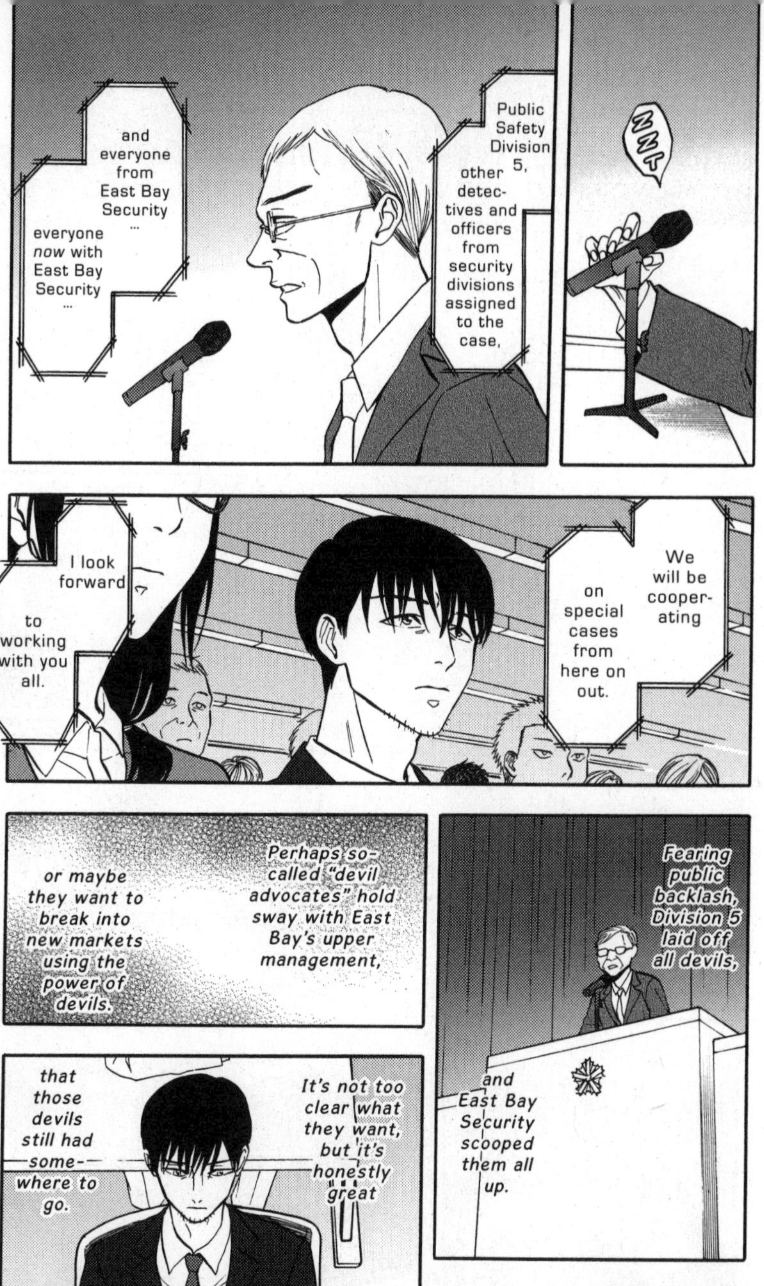
NNT
Public Safety Division 5, other detectives and officers from security divisions assigned to the case,
and everyone from East Bay Security...
everyone *now* with East Bay Security...
We will be cooperating on special cases from here on out.
I look forward to working with you all.
Fearing public backlash, Division 5 laid off all devils,
and East Bay Security scooped them all up.
Perhaps so-called "devil advocates" hold sway with East Bay's upper management,
or maybe they want to break into new markets using the power of devils.
It's not too clear what they want, but it's honestly great
that those devils still had somewhere to go.

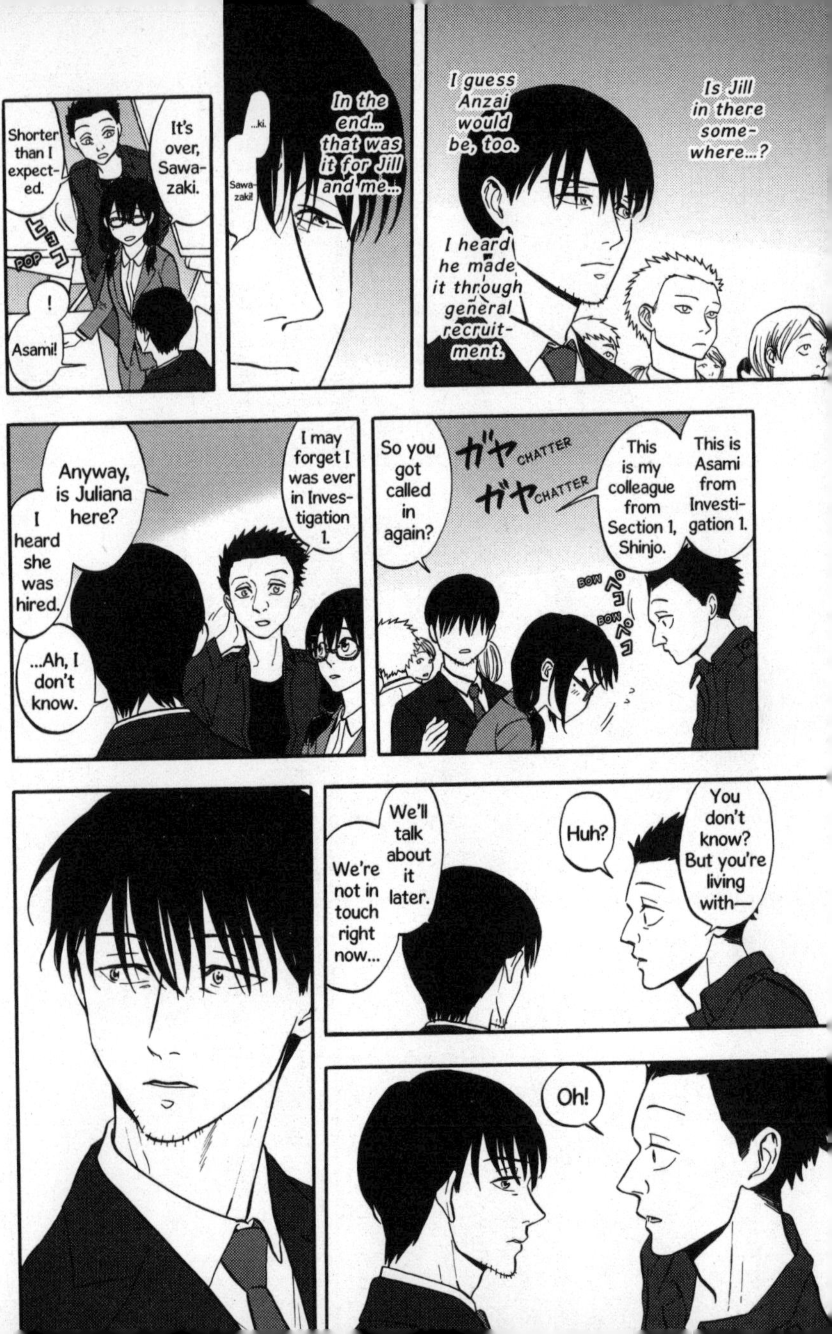

Is Jill in there somewhere...?
I guess Anzai would be, too.
I heard he made it through general recruitment.
In the end... that was it for Jill and me...
...ki.
Sawazaki!
It's over, Sawazaki.
Shorter than I expected.
ヒョコ POP
!
Asami!
This is Asami from Investigation 1.
This is my colleague from Section 1, Shinjo.
ガヤ CHATTER
ガヤ CHATTER
So you got called in again?
ペコ BOW
ペコ BOW
I may forget I was ever in Investigation 1.
Anyway, is Juliana here?
I heard she was hired.
...Ah, I don't know.
You don't know? But you're living with—
Huh?
We'll talk about it later.
We're not in touch right now...
Oh!

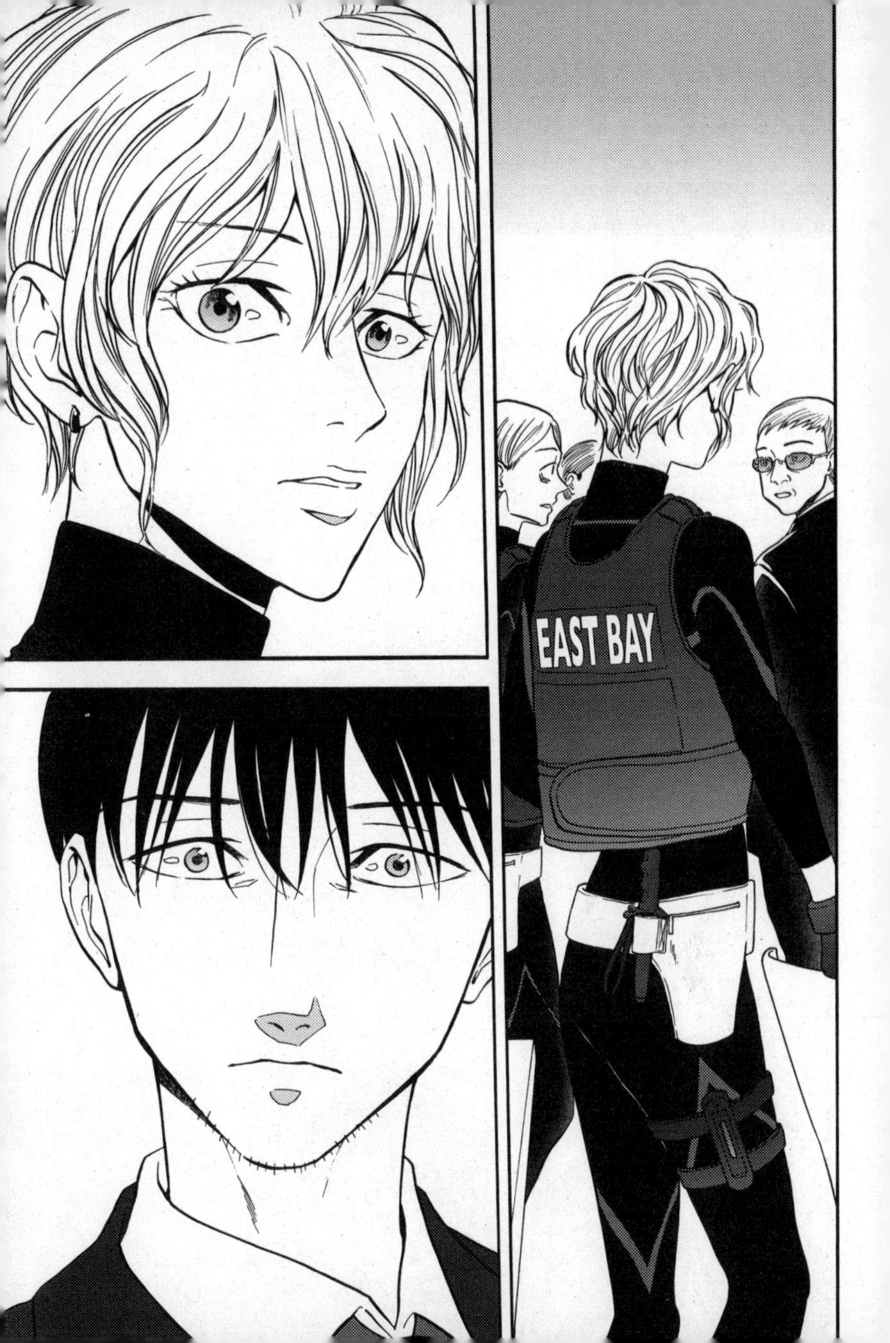
EAST BAY

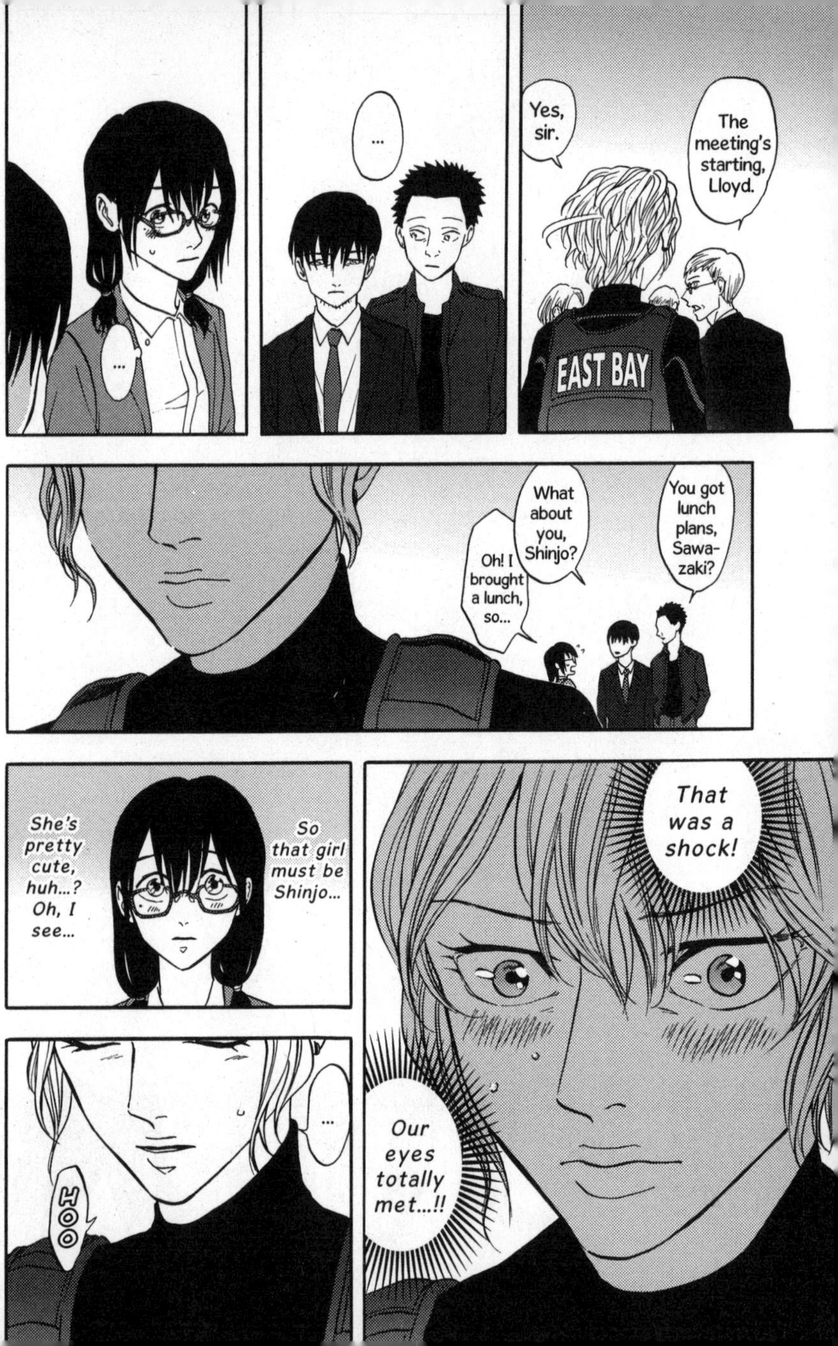

The meeting's starting, Lloyd.
Yes, sir.
EAST BAY
...
...
You got lunch plans, Sawa-zaki?
What about you, Shinjo?
Oh! I brought a lunch, so...
That was a shock!
Our eyes totally met...!!
So that girl must be Shinjo...
She's pretty cute, huh...? Oh, I see...
...
HOO

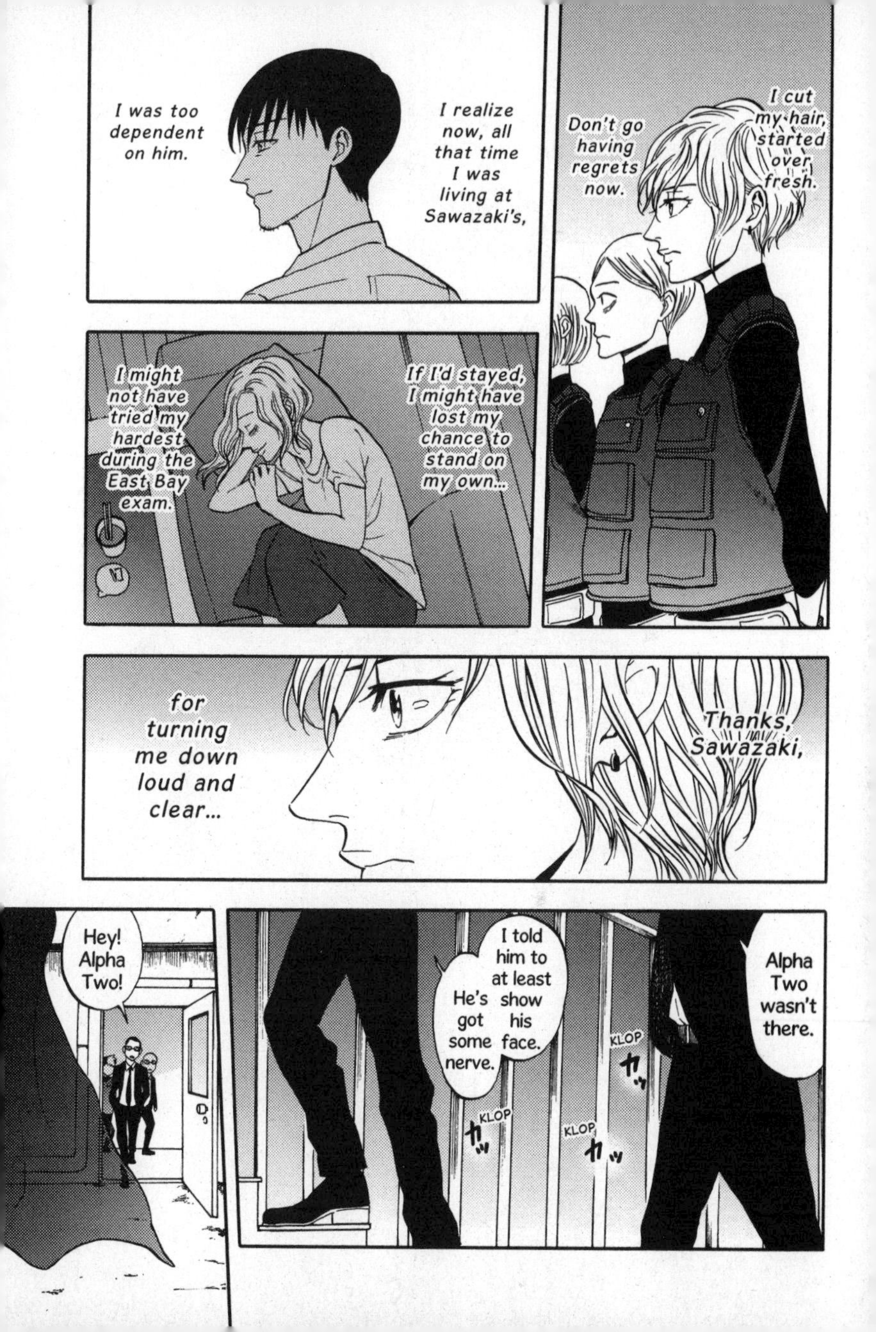

I cut my hair, started over fresh.
Don't go having regrets now.
I realize now, all that time I was living at Sawazaki's,
I was too dependent on him.
If I'd stayed, I might have lost my chance to stand on my own...
I might not have tried my hardest during the East Bay exam.
Thanks, Sawazaki,
for turning me down loud and clear...
Alpha Two wasn't there.
KLOP
カッ
I told him to at least show his face.
He's got some nerve.
KLOP
カッ
KLOP
カッ
Hey! Alpha Two!

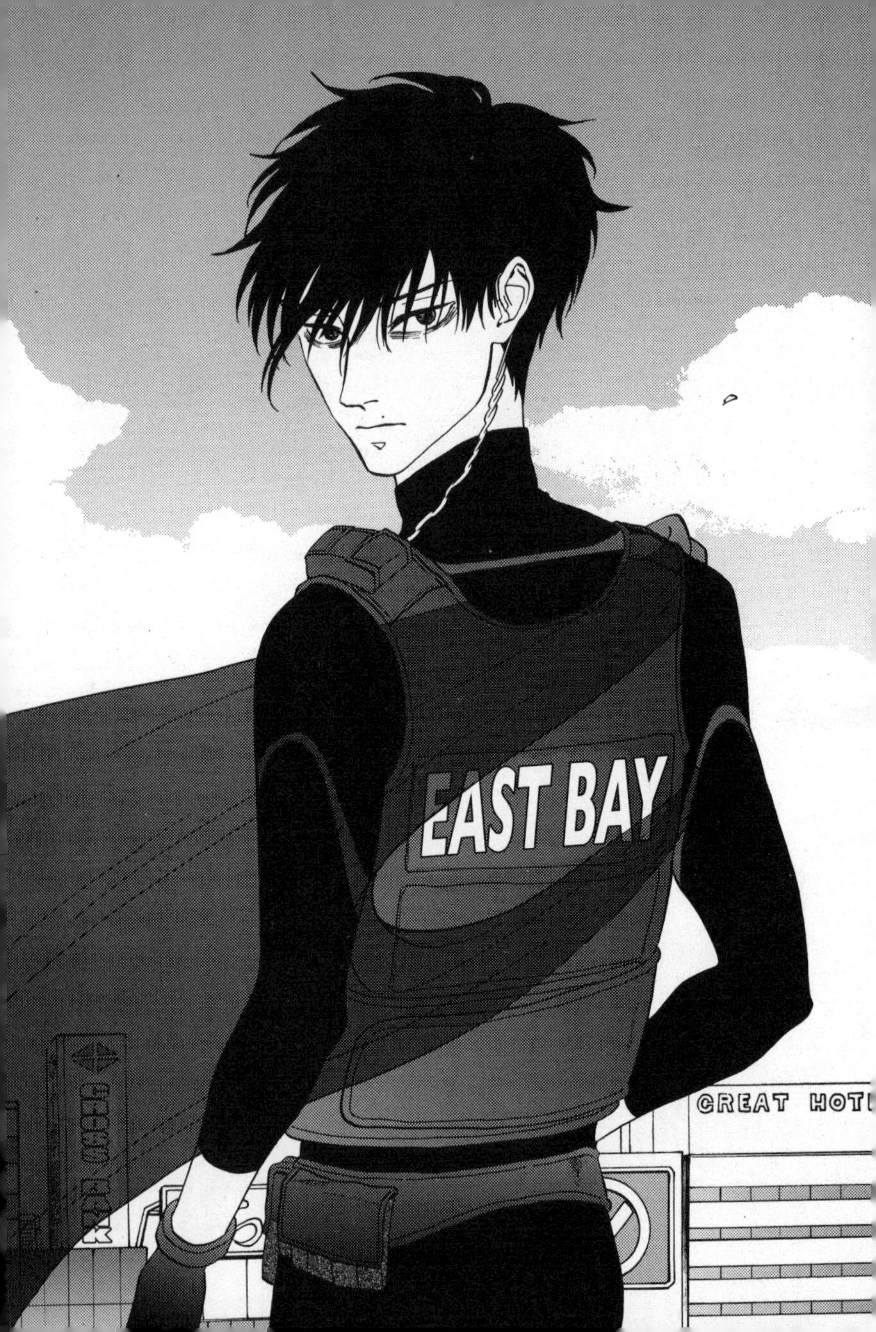
EAST BAY
GREAT HOT

Line 57
New Front

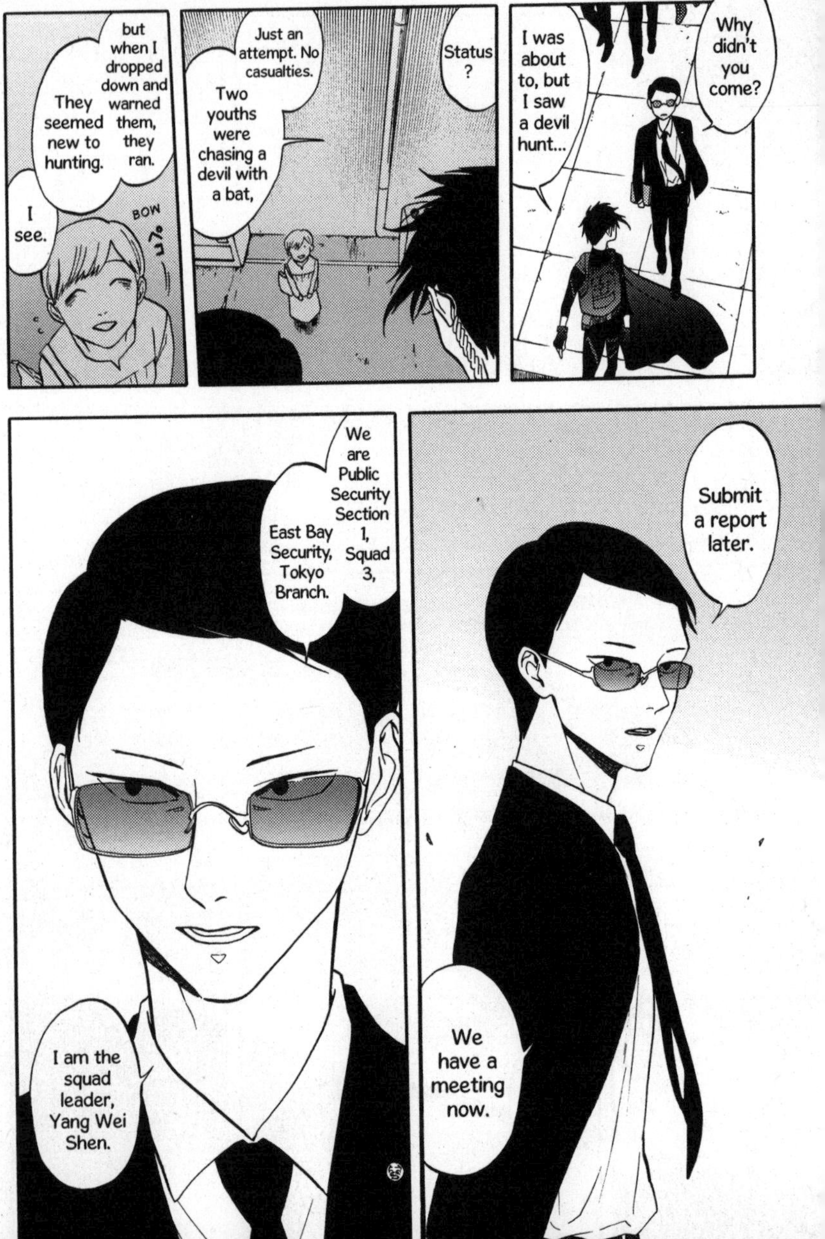
Why didn't you come?
I was about to, but I saw a devil hunt...
Status?
Just an attempt. No casualties.
Two youths were chasing a devil with a bat,
but when I dropped down and warned them, they ran.
They seemed new to hunting.
BOW
ペコ
I see.
Submit a report later.
We have a meeting now.
We are Public Security Section 1, Squad 3,
East Bay Security, Tokyo Branch.
I am the squad leader, Yang Wei Shen.

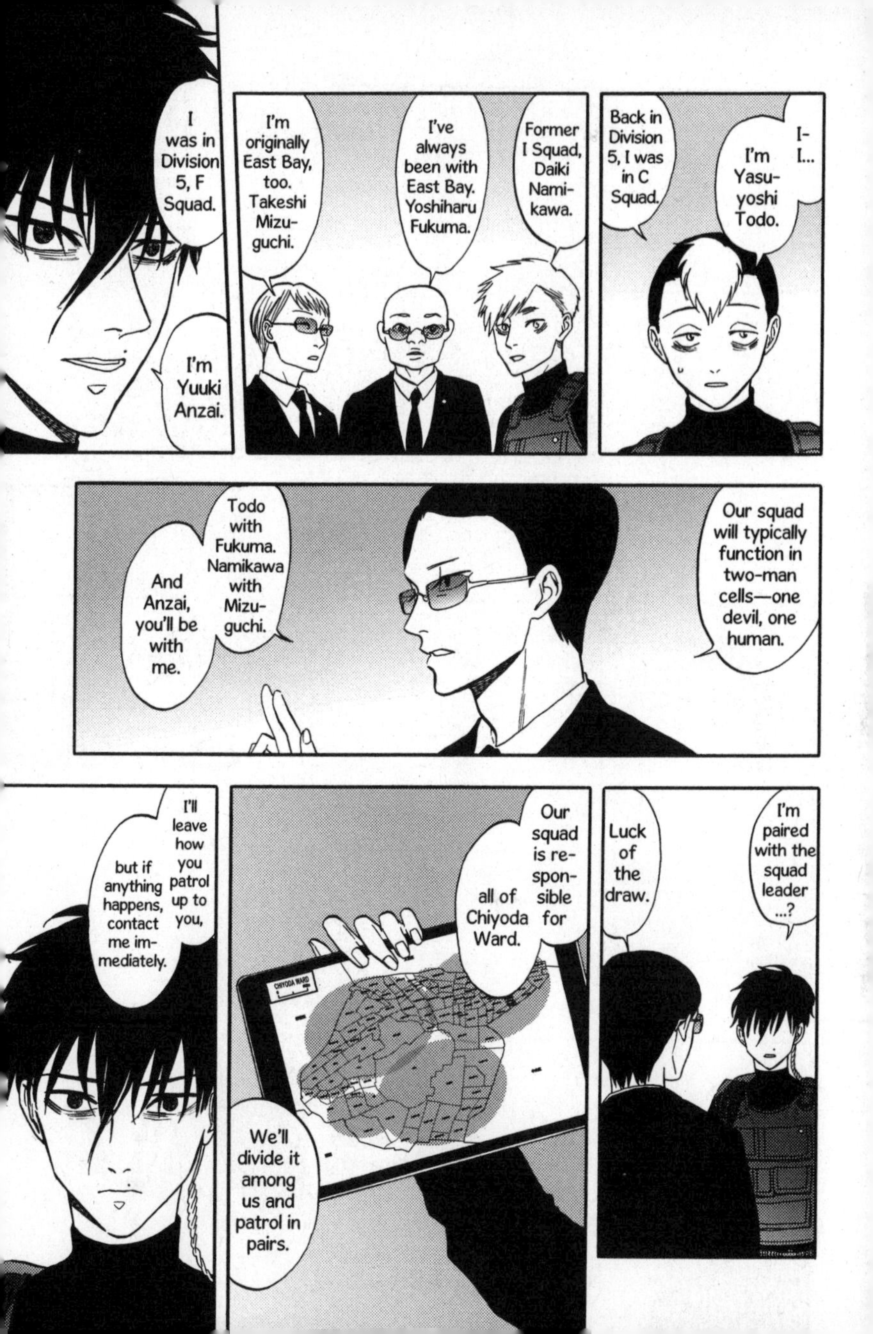
I— I...
I'm Yasuyoshi Todo.
Back in Division 5, I was in C Squad.
Former I Squad, Daiki Namikawa.
I've always been with East Bay. Yoshiharu Fukuma.
I'm originally East Bay, too. Takeshi Mizuguchi.
I was in Division 5, F Squad.
I'm Yuuki Anzai.
Our squad will typically function in two-man cells—one devil, one human.
Todo with Fukuma. Namikawa with Mizuguchi.
And Anzai, you'll be with me.
I'm paired with the squad leader ...?
Luck of the draw.
Our squad is responsible for all of Chiyoda Ward.
CHIYODA WARD
We'll divide it among us and patrol in pairs.
I'll leave how you patrol up to you,
but if anything happens, contact me immediately.

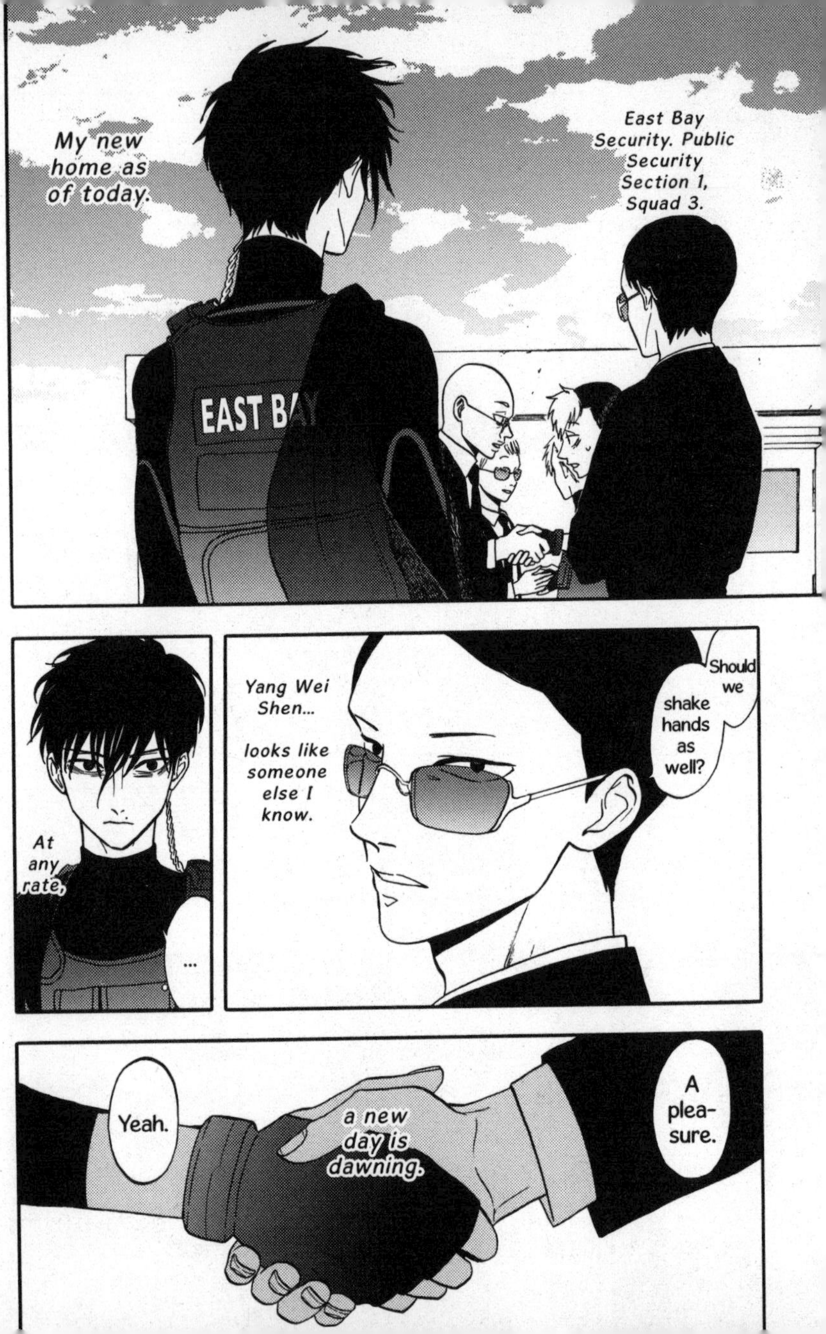
East Bay Security. Public Security Section 1, Squad 3.
My new home as of today.
EAST BA
Should we shake hands as well?
Yang Wei Shen...
looks like someone else I know.
At any rate,
...
A pleasure.
a new day is dawning.
Yeah.

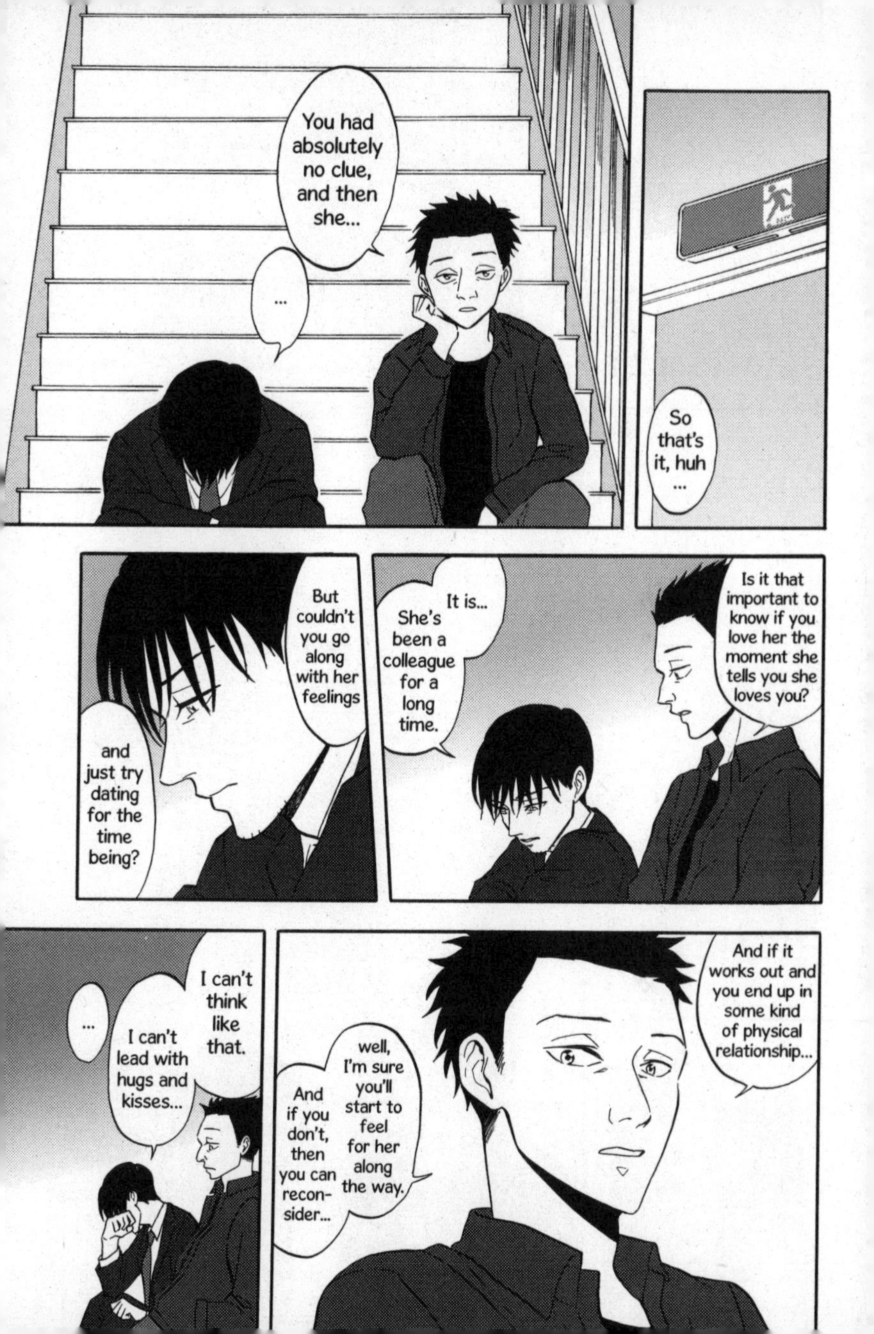
So that's it, huh ...
You had absolutely no clue, and then she...
...
Is it that important to know if you love her the moment she tells you she loves you?
It is... She's been a colleague for a long time.
But couldn't you go along with her feelings
and just try dating for the time being?
And if it works out and you end up in some kind of physical relationship...
well, I'm sure you'll start to feel for her along the way.
And if you don't, then you can reconsider...
I can't think like that.
I can't lead with hugs and kisses...
...

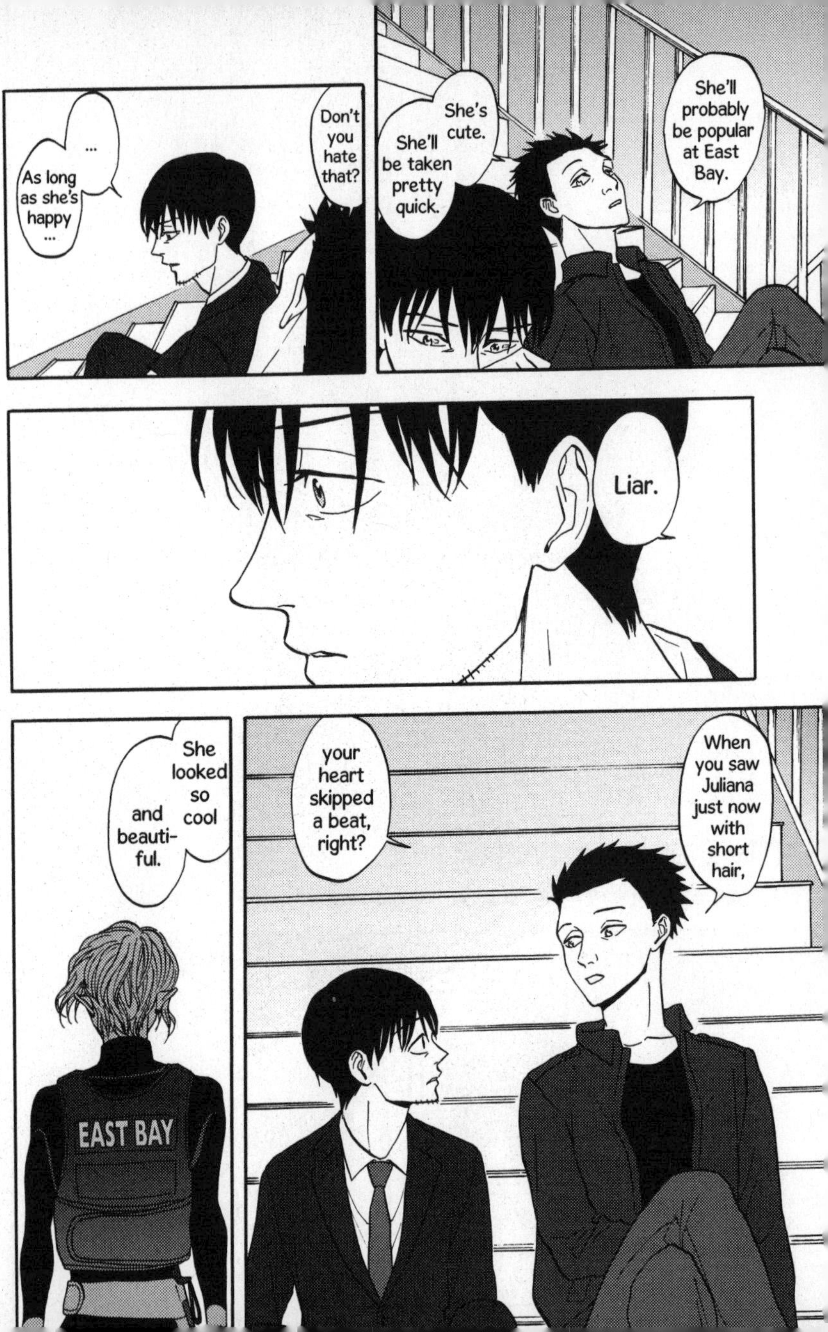
She'll probably be popular at East Bay.
She's cute.
She'll be taken pretty quick.
Don't you hate that?
...
As long as she's happy ...
Liar.
When you saw Juliana just now with short hair,
your heart skipped a beat, right?
She looked so cool and beautiful.
EAST BAY

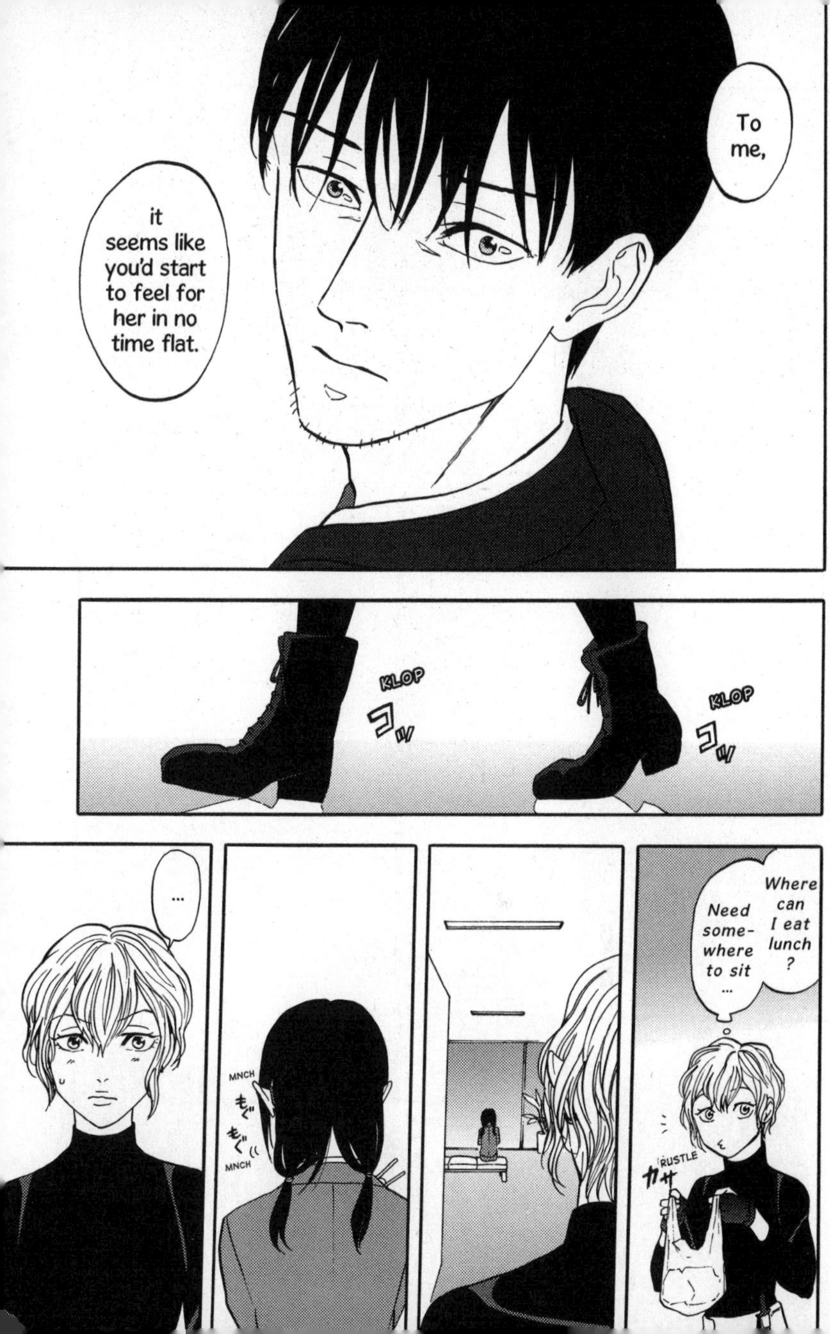
To me,
it seems like you'd start to feel for her in no time flat.
KLOP
コッ
KLOP
コッ
Where can I eat lunch?
Need some-where to sit ...
RUSTLE
カサ
MNCH
もぐ
もぐ
MNCH
...

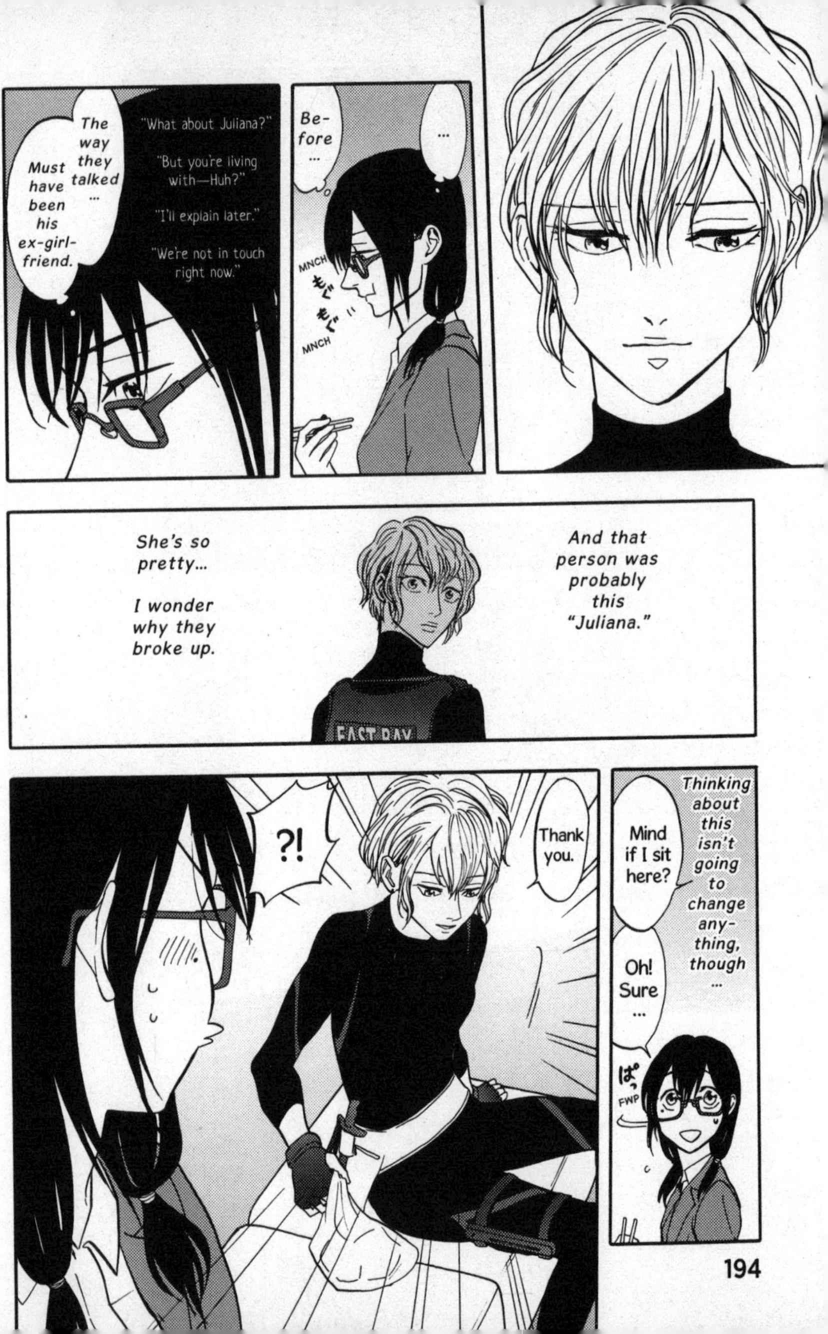

...
Be-fore...
MNCH もぐもぐ MNCH
"What about Juliana?"
"But you're living with—Huh?"
"I'll explain later."
"We're not in touch right now."
The way they talked...
Must have been his ex-girl-friend.
And that person was probably this "Juliana."
She's so pretty...
I wonder why they broke up.
Thinking about this isn't going to change any-thing, though...
Mind if I sit here?
Oh! Sure...
ぱっ FWP
Thank you.
?!

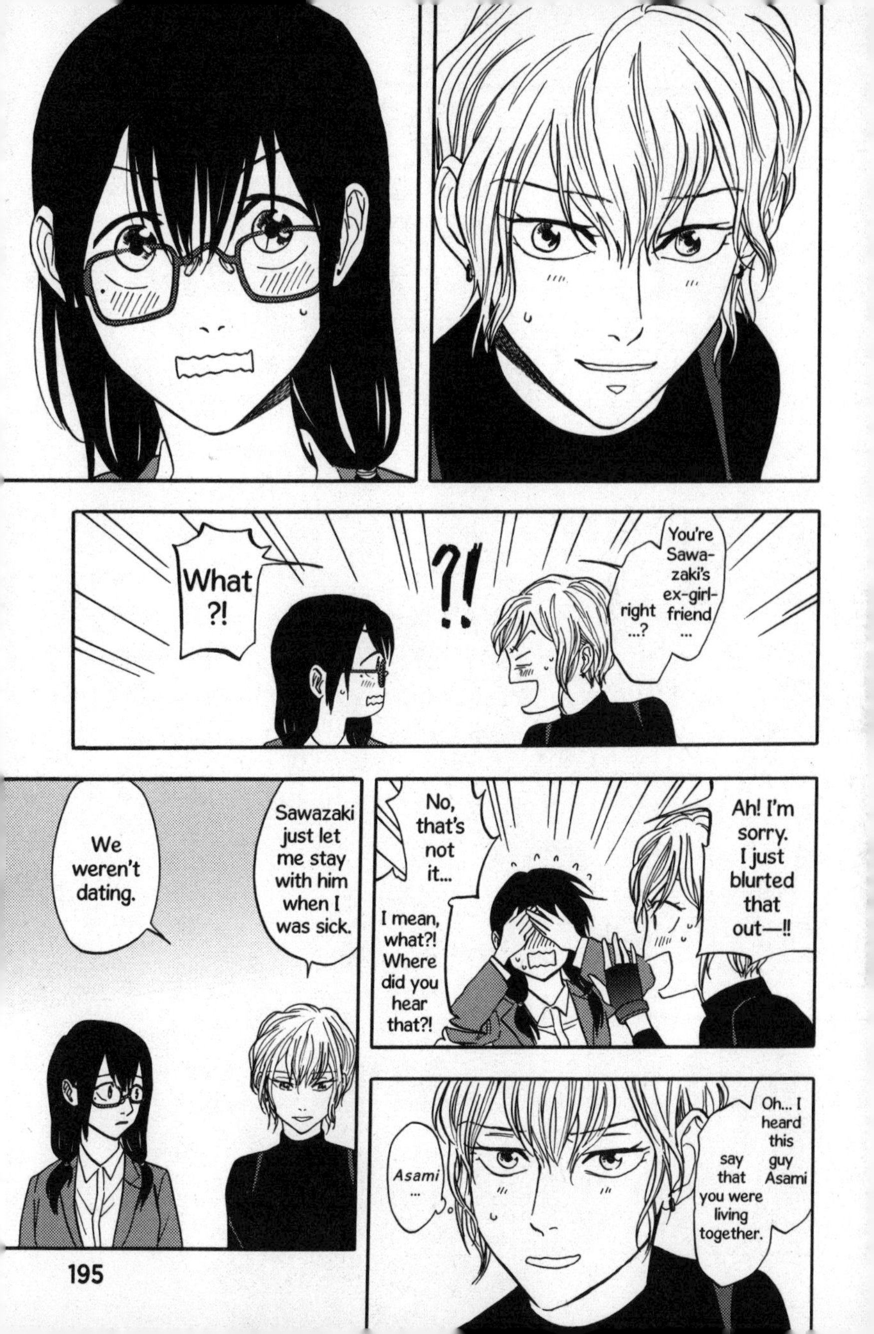
You're Sawazaki's ex-girl-friend ... right ...?
?!
What ?!
Ah! I'm sorry. I just blurted that out—!!
No, that's not it...
I mean, what?! Where did you hear that?!
Oh... I heard this guy Asami say that you were living together.
Asami ...
Sawazaki just let me stay with him when I was sick.
We weren't dating.

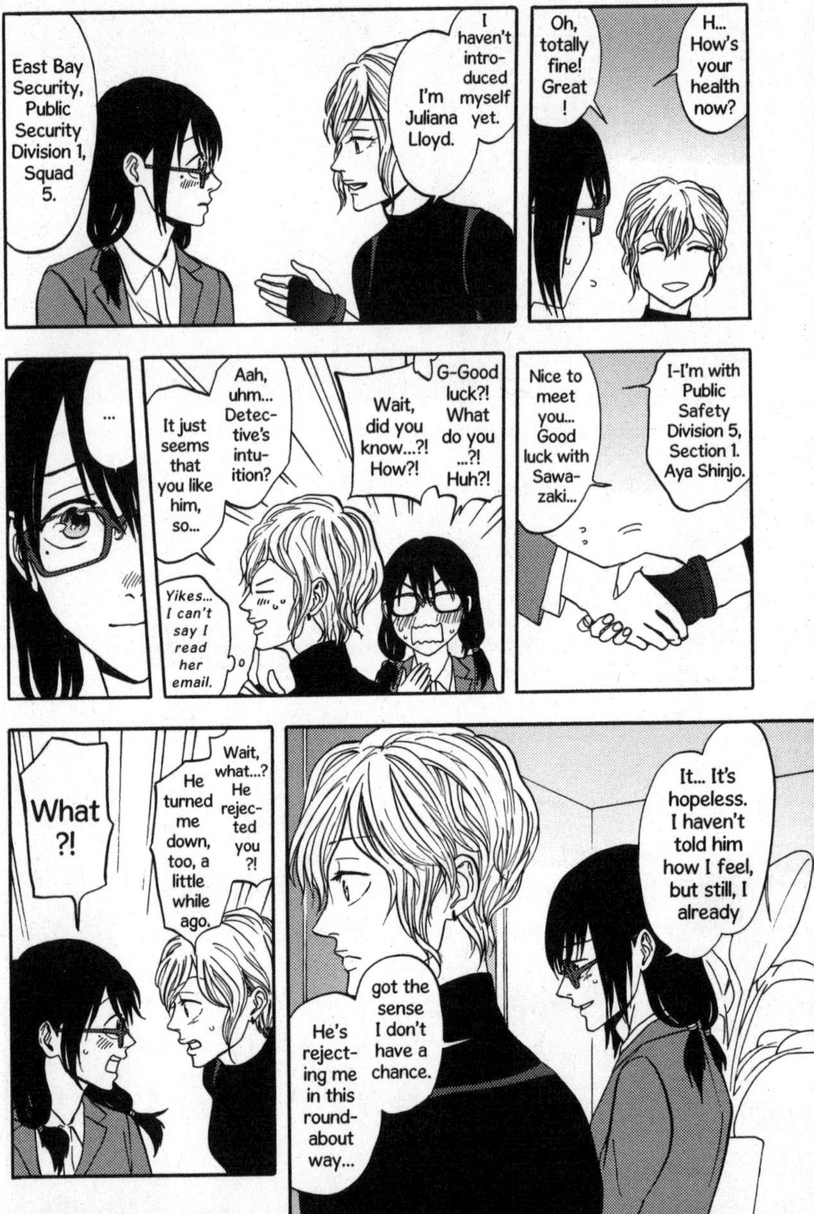
H... How's your health now?
Oh, totally fine! Great!
I haven't introduced myself yet.
I'm Juliana Lloyd.
East Bay Security, Public Security Division 1, Squad 5.
I-I'm with Public Safety Division 5, Section 1. Aya Shinjo.
Nice to meet you... Good luck with Sawazaki...
G-Good luck?! What do you ...?! Huh?!
Wait, did you know...?! How?!
Aah, uhm... Detective's intuition?
It just seems that you like him, so...
Yikes... I can't say I read her email.
...
It... It's hopeless. I haven't told him how I feel, but still, I already
got the sense I don't have a chance.
He's rejecting me in this roundabout way...
Wait, what...? He rejected you?!
He turned me down, too, a little while ago.
What?!

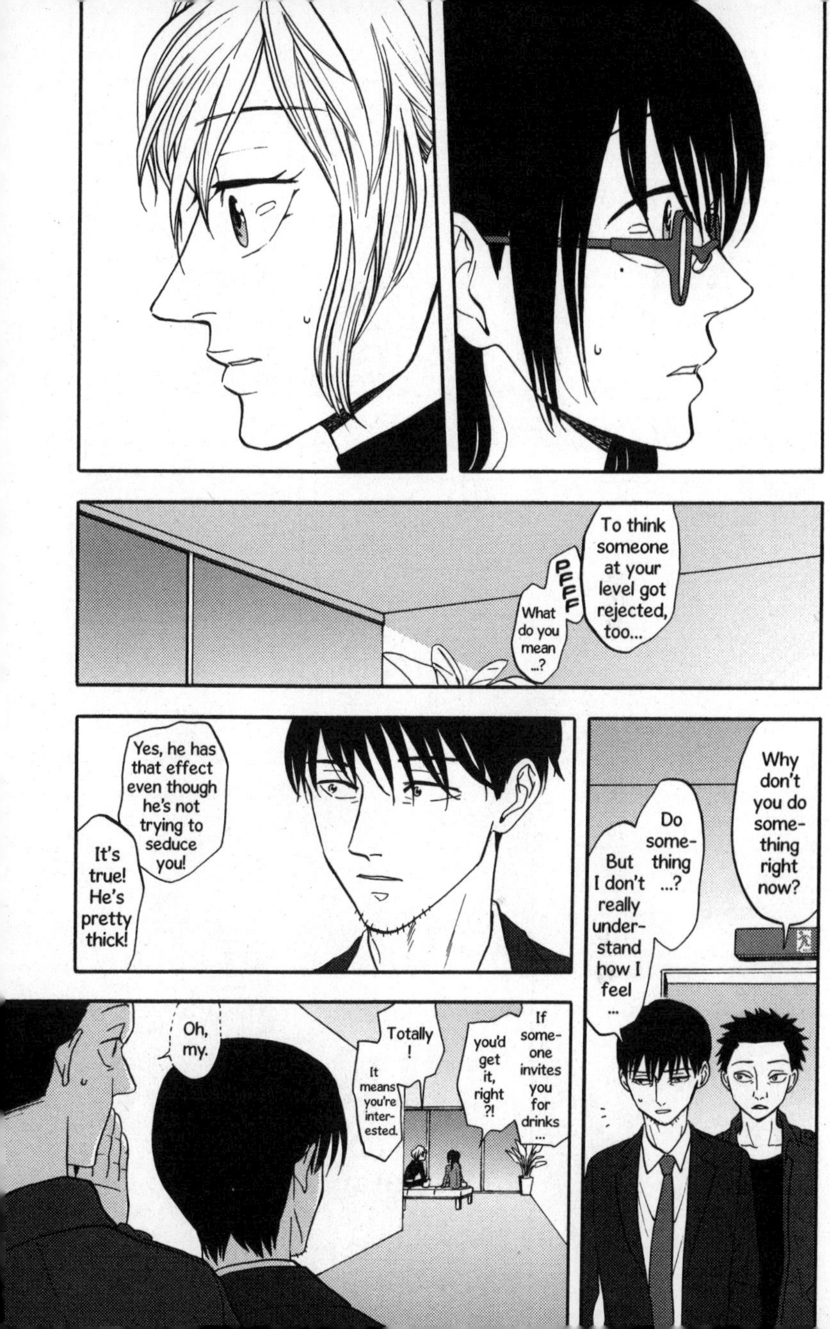

To think someone at your level got rejected, too...
PFFF
What do you mean ...?
Why don't you do some-thing right now?
Do some-thing ...?
But I don't really under-stand how I feel ...
Yes, he has that effect even though he's not trying to seduce you!
It's true! He's pretty thick!
If some-one invites you for drinks ...
you'd get it, right?!
Totally!
It means you're inter-ested.
Oh, my.

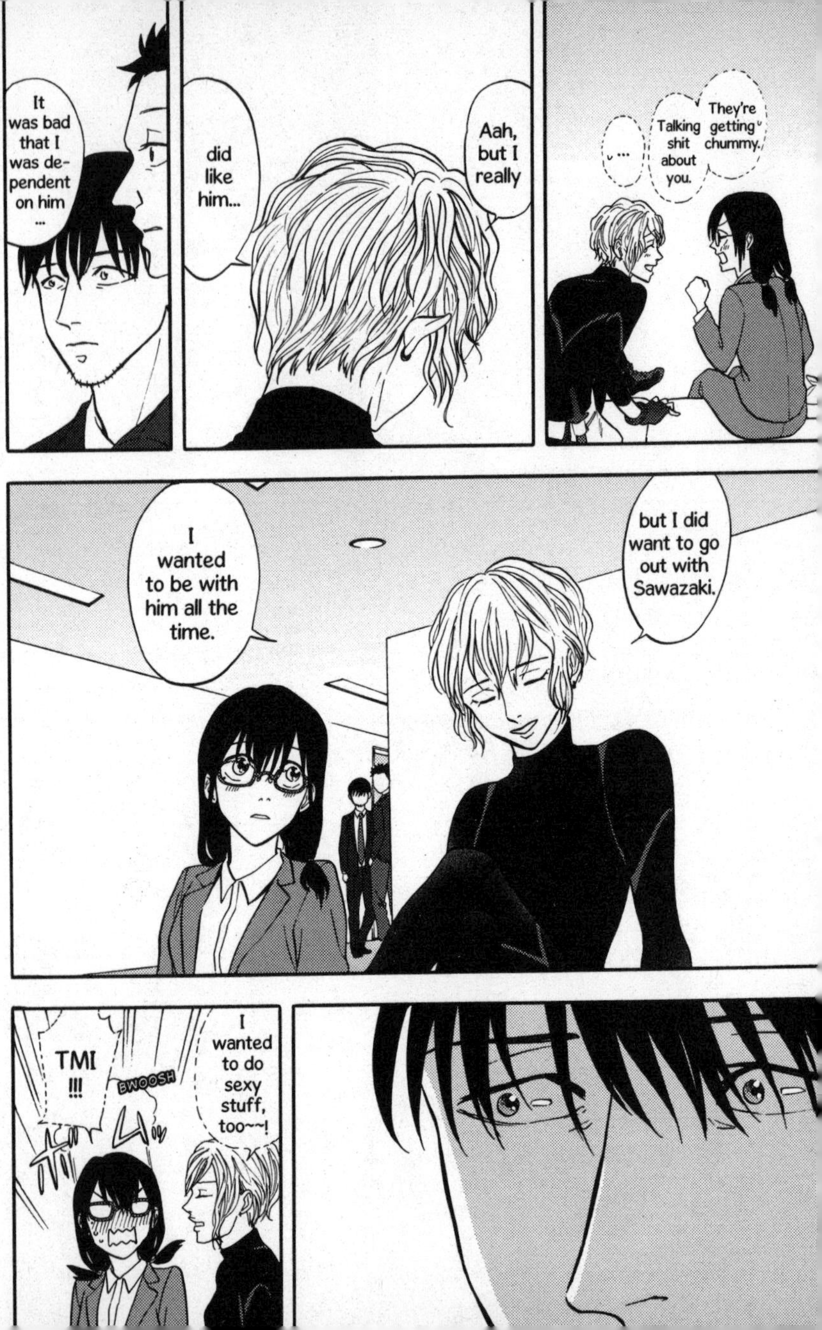

They're getting chummy.
Talking shit about you.
...
Aah, but I really
did like him...
It was bad that I was de-pendent on him ...
but I did want to go out with Sawazaki.
I wanted to be with him all the time.
I wanted to do sexy stuff, too~~!
BWOOSH
TMI !!!

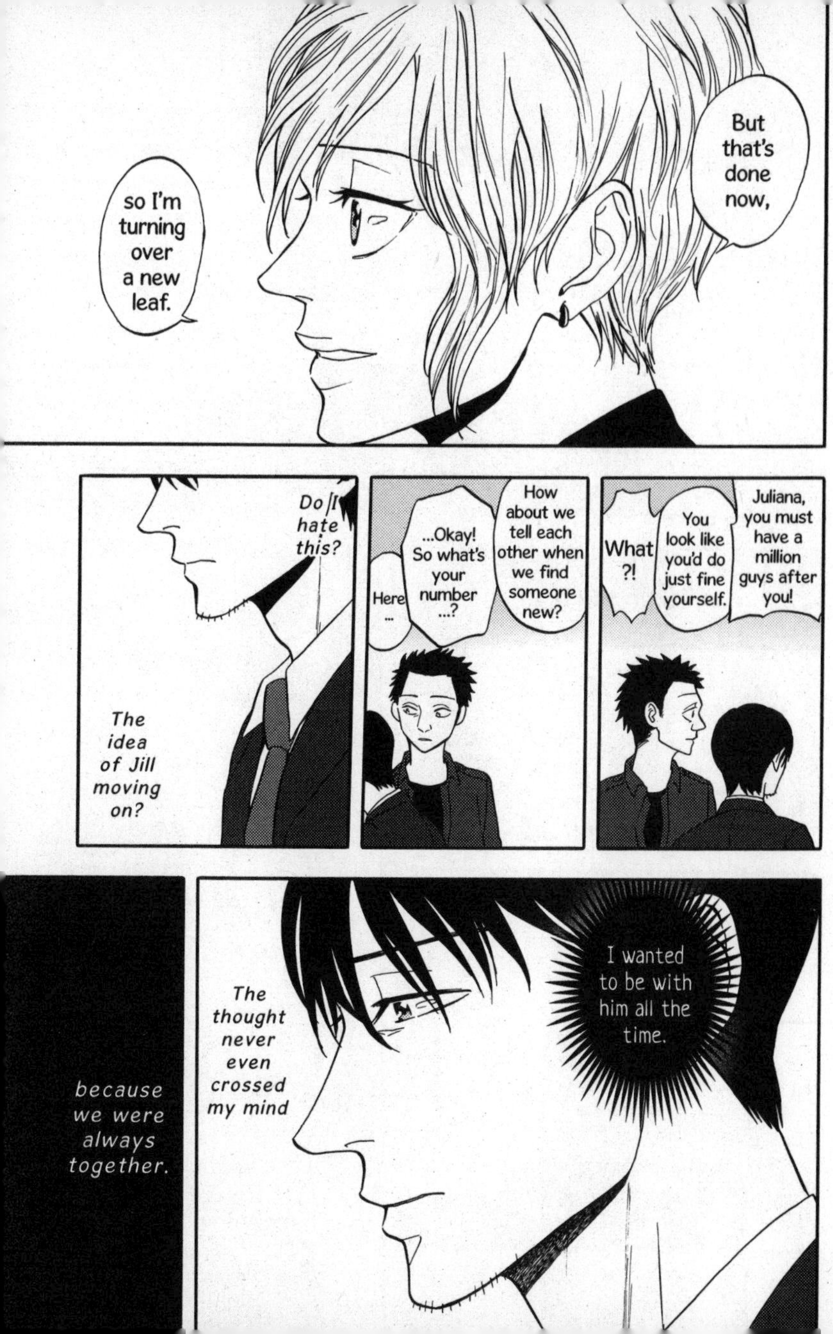

But that's done now,
so I'm turning over a new leaf.
Juliana, you must have a million guys after you!
You look like you'd do just fine yourself.
What?!
How about we tell each other when we find someone new?
...Okay! So what's your number ...?
Here ...
Do I hate this?
The idea of Jill moving on?
I wanted to be with him all the time.
The thought never even crossed my mind
because we were always together.

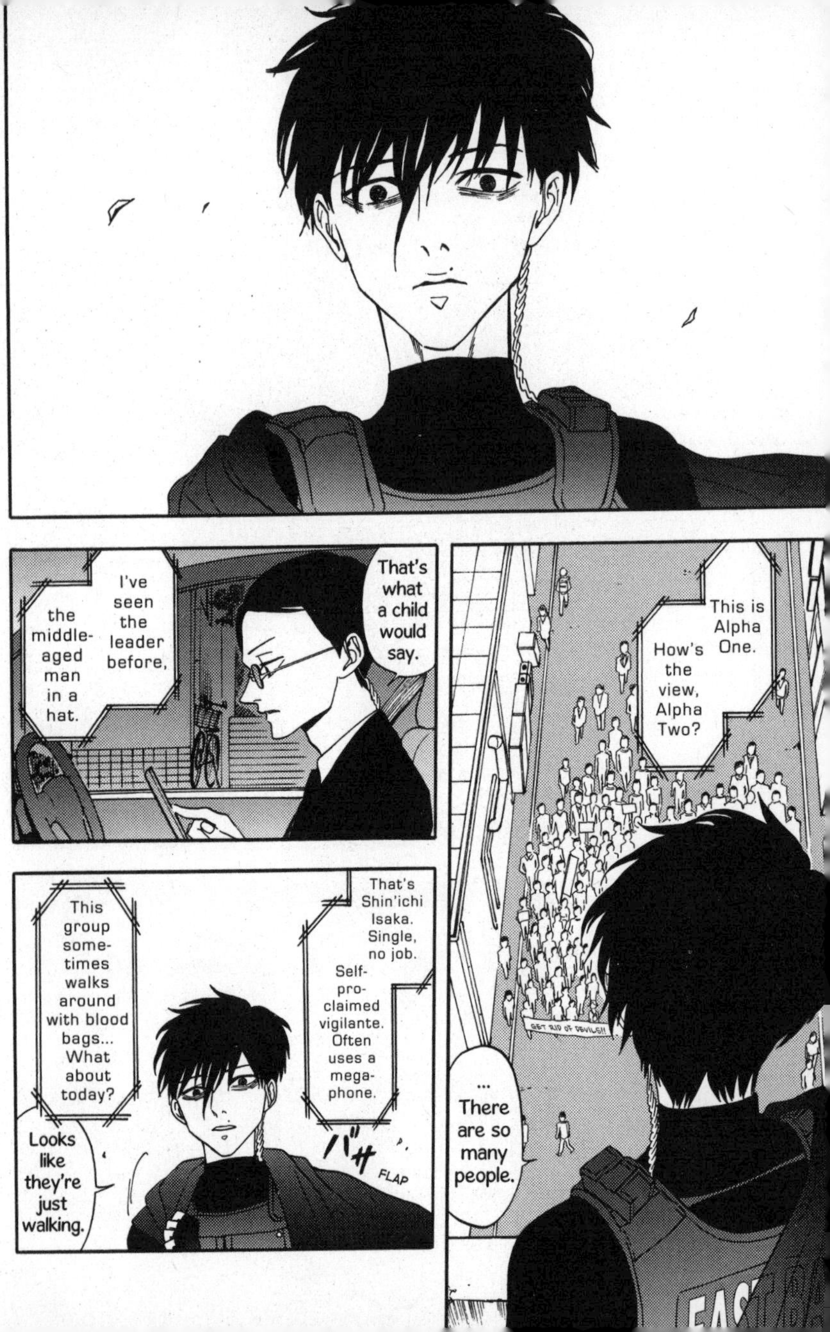
This is Alpha One.
How's the view, Alpha Two?
GET RID OF DEVILS!!
... There are so many people.
That's what a child would say.
I've seen the leader before,
the middle-aged man in a hat.
That's Shin'ichi Isaka. Single, no job.
Self-proclaimed vigilante. Often uses a megaphone.
This group sometimes walks around with blood bags... What about today?
バサ
FLAP
Looks like they're just walking.

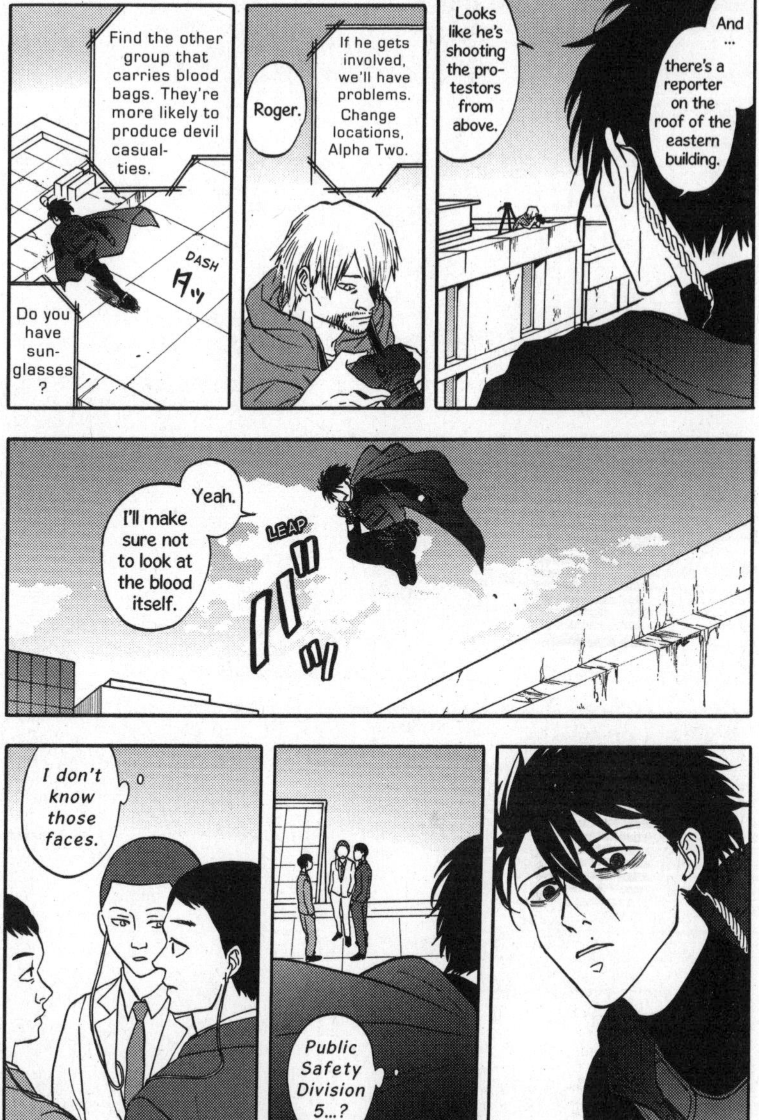
And ... there's a reporter on the roof of the eastern building.
Looks like he's shooting the pro- testors from above.
If he gets involved, we'll have problems. Change locations, Alpha Two.
Roger.
Find the other group that carries blood bags. They're more likely to produce devil casual- ties.
DASH
ダッ
Do you have sun- glasses ?
Yeah. I'll make sure not to look at the blood itself.
LEAP
Public Safety Division 5...?
I don't know those faces.

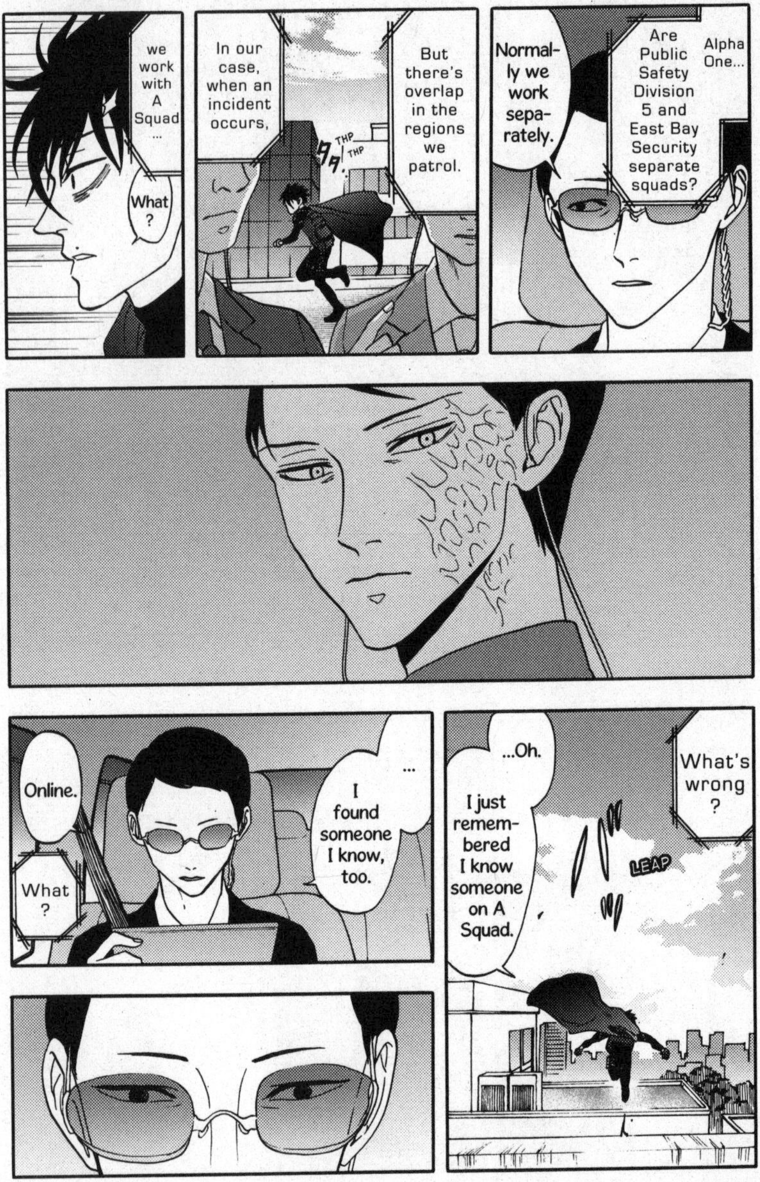

Alpha One...
Are Public Safety Division 5 and East Bay Security separate squads?
Normally we work separately.
But there's overlap in the regions we patrol.
In our case, when an incident occurs,
THP THP
we work with A Squad ...
What?
What's wrong?
...Oh.
I just remembered I know someone on A Squad.
LEAP
... I found someone I know, too.
Online.
What?

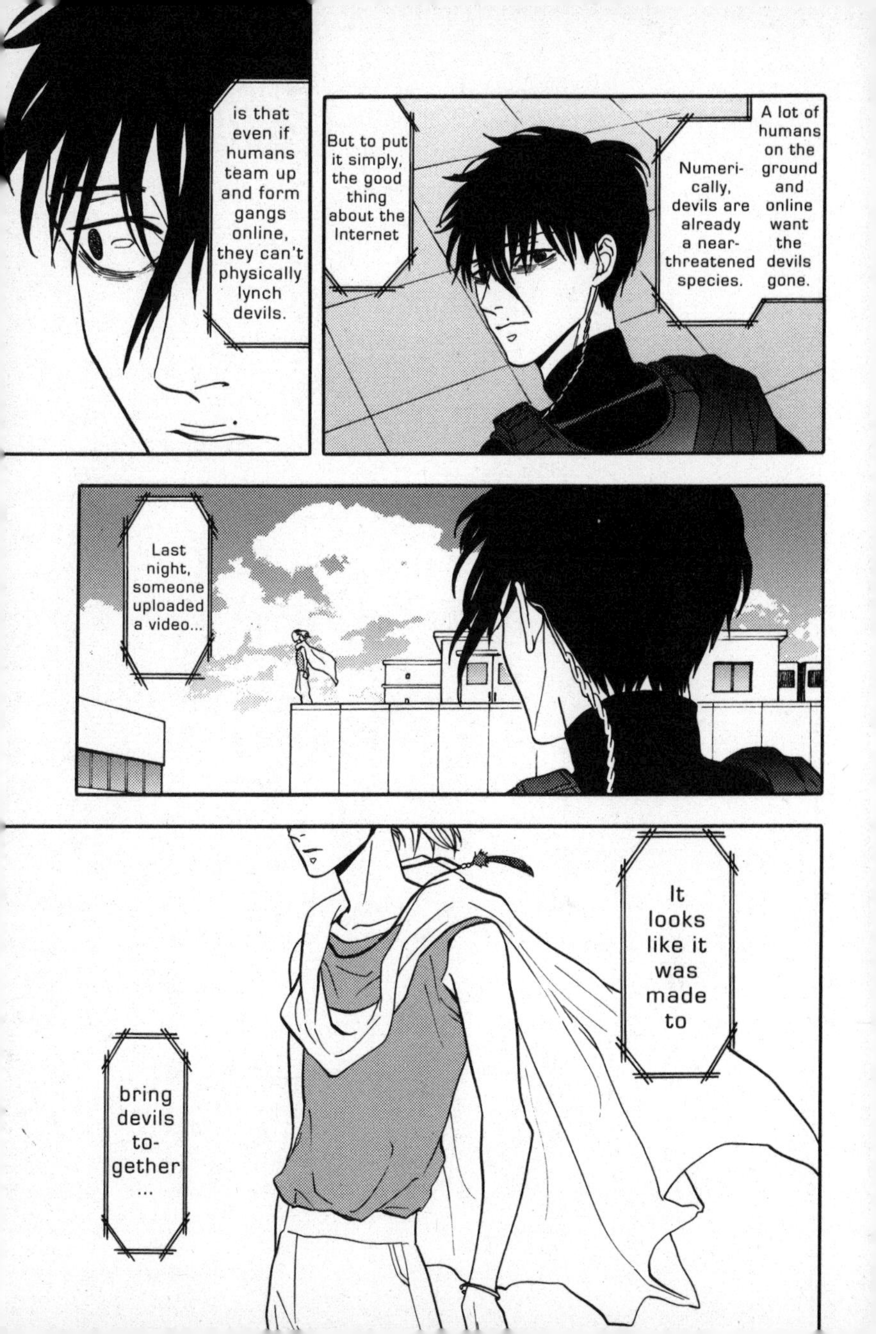
A lot of humans on the ground and online want the devils gone.
Numerically, devils are already a near-threatened species.
But to put it simply, the good thing about the Internet
is that even if humans team up and form gangs online, they can't physically lynch devils.
Last night, someone uploaded a video...
It looks like it was made to
bring devils together...

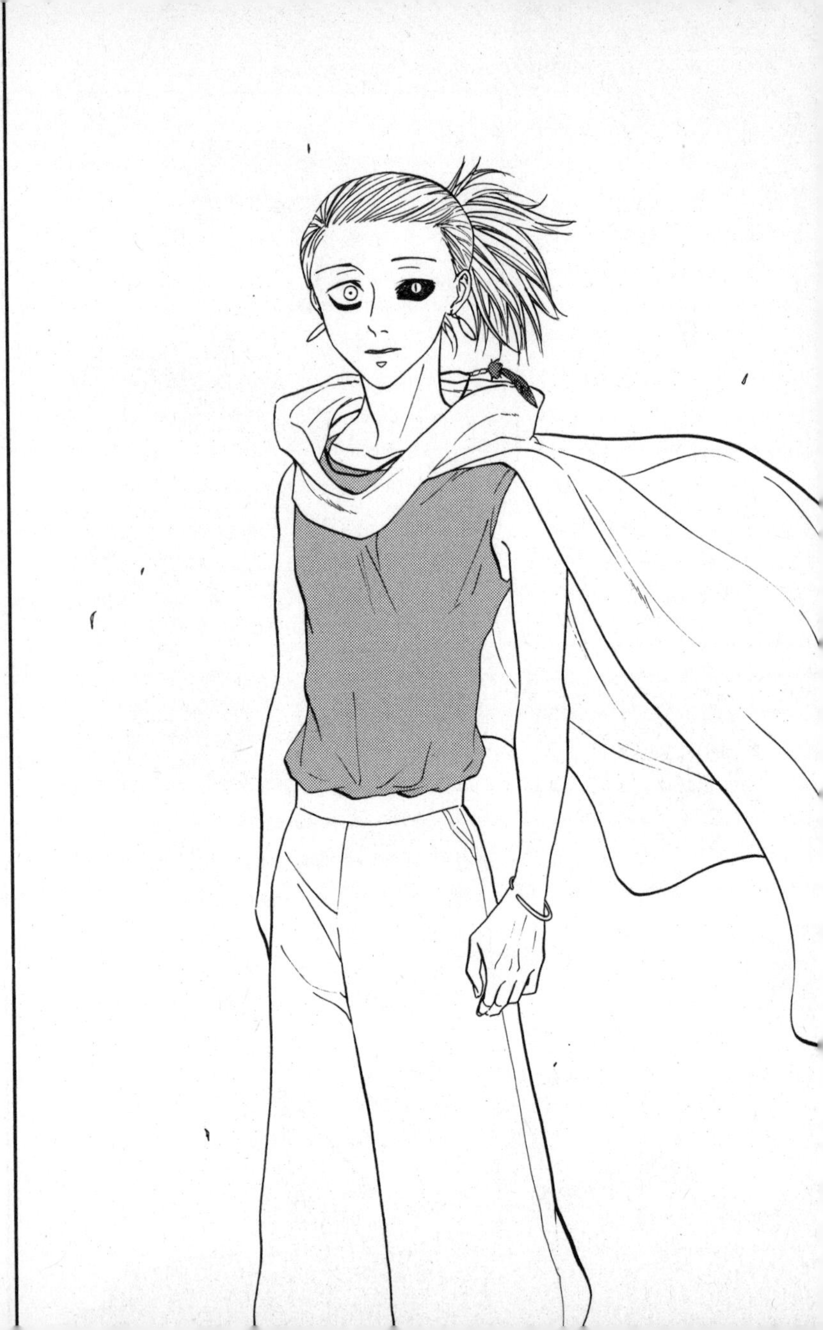

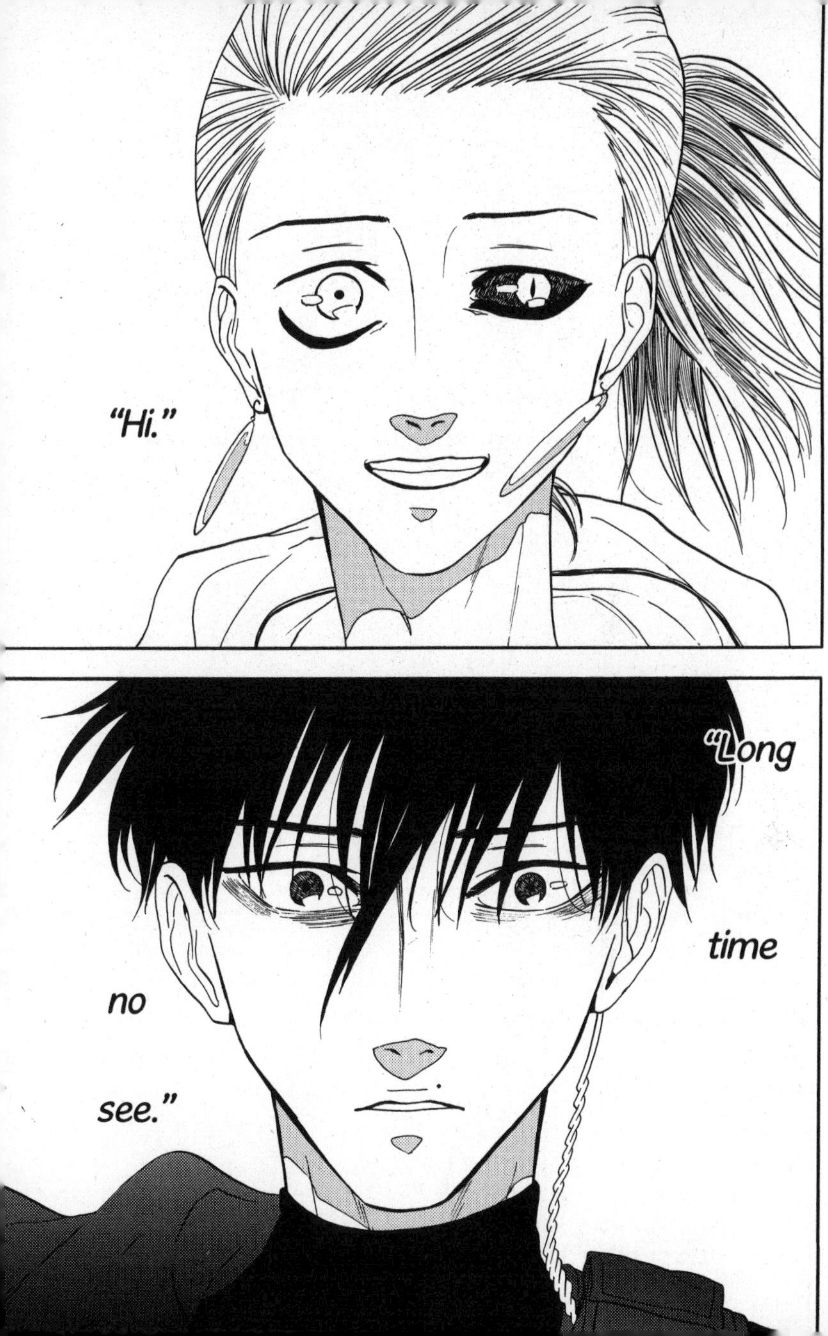
"Hi."
"Long time no see."

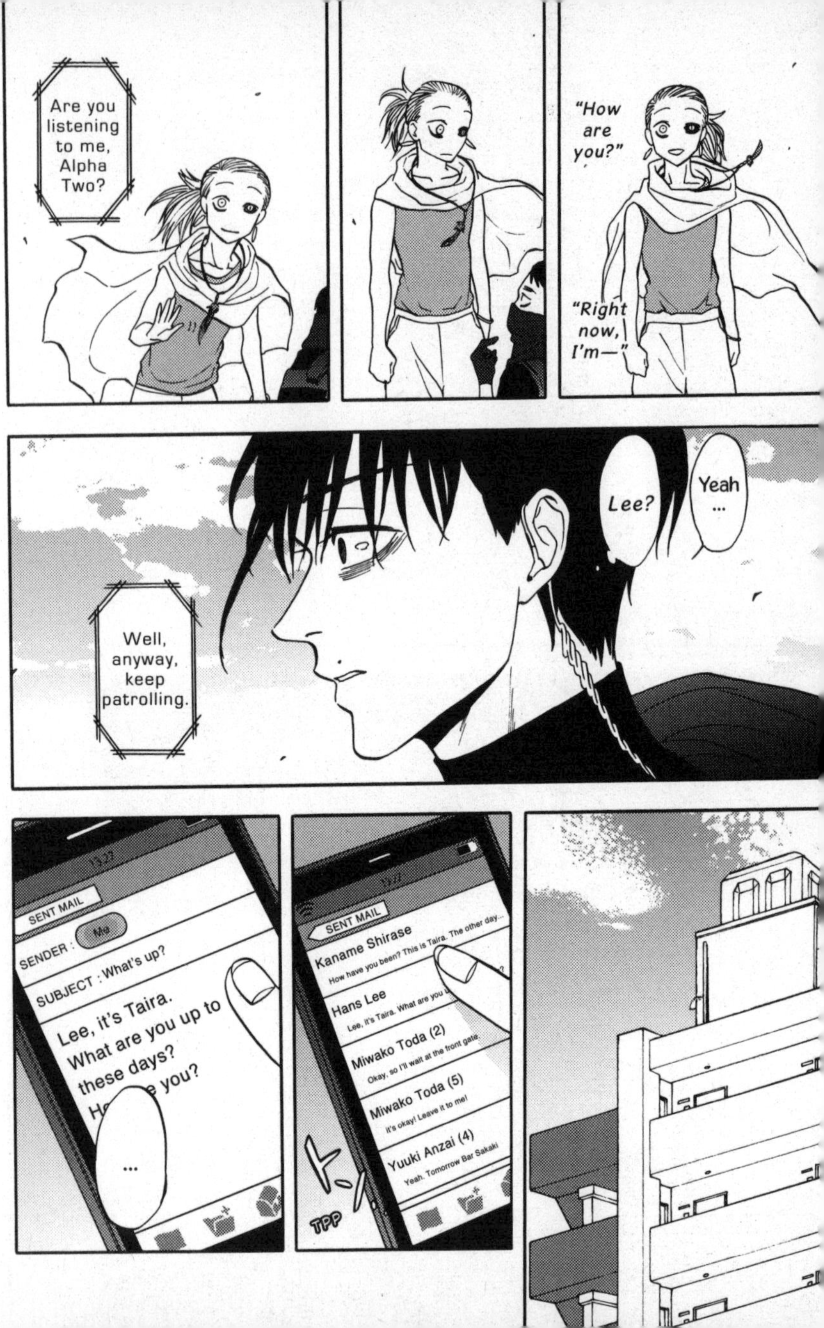
"How are you?"
"Right now, I'm—"
Are you listening to me, Alpha Two?
Lee?
Yeah ...
Well, anyway, keep patrolling.
SENT MAIL
Kaname Shirase
How have you been? This is Taira. The other day...
Hans Lee
Lee, it's Taira. What are you
Miwako Toda (2)
Okay, so I'll wait at the front gate.
Miwako Toda (5)
It's okay! Leave it to me!
Yuuki Anzai (4)
Yeah. Tomorrow Bar Sakaki
TPP
SENT MAIL
SENDER : Me
SUBJECT : What's up?
Lee, it's Taira. What are you up to these days?
...

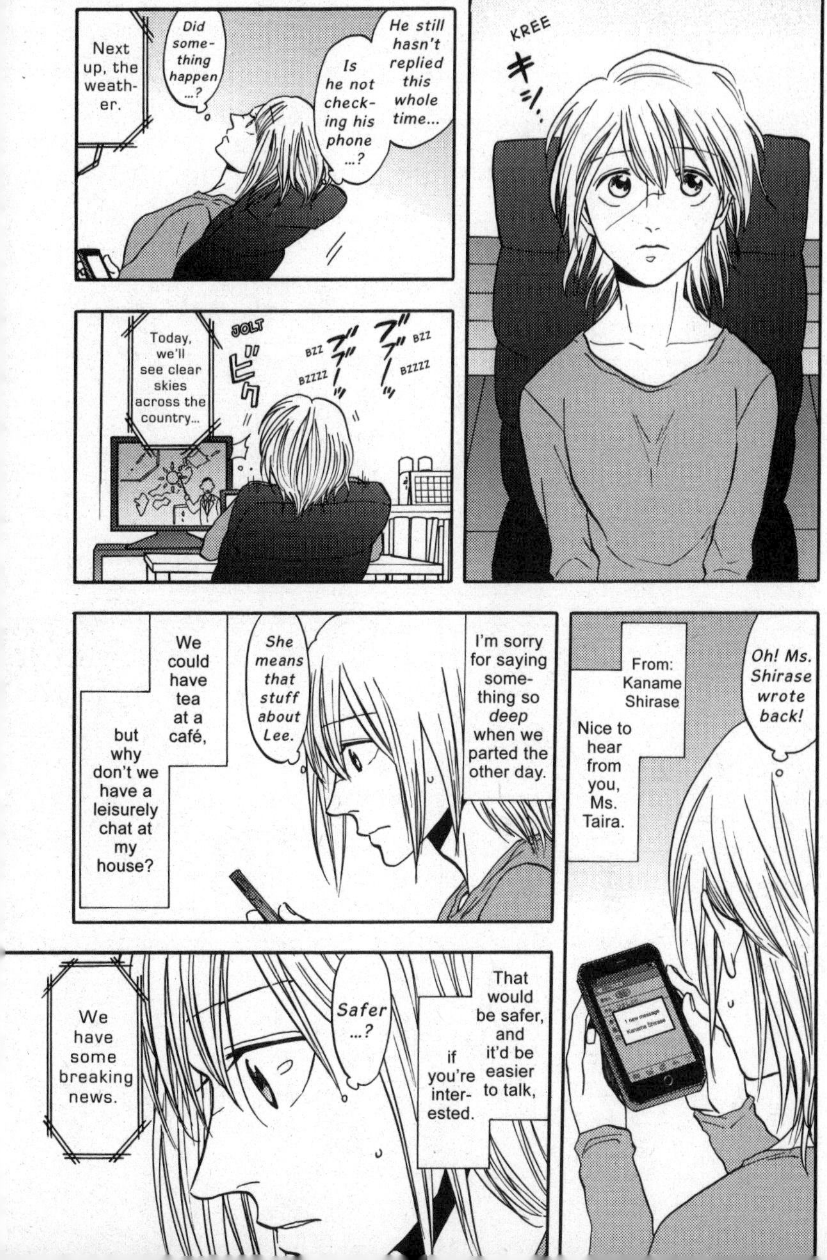
KREE
He still hasn't replied this whole time...
Is he not checking his phone ...?
Did something happen ...?
Next up, the weather.
BZZ
BZZZZ
BZZ
BZZZZ
JOLT
Today, we'll see clear skies across the country...
Oh! Ms. Shirase wrote back!
From: Kaname Shirase
Nice to hear from you, Ms. Taira.
1 new message
Kaname Shirase
I'm sorry for saying something so *deep* when we parted the other day.
She means that stuff about Lee.
We could have tea at a café,
but why don't we have a leisurely chat at my house?
That would be safer, and it'd be easier to talk,
if you're interested.
Safer ...?
We have some breaking news.

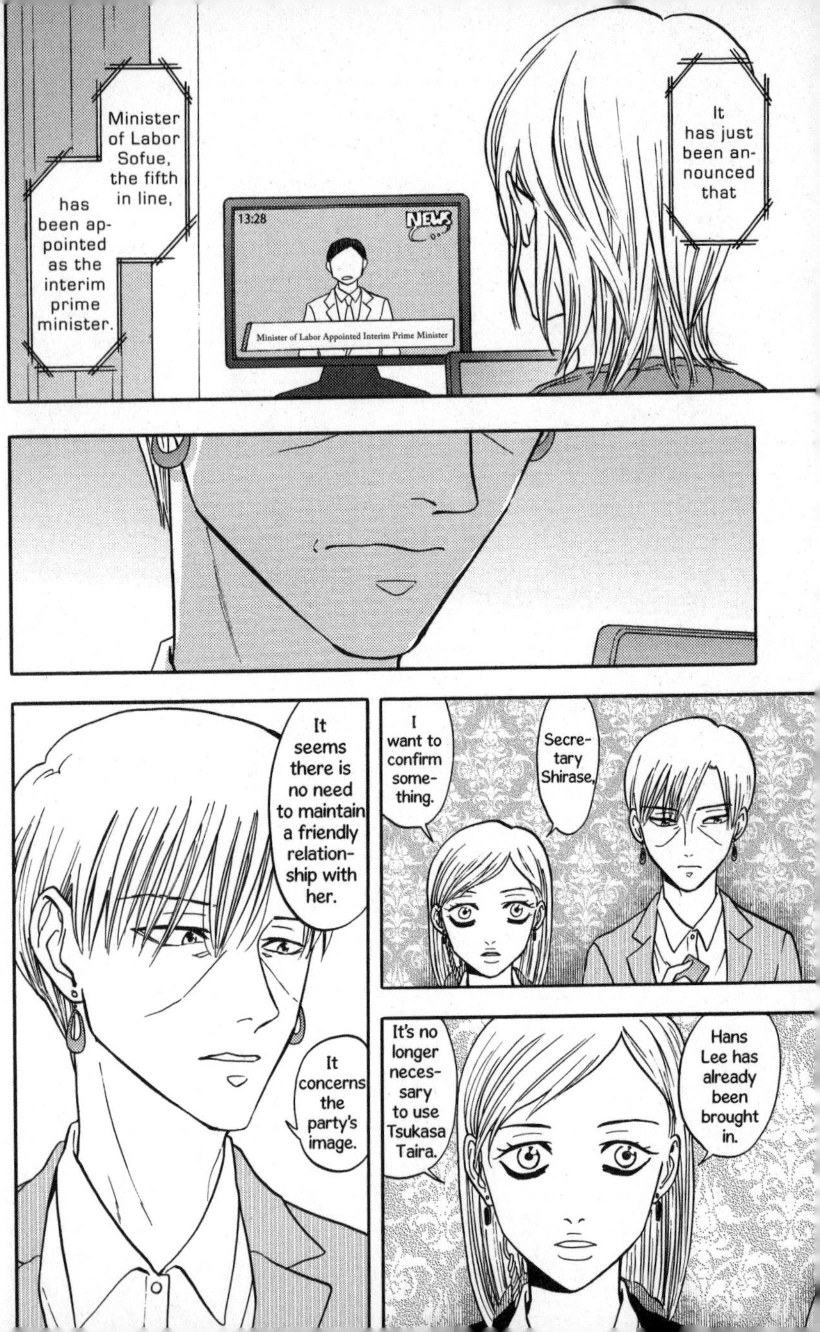
It has just been announced that
Minister of Labor Sofue, the fifth in line, has been appointed as the interim prime minister.
13:28
NEWS
Minister of Labor Appointed Interim Prime Minister
Secretary Shirase,
I want to confirm something.
Hans Lee has already been brought in.
It's no longer necessary to use Tsukasa Taira.
It seems there is no need to maintain a friendly relationship with her.
It concerns the party's image.

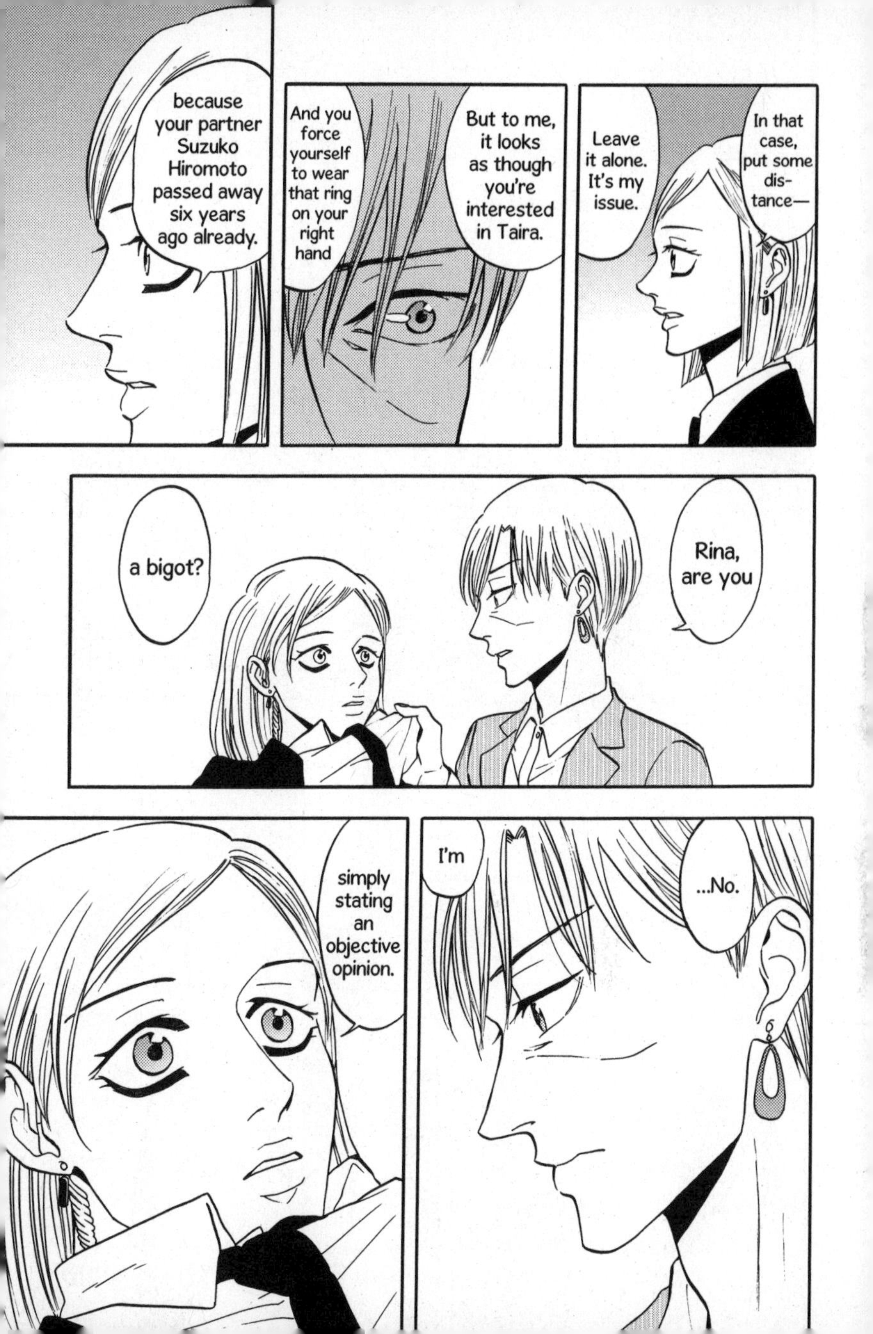
In that case, put some dis- tance—
Leave it alone. It's my issue.
But to me, it looks as though you're interested in Taira.
And you force yourself to wear that ring on your right hand
because your partner Suzuko Hiromoto passed away six years ago already.
Rina, are you
a bigot?
...No.
I'm
simply stating an objective opinion.

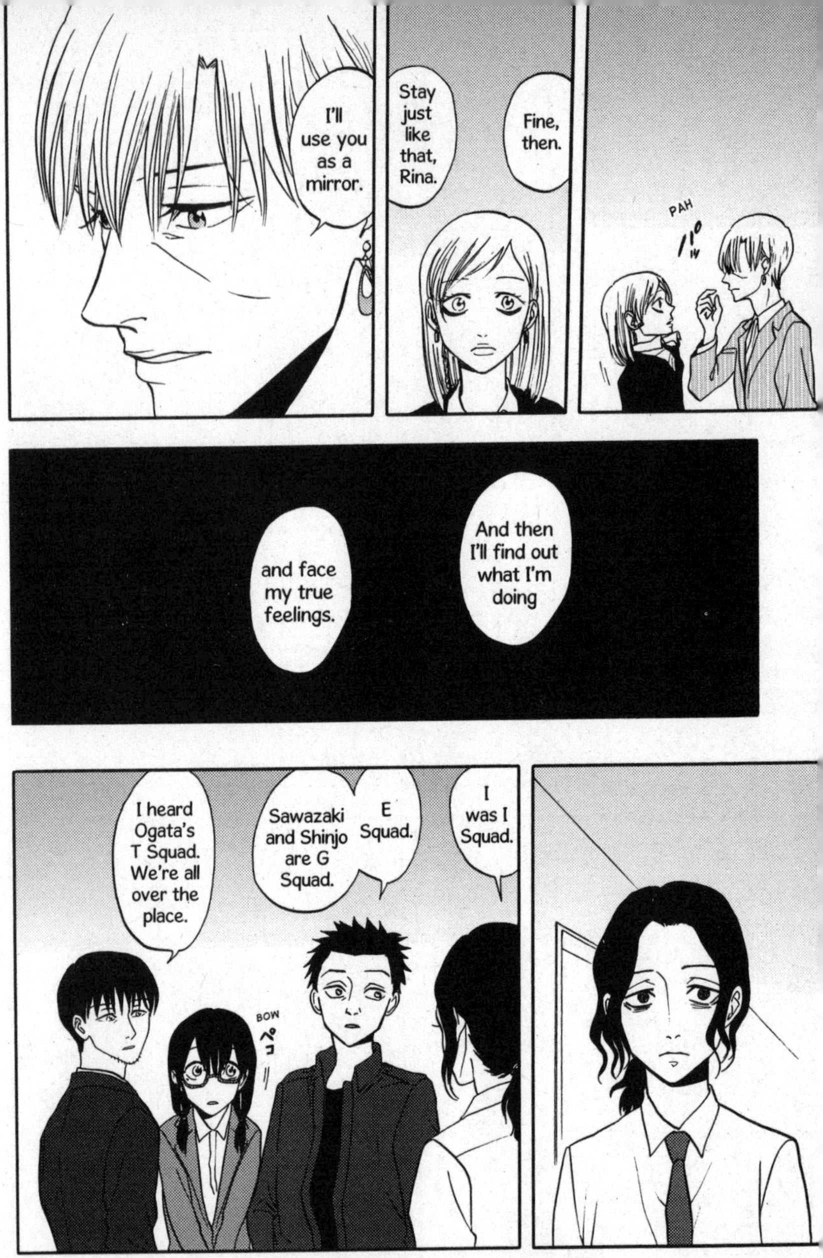
Fine, then.
PAH
Stay just like that, Rina.
I'll use you as a mirror.
And then I'll find out what I'm doing
and face my true feelings.
I was I Squad.
E Squad.
Sawazaki and Shinjo are G Squad.
I heard Ogata's T Squad. We're all over the place.
BOW

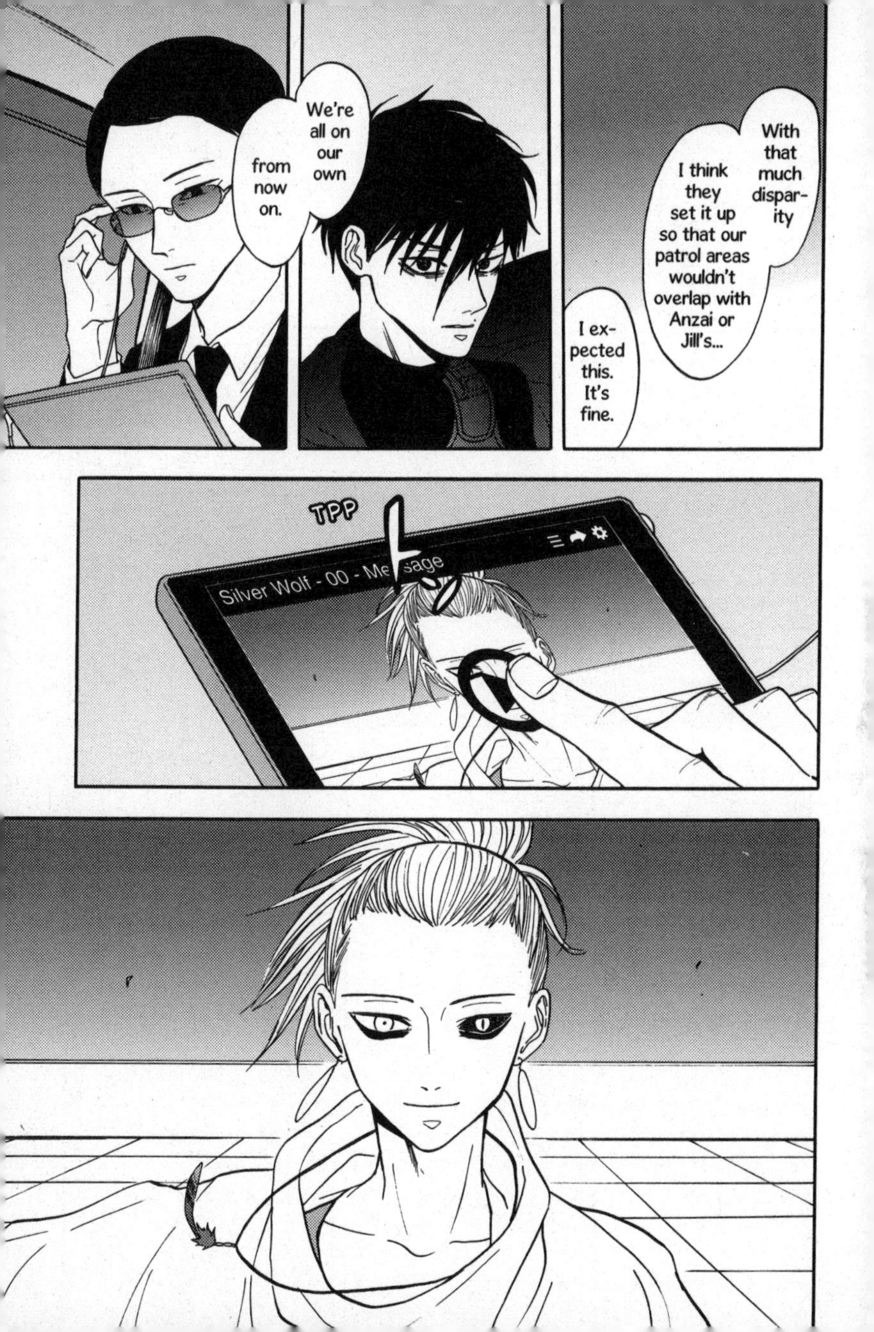
With that much disparity
I think they set it up so that our patrol areas wouldn't overlap with Anzai or Jill's...
I expected this. It's fine.
We're all on our own from now on.
TPP
Silver Wolf - 00 - Me sage

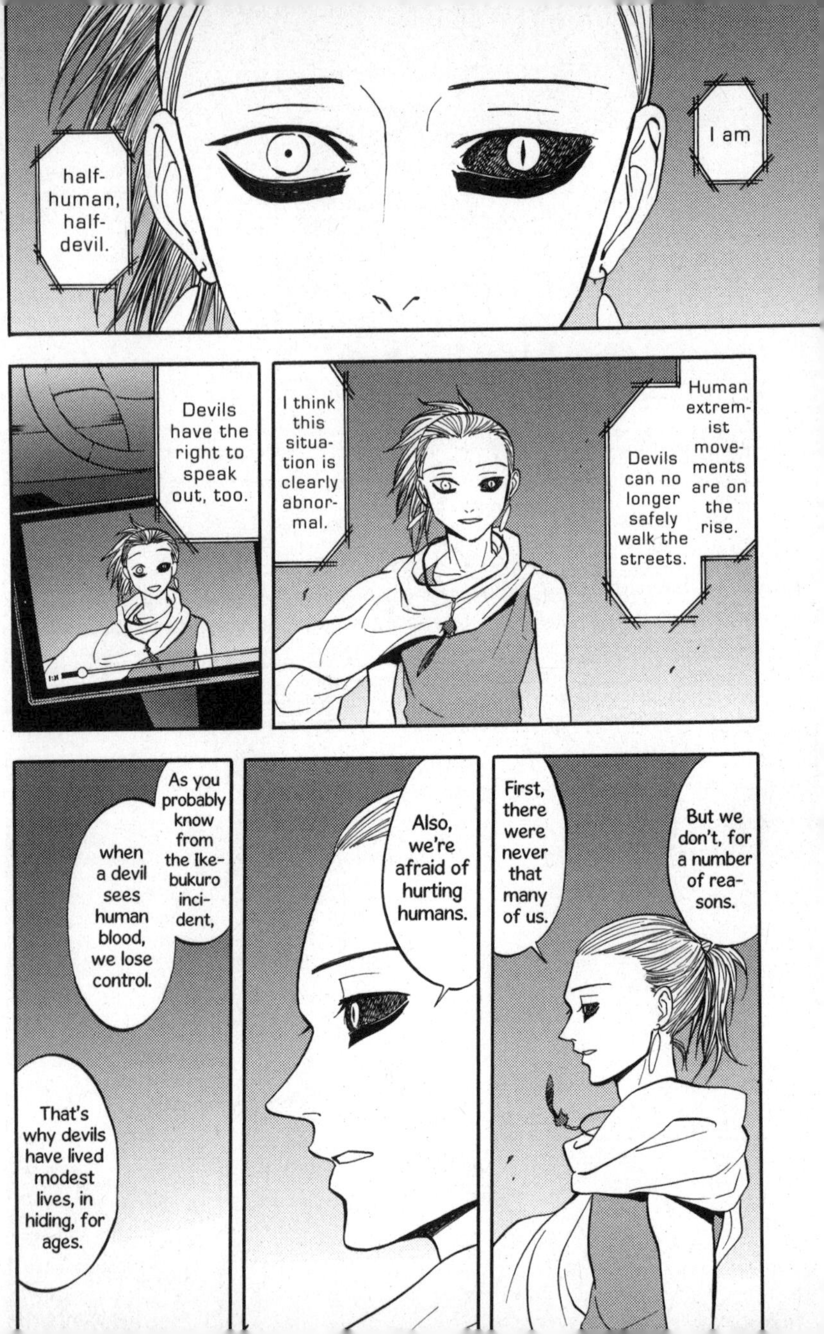
I am
half-human, half-devil.
Human extremist movements are on the rise.
Devils can no longer safely walk the streets.
I think this situation is clearly abnormal.
Devils have the right to speak out, too.
But we don't, for a number of reasons.
First, there were never that many of us.
Also, we're afraid of hurting humans.
As you probably know from the Ikebukuro incident,
when a devil sees human blood, we lose control.
That's why devils have lived modest lives, in hiding, for ages.

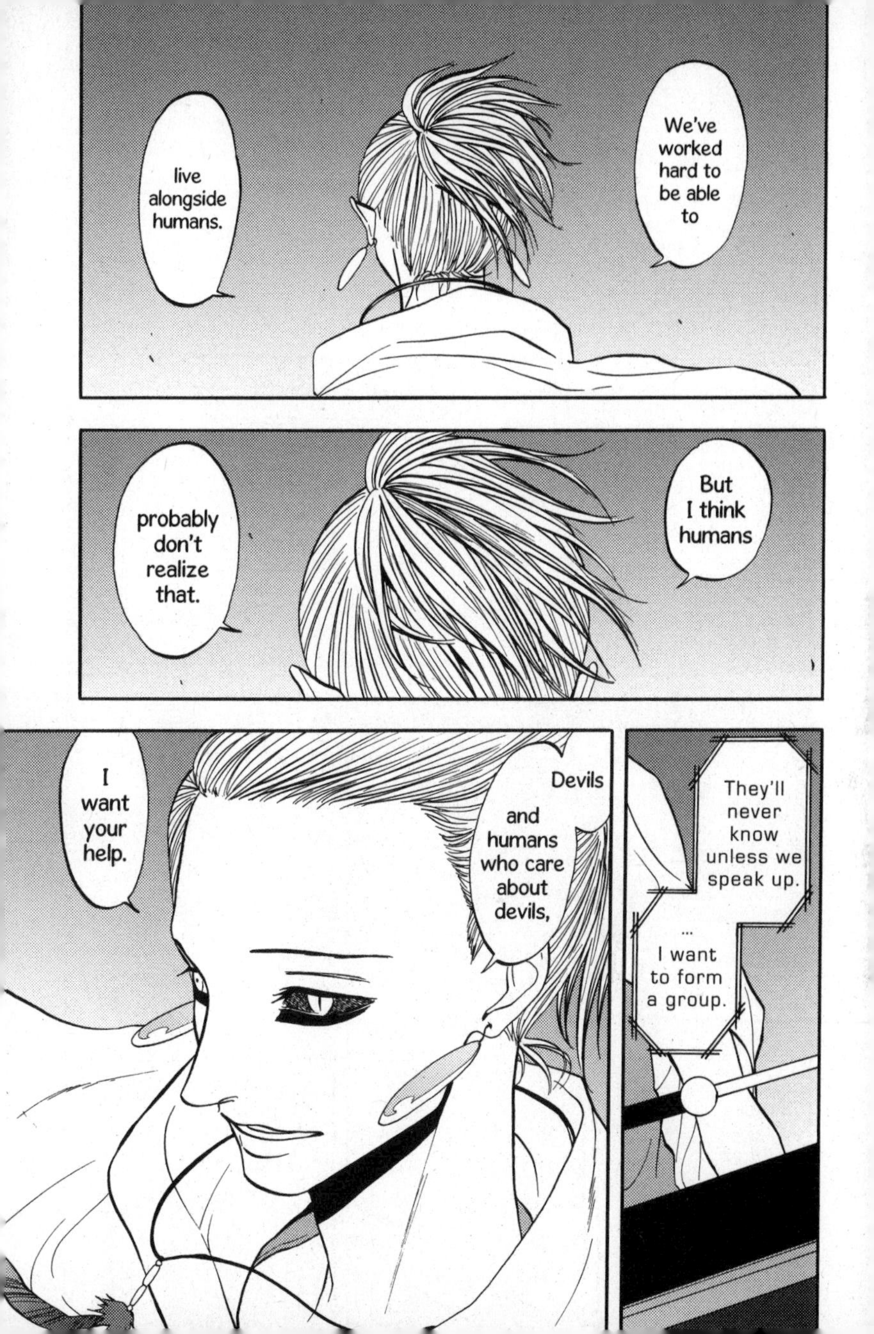
We've worked hard to be able to
live alongside humans.
But I think humans
probably don't realize that.
They'll never know unless we speak up.
... I want to form a group.
Devils and humans who care about devils,
I want your help.

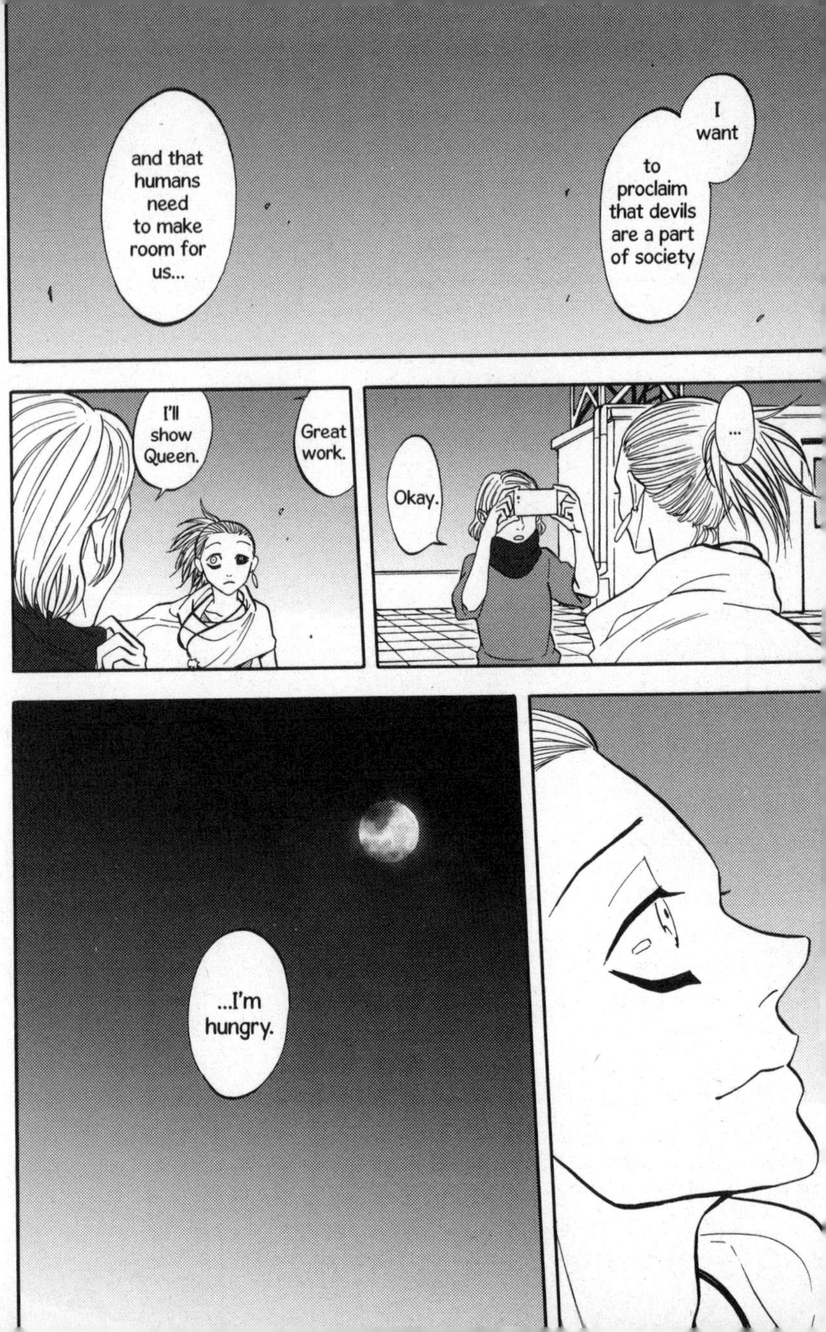
I want to proclaim that devils are a part of society
and that humans need to make room for us...
...
Okay.
Great work.
I'll show Queen.
...I'm hungry.

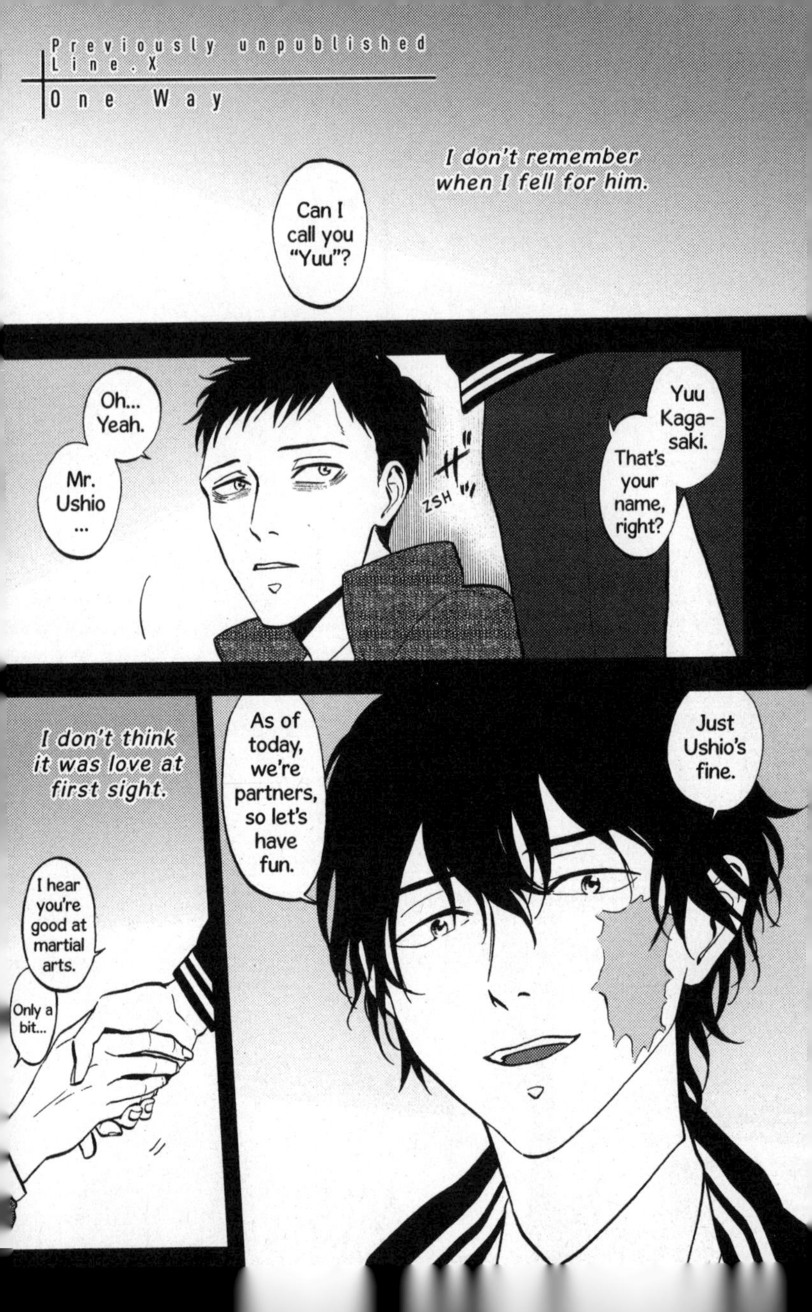
Previously unpublished
Line.X
One Way
I don't remember when I fell for him.
Can I call you "Yuu"?
Yuu Kaga-saki.
That's your name, right?
ZSH
Oh... Yeah.
Mr. Ushio ...
Just Ushio's fine.
As of today, we're partners, so let's have fun.
I don't think it was love at first sight.
I hear you're good at martial arts.
Only a bit...

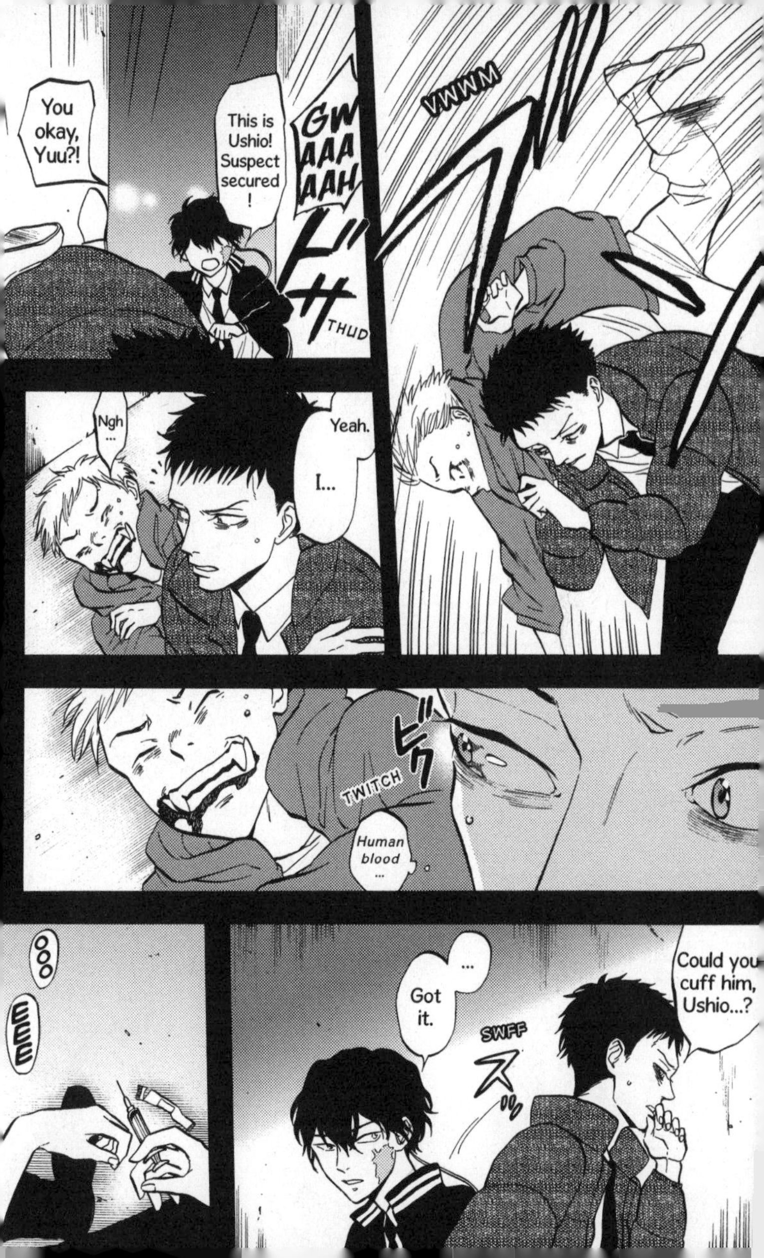
VWWM
GW
AAA
AAH
This is Ushio! Suspect secured!
You okay, Yuu?!
ドサ
THUD
Yeah.
I...
Ngh...
ビク
TWITCH
Human blood...
Could you cuff him, Ushio...?
SWFF
ス
... Got it.
OOO
EEE

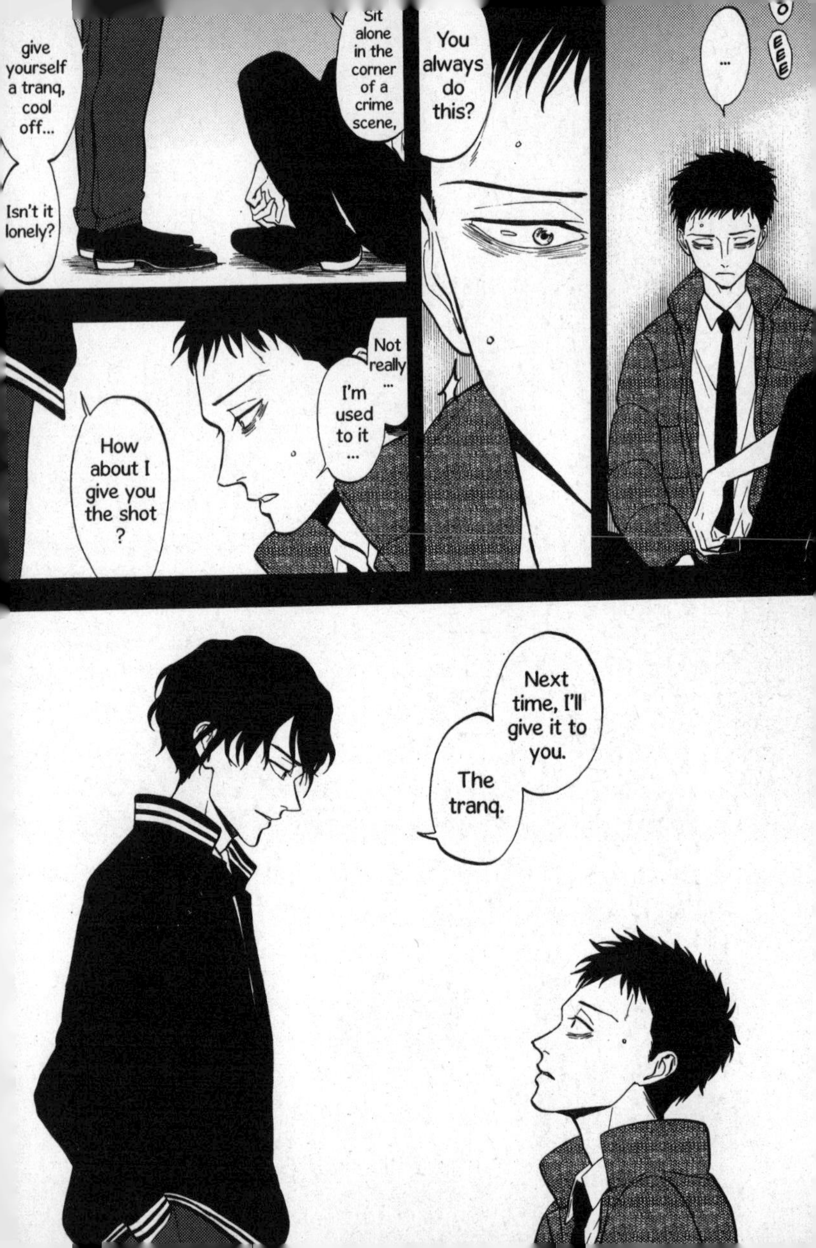
OEEE
...
You always do this?
Sit alone in the corner of a crime scene,
give yourself a tranq, cool off...
Isn't it lonely?
Not really...
I'm used to it...
How about I give you the shot?
Next time, I'll give it to you.
The tranq.

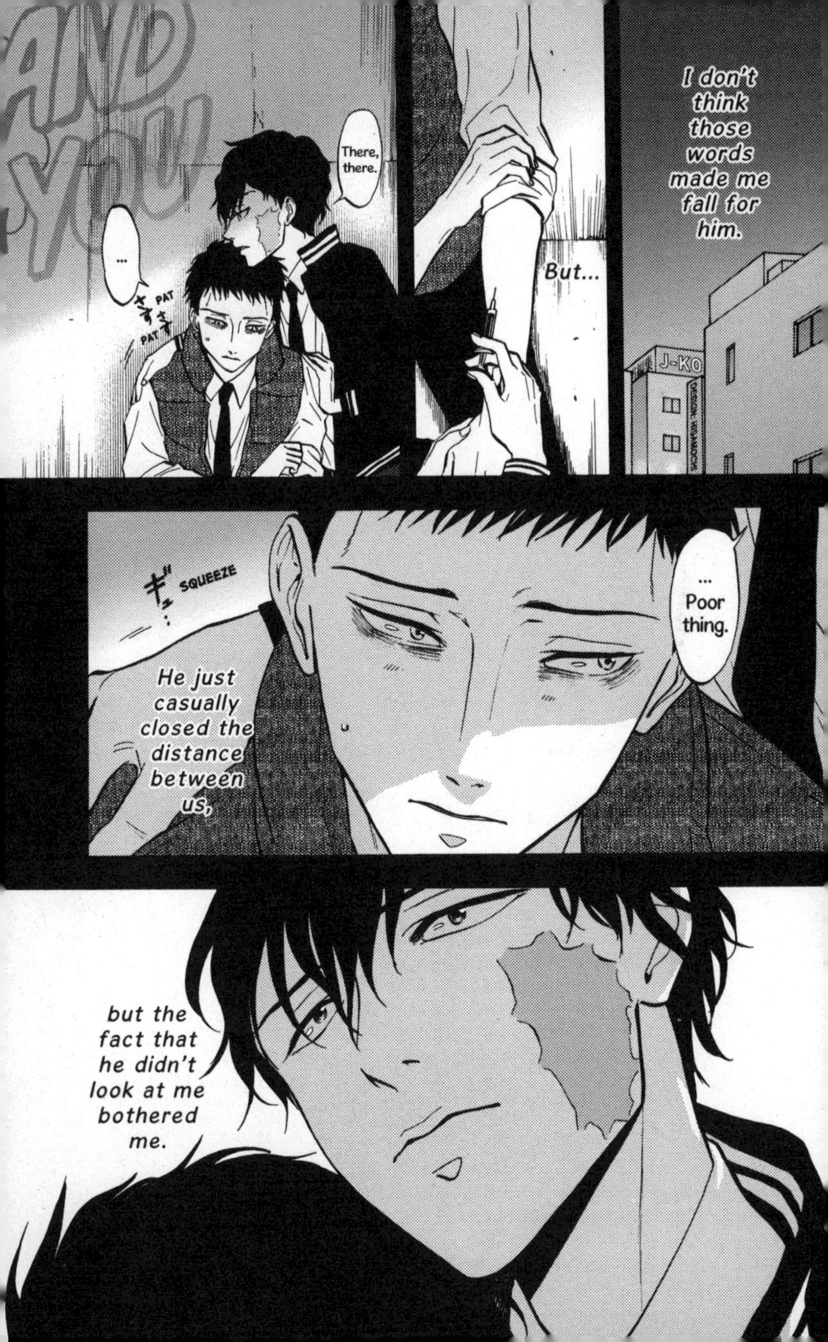
I don't think those words made me fall for him.
But...
There, there.
...
PAT PAT
AND YOU
J-KO
... Poor thing.
SQUEEZE
He just casually closed the distance between us,
but the fact that he didn't look at me bothered me.

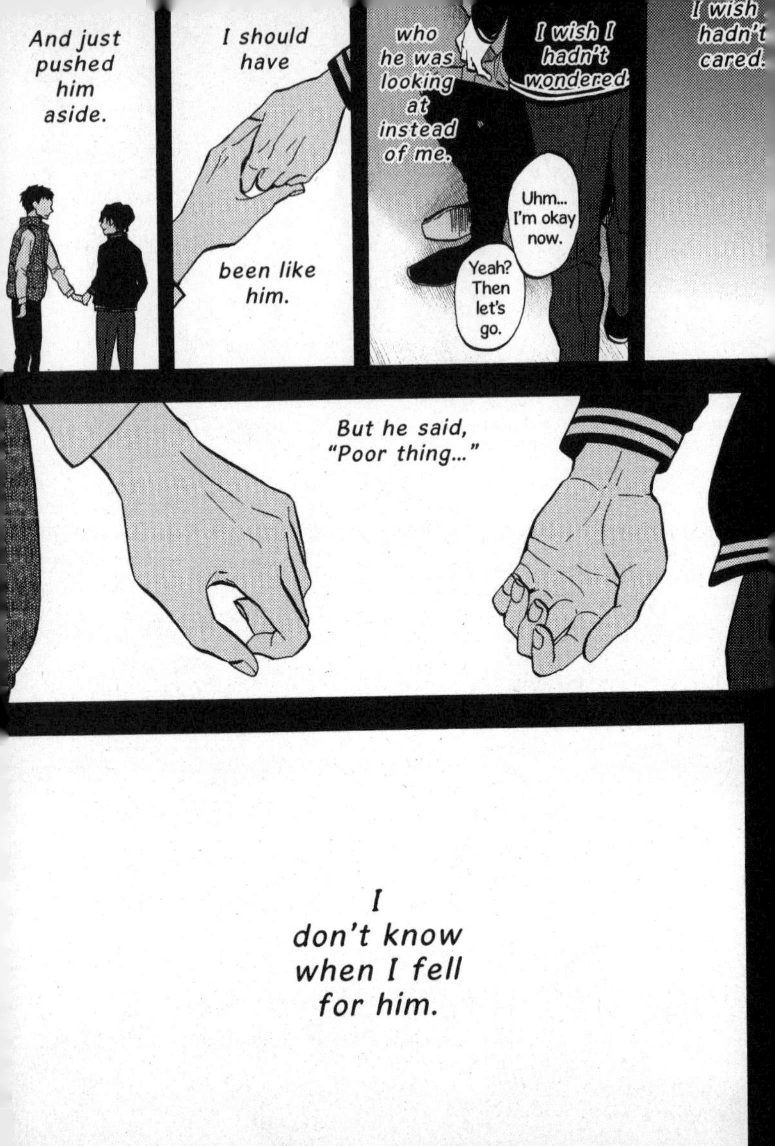
I wish hadn't cared.
I wish I hadn't wondered
who he was looking at instead of me.
Uhm... I'm okay now.
Yeah? Then let's go.
I should have been like him.
And just pushed him aside.
But he said, "Poor thing..."
I don't know when I fell for him.

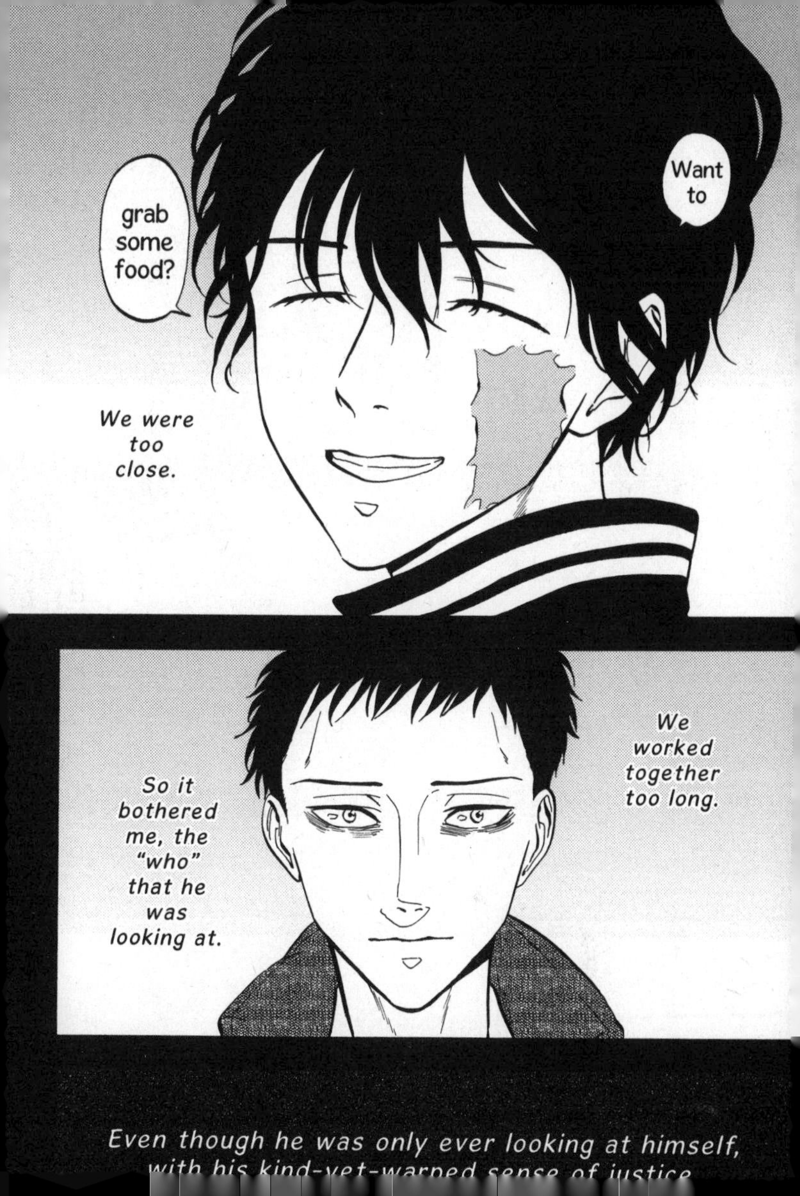
Want to
grab some food?
We were too close.
We worked together too long.
So it bothered me, the "who" that he was looking at.
Even though he was only ever looking at himself,
with his kind-yet-warped sense of justice

Work Party Hotpot

(December 1997)

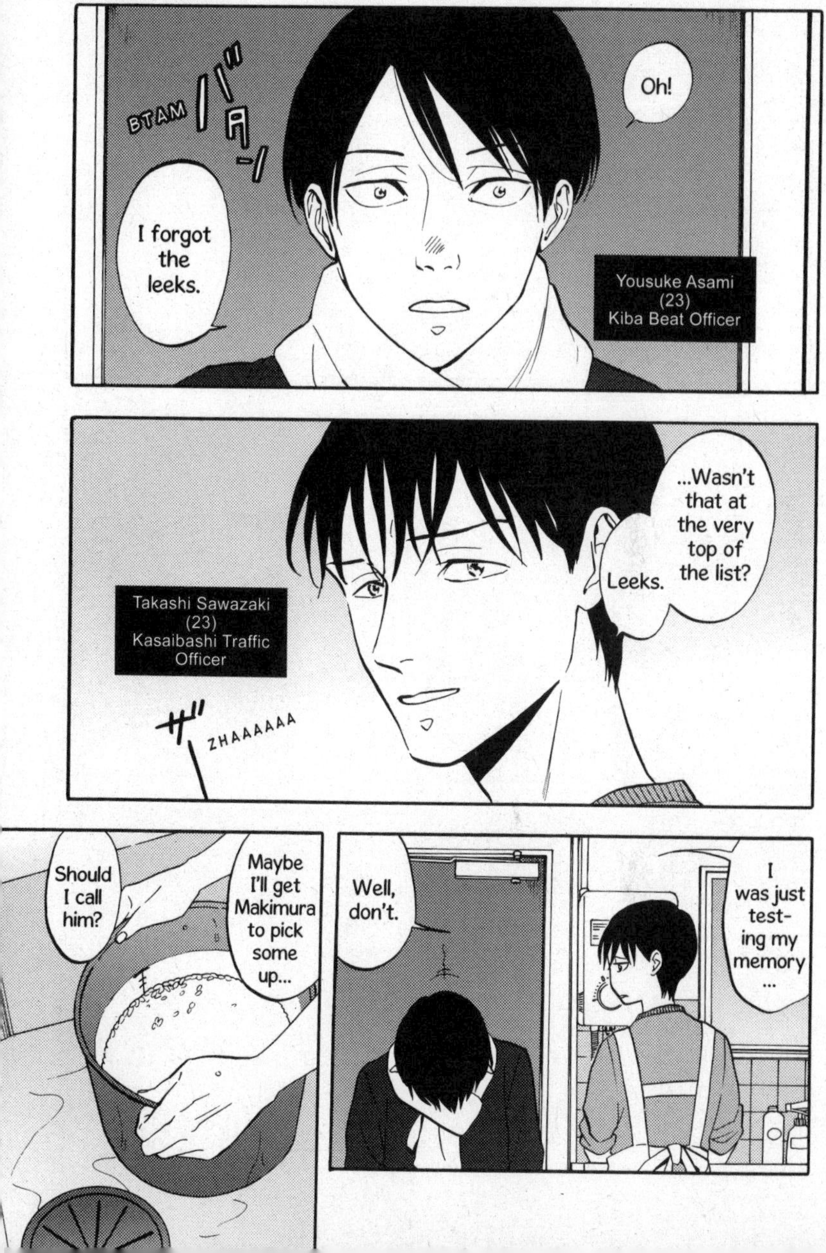
Oh!
BTAM
Yousuke Asami (23) Kiba Beat Officer
I forgot the leeks.
...Wasn't that at the very top of the list?
Leeks.
Takashi Sawazaki (23) Kasaibashi Traffic Officer
ZHAAAAAA
I was just test-ing my memory...
Well, don't.
Maybe I'll get Makimura to pick some up...
Should I call him?

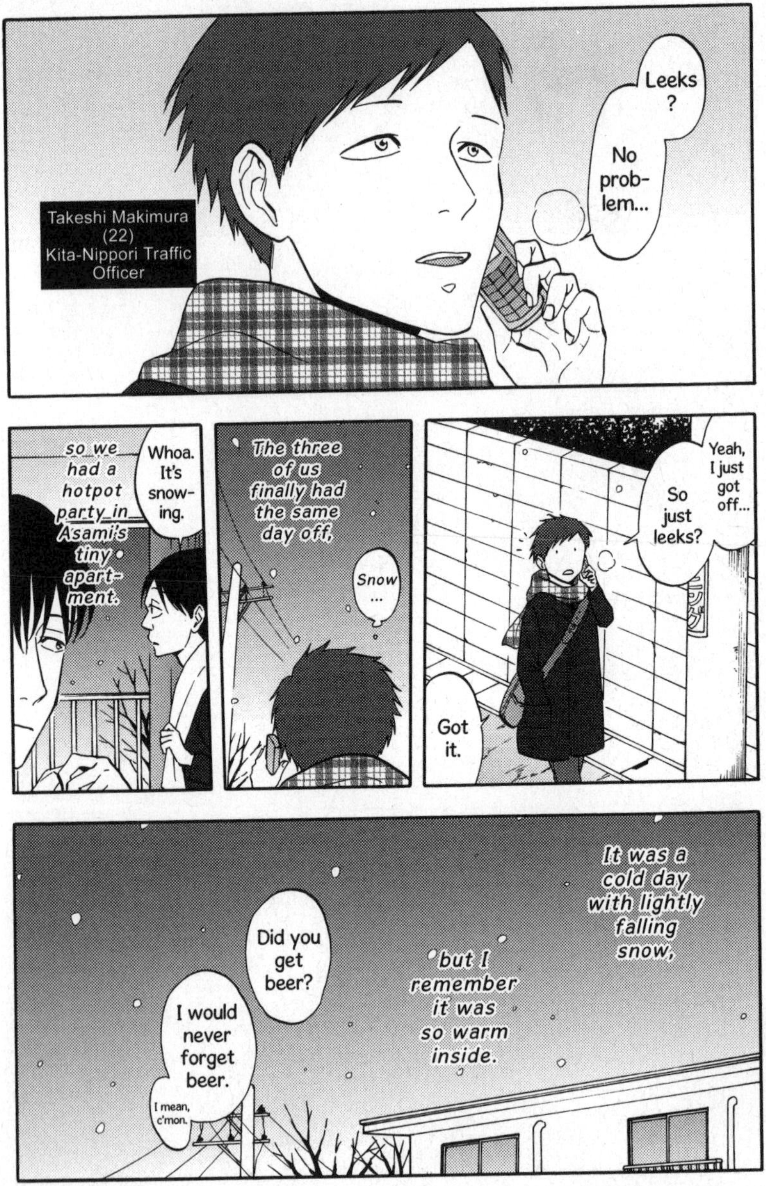
Leeks? No problem...
Takeshi Makimura (22) Kita-Nippori Traffic Officer
Yeah, I just got off...
So just leeks?
Got it.
The three of us finally had the same day off,
Snow...
Whoa. It's snowing.
so we had a hotpot party in Asami's tiny apartment.
It was a cold day with lightly falling snow,
but I remember it was so warm inside.
Did you get beer?
I would never forget beer.
I mean, c'mon.

NEXT VOLUME

Queen's reign of terror is not yet over.

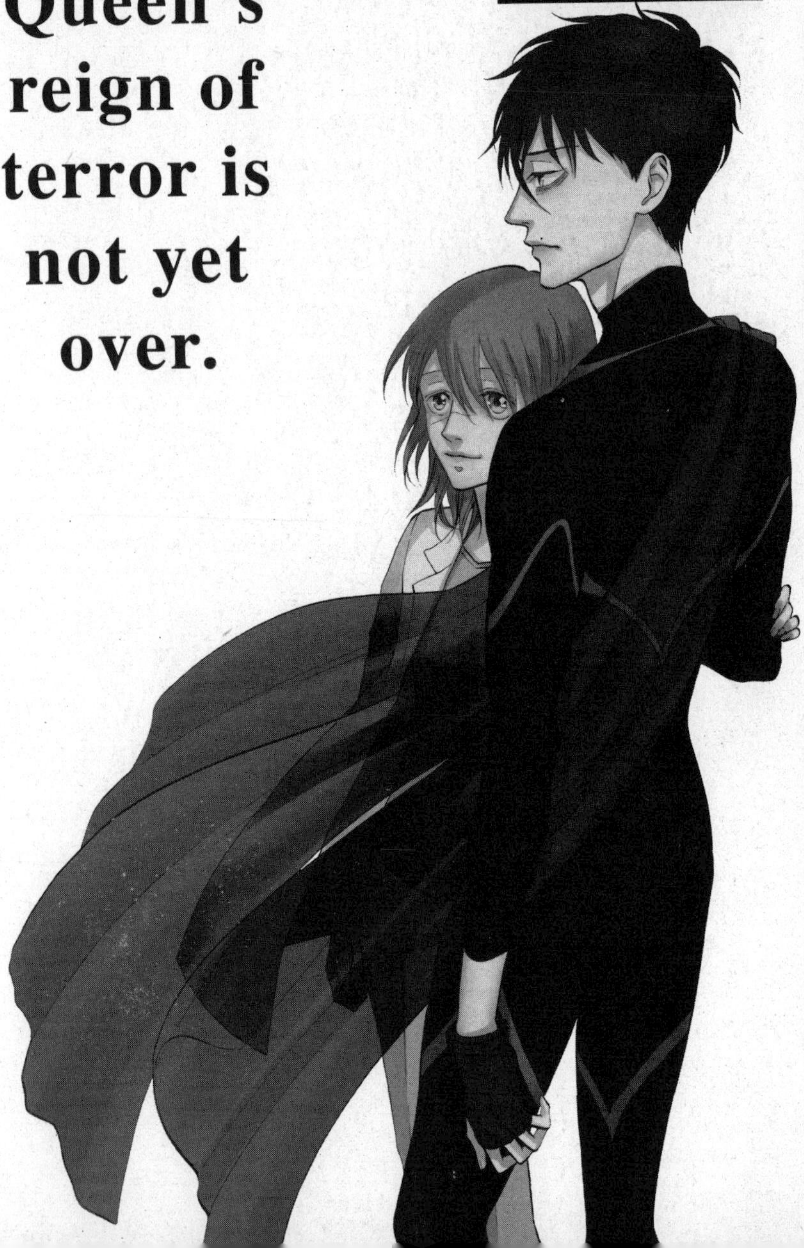

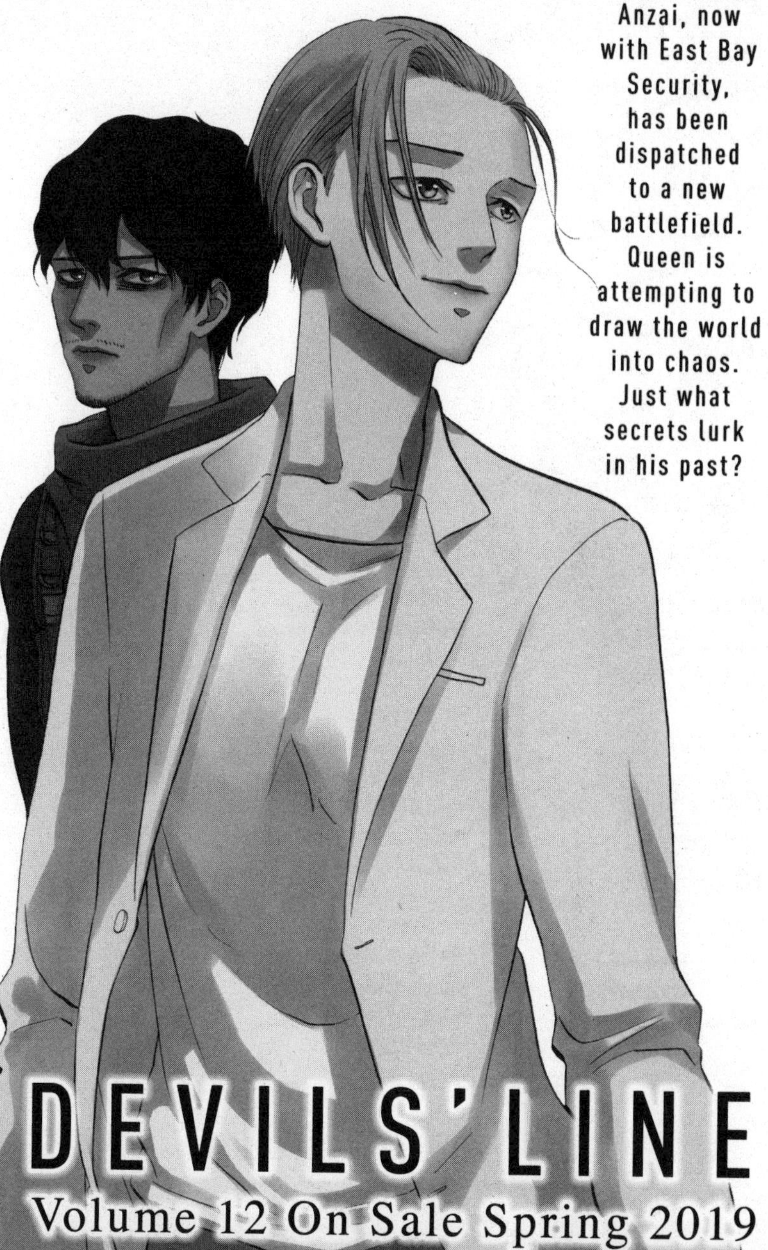
Anzai, now with East Bay Security, has been dispatched to a new battlefield. Queen is attempting to draw the world into chaos. Just what secrets lurk in his past?
DEVILS' LINE
Volume 12 On Sale Spring 2019

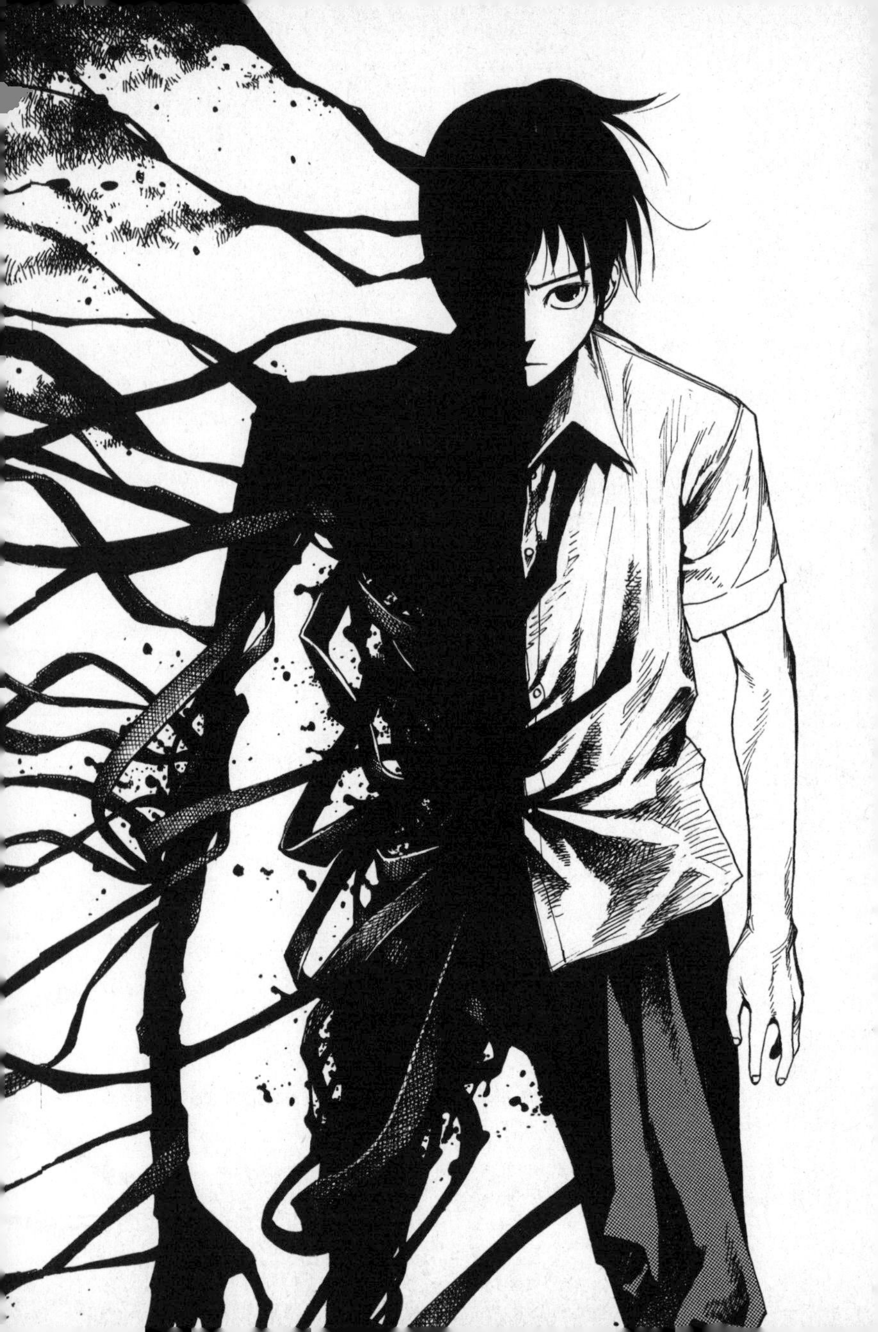

AJIN

DEMI-HUMAN

GAMON SAKURAI

SAY YOU GET HIT BY A TRUCK AND DIE.
YOU COME BACK TO LIFE. GOOD OR BAD?

FOR HIGH SCHOOLER KEI—AND FOR AT LEAST FORTY-SIX OTHERS—
IMMORTALITY COMES AS THE NASTIEST SURPRISE EVER.

SADLY FOR KEI, BUT REFRESHINGLY FOR THE READER, SUCH A FEAT
DOESN'T MAKE HIM A SUPERHERO. IN THE EYES OF BOTH THE GENERAL
PUBLIC AND GOVERNMENTS, HE'S A RARE SPECIMEN WHO NEEDS TO BE
HUNTED DOWN AND HANDED OVER TO SCIENTISTS TO BE EXPERIMENTED
ON FOR LIFE—A DEMI-HUMAN WHO MUST DIE A THOUSAND DEATHS
FOR THE BENEFIT OF HUMANITY.

VOLUMES 1-11 AVAILABLE NOW!

Story by NISIOISIN
Retold by Mitsuru Hattori

Legendary novelist NISIOISIN partners up with Mitsuru
Hattori (*SANKAREA*) in this graphic novel adaptation of
one of NISIOISIN's mystery novels.

An aspiring novelist witnesses a tragic death, but that is only the
beginning of what will become a string of traumatic events involv-
ing a lonely elementary school girl.

All 3 Volumes Available now!